SHARING THE BURDEN?

NATO and Its Second-Tier Po\

Since the fall of the Berlin Wall, NATO's middle powers have been pressured into shouldering an increasing share of the costs of the transatlantic alliance. In *Sharing the Burden?* Benjamin Zyla rejects the claim that countries like Canada have shirked their responsibilities within NATO.

Using a range of measures that go beyond troop numbers and defence budgets to include peacekeeping commitments, foreign economic assistance, and contributions to NATO's rapid reaction forces and infrastructure, Zyla argues that, proportionally, Canada's NATO commitments in the 1990s rivalled those of the alliance's major powers. At the same time, he demonstrates that Canadian policy was driven by strong normative principles to assist failed and failing states rather than a desire to ride the coat-tails of the United States, as is often presumed.

An important challenge to realist theories, *Sharing the Burden?* is a significant contribution to the debate on the nature of alliances in international relations.

BENJAMIN ZYLA is an assistant professor in the School of International Development and Global Studies at the University of Ottawa.

Sharing the Burden?

NATO and Its Second-Tier Powers

BENJAMIN ZYLA

UNIVERSITY OF TORONTO PRESS
Toronto Buffalo London

© University of Toronto Press 2015
Toronto Buffalo London
www.utppublishing.com
Printed in the U.S.A.

ISBN 978-1-4426-4750-3 (cloth)
ISBN 978-1-4426-1559-5 (paper)

Printed on acid-free, 100% post-consumer recycled paper with vegetable-based inks.

Library and Archives Canada Cataloguing in Publication

Zyla, Benjamin, author
Sharing the burden? : NATO and its second-tier powers / Benjamin Zyla.

Includes bibliographical references and index.
ISBN 978-1-4426-4750-3 (bound). – ISBN 978-1-4426-1559-5 (pbk.)

1. North Atlantic Treaty Organization – Military policy.   2. North Atlantic Treaty Organization – Canada – Case studies.   3. Canada – Military policy – Case studies.   4. Middle powers – Case studies.   I. Title.

UA646.3.Z95 2015   355'.031091821   C2014-907041-1

This book has been published with the help of a grant from the Federation for the Humanities and Social Sciences, through the Awards to Scholarly Publications Program, using funds provided by the Social Sciences and Humanities Research Council of Canada.

University of Toronto Press acknowledges the financial assistance to its publishing program of the Canada Council for the Arts and the Ontario Arts Council, an agency of the Government of Ontario.

 Canada Council   Conseil des Arts
for the Arts   du Canada

 ONTARIO ARTS COUNCIL
CONSEIL DES ARTS DE L'ONTARIO
an Ontario government agency
un organisme du gouvernement de l'Ontario

University of Toronto Press acknowledges the financial support of the Government of Canada through the Canada Book Fund for its publishing activities.

Contents

Acknowledgments

It was Harald v. Riekhoff, Elinor Sloan, and Joel J. Sokolsky who first prompted my interest in Canadian foreign policy, the transatlantic alliance, and questions of international conflict and crisis management. In many ways, they made Canada – as the "odd one out" in transatlantic relations – so interesting to a young German fellow that I decided to spend about the next 10 years researching its role in the North Atlantic Treaty Organization (NATO). I owe a great debt, especially to Dr. Sokolsky. His strong support for the idea of this research topic from Day One and his unwavering encouragement and belief in my academic potential, combined with his knowledge and scholarship on Canadian foreign policy and his scholarly wisdom, have been an inspiration to me.

I also want to thank Ugurhan Berkok not only for those great soccer matches we had on the fields in and around Kingston, Ontario, but also for sharpening my analytical research skills in the field of international political economy and getting me "hooked" on the burden-sharing idea. Thank you also to many colleagues and friends who have provided invaluable comments, feedback, and support throughout the various stages of this project: Bryan Berezuik, Jane Boulden, Andrea Charron, Houchang Hassan-Yari, Ron Haycock, Lawrence McDonough, Brian McKercher, Philippe Lagassé, David Last, Gregory Liedtke, Joseph T. Jockel, Sean Kay, Jamie Shea, and Charles C. Pentland. I am also grateful to the two anonymous reviewers for their comments and suggestions on the draft manuscript. The usual disclaimer, of course, applies: I remain solely responsible for all errors of fact or interpretation.

This research project would not have been possible without the generous financial support of a number of institutions and funding agencies. Above all, I am thankful to the Social Sciences and Humanities

Research Council of Canada (SSHRC) for its generous support while I was holding a SSHRC Postdoctoral Fellowship. I also thank the government of Canada for its support through the R.B. Byers Postdoctoral Fellowship as well as the Canadian Federation for the Humanities and Social Sciences for awarding me a grant under the Aid to Scholarly Publications Program.

Earlier research for this book also benefited from the support of the International Council for Canadian Studies and its Government of Canada Award as well as the German Academic Exchange Service.

The manuscript travelled with me, in its various stages, to a number of institutions in Canada and abroad. I started work on it as a postdoctoral fellow at the Queen's Centre for International Relations (QCIR; now the Centre for International and Defence Policy) at Queen's University in Kingston. In many ways, QCIR allowed me the time to think and expand upon my arguments, and it provided a wonderful and supportive host environment. This is also when I was introduced to Daniel Quinlan of University of Toronto Press. His strong encouragement in getting this book off the ground and supporting it from the first day we met until the final word was written deserves acknowledgment. A few months into my fellowship at QCIR, I had the opportunity to be a visiting fellow at the Europe Center at the Freeman Spogli Institute for International Studies at Stanford University in California. The hospitality and generosity of the Center were outstanding, as were the reference librarians, who helped me find missing raw data on burden sharing, particularly data that other NATO member states considered classified information.

At the University of Ottawa, I am fortunate to be a member of a supportive, stimulating, and collegial department. I am particularly thankful to Paul Haslam and Dean Mérette for granting me a semester of academic leave to be a visiting professor at the École normale supérieure de Lyon, where I put the finishing touches on the manuscript and improved my French-language skills. My time in Lyon also allowed the ideas developed in this book to be introduced to and successfully tested in a very different academic community in Europe.

I would not have been able to produce much of the primary information, especially the information in the civilian burden-sharing chapters, without the help of numerous interview partners who shared their time and insights with me, especially those at the Canadian delegation to NATO, the German Embassy, and members of the international staff at NATO Headquarters in Brussels as well as various government officials in Berlin, Bonn, Brussels, and Ottawa. Unfortunately, they must remain anonymous. I also thank the reference librarians at Library and Archives Canada in Ottawa, NATO Headquarters, the European Parliament, the European Commission, and various European universities for giving me access to their collections and helping me find data on NATO burden sharing. Thanks also to Marie-Isabelle Beye for her research assistance

Finally, I would like to thank my friends and family, whom I so often neglected in researching and writing this book, for their ongoing love and support. I am particularly grateful to my parents, to whom I dedicate this book. They have always stood by my side and offered love, inspiration, constant encouragement, advice, and wisdom. My appreciation also goes to my partner, Elke Winter. She lived through this manuscript's highs and lows and believed in me during those moments when I had little idea where my work would take me. Your love, friendship, and support mean so much to me!

Gatineau, 30 July 2013

SHARING THE BURDEN?

NATO and Its Second-Tier Powers

1 Introduction

The end of the Cold War shifted the tectonic plates of global order. After 1989, geopolitics was no longer about balancing against or bandwagoning with other powers; it was about extending a helping hand to former enemies, engaging societies in Central and Eastern Europe (CEE) on a sociopolitical-economic level, and practising policies of enticement to lure those states into the Western community. International security institutions underwent their own transformation, changing their mandate from collective defence to international crisis management.[1]

This shift in global order, in turn, shook the hierarchy of power in international politics. It gave new meaning and roles to second-tier powers[2] (especially in the governance of regional order in Europe) and helped them rediscover the value of practising multilateralism through these international institutions, which were now seen as intermediaries that could foster and manage transnational cooperation. No longer were debates within these institutions limited to how to balance the superpower or how to deploy material powers to the extended regions

---

1 The literature on this topic is extensive; see, e.g., Pease 2008; Rosenau and Czempiel 1992; Ruggie 1993b; Russett and Oneal 2001.
2 This term has gone through distinct cycles of popularity (see Ravenhill 1998). It refers to a group of states that rank below the great powers in terms of material capabilities and ability to project their powers around the world. These countries have an impact in either specific regions or issue areas and have a "tendency to pursue multilateral solutions to international problems," "to embrace compromise positions in international disputes," and "to embrace notions of 'good international citizenship' to guide diplomacy" through international institutions (Laura Neak, quoted in Bishai 2000); see Cooper, Higgott, and Nossal 1993, 19; Keohane 1969, 298; Holbraad 1984.

of the world. By focusing on new, original, and concrete ways of managing the emerging security order in Europe, second-tier powers enhanced the value of their membership in those organizations. To their own surprise, their voices were heard more often, and their ideas gained more traction, in international institutions like the United Nations (UN) and the North Atlantic Treaty Organization (NATO).

At the same time, while acquiring a new prominence in international politics, NATO's second-tier powers, including Canada, experienced tremendous internal institutional pressure, mainly from the major powers, to shoulder a greater share of the Atlantic burden.[3] The "big players" asserted that they had provided a disproportionate share of public security goods to maintain regional order in Europe during the Cold War and that since the Cold War was over, it was time for second-tier powers to assume a larger role in providing collective security and defence.[4] Put another way, while second-tier powers played a rather tangential role in world order during the Cold War, after the Cold War ended they became an integral part of the discussion on the future of that order, especially with the growing threat of regional (dis)order posed by ethnic conflicts in south-eastern Europe.

This book examines that discussion about regional order in the "new" Europe and specifically the extent to which second-tier powers shared the burden of the collective defence alliance[5] – defined as the "actual contribution of each nation to collective defence and the fairness of each state's contribution"[6] – and NATO's new mandate of crisis management in the post–Cold War era, from 1989 to 2001. In addition to this general discussion, a case study approach examines Canada as a second-tier power and its particular contributions to NATO burden sharing. It focuses on the social actions of sharing Atlantic burdens rather than burden sharing itself, which is a static outcome of those actions. The book takes the point of view that sharing the burden of an

---

3 See, e.g., Bennett, Lepgold, and Unger 1997; Coker 1990; Forster and Cimbala 2005; Joffe 1987.
4 See, e.g., Asmus, Kugler, and Larrabee 1993; Kupchan and Kupchan 1991, 1995; Yost 1998. For a critique of this argument, see Joffe 1992; Mearsheimer 1995.
5 I follow Michael Barnett and Jack Levy (1991, 370) here, who defined alliances as "a formal or informal relationship of security cooperation between two or more states and involving mutual expectations of some degree of policy coordination on security issues under certain conditions in the future."
6 Hartley and Sandler 1999, 669.

international institution is an action directed towards a specific set of social purposes at the national and international levels,[7] purposes it defines as regional order, peace, security, and prosperity in Europe, whereby *sharing* assumes that a country has trust in that institution or security community. Thus, the book does not analyse the preferred policies of NATO burden sharing; rather, it examines the practice of burden sharing in very specific contexts, including the national preferences of states for sharing Atlantic burdens.

The book places these discussions in the narrow context of the immediate post–Cold War era and its imposing demands for collective crisis-management capabilities, and it asks the following questions: How did the second-tier powers' national preferences explain their motivations and behaviour in the alliance's burden-sharing regime in the 1990s? With reference to the case study, how did Canada's patterns of national state preferences shape its practice of sharing Atlantic burdens? Moreover, what did states – and second-tier powers, in particular – do to share the burden of providing regional order in Europe in the 1990s? How and why, if at all, did they shoulder and manage that burden? This book also addresses the following more general sub-questions: What does sharing the burden actually mean in the new world order? Are commonly used burden-sharing indicators adequate to objectively measure these commitments? Finally, given the new security environment immediately after the Cold War, what, if anything, does this mean for the traditional classification of states into super-, major, second-tier, and third-tier powers?

This book is not meant to contribute to the literature on international political economy; it does not use economic theories, models, or methods of burden sharing and thus does not speak the language of economists. But it does contribute to the literature on international security affairs, international institutions, transatlantic relations, and foreign policy analysis (especially Canadian).

While international institutions are, generally, indicators of the patterns and structure of global order, NATO – formed in 1949 as an

---

7 The book thus builds on earlier scholarship in this field. Bruce Russett (1970, 157), e.g., noted that "how a nation will in fact distribute the burdens of defense spending is fixed less by inexorable laws of economics than by the nation's political system and the values of its people." Yet his work compares the extent of defence spending only to that in areas such as health, education, and social welfare.

international institution[8] ensuring regional order in Europe – is a crucial place to start the analysis, for at least three reasons. First, as an institution that manages security governance, NATO is widely respected for successfully providing the public goods of collective security and defence, stability, and order in Europe and, increasingly, abroad.[9] It is precisely this proven track record that has made NATO such a valued institution in international security affairs.

Second, the 1990s saw international institutions becoming more active in managing and maintaining international security affairs. Therefore, examining the patterns of power in regional order and determining who shares the burdens should be a meaningful exercise. Starting with the UN, NATO, and the Organization for Security and Co-operation in Europe (OSCE),[10] international institutions were rejuvenated and filled with a sense of new activism, while slowly overcoming the ideological stalemates of the Cold War years.

Third, although managing this new world order was initially entrusted to the UN, its failure to contain ethnic conflicts in the Balkans caused member states to transfer their trust to other security institutions like NATO, which had effectively managed regional order in Europe for decades. Throughout years of significant geopolitical turmoil, NATO has been one of the most resilient of international institutions.[11] In spite of larger historical changes – the period of détente, France's withdrawal from the integrated military command system,[12] the missile gap in Europe, a continuously integrating European Union (EU) – NATO has shown perseverance of mandate, scope, and

---

8 A commonly accepted definition is that international institutions are "sets of rules that stipulate the ways in which states should cooperate and compete with each other" (Mearsheimer 1994–95, 8). This definition, however, is not universally accepted. At the heart of the debate are distinctions between "international institutions" and "international regimes" (for an overview, see Keohane 1988, 1989a, 3–4). Hasenclever et al. (1997) hold that "institutions" has now largely replaced "regime" in the scholarly literature.

9 See, e.g., Duffield 1994–95; McCalla 1996; Wallander 2000; Williams and Neumann 2000.

10 With the 1990 Charter of Paris, the Conference on Security and Co-operation in Europe was renamed the OSCE. For an excellent introductory history of both organizations, see Galbreath 2007.

11 See Lindley-French 2006.

12 France withdrew in 1967 under President Charles de Gaulle; it rejoined in 2009.

membership as well as endurance in pursuing its objectives and adjusting to new geopolitical realities.

Thus, examining the practice of sharing NATO's collective burden can be considered a yardstick for the extent, structure, and patterns of the burdens that its members incurred. It also provides insight into questions of why and how much second-tier powers contributed to the governance of regional order in Europe at times when the vast majority of NATO's assignments were focused on maintaining continental security in Europe rather than abroad, as was increasingly the case after 9/11 (e.g., in Afghanistan and Libya).[13]

By 1999, NATO consisted of 19 member states.[14] Devoting equal attention to all of them would be an overwhelming task and is beyond the scope of this book; instead, it looks solely at second-tier NATO powers. Specifically, it examines Canada as a representative of those second-tier powers while making cross-references and comparisons to its peers, such as Norway, Spain, and the Netherlands. The Canadian case study is also used to relocate the issue of burden sharing from economics to the mainstream debates of international relations (IR).[15]

The choice for this case study is appealing because Canada is the only North American country that has used NATO as a conduit for pursuing its commitments to world order and regional security governance in Europe.[16] The other North American partner, the United States, enjoys a far stronger, more extensive, and more multidimensional commitment to upholding global order. Consequently, it can be said that the US operates in a separate league of states, one that renders comparisons to any other NATO member state useless. Indeed, this study confirms that the United States truly deserves the status of a

---

13 It is also in this sense that this book builds on the existing scholarship on alliance behaviour, such as Bennett, Lepgold, and Unger 1994; Snyder 1997; Walt 1987; Kupchan 1988.

14 On 4 April 1949, Belgium, Canada, Denmark, France, Iceland, Italy, Luxembourg, the Netherlands, Norway, Portugal, the United Kingdom, and the United States became the founding members of NATO. On 18 February 1952, Greece and Turkey joined, followed by the Federal Republic of Germany on 6 May 1955 and Spain on 30 May 1982. Post–Cold War enlargement took place on 12 March 1999, when the Czech Republic, Hungary, and Poland joined, followed by Bulgaria, Estonia, Latvia, Lithuania, Romania, Slovakia, and Slovenia on 29 March 2004 and Albania and Croatia on 9 July 2008.

15 For the latest lack thereof, see Sandler and Shimizu 2014.

16 On this notion, see Sokolsky 1989.

superpower because its share of the collective burden in many absolute force share indexes exceeds those of all of its allies combined.

The Argument

This book sets out four arguments. First, I argue that despite having relatively limited resources, second-tier states joined the institutional activism of the 1990s, contributing a substantial amount to regional order in continental Europe. Contrary to the assumptions held by collective action theorists, second-tier powers shouldered a proportionate share of the Atlantic burden in the new Europe – in spite of, and occasionally even exceeding, domestic and societal limitations such as economic recessions. Second-tier powers like Canada showed strong preferences for remaining active and committed agents rather than practising free riding[17] and made an essential, although not always easily quantifiable, contribution to collective security through military and non-military means (e.g., diplomacy, foreign aid).

Part and parcel of this misunderstanding is that in the new world order, commonly accepted measures for determining Atlantic burdens are outdated. The conventional indicator used to calculate a state's share of the Atlantic burden is its total defence expenditure as a percentage of its gross domestic product (GDP).[18] Even at the end of the Cold War, NATO continued to argue that the GDP/percentage of defence spending indicator "is the best known, most easily understood, most widely used and perhaps the most telling measure. It broadly depicts defence input in relation to a country's ability to contribute."[19]

But the fact that an indicator is commonly accepted does not mean that it is accurate or that it captures contemporary trends and developments in international security affairs. And while the GDP indicator emphasizes the economic costs of collective action, it excludes, for example, the political and diplomatic costs at home and abroad as well as the calculations of national decision makers based on domestic preferences about

---

17 *Free riding* assumes that states acting rationally will not contribute more to the collective good than they would gain from that good if it were supplied to all alliance members.

18 This indicator is commonly used in the literature as an index of national power. See, e.g., Merritt and Zinnes 1988; Singer 1988; Oneal 1990a, 1990b; Oneal and Elrod 1989; Palmer 1991.

19 North Atlantic Treaty Organization 1988, 10.

engaging their country in international politics.[20] Moreover, the nature of the public good produced by NATO has changed since the Cold War's end; allies no longer enjoy a pure public good or compete for the benefits resulting from acquiring military capabilities[21] or for private benefits,[22] especially from European allies. All this suggests an incomplete – or highly selective – picture of the conventional burden-sharing regime using GDP/level of defence spending as a benchmark.

Second, to increase the explanatory value of the burden-sharing debate, especially in the context of the post–Cold War era, I argue that indicators ought to be divided into military and non-military, or civilian.[23] The military indicators of Atlantic burden sharing are discussed in Part II, and the civilian indicators are introduced in Part III; they build on and significantly expand the existing scholarship on this topic.[24] Moreover, this book holds that only a large number of multi-dimensional and cross-level indicators can come close to objectively determining the precise share of the Atlantic burden and thus to ensure distributive justice among the allies. This is relevant for the case study employed in this book as the idea of a transatlantic security cooperation being structured into two pillars – the United States and Europe – threatens to make Canada the "odd one out" in NATO.[25]

Third, I argue that studying the practice of sharing NATO burdens requires a contextualization of these social actions; above all, practices are indicative of the societal predispositions (or preferences) that lead to state actions in NATO's burden-sharing regime.[26] In this sense, the book applies a bottom-up view to politics, whereby the demands and preferences of individuals and groups are considered analytically

---

20 Moreover, as Sandler and Forbes (1980) have shown, the association between GDP and the percentage of military defence expenditures to GDP was not statistically significant after 1966.
21 Murdoch and Sandler 1982, 1984; Sandler and Cauley 1975; Sandler and Murdoch 1986.
22 Oneal 1990b, 385; Oneal and Diehl 1990.
23 For the argument that the end of the Cold War has brought an end to the exclusivity of the military dimension in the burden-sharing debate see Chalmers 2001, 569. In this sense, this book builds on the most recent scholarship on Atlantic burden sharing, which has attempted to introduce indexes such as exposure to Atlantic risk factors or casualties into the discussion; see Sperling and Webber 2009.
24 Boyer 1993; Sandler and Forbes 1980. Oneal (1990a) has grouped military and foreign aid contributions together as a way to measure Atlantic contributions.
25 Jockel and Sokolsky 1986, 2008; Pentland 2003–04.
26 For a similar argument see Foucault and Mérand 2013.

before policy making (and thus policy outcomes such as burden sharing). It also offers a new epistemology (for details, see below) to conventional liberal IR theory and studies the patterns of national state preferences *for* sharing NATO burdens.

While the case study focuses on Canada as a second-tier power, the book shows that the old paradigm of using the scope and extent of military capabilities to determine the position of a state in the hierarchy of international politics is not enough to explain its foreign policy actions and commitments in the new world order. This is because the international security system underwent significant transformational changes, and the "traditional currency" of international politics – state power and thus influence – was given new meaning, after the Cold War ended. In turn, this new definition of national power imposed new roles, responsibilities, and self-perceptions on armed forces and government officials that traditional burden-sharing indicators did not reflect.

In contrast to other works on burden sharing, this book places its analysis in the post–Cold War era and examines the (domestic) preference formation of Canada's foreign policy towards NATO and European security governance. The empirical analysis that resulted from qualitatively reviewing the government's discourses concerning Canada's NATO operations found that it was to a large degree driven by what Arnold Wolfers called an "external responsibility" – that is, a felt obligation to promote international economic, social, or political conditions to uphold the values of human rights and security, democracy, freedom, and the rule of law.[27] Wolfers suggested that only major powers and superpowers are expected to hold this external responsibility because they have a surplus of resources and the ability to make them readily available to the international community. The case study here builds on Wolfer's hypothesis by showing that, in relative terms, second-tier powers like Canada also felt an external responsibility and practised burden-sharing behaviour that is contrary to free riding.

To bolster this argument, the book uses liberal IR theory as its framework and relies on Max Weber's epistemology of *erklären* ("explaining") and *verstehen* ("understanding") to provide an "explanatory understanding"[28] of the value-rational and instrumentally rational[29]

---

27 Wolfers 1962, 73–7.
28 Or, in the words of Bloomfield and Nossal (2007), "explicative understanding."
29 Weber (1947, 115) also made a distinction between social actions that are *wertrationell* ("value-rational") and *zweckrationell* ("instrumentally rational").

motivations that led to the social practices of burden sharing in the first place (including changes to it); in this way, the book challenges the realist-dominated literature on alliances.[30] This liberal IR framework helps us gain access to the formation and patterns of Canada's national preferences towards NATO burden sharing by taking human nature into account and thus overcoming the realists' ontological straightjacket, which assumes that states are unitary actors in world politics.

This theoretical framework also allows us to examine whether particular types of state preferences and variations on them, including individual rights (ideational liberals), commercial interests (early commercial liberals), domestic institutions (republican liberals), or an interplay of the three affect the foreign policies of second-tier powers. Above all, national state preferences develop out of contention among domestic individuals or groups.[31] They are, as Ira Katznelson and Barry R. Weingast remind us,[32] caused by historical processes and thus indicate that they rely on agency. In turn, the purpose of theory (and its development) is to analyse how historical developments cause a particular set of preferences held by a given actor.[33] Preferences thus rely on agency; they are induced by human interaction and show patterns that can be studied.[34] Moreover, they highlight the ethical dimension of national statecraft and reveal the social and political dimension of states' NATO burden-sharing behaviour as well as NATO's general collective action problems.[35]

---

30 Broadly speaking, this literature argues that alliances are not driven by principles, norms, or values, but rather by states seeking to promote and foster their national interests and state security or to address an external threat. For a good overview of this type of literature, see Holsti, Hopmann, and Sullivan 1973; Levy 1981; Liska 1962.

31 Moravcsik 1998, 22.

32 Katznelson and Weingast 2005, 3.

33 Ibid.

34 See also Hall 2000.

35 It is precisely in this sense that this book builds on the argument by Bennett, Lepgold, and Unger (1994, 72), who stated that "whether states free-ride, are entrapped, keep their distance or reveal their preferences depends in part on state autonomy, societal preferences and bureaucratic politics." See also Barnett and Levy 1991. This book goes one level deeper and examines the domestic preference formation of one particular state.

The explanatory capabilities of liberal IR theory mixed with Weber's epistemology are thus superior to its realist and neo-liberal competitors, which assume – among other things – that state preferences remain static and stable over time. In short, examining Canada's preference formation ensures a rigorous methodological approach and establishes causality between domestic preferences and state actions. Of course, preferences are considered to be *causally* independent of political strategies pursued by other actors and thus occur before any interactions that are taking place in the political marketplace.[36] Preferences are not the same as policy options.

The fourth argument I make is that formulating and executing national security policies in the post–Cold War era required new and different capabilities. They were grounded in a new definition of security, one that was no longer a one-dimensional concept but instead considered a range of political, economic, diplomatic, and military factors. These policies made increasing use of soft power resources,[37] not simply military capabilities. They were largely the product of a change in societal predispositions towards issues of national security that rested on the social dictum of cashing in the peace dividend[38] and realizing the benefits of Cold War security investments. It is precisely these domestic preferences that liberal IR theory helps explain, enabling us to determine whether the foreign policies of second-tier powers were shaped by individual rights, commercial interests, (domestic) institutions, or an interaction among all three. Against this background, I charge that second-tier states did not exclusively engage in cost-benefit analysis in the post–Cold War order but rather exhibited a combination of material and non-material (or social) interests (e.g., ethics) in their foreign policy decisions.[39]

Although the book concentrates on the 1990s, it is also relevant to contemporary debates over troop contributions and levels of foreign aid sent to, for example, NATO's International Security Assistance

---

36 Moravcsik 1998, 24–7. In turn, representative institutions of the state decide how social coalitions and individuals are represented in the Canadian political system.

37 For a definition and discussion, see Nye 2004, 2005a, 2008.

38 For a discussion of this concept, see Brömmelhörster 2000; Russett 1993; Markusen, DiGiovanna, and Leary 2003; Chan 1995.

39 It is in this area that this book contributes to the most recent debate in IR scholarship: on whether state preferences are positive-sum or zero-sum and thus whether they pursue absolute or relative gains. See Grieco 1988; Morrow 1994.

Force in Afghanistan (ISAF). As in the 1990s, current debates about Afghanistan need to be placed in the context from which they obtain their meanings. In light of the widely marketed whole-of-government approach[40] – a combination of a country's foreign, defence, and development policies – analysts of Atlantic burden sharing need more than ever to distinguish between military and civilian indicators. Such a focus would more adequately and objectively assign meaning to sharing collective burdens.

Methodology, Methods, and Sources

Before we examine the book's theoretical, conceptual, and empirical analyses, it is important to explain the methodology used and, briefly, how the empirical data was processed.

Methodology

Generally speaking, methodology refers to "the ways we acquire knowledge."[41] Sharing Atlantic burdens can be understood as a complex set of interactions among a number of actors that are themselves embedded in a complex set of structures, norms, and values and that, in this process, develop preferences. Individual actors never act in a vacuum so that the evolution of foreign policy cannot be fully explained by analysing individual actions. Rather, it needs a multi-level analysis ranging from the individual through the societal to the international level. Max Weber's epistemology of *explaining* and *understanding* is used throughout this book to trace the factors that explain the social actions of sharing NATO's burdens without excluding either explanatory or ideational factors.[42] It also allows us to *understand* the formation of state preferences.

Weber argued that social actions are in need of an explanatory understanding; they need to be interpreted from within the context in which a policy was drafted and from which it obtained its meaning.

---

40 This literature is extensive; see, e.g., de Coning 2007; Eide et al. 2005; Friis and Jarmyr 2008; Gross 2008; Holland 2009; Patrick and Brown 2007; Smith 2004; Viggo 2008; Whelan 2003.

41 Moses and Knutsen 2007, 5.

42 Hollis and Smith 1990.

Explanatory understanding dissolves the dualism between *explaining* and *understanding* in the social sciences. Using this epistemology allows us to go beyond simple policy statements, statistical data, primary sources, and interview transcripts and to include subjective norms and values in the analysis without abandoning the notion of causal explanations and individual actions. An objective analysis provides knowledge about the causality of social reality – that is, it allows for an objective explanation of social facts.[43] It is precisely this mutual ground that this book attempts to provide, thereby offering a novel contribution to the literature on NATO burden sharing and liberal IR theory.

State preferences have two characteristics: they signify stable elements that are internal to states; and, as Andrew Moravcsik has convincingly shown,[44] they are revealed in a state's decision making and can thus be observed and studied in government documents. This book exploits both characteristics.

Methods

While we cannot engage in a comprehensive discussion of the methods used in this study, it is important to briefly explain the essential methods and approaches.

First, the research used a case study approach to examine the issue of NATO burden sharing in the immediate post–Cold War era.[45] Case studies, as Jonathan Moses and Torbjørn Knutsen remind us, are "histories with a point. They are 'cases of something' – and the thing under study is interesting, relevant or 'in focus' because of a larger theoretical concern or a specific research design."[46] At the same time, case studies look beyond the immediate object of analysis and deduce generalizations – that is, they go beyond the empirical analysis and produce

---

43 See, e.g., Weber 1947.

44 Moravcsik 1998.

45 I follow here Lijphart's typology of case studies (1971, 691). He distinguished between (1) theoretical, (2) interpretive, (3) hypothesis generating, (4) theory-confirming, (5) theory-infirming, and (6) deviant case studies. The case study used in this book is at the intersection of 3 and 6 (or mis-fitting case study) – it aims to show how a particular case does not easily fit an existing universal claim and tests a central theoretical claim.

46 Moses and Knutsen 2007, 132.

general statements about a larger phenomenon or issue. This larger context is NATO burden sharing in the 1990s.

A second method was to apply thematic (qualitative) content analysis to primary sources. This is, at the most basic level, a method whereby a researcher attempts to carve out themes in the material being analysed.[47] It belongs to the qualitative family of social science methods and enables the researcher to analyse large amounts of documents and text in an objective and systematic manner.[48] The primary sources included Canadian Cabinet documents and correspondence, unpublished departmental memos and research reports, ministers' speeches, and reports and cables (situation and otherwise) sent from Canadian personnel (most notably those at NATO Headquarters, London, Berlin, and Washington) to Ottawa – retrieved from archives using access to information requests. Thematic content analysis was applied to search for themes and patterns in an inductive ("letting the data speak") as well as deductive way (applying a specific hypothesis derived from liberal IR theory). This method brings out the meaning of the text and reveals the social, political, and historical context(s) in which it was produced and from which it obtained its meaning(s); it provides insights into how people and institutions make sense of something that happened.

Third, the research relied on semi-structured interviews with government officials, bureaucrats, diplomats, and others involved in transatlantic affairs.[49] These interviews gave insights into Canada's foreign policy thinking as well as explanations of its decision-making processes and patterns, and thematic content analysis was also applied to them. Because the interviewees were asked about highly sensitive and often classified information, the names of most interviewees have been kept confidential at their request.

---

47 Klotz and Prakash 2008.
48 Berelson 1952, 18; Holsti 1969, 14.
49 Because the politics of NATO burden sharing is a highly classified issue, primary source material is regarded as top secret and is not normally made available to researchers. This was particularly the case for this book, given its contemporary nature. On the other hand, NATO's archival material is not subject to the usual 30-year retention period, but NATO documents can be made available only when all of its member states concerned with the file unanimously agree to release them.

The Data

The information in this book is based primarily on data gathered formally and informally from various institutions and government organizations. Much of the non-military data, for example, was collected during a research trip to NATO Headquarters in Brussels in the spring of 2007 and takes the form of interviews with diplomatic officials and members of the International Staff.[50] These interviews made it possible to place the raw data in the context of larger political developments occurring at the highest levels, and they became a crucial source of information for analysing the political processes and interests of the agents involved.

A second important source of data was the reports commissioned by government agencies in the United States, Germany, Canada, and the EU. Particularly helpful was the US *Report on Allied Contributions to the Common Defense* as well as the *Military Balance*, a journal published each year by the International Institute for Strategic Studies. For the case study, it was particularly difficult to collect data on Canada's soft power resources and its intangible contributions to collective security, so where necessary, Access to Information and Privacy requests were filed to declassify government documents and open the "black box" of government thinking and decision making.

Reports on burden sharing published by parliamentary committees, think tanks, and civil society organizations were another important source for this book. This information was mainly secondary, but it helped fill smaller gaps in either the existing literature or the information provided by the interviewees. Public opinion polls were a useful tool for gaining insight into the thinking of domestic society on issues related to foreign and defence policy. They were particularly important for studying societal processes using a liberal framework of analysis.

Analysis and Processing

In theory, any contribution made by a NATO member state that enhances peace and stability is part of that nation's burden-sharing effort. While many components of defence effort are measurable, others are much more subjective and do not readily lend themselves to quantification. Consequently, even the most sophisticated analytical techniques

---

50 Names are provided when the interviewees consented to it.

cannot provide a definitive solution to the fair-share problem. In addition to interpretations, they require an explanatory understanding.

There is no single, universally accepted formula for calculating each nation's "fair share" of the collective burden. National contributions assume many forms, requiring different measures and analyses. Any such calculation would have to take account of the many disparate factors that determine the level of a nation's defence effort and ability to contribute. Identifying which factors to count and deciding how each should be weighed relative to the others is a difficult task. Some forms of burden sharing, such as defence spending and military hard power (discussed in Part II), are quantifiable and permit relatively precise calculations. Other important but less tangible contributions – such as commitments to enlarging the alliance, helping shape new internal regimes such as the North Atlantic Cooperation Council (NACC) and the Partnership for Peace (PfP) program, both discussed in Part III – must be evaluated more subjectively.

After collecting the data, I aggregated it for easy cross-level and multi-country comparisons in the following ways (presented in the tables throughout the book):

- **Total contributions** – The total amount of contributions that a country made in a given time period.
- **Average** – The calculated average (arithmetic mean) of those contributions during that time. (From 1990 to 1998, the average was calculated by dividing the total contributions by the 16 NATO members at the time; from 1999 to 2001, the denominator was increased to 19 because the alliance added three members in 1999.)
- **Rank** – Calculated in descending order, starting with the state contributing the highest amount; it is useful for making cross-index comparisons.
- **Percentage of total** – The percentage that a country accomplished as a share of the total.
- **Percentage of total without the United States** – This additional category bolsters the argument that the United States is NATO's sole superpower and is thus in a category by itself.

Cautionary Note and Caveats

When I was researching and processing the data, a number of difficulties arose. First, while I attempted to collect the data for every year from

1989 to 2001, it was not always obtainable. Often, this lack of data resulted from top-secret classifications of NATO documents or those of
the member states – for example, numbers for NATO's common budgets were not available for the years 1989–95. In those cases, the available data was presented and used for the calculations; this approach, of
course, hinders an objective analysis of the primary sources.

Second, the UN and NATO member states use different accounting
practices, and best efforts were made to use comparable data sets. The
resulting figures provide a useful snapshot of the costs incurred by the
NATO allies in responding to continental crisis-management goals.

Third, despite the most diligent selection of indicators that emerged
from the empirical data set, there are even more that I could have used.
Nevertheless, I have divided them into the two categories of analysis
mentioned earlier, military and civilian.

Organization of the Book

The book is divided into three parts. Part I, "Frameworks," lays out the
theoretical and conceptual foundations. Chapter 2 traces how the issue
of NATO burden sharing is discussed in the literature. It concludes by
formulating a number of conceptual and methodological criticisms and
calling for a reinterpretation of the new world order in general and the
practice of NATO burden sharing in particular. These criticisms, to be
honest about my research design, were formulated after consulting the
empirical material. In other words, they are the result of an inductive
research approach, whereby the empirical evidence spoke for itself, and
it revealed a number of theoretical, conceptual, and empirical flaws in
the existing scholarship on NATO burden sharing.

In addition, the data suggested that liberal IR theory might be useful
in explaining the practice and preference formation of the burden-
sharing behaviour of NATO second-tier powers. The second part of
chapter 2 introduces this theoretical framework and its main ontological and epistemological assumptions, and it traces the historical roots of
liberal IR theory as well as its contemporary branches. It also discusses
in detail why liberal IR theory is empirically more powerful, analytically more fundamental, and conceptually more parsimonious than its
main theoretical competitors.

Chapter 3 discusses the conceptual puzzle of the new world order by
evaluating the changing patterns and facets of world order in the post–
Cold War era. It also carves out the distinct features of that new order,

including the scope, meaning, and roles that it prescribed for social actors and NATO burden sharing in particular.

Part II, "Military Burdens," traces the historical record of, and share of collective burdens incurred by, international institutions in all peace operations in the Balkans. Chapter 4 starts by evaluating the role of the EU and the UN in managing the evolving crisis in southeastern Europe. After recounting the UN's failure to contain the ongoing violations of human atrocities in the Balkans, chapter 5 shifts its focus to the NATO-led peace operations, discussing the share of the collective burdens incurred and commitments made to the Implementation Force, Stabilization Force, and Kosovo Force.

Part III, "Civilian Burdens," analyses the non-military aspects of Atlantic burden sharing. Chapter 6 focuses on the intangible roles and share of the burden that second-tier powers carried in the course of NATO's expansion into Eastern Europe. Chapter 7 examines, first, "soft military indicators," such as the level of UN peacekeeping personnel, then "hard civilian indicators," such as NATO's common budgets and foreign aid. Chapter 8 summarizes the empirical findings of the Canadian case study and explores their theoretical as well as practical implications for scholars and practitioners. This concluding chapter then evaluates the theoretical and practical implications of this research for academics and policymakers alike.

PART I

Frameworks

2 Theoretical Framework

Introduction

Atlantic burden sharing has been a contentious issue since the birth of NATO in 1949[1] and has produced a wealth of scholarship across a number of disciplines. Each discipline has claimed to have the best theoretical tools to study burden sharing, and each has used insights from the others to further advance and refine its theoretical and conceptual models. The purpose of this chapter is to set out the theoretical framework for this book. Before doing so, however, it looks at the conventional thinking on Atlantic burden sharing and reviews some of the key works on this issue in the field of IR.

Conventional Thinking on Burden Sharing

The literature in the field of IR distinguishes between at least two competing sets of order.[2] On the one hand, analysts observe a widening agenda of world order that links the state, the economy, and transnational actors. This line of thought addresses issues like human security, globalization, human rights, and international environmentalism. Here the analysis focuses on individuals and their livelihoods rather than states, thus denoting a liberal conception of order.

The second way of thinking about global order is largely state-centred and is concerned with traditional concepts of statecraft, such as the

---

1 See, e.g., Lundestad 1998, 2003, 63–110.
2 Bull 1977; Cox and Sinclair 1996; Miller and Vincent 1990.

balance of power regimes,[3] the nature of the international structure of states, and the polarity of the international system. This model has spawned a significant debate in IR about the polarity of the post–Cold War system.[4] Order is judged to be an aspect of the international state system, while the exercise of international politics is concerned with the distribution of material power and how, if at all, the power resources of states shift in the international system from one pole to another. International politics is governed by the balance-of-power regime, in which states either rival each other (balance) or bandwagon[5] with a power bloc in the system.

Stephen Walt found that states usually balance and rarely bandwagon.[6] *Balancing* refers to a social act in which weaker states join either a stronger power or a coalition of powers. While these revisionist states operate under conditions of anarchy,[7] the distribution and alignment of material-power capabilities in the system establish the states' motivations for challenging the existing global order.[8] Such logic implies that security is the most important value in an anarchical system. At the same time, it prescribes a hierarchy of international politics in which a limited number of great powers dominate the structure of the international system and a larger number of second-tier powers engage in either balancing or bandwagoning behaviours. Yet the reason that states wage war is that they are concerned about their own survival.[9] In this sense, power is considered to be a means of achieving greater national security.

In the context of NATO, this (neorealist) logic implies that an ally with little military strength will gain little security benefit from the

---

3 A discussion of the balance of power is found in Claude 1962; Gulick 1955; Haas 1953; Morgenthau 1948.
4 See Hyde-Price 2007; Ikenberry 1996, 2002; Krauthammer 1990/91; Layne 1993; Mastanduno 1997; van Oudenaren 2005.
5 Jervis and Snyder 1991; Kaufman 1992; Walt 1987. For a critique of bandwagoning relying on the domestic-sources school of alliances, see David 1991, 1992/93; Larson 1991; Levy and Barnett 1991.
6 Walt 1987, 265.
7 *Anarchy* refers to a system of IR that operates without a government and thus without political authority; see Brown, Lynn-Jones, and Miller 1995; Buzan, Jones, and Little 1993; Oye 1986.
8 For neorealists, the distribution of power is the key independent variable in understanding international outcomes such as war, peace, alliance politics, and the balance of power.
9 Waltz 1979.

alliance, whereas a very strong ally can provide a surplus of security and is thus expected to dominate it. Put differently, the distribution of alliance benefits is the result of the relative capabilities of states.[10] In terms of alliance management (e.g., inter-alliance bargaining over military planning, preparedness, and coordination in the event of crisis), allies that value the alliance the least or have better alternatives will be more inclined to lobby other allies for stronger alliance commitments or offer some side payments in alliance negotiations.[11]

A popular example of this power-based theory of international regimes and cooperation is the hegemonic stability theory,[12] which argues that the effectiveness of international regimes and institutions[13] depends on the unipolar configuration of power in particular issue areas. Scholars of this school have debated the specific role that power plays in the set-up and maintenance of international regimes, which have far-reaching implications for predictions of regime content. These debates have also led to different conceptions of power. Stephen Krasner, for example, held that power is the *means* of national statecraft predicting distributional biases. Joseph Grieco, on the other hand, focused on power as an *end* of foreign policy and suggested that regimes generally experience a balanced distribution of gains resulting from cooperation; if not, they are destined to collapse and disappear.

This simplified story of the structure of world order is by no means new. The consensus of this literature is that rising states pose problems for global order because they are believed to hold revisionist ambitions and want to challenge the status quo of world politics. At the same time, such a view provides scholars and analysts of international politics with a clear idea of which objects of analysis are worth examining and which are not: the focus is on major powers, and unless second-tier states are engaged in serious balancing activities or show revisionist

---

10 This is suggested by the sociological-psychological literature on coalition theories; see Caplow 1968.

11 There are two principal sources of conflict in alliance politics (or bargaining): alliance entrapment and alliance abandonment; see Mastanduno 1981, 151–2; Snyder 1984. They have been labelled the "alliance security dilemma" but may better be described as "trade-offs"; see Snyder 2002, 113.

12 van Ham 1992.

13 The effectiveness of an international regime requires two things: that its members abide by its rules and norms and that it is able to fulfil the objectives it has been given. In contrast to regime effectiveness, scholars use regime robustness to measure resilience when exogenous influences are changing.

ambitions for the international system, they are, from a conceptual point of view, irrelevant.[14]

It is hardly surprising, therefore, that second-tier powers were not the primary focus of burden-sharing studies during the Cold War.[15] Relying on the public goods model, the seminal study of Olson and Zeckhauser suggested that alliances are institutions that provide the common public good[16] of collective defence. They noted that "when a nation decides how large a military force to provide in an alliance, it must consider the value it places upon collective defense and the other, nondefense, goods that must be sacrificed to obtain additional military forces."[17] Following deductive reasoning, public goods theorists have pointed out that if collective defence is assumed to be a purely public good,[18] then the benefits of that public good are expected to be non-rival and non-excludable.[19] This means that preventing one member of the group from consuming the good is not feasible economically and that unless side payments or coercion is applied, large groups are likely to produce collective goods.[20]

This model[21] provided two insights into the burden-sharing debate. First, theorists noted that the more powerful states shoulder disproportionately higher contributions to the collective burden.[22] In 1970, for example, the United States contributed more than 70% to NATO's

---

14 See Wight 1973, 1977; Wight, Bull, and Holbraad 1978.

15 Others have also shown that the hegemonic stability theory can be considered an application of Olson's theory of collective action; see Oneal and Elrod 1989, 448.

16 A *public good* is defined as the common interest of a group of individual actors; see Olson 1965; Olson and Zeckhauser 1966.

17 Olson and Zeckhauser 1966, 268.

18 Samuelson 1954.

19 A public good is considered non-rival when a unit of that public good can be consumed by one state without diminishing its availability and thus its benefits for others. The benefits of a public good are non-excludable "if they cannot be withheld at an affordable cost by the good's provider"; see Sandler and Hartley 1999, 29.

20 The opposite applies as well: the smaller the group, the greater the prospect of finding collective goods because it is assumed that at least one member of the group has sufficient interest in the good to provide payments towards it, even though not all members may share the costs; see Olson 1965, 49–50.

21 The model has been further developed by Hansen, Murdoch, and Sandler 1990; Murdoch and Sandler 1982, 1984, McGuire 1990; Russett 1970; van Ypersele de Strihou 1967.

22 This is also known as an exploitation hypothesis (McGuire 1990, 29); see also Sandler and Hartley 1995, ch. 2.

defence spending, while the next largest allies – Germany, France, and the United Kingdom – each assumed less than 6%.[23] Analysts used this opportunity to make a causal link between the level of national defence spending and the issue of burden sharing.[24]

The second insight was that because of the imbalance of power in an alliance, there is a systematic tendency among second-tier states to contribute less to the collective benefit of the public good than they receive from it. This free riding, or exploitation, occurs when non-payers of the public good continue to enjoy it despite their lack of payments. Receiving the benefits of the public good regardless of whether a payment towards that good was made can produce negative effects for the collective welfare of the alliance. Still, the public good can be provided under two conditions.[25] First, those allies that value the public good the most are expected to contribute to providing it, while those that do not are assumed to engage in free riding. (Olson calls this the "privileged group.") In this case, individual states have an incentive to not reveal their demand for the good and thus conceal the value they attach to it. Second, the public good can be provided when the group of states is relatively small.

At the same time, following this line of argument suggests that an internal asymmetry of an alliance can work to its advantage because only an outstanding economic and political power has the ability to lead the group and force payments on its members to ensure the alliance's effectiveness and robustness.

A variant of this theory of collective action – called the joint product model – expands on Olson's theory of collective state action and holds that states contribute to the public good not only exclusively for public but also for private benefits.[26] Private benefits provided in collective-action situations are not equally available to all members of a group; they are often enjoyed only by a few selected states. Following this logic, one could expect that some states contribute to the public good

---

23 Most of NATO's data on defence spending is published in various reports and press releases (e.g., by the Defence Planning Committee, http://www.nato.int/cps/en/natolive/topics_49198.htm).

24 Olson and Zeckhauser's model was verified; see Oneal 1990a, 1990b; Oneal and Elrod 1989.

25 Olson 1965, 2, 49–50.

26 Russett 1970, 109–10. Others have shown that when private benefits increase in importance, the likelihood of free riding declines; see Sandler and Forbes 1980, 430.

precisely because they are striving to receive private goods (or benefits) from major states while attempting to avoid perceptions of free-riding.[27] However, the possibility of receiving private benefits makes the public good impure. A number of scholars have built on this finding by noting a variation in the purity of collective goods.[28] A public good, for example, can be public within a country but private among countries, or it can be impure both within and among countries.[29]

Hegemonic stability theorists borrowed insights and logic from collective action theorists by arguing that hegemonic stability theory can be seen as a specific theoretical account of international regimes and as a special case of Olson's theory of collective action.[30] The theory also has roots in the field of economics and seeks to explain under which conditions, as well as when and why, states pursue cooperation in international regimes.[31] Hegemonic stability theory holds that when conditions of a unipolar power structure in a regime disappear, the regime itself is likely to break down and become ineffective. It also asserts that regimes are established and maintained by actors who hold outstanding power resources (or a preponderance of power) that are relevant to the particular issue area. In turn, regimes decline or decrease their effectiveness – that is, when members stop abiding by its norms and rules[32] – when power resources become more equally distributed across the group.[33]

While it pushed the explanatory relevance of realist scholarship in IR, hegemonic stability theory was not without its critics. Most prominent among the challengers who questioned its very basic assumptions was Duncan Snidal. He introduced two new variants of hegemonic stability theory that are relevant for burden-sharing studies. The first was that of a "benevolent leader" that provides the public good unilaterally, while other states of the group are alleviated from their payments towards this good or to maintain the regime.[34] However,

---

27 A good overview of this variant of collective action theory is found in Hartley and Sandler 1999; Betts 2003.
28 Murdoch and Sandler 1982; Sandler 1977; Sandler and Cauley 1975; Sandler, Cauley, and Forbes 1980.
29 Pauly 1970.
30 Hasenclever, Mayer, and Rittberger 1997, 86, 88.
31 Kindelberger 1973.
32 Young 1994; Underdal 1992.
33 Keohane 1980.
34 Snidal 1985.

this "exploitation of the great by the small," he noted, does not necessarily mean that the hegemon's net gains from providing this good – that is, the benefits it receives from the good minus its contributions – is smaller than those received by the free-riding countries. The hegemon's net benefits may well exceed those of the free riders, which pay rents to the hegemon.

This insight underlines the interest-based nature of this variant of the hegemonic stability paradigm. However, it does not suggest that states would not cooperate at all; they do so, for example, by adjusting their policies to achieve common goals in the context of agreed-upon rules or regimes.[35] Hegemonic stability theory does not rule out first-order cooperation at the international level (cooperation in specific issue areas that are mutually beneficial) as it tries to explain such cooperative behaviour in itself.[36] However, second-order cooperation is logically impossible for hegemonic stability theorists, especially when it comes to questions of rule making and enforcement.

The second variant of the conventional hegemonic stability model that Snidal introduced is the coercive leadership model. In line with Robert Gilpin's work on war and peace, Snidal assumes that the global hegemon is compelled to produce international public goods.[37] However, what distinguishes Snidal's two variants is that in the latter version, the hegemon is not assumed to bear the costs of providing the public good itself because its interests in the good are so high. Rather, because of its superior power predispositions, the global hegemon forces other states in the group to contribute to providing the good. This means that the hegemon can effectively "tax," or sanction, those states for their inability or unwillingness to share the burden.[38] This taxation can occur to different degrees and at different levels of coercion

---

35 This phenomenon is sometimes called "first-order cooperation." When costs to provide these rules are provided by two or more states, the literature speaks of "second-order cooperation"; see Axelrod and Keohane 1986; Zangl 1994.

36 Keohane 1980, 132.

37 Gilpin 1981.

38 Some analysts have asserted that the exploitation hypothesis may be inconsistent with the realist's assumptions that states generally have a low tolerance for relative losses (a stance that would align realist and especially neo-liberal theories). However, contrary to neo-liberal assumptions, the distribution of interests in the benevolent leadership model is based on power and resources and thus their distribution. Also, the exploitation hypothesis does not imply that the hegemon necessarily experiences a loss relative to other states (even though this may be the case).

(e.g., persuasion, bribes). Snidal's two models are not necessarily exclusive: a combination of coercion and benevolence may occur.[39]

Another example of the power-based theory of international regimes is the power transition research program, which put forward a slightly different realist explanation of alliance behaviour. While sharing most of the assumptions held by realism, power transition theorists particularly reject the prevalence of the balance-of-power regime of classical and neorealist thinkers. Most prominent among them are Organski (classical power transition theory), Gilpin (hegemonic transition theory), Modelski and Thompson (theory of long cycles of global leadership and decline), and Doran (power cycle theory).[40] All of these variants of the power transition research paradigm share the assumption that concentrations of power in hegemonic states have a stabilizing rather than a weakening effect on the international system. Hegemons, in other words, contribute to peace, rather than inflicting war, and prevent the creation of coalitions against dominant states.[41]

Organski was one of the founders of this research program, and he made two distinct contributions to the literature. First, by focusing on the strongest states, he rejected the explanation that an equal distribution of capabilities among allies contributes to peace. Instead, he argued, this equal distribution leads to war.[42] A dominant power that functions as the system's hegemon provides stability and order within a group of states by establishing rules that direct political, economic, and military relations, and it derives these rules from its relative wealth and capabilities. Hegemony emerges, according to Organski, from the uneven patterns of industrialization and wealth, and it provides the causal explanation of why other states challenge the dominant state's leadership. The transition period between one state losing its dominance and another one taking its place marks the crucial point where war between two contending great powers is most likely.[43] "This war is fought for control of the 'rules of the game,' or status quo, of the international

---

39 See Yarbrough and Yarbrough 1987. For a critique of Snidal's models, see Alt, Calvert, and Humes 1988; Lake 1993.
40 Kugler and Lemke 1996; Gilpin 1981, 1988; Modelski and Thompson 1989; Organski 1958; Doran 1980, 1989.
41 Levy 1994 calls this "hegemonic realism."
42 Organski 1958, 313–30.
43 This finding has been extended to all major powers; see Houweling and Siccama 1988.

system, with the expectation that victory by the challenger will be followed by a restructuring of international diplomatic, economic, and military relations."[44] Relative power capabilities[45] and the degree of satisfaction of states function as key independent variables in the power transition research program. In other words, states with insufficient power capabilities or high degrees of satisfaction with the status quo show little motivation to challenge the existing international order.[46]

Another distinction between Organski's power transition theory and prevalent neorealist explanations is that it rejects conditions of anarchy as the primary ordering principle of international politics and insists on a hierarchical international order that is defined by the distribution of power and the practices of hegemonic states.

Doran's power cycle theory goes a step further and attempts to unite the structural with the behavioural variables to explain state actions. It reconciles "realism and idealism in conceptualizing foreign policy role as coequal in significance with power in matters of statecraft."[47] However, contrary to Organski and Kugler, Modelski, and Gilpin, who identify major war as the medium by which a new hierarchy of the international system is created, Doran finds that causation follows the opposite route: from a transformation of the system to war. War is not a necessary ingredient of systemic change; rather, evolutionary developments take place through the processes of complementarity and competitiveness, which make states rise or decline (i.e., compete or cooperate) in terms of their "relative share of the total power in the central system."[48] This in turn explains the cyclical redistribution of power in the international system.[49]

---

44 Lemke 1997, 24.
45 Different measures were applied here. Organski and Kugler (1980) settled on gross national product. Howeweling and Siccama (1988) as well as Lemke and Werner (1996) test the power transition theory based on Doran and Parson's relative capability index (1980).
46 See Organski and Kugler 1980, 42–5, 50–2. For an application of this logic to alliances, see Kim 1989, 1991, 1992. Unlike balance of power theories, power transition theory excludes alliances and treats internal growth as the sole source of power and international change. (Balance of power theory does both.)
47 Doran 2003, 14.
48 Doran 2005, 687.
49 Doran 1971, 2–12. Complementarity denotes a situation whereby governments join forces because of their comparative advantage; competitiveness is, in a way, the opposite: states clash over certain behaviour or attitudes.

The foreign policy role of states – the dynamic (and systemic) variable of power cycle theory – references the expected foreign policy behaviour and position of the state in the international system. To be legitimate, a foreign policy role requires systemic acceptance by other states.[50] It is partially determined by the power of the state, and it needs to be in sync with it (i.e., maintain a dynamic equilibrium) to ensure the stability of the system.[51]

Conceptual and Theoretical Limitations of These Models

The end of the Cold War created problems for these static models of collective action, regimes, and world order. Some allies took the opportunity to point out the imbalance in the Atlantic burden-sharing regime. The United States, as mentioned earlier, claimed that it had assumed a disproportionately large share of the burden and that it was time for second-tier powers to increase their share.[52] Germany responded, complaining that its national contribution to the common defence was distorted because of the use of the GDP/percentage of defence spending indicator. It argued that it had shouldered, for example, the costs of protecting American military installations in Germany and provided more than 130,000 housing units for allied servicemen[53] but that these expenses were not reflected in the GDP indicator.[54] These two examples give weight to the need to revisit the practice of using this indicator to determine a country's share of the Atlantic burden.

On the conceptual level, the public goods model did not adequately explain Atlantic burden-sharing behaviour, for a number of reasons. First, the public good of collective defence was redefined after the Cold War, when at its seminal London summit in 1990 the alliance downgraded the importance of collective defence over crisis management.

---

50 Doran 2003, 30.
51 For details, see Doran 1991, ch. 7.
52 United States, Committee on Armed Services 1988. US overspending on the defence of Western Europe also gained traction in the 1988 presidential campaign; see "Sharing (Which?) NATO Burdens," *New York Times*, 16 June 1988; "NATO's Smiling Summiteers," *New York Times*, 8 March 1988.
53 Boyer 1993, 83.
54 The GDP indicator is still used today.

The general geopolitical situation in Europe and the evolving ethnic conflicts in the Balkans in particular amply reinforced this shift and justified the need for extraterritorial forces to project NATO's collective values and beliefs. With the escalating intra-state wars in south-eastern Europe, preventing genocide or the mass murder of ethnic groupings, exporting political and socio-economic values to evolving democratic societies in CEE, and maintaining a stable European order became NATO's "new" public goods (also called milieu goals).[55]

A second reason for the failure of the public goods model was that while it was heavily influenced by rational choice thinking and economic modelling, it had limited value for explaining and understanding state behaviour because it focused so explicitly on static material power as a military component of national statecraft rather than what power is actually about. While realist IR theorists focus exclusively on major wars and the balancing behaviour of states, they deny an analytical perspective below the surface of the state or any unpacking of the value and instrumentally rational motivations and interests of social agents. The materialistic ontology neglects the social dimension of power, and excludes factors like status, prestige, recognition, the values of freedom and democracy, the rule of law, international justice, and the effects that (international) rules and principles can have on the behaviour of states. On the issue of burden sharing, the decision of states to free ride, keep a distance, or invoke notions of state sovereignty depends on societal preferences.[56] States do not necessarily seek relative gains; in fact, in their foreign policies, they often tend to pursue absolute gains. Furthermore, the collective action model shows the deficiencies of explaining other states' behaviour.[57]

Third, Olson and Zeckhauser's theory and logic of collective action employs a number of assumptions that make it barely applicable to a real-world setting. First and foremost, it assumes that the defence of

---

55 For a similar argument, see Dorussen, Kirchner, and Sperling 2009, 793.
56 Whether this burden-sharing commitment is of a military, economic, or political nature also depends on these domestic variables; see Bennett, Lepgold, and Unger 1994, 72; see also Putnam 1988. It also depends on how much states have contributed to other international organizations that occupy a political space of "regime complexity"; see Bennett, Lepgold, and Unger 1994; Dorussen, Kirchner, and Sperling 2009.
57 Sandler and Hartley 1999, ch. 2.

the NATO alliance is a *pure* public good – that is, fully joint and non-excludable – and that alliances produce only a single public good: collective defence. Furthermore, it assumes that alliance defence is produced equally and efficiently among all allies and that the costs are exclusively economic rather than political –or social, for that matter. However, this is an oversimplification that ignores the potential benefits of multinational cost variation and thus the comparative advantage that states may have in producing collective goods. It also disregards, as Mark Boyer argues, the possibility of trading between smaller and major powers in providing the public good. In other words, collective action theorists' assumption is one-dimensional: it excludes the possibilities that allies produce more than one public good and that they trade those goods among themselves.[58]

The collective action model presumes that allies decide on the size of their contributions in isolation[59] and that they are engaged in only one activity at a time.[60] This distorts the practice of burden sharing and goes against mainstream arguments in the literature as to why nations join alliances. These assumptions are also analytically restrictive because states in an alliance regularly engage in negotiations and arguments with their allies based on their national preferences. Put differently, and to paraphrase Mark Boyer, alliances are by nature cooperative, and their national preferences determine the extent to which they contribute to a burden-sharing regime.[61] By joining an alliance, states give up a certain degree of national sovereignty; this implies that they have an interest in negotiating the benefits of that membership, which requires negotiation and cooperation with the allies to reduce uncertainty.[62] States in an alliance also constantly seek trade-offs between domestic and international policy goals, and they make choices from a number of available alliance goods.

Fourth, the public goods model fails to account for the possibility that it is affected by the changing global order. This explains the model's rather static nature and the fact that it is not receptive to situational change. A number of analysts have pointed out, however, that the international order of the post–Cold War era is much more integrated,

---

58 Boyer 1993, 32.
59 Russett 1970; Sandler 1977.
60 Strange 1987b.
61 Boyer 1993, 38; Kimball 2010. For a rebuttal, see Sandler and Forbes 1980, 431–4.
62 Axelrod 1984.

cohesive, and successful than it was during the Cold War.[63] It is a bloc of power representing a cohesive set of values that pulls other states into the Western community. Thus, it renders the old story of challenging the existing order obsolete.

The new world order in the 1990s was guided by the logic of socialization and internalization.[64] It was not about increasing power capabilities, engaging in the balance of power, or bandwagoning politics. Above all, the Western order held a set of values that pulled non-Western states into its sphere. The dominant underlying expectations, particularly among members of the US foreign policy elite, were that non-Western states could be enticed and subsequently brought into the Western community of states. It is precisely in this sense that liberal IR theory helps us establish causality between state preferences and state behaviour and understand the intersubjective social structures of agents (i.e., how non-democratic states, especially in CEE, became cooperative rather than competitive and what that meant for NATO member states and their practice of burden sharing). In other words, it is not merely the cost-benefit analysis that can determine an actor's behaviour but rather its norms and values and the logic of appropriateness.[65]

Fifth, as numerous studies have shown, the collective action model does not withstand empirical analysis, especially the strong free riding, or no provision, of the public good hypothesis.[66] The free-riding assumption does not hold in other issue areas either. Eiko Thielemann, for example, has shown that certain northern European countries have contributed to an exceptional degree to the protection of refugees, something that cannot be explained by their size, relative capabilities, or immediate exposure to trans-European refugee movements.[67] More

---

63 Foot, Gaddis, and Hurrell 2003; Hurrell 2007; Hurrell and Kingsbury 1992; Hurrell and Woods 1999.
64 See Gheciu 2005b; Christiansen, Jørgensen, and Wiener 2001; Schimmelpfennig 1999, 2003.
65 In the context of international regimes, the logic of appropriateness denotes that human action follows rules of institutions because they are seen as natural, expected, and legitimate and because social actors want to fulfil their obligations, role, or identity in a political community. They do what "they see as appropriate for themselves in a specific type of situation" (March and Olsen 2004, 3).
66 See Marwell and Ames 1979, 1980, 1981; Alfano and Marwell 1981; Scherr and Babb 1975; Bohm 1972; Sweeney 1973.
67 Thielemann 2003.

recently, scholars have argued that in European security governance regimes, poorer European countries have not exploited the richer states.[68]

Sixth, as Duncan Snidal reminds us, from a theoretical point of view the non-excludability assumptions of regime theory vary greatly over issue areas.[69] Indeed, excludability is not an impossibility, thus calling into question the relevance of, especially, the hegemonic stability theory in certain issue areas. John Conybeare, for example, has shown that the non-excludability principle does not fit into many economic issue areas,[70] making hegemonic stability theory highly selective and thus less prone to generalizations. Other empirical tests have shown that in the absence of hegemony, a number of regimes can be identified.[71]

Seventh, as Joanne Gowa charges, hegemonic stability explanations neglect the security externalities of economic cooperation;[72] their ontological assumptions do not include the context of cooperation under hegemony. Indeed, numerous studies have shown that the societal transformation processes occasioned by the shake-up of the external security environment at the end of the Cold War gave new meanings to the values of security, diplomacy, and power.[73] It transformed the roles, functions, interests, and responsibilities of states and international institutions and provides an insight into why states prefer cooperation to balancing.

It is against this backdrop that we need to explain and understand the social actions of burden sharing and the preference formation of states. Above all, the transformation processes challenge the power-lust and zero-sum-game argument of realist theorists, whose main tenets rest on the notion that the extent of national defence spending as a percentage of a country's total GDP automatically determines the degree of its international material capabilities and, as a result, influence. While this logic is based on ontological assumptions of an anarchic

---

68 Dorussen, Kirchner, and Sperling 2009.

69 Snidal 1985, 595–7. For a similar argument rejecting the non-rivalry and non-excludability assumption in conventional collective action theory, see Duffield 1996, 348–9; Russett 1970, 70; Goldstein 1995, 40.

70 Conybeare 1984, 8.

71 Young and Osherenko 1993, 230.

72 Gowa 1989, 322–4.

73 Some scholars have argued that the end of the Cold War can be equated with a revolution in international affairs; see Halliday 2001, 19–22.

world, the pre-eminent role of states in international affairs, the need for security, and the necessity for large military capabilities as a means of projecting power all render these assumptions inconsistent in a new world order. This is especially true given that nearly all of NATO's Cold War enemies became its friends and open to engagement with the West.

Eighth, the power transition research paradigm is not very relevant to our case study because the issue of power distribution resulting from industrialization and the degree of satisfaction with the status quo of the international system do not really apply. Despite fears of a strategic vacuum developing in CEE after the withdrawal of the Soviet Union at the end of the Cold War, no war was likely during the power shift in those regions because the Soviet Union's ambition to challenge the status quo was declining.

This speaks to several other minor explanatory weaknesses of the power transition paradigm. To start with, it does not allow us to predict which state initiates a war or when, why, or who carries the burdens of that war. It can explain the structural conditions that are conducive to war, but not the causal mechanisms that cause states to start wars.[74] In addition, the paradigm shares major ontological assumptions with realists, who deny a more in-depth analysis of how the foreign policy behaviour of states comes about (i.e., how policy is made) and, in particular, what preferences states hold on foreign policy issues. Moreover, its power cycle variant relies heavily on assumptions of rationality, whereby at any time, the international system can be described as the result of all states being on different power cycles (or curves). Thus, the system is determined by changes in states' share of the total systemic power.

Finally, rationalists' static assumptions (particularly those held by the realist, neorealist, and neo-liberal schools of IR) about states' interests or preferences paint a rigid picture of international behaviour that states are bound to follow. The rationalists assume that a social actor's preferences remain stable, and this helps theorists construct epistemologically motivated IR theories.[75] There are, however, at least three problems with this rationalist mode of explanation. First, it denies an analytical perspective on the processes and ways in which

74 DiCicco and Levy 2003, 144.
75 Hasenclever, Mayer, and Rittberger 1997, 23–4.

national preferences (or interests) are formed[76] and thus prevents a deeper explanation of social behaviour.[77] If changed too quickly, it argues, preferences degenerate "to a generalized post hoc revealed-preference exercise, where actions are assumed to reflect prevailing fluctuations in preferences."[78]

Moreover, this static model of the so-called national interest does not seem overly convincing in the post–Cold War security environment because the international system had changed considerably, and thus it can be assumed that at least some (if not all) states' preferences have changed accordingly. Rationalist theories of preference formation noted above do not seem to take these changes into account. This is particularly troubling considering NATO's burden-sharing regime in the immediate post–Cold War era. As this book will show, liberal theories of preference formation hold greater prospects for explaining the changes in the national preference formation of NATO member states and thus their burden-sharing behaviour in the 1990s.

Methodological Criticisms

During the research on NATO burden sharing (defined as the "actual contribution of each nation to collective defence and the fairness of each state's contribution"[79]), a number of methodological deficits and inaccuracies became apparent in NATO's reliance on a state's level of defence spending as a percentage of its GDP.

The first deficit results from international institutions' different accounting practices and methods of aggregating data, which inherently complicate the collection of comparable statistical data, especially for NATO and the UN. A selected group of NATO members, for example, report the costs incurred from conscription as part of their national

---

76 Here this study builds on an argument put forward by Graham Allison (1971), who said that to assume that states are rational utility maximizers is to say that states have achieved a Pareto-optimal result at the national level; this is a claim that simply cannot be supported empirically.

77 Some neorealist and neo-liberal scholars go so far as to argue that national preferences are stable not only over time but also across actors; see Keohane 1989a; Powell 1991; Waltz 1979.

78 Snidal 1986, 43. A related problem in alliance research is that there is no theory of bargaining among allies, only one among adversaries; see Schelling 1960.

79 For a greater discussion, see Hartley and Sandler 1999, 669.

defence budgets; however, not all allies have conscripted armies, so comparing the aggregated data naturally produces imprecise results. (The United States, the United Kingdom, and Canada have voluntary armies, while Norway and Turkey, to name just two countries, rely on conscription; this puts them at a disadvantage when measuring the efficiency and effectiveness of their armed forces.)[80] Other allies add capital expenditures for pensions to their defence budgets as well as the costs of research and development.

Second, this practice results in imprecise data sets, and this contributes to an inaccurate analysis of the whole burden-sharing debate. Hence, the collected and aggregated data that is provided by international security organizations like NATO or the UN is of limited explanatory value; at the very least, it requires cautionary use as well as an analysis and interpretation of their context. Also, measuring defence budgets as a percentage of GDP does not reflect variations in income levels among NATO allies and thus violates the fundamental principles of distributive justice.

Fourth, the GDP indicator does not give any information about how NATO member states structure their forces to execute the new NATO missions that were envisioned in the alliance's 1991 Strategic Concept, which placed greater emphasis on more flexible and mobile rapid reaction forces and crisis management. This relates to the earlier point about the efficiency versus the effectiveness of armed forces and, once again, calls for an interpretation of the context.

Moreover, while smaller allies, in particular, are unable to devote a sizable amount of their armed forces or military equipment to collective defence, they concentrate their efforts on contributions to international peace operations and non-military assistance to CEE. Thus, they contribute indirectly to collective defence, but this commitment is not reflected in the conventional GDP indicator.

Finally, the GDP yardstick does not reflect the actual costs of national defence spending. The contributions of Greece and Turkey, for example, which spend about 4.5% and 4.1%, respectively, of their GDP on defence, are deceptive, especially when they are weighed against their collective benefit for the entire alliance. Indeed, it shows that these states have received a private rather than a collective benefit from their large conventional forces.

---

80 Lis and Selden, 2003.

Because of these conceptual and methodological deficits, one might conclude that the ontological and epistemological assumptions of collective action theorists do not hold much explanatory power for the debate on burden sharing in the post–Cold War era. Above all, this "obscures a contextualization"[81] of a member state's strategic situation and commitment to Atlantic burden sharing. As a result, the context of the social actions of sharing Atlantic burdens needs to be considered in order to understand the underlying motivations for sharing the burden in the first place. To do this, we need to study the evolution of national preferences.

General Ontological Assumptions of Liberal IR Theory

Having reviewed the various strands of the theoretical literature, the remainder of this chapter discusses the evolution of liberal IR theory and why it is used as the theoretical framework of this book.

The greatest benefit of using liberal IR theory is that it contributes to an understanding of foreign policy by focusing on how individuals, their ideals and values, as well as social forces and the political institutions of democracy and representation, shape the foreign relations of states. It thus provides a multi-causal explanation of state behaviour(s). It assumes that political action (and change) is embedded in domestic and transnational society, which is composed of rationally acting but socially diverse individuals who have different preferences for outcomes. It further assumes that these individuals define their material and non-material interests independently of politics and exploit them. It is thus a powerful framework for explaining how national preferences causally affect the foreign policy behaviour of states and how states in an alliance create and maintain a "zone of peace."[82] In contrast to realism,[83] liberal IR theory is interested in the type and number of actors involved in the decision-making process and allows for the interplay of varying ideas, people, and structures in that process.

---

81 Hartley and Sandler 1999, 668; see also Sandler and Hartley 1999.
82 Doyle 2008.
83 There are two reasons for this contrast. First, realism ontologically renounces opening the "black box" of preference formations by assuming the unity of states. However, states and thus their foreign policy decisions are highly decentralized and fragmented entities, and, in contrast to realist security interests, liberals promote individual rights and freedoms transnationally. For a detailed discussion of realist

Ontologically, liberal IR theory posits that humans generally have good characters and that progress in international affairs is possible; it focuses on cooperation between principals and agents (rather than power and power capabilities) and on the domestic interests and structures of states (or both). It thus attributes less to the influence of external factors on the state but rather sees the relationship between state and society (domestic and transnational) as the centre of its research program; in this sense, it leaves room for domestic determinants as explanatory values of state behaviour (e.g., in the Canadian case, the budgetary crisis in the early 1990s and the threat to national unity in 1995). As a result, and combined with a Weberian methodology, which is a novel contribution, liberal IR theory provides better *explanations* and *understanding* of foreign policy behaviour (e.g., NATO burden-sharing practices) and how absolute gains rather than relative gains are the primary motivation of this behaviour.

To fully appreciate contemporary liberal IR scholarship, one needs to trace its origins to the liberal political thought of the 17th century. The basic tenet of classical liberal thinking is a belief in individual rights, private property, and representative government;[84] it places a high value on human and humanitarian rights, liberty, freedom, democracy, and the rule of law as well as social forces such as capitalism and liberal market economies.[85] It respects international laws, other peaceful states, and international norms, and it regards individuals, not states, as the primary actors in international politics.[86] Much like realism, liberal IR theory assumes that the nature of the international system is anarchic but that it is non-repetitive, or cyclical.[87]

---

ontology, see Brooks and Wohlforth 2008; Donnelly 1992; Gilpin 1981; Jervis 2003; Kaufman, Little, and Wohlforth 2007; Walt 1987; Waltz 1979; Wohlforth 1993. Second, while downplaying economic gains, realism's assumptions of self-help, security interests, and state power imply that "states do not willingly place themselves in situations of increased dependence" (Waltz 1979, 107).

84 Doyle 1997.

85 Against this backdrop, liberal IR theory also complicates the study of foreign policy; see Moravcsik 1997; Nincic 1992; Zacher and Matthew 1995. Broadly speaking, the literature distinguishes between social welfare liberals and laissez-faire liberals: the former is committed to judicial freedom, democratic control of government, the right to private property, and the economic forces of supply and demand; the latter leans towards a highly constrained role of the state in economic relations; see Locke 1988.

86 Zacher and Matthew 1995, 119.

87 Donnelly 1992; Gilpin 1986; Holsti 1985.

The objective of liberal IR theory, then, is to examine whether and how particular types of state preferences and their variations impact the foreign policies and behaviours of states – in our case, second-tier powers like Canada.[88] It provides a theoretical framework for various strands of contemporary liberal theory – the ideational, commercial, republican, sociological, and institutional liberal schools[89] – which should not be seen in competition with one another but rather as complementary.

Strands of Liberal IR Theory

Identity and Nature of Social Orders (Ideational Liberals)

John Locke is considered to be one of those ideational liberals who focused on human rights and the obligation of the state to uphold the "life, liberty, and property" of its subjects.[90] The rights of states, he charged, are simply an extension of the rights of individuals, ceded to the state; they are based on a social contract between the individual and the state. Individuals make the state the ultimate representative of civil society, which in turn enforces their rights to the best of its abilities. These rights are the product of a deep appreciation for equality and respect for other human beings. Conversely, it is the natural duty of individuals to respect these rights, by force if necessary, and punish those who intend to violate them. It is these duties that lead states to maintain peace with each other in a community of states.[91] Moreover, individuals create a "Commonwealth" in which "federative powers" – that is, the power to adopt and pass laws as well as to implement them – are shared among the Executive, the Legislative, and the Judiciary.[92] In such a federation, states have the constitutional right (legitimacy) to act on behalf of civil society, nationally as well as internationally. In turn, civil society holds the government accountable for its actions.

---

88 Doyle 2008, 59.
89 I follow here the distinction made by Moravcsik 2003, 167. For a discussion on the
     variants, see Doyle 1997; Moravcsik 2003; Zacher and Matthew 1995.
90 Locke 1988.
91 Doyle 2008, 60.
92 Locke 1988, ch. 8, 9, and 12.

Lockean states remain at peace unless a state breaks the law or is attacked. Threats to peace are based on ignorance, partiality, and revenge as well as weakness and fear among agents.[93] Accordingly, the primary objective of the state is to avoid these opportunities for war and to pursue opportunities for improved regulation in order to maintain a stable political, social, and economic environment in which individuals can pursue their chosen goals.

Commerce and Cross-Border Transactions (Commercial Liberals)

Adam Smith (1723–90) is considered the father of liberal, or laissez-faire, economic thinking; he believed that governments have a very restricted role in the governance of national economies and that free and unrestricted markets hold the best prospects for generating mutual gains.[94] Consumers and society enjoy "natural rights" that allow them to pursue their own interests without government intervention. Indeed, the individual freedom of people produces "a natural progress of things" and a division of labour. A free market economy guarantees that the consumer is led by an "invisible hand"[95] and that manufacturing is stimulated and controlled by the supply and demand chain.

Smith noted that states have only three duties: to protect society from the hostile invasion of another country, to ensure the functionality and impartiality of the judiciary, and to maintain public institutions[96] as a condition for domestic stability.[97] Only on very rare occasions does the free market exchange of goods and services require the interference of the state (e.g., to protect ports and maritime commerce). The idea of a large standing army is foreign to liberals: soldiers are considered labourers who are taken away from the processes of production, and the size of the armed forces should therefore be kept to a minimum. The use of force is allowed only in exceptional circumstances (e.g., to fight

---

93 Locke called this condition a "troubled peace." States create regimes to overcome these Lockean "inconveniences" by a Common Court of Judicature; see Bentham 1927, 42–3; Keohane 1984, ch. 6.

94 Francois Quesnay, Anne Turgot, and Thomas Paine endorsed this view; see Domke 1988; Howard 1978.

95 Smith 1976.

96 Ibid., Book V, ch. 1. He refers here to public goods like roads, bridges, and other infrastructure.

97 Locke (1963, 406) held that states' powers are bound by established rules and laws.

aggressors); establishing colonies and setting tariffs are prohibited because they are seen as causing war rather than promoting peace.

Joseph Schumpeter (1883–1950) built on Smith's philosophy and offered a modernized version of liberal market theories. For Schumpeter, a
combination of laissez-faire market capitalism and liberal democracy
creates a lasting liberal peace.[98] He thus considers peace the structured
outcome of capitalist democracies. In his studies on empires and the politics of imperialism, he found that the more capitalism and democracy
develop, the more the signs of imperialism are likely to disappear. Like
Smith, he concluded that only democratic capitalism leads to peace: it
trains individuals to be rational, individual, and knowledgeable about
democracy and to calculate the costs and benefits of their actions.

Because people's daily preoccupation is to ensure the accumulation of
wealth in the process of economic production, they are not interested in
waging war because it would be they who would have to pay the costs
(i.e., through higher taxes).[99] Moreover, war decreases the chances of developing lasting free trade relationships with other countries, thus reducing access to raw materials abroad for the production of goods at home.
Only businesses related to the military industrial complex and military
aristocrats would benefit from states waging wars, not civil society.[100]

Contemporary commercial liberals seek to explain the individual
and collective behaviour of states using the patterns of market incentives faced by domestic and transnational actors.[101] Specifically, they
argue that market societies oppose wars and conflicts and that transnational market relations and commercial societies are pacifying forces.[102]
While commercial liberals believe in the importance of republican institutions for guaranteeing rights and freedoms, they hold that the deeper
cause of peace is transnational commerce.[103] The core of this strand of

---

98 Schumpeter 1951, 1946, 3–98. A "liberal state" does not in any way imply an ideological preference for state representation or political party (e.g., the Liberal Party
of Canada).

99 Humphrey 1983, 94–5.

100 Schumpeter 1951, 70–5.

101 Some argue that they focus on Waltz's "second image," which highlights the pacifying market of social forces; see Keohane and Nye 1977; Oneal et al. 1996; Oneal
and Russett 1997; Rosecrance 1986.

102 Others (Ohmae 1990; Vernon 1971) argue that multinational corporations cause
a loss of control and sovereignty.

103 Oneal, Russett, and Berbaum 2003. Kim and Rousseau (2005) disputed this pacifying effect of economic interdependence.

liberalism is functionalist in the sense that "changes in the structure of the domestic and global economy affect the costs and benefits of transnational economic exchanges."[104]

Representation and Cosmopolitanism (Republican Liberals)

For republican liberals, the type and conditions of the political system are essential for maintaining transnational peace and order;[105] this includes how states perceive each other.[106] John Owen put it succinctly. "When liberals run the government, relations with fellow democracies are harmonious. When illiberals govern, relations may be rockier."[107]

Joseph Schumpeter and Adam Smith held that a combination of free market forces and democratic institutions of government is the primary precondition for a lasting peace among states; however, their thinking held weak explanatory powers for the existence of long-lasting peace among democracies and the strong likelihood that liberal states would go to war with non-liberal states. With his concept of a "perpetual peace," Immanuel Kant tried to build a bridge from Locke to Schumpeter and Smith, arguing that republican representation (elected legislatures, accountable governments, and separation of powers among institutions of government), combined with respect for freedom, human and individual rights, and transnational interdependence (trade and social interconnectedness), are the preconditions for such a peace.

Kant called these conditions "definitive articles" because they form the integral components of a liberal republic. The first article speaks to the civil constitution of the state, which needs to be republican; in such a republic, individual rights and freedoms must be guaranteed. The second article refers to the pacific federation of free and liberal states,[108] while the third establishes a cosmopolitan (or international) law. When all states have adopted these definitive articles and consented to a "metaphorical treaty," perpetual peace is achieved.

---

104 Moravcsik 2003, 171. This "commercial realism" is found primarily in regional analysis (e.g., in the EU and North America).
105 The literature examining the correlations between liberal democracy and international peace is extensive; see, e.g., Souva and Prins 2006; Chan 1984, 1997; Ray 1997.
106 Russett and Starr 2000.
107 Owen 1994, 89.
108 Kant 2006, 105.

Transplanted to a modern context, Kantian internationalism guarantees the pre-eminence of the principles of international law and distinguishes among the outcomes of state actions by the differences in their interaction. Only states have the right to use force, have a "positive duty" to defend other members of the pacific community, and can override the sovereignty of other states to rescue individuals from oppressive and brutal regimes (or even change them).[109] In doing so, however, liberal states ought to refrain from employing armed interventions; rather, they should use the scope of their transnational economic relations to induce economic and political reforms, particularly in those states that are undecided about the benefits of democracy.

Modern scholarship that is inspired by Kant's idea of perpetual peace includes the democratic peace theory (DPT),[110] which is perhaps the most important conceptual challenge to realism to date.[111] It holds that liberal democracies are less likely to go to war against each another[112] when states create a zone of peace among themselves.[113] DPT is itself divided into normative and structural theories; the structural branches study the institutional constraints of liberal states, while normative accounts focus on the norm that fighting wars is unjust.[114] DPT holds that the primary foreign policy objective of liberal democracies is to save the liberal community itself and increase the conditions under which the zone of peace can grow. As a means to this end, liberal states are expected to form alliances with other liberal states and manage such an

---

109 However, the process of democratization needs to be coupled with liberal values and principles as well as transnational interdependence (Keohane 1990). The statistical evidence was challenged by Mansfield and Snyder (1995), who suggested expanding international institutions to overcome this dilemma; see also Enterline 1996.

110 Owen 1994; Babst 1972; Bueno de Mesquita, Jackman, and Siverson 1991; Bueno de Mesquita and Lalman 1992b; Garnham 1986; Maoz and Abdolali 1989; Morgan and Schwebach 1992; Rummel 1983; Russett 1993; Small and Singer 1976; Streit 1939; Weede 1984.

111 Recently, numerous auxiliaries have been developed; see Ray 2003, 221; Elman and Elman 2003.

112 Russett and Oneal (2001) empirically discuss the extent and degree of types of democratic societies.

113 The first to observe this was Streit (1939). More recent scholarship on DPT in general includes Babst 1972; Oneal et al. 1996; Kim and Rousseau 2005; Zeev and Abdolali 1989; Bennett 2006.

114 Dixon 1993, 1994; Raymond 1994.

alliance in the spirit of multilateralism.[115] Recent scholarship on NATO has shown that Western states have functioned as role models for states from CEE, which have aspired to their democratic values and free market principles.[116] Thus, from the point of view of DPT's normative elements, the simplest and most effective mode of liberal expansionism is to be "attractive" to others.[117]

But this is not to say that democracies never wage war.[118] They *do* go to war, and they can be hostile and offensive to other countries, particularly if those countries are not liberal democracies – democratic states were active participants in 24 of 56 interstate wars with non-liberal states[119] – and statistically they are more likely to win.[120] Today, more than 102 liberal states make up the zone of peace,[121] showing that DPT is the most progressive and quantitatively oriented research program in IR. As Jack Levy noted, "the absence of wars between democracies comes as close as anything to an empirical law in international relations."[122]

At the same time, however, liberal democratic societies are complaisant; they neglect to preserve existing conditions in a changing international environment – by failing to support their allies, oppose their enemies,[123] or fund their armed forces to defend themselves in a situation

---

115 Russett and Starr, 2000; Keohane 1990.
116 Head, PfP Division, NATO Headquarters, interview by the author, Brussels, May 2007; see also Snyder 1990.
117 Schimmelpfennig 2003.
118 Snyder 2000, 277; Rummel 1979; Snyder and Mansfield 1995. Other quantitative studies are Chan 1984; Bueno de Mesquita and Lalman 1992b; normative ones are Morgan and Campbell 1991; Dixon 1994. Hume (1963) calls the aggression of liberal states against non-liberal states "imprudent vehemence."
119 Doyle 1983b. For further reading, see Hume 1963.
120 Maoz and Russett 1993.
121 Doyle 1997, 88.
122 Levy 1989; see also Ray 1988. However, DPT scholars disagree about why democracies do not go to war with one another: (1) it is because of parliamentary control mechanisms (Mayhew 1974; Bueno de Mesquita, Jackman, and Siverson 1991; Siverson and Emmons 1991; Downs 1957; (2) institutions act as checks and balances (Russett 1993; Doyle 1983b); (3) there are repercussions for transnational commerce (Gelpi and Grieco 2008); (4) they follow liberal democratic values and norms (Risse-Kappen 1996).
123 Critique on DPT comes mainly from realists, who argue that definitions of *democratic* vary and that illiberal leaders in democracies can threaten other states; see Layne 1994; Mearsheimer 1990.

of war or aggression. Once liberal states have established a zone of peace, they tend to become satisfied, neglecting or ignoring changes in the zone.

Sociological Liberalism

The school of sociological liberalism examines the preferences and interdependence[124] of dominant societal actors as predispositions of state actions and thus as causes of interstate cooperation and conflict. The national preferences of states and the process by which they are shaped determine the likelihood and nature of transnational cooperation and conflict. In foreign policy, in other words, the social identity of states matters.[125] Policy analysts focus their attention on transnational relations, especially on the linkages and networks between citizens and societal groups, because they can affect the behaviours and policymaking processes of states.[126]

Andrew Moravcsik goes further and argues that states act like a "transmission belt"[127] – they manage the diverse goals, interests, and preferences of actors within the state, and this then leads to policy decisions.[128] Preferences (or interests) are analytically different from strategies or strategic settings; they are fundamental interests that shape the behaviour of states in international politics.[129] Because the state comprises numerous individuals and thus represents a multitude of interests, actors are believed to have preferences for outcomes (e.g., wealth, peace), leading them to pursue strategies, or means, to achieve their ends.[130]

---

124 Karl Deutsch is credited with being the father of sociological liberalism, arguing (1957) that the more frequently transnational ties occur, the more people and groups of society become integrated or interdependent with one another. The emerging cultural homogeneity causes a "we-feeling" (community) among states.

125 Here there is an interesting overlap between liberal and constructivist IR theory. Constructivists focus more on the social than the material origins of socialization of particular preferences (Risse-Kappen 1996); liberals have no distinct position on the origins of social identities (rooted in history or other forms of interaction).

126 This has been called the "CNN effect"; for a discussion, see Gilboa 2005; Jakobsen 2000.

127 Moravcsik 2003, 163.

128 However, this study does not analyse the bargaining processes or institutional choices that are made among allies.

129 This has become known as the structural liberal theory of IR; see Moravcsik 2003.

130 Preferences are assumed to be constant. They may not be directly observable but can be studied empirically (Frieden 1999, 40–7).

In short, actors need to have a social purpose and rank their preferences and outcomes in a given environment. It is therefore important to analyse whether it is preferences or the environment that is causally responsible for behavioural outcomes. Put differently, actors might rank their preferences and form strategies to achieve them depending on the environment in which they are embedded.[131] Moreover, societal actors compete for the best ideas and concepts, while individuals and institutions of the state, as well as bureaucrats and interest groups, represent a subset of domestic society. Consequently, they are the most important unit of analysis for all liberal IR theorists.[132]

This points to the bottom-up, or "inside out,"[133] principle of liberal IR theory and explains how ideas and preferences are exchanged in the political marketplace. Individuals and groups – not states or identities – form the basis of interstate power and influence so that the exchange of societal interests and pressures determines which preference is most likely to influence policy choices.[134] Preferences shape the way states define their foreign policy interests, and states are expected to have different preferences on policy issues.[135] However, a variation in representative institutions indicates which group or groups most influence the policymaking process(es).

Liberal IR scholars attempt to understand the social purposes that each state has acquired through society, while rejecting the automatic harmony and unity of state actors. They also make no distinction between domestic and international politics[136] and assume that international conditions are in a state of "troubled peace."[137] Moreover, structural liberals focus on the distribution of preferences (rather than power capabilities, as realists do), believing that states pursue their preferences in competition with other states and that this is the source of transnational conflicts.[138]

---

131 This is a long-debated issue in IR; see details in Bueno de Mesquita and Lalman 1992b; Levy 1990–91.
132 Doyle 2008.
133 Panke and Risse 2007, 91.
134 Lindblom 1977.
135 Moravcsik 1993; Putnam 1988; Rittberger and Freund 2001.
136 Ibid.
137 Doyle 1997, 219.
138 Hegre et al. 2001; Rummel 1997.

Institutional Liberalism

This school of liberal IR theory was pioneered by the works of, for example, Alfred Zimmern and David Mittrany, who argued that international organizations not only facilitate but also promote cooperation among states without making hegemony a precondition for such cooperation.[139] Indeed, mutual interests can facilitate cooperation, joint gains, and thus the growth of international regimes. Others have argued that international organizations are independent international social actors and not merely agents of the state.[140] They influence states' political agendas and leaders, at times even pursue their own policies, and foster mutual trust, respect, and transparency by increasing the flow of information among their membership.[141] Institutions thus reduce the influence of external factors (e.g., fear, suspicion, cheating),[142] reinforce peaceful relations among democratic states, and increase the ability to monitor their membership.[143]

The Explanatory Value of Using Liberal IR Theory

Liberal IR theory can explain a number of phenomena where other IR theories struggle. First, it provides plausible theoretical explanations of why and how states' foreign policies change. In contrast, neither its main theoretical competitors, such as realism (and its various branches), nor the historical institutionalist research program can explain "all the way down" what causes states' foreign policies to change, especially on issues where they conflict or cooperate with other states. Instead, other theorists use explanatory proxies, such as relative power capabilities or the distribution of information, to explain these changes.

Because questions of change have become particularly pertinent for the practice of burden sharing by second-tier powers in the post–Cold

---

139 Young 1989, 200; see also Keohane 1984.
140 Mansfield and Pevehouse (2000) have shown that effective international organizations are integral to spreading liberal democratic values and thus to promoting international peace.
141 Keohane 1984, 257.
142 Baldwin 1993; Keohane 1989a; Powell 1991; Snidal 1991; Stein 1990.
143 Russett and Oneal 2001.

War era, liberal IR theory is expected to provide deeper plausible explanations for historical changes in NATO's burden-sharing regime, and
it does explain the differences in the nature of orders. In contrast, neither realism nor historical institutionalism has been able to produce
persuasive explanations for long-term changes in NATO's burden-
sharing regime; and neither has been able to persuasively account for
or incorporate into its research program significant historical changes,
such as the end of the Cold War or the global rise of democratic states.
The realist research program, in particular, has a tendency to reduce
international political events to systemic or cyclical questions of power balancing and alignment, while neglecting phenomena such as
transnational movements and commerce, democratization, economic
growth, and social networks.

Second, liberalism opens the "black box" of states' decision-making
processes, thus eliminating any unitary assumptions of state actions. It
holds that states represent social collectivities, which in turn shape state
preferences. States represent societal preferences through institutions
that consistently process the demands and interests of social groups. As
Andrew Moravcsik reminds us, "the state is not an actor but a representative institution, constantly subject to capture and recapture, construction and reconstruction, by coalitions of social actors."[144] In other words,
institutions process the interplay and exchange of the particularistic
material and ideational interests of groups and actors in civil society,
exchanging and transmitting political ideas. The "ends" of this transmission process can be called "state preferences" – in Canada's case, the
decision to share the military or civilian burdens of NATO represents
the basic national interests of Canadians.

This is not to say that this preference-formation process is harmonious or balanced. Societal groups differ extensively in their relative capabilities and resources, membership, and representation. In an ideal
setting, following this logic also helps to define which social actor (or
groups of social actors) influences the preferences (or national interests)
of states. Above all, state preferences do not follow any pre-assigned
order or hierarchy; a number of preferences can operate alongside one
another. In short, liberal theories are able to crack the "hard shell," or
"black box" of the state. In building on this insight, we went a step

---

144 Moravcsik 2003, 163.

further and broke up the rationalist assumptions of liberal IR theory based on a Weberian methodology to provide much deeper explanations and understanding of the social action of burden sharing.

Third, a key assumption of liberal IR theory about world politics is that states' preferences are influenced not only by their civil society but also by their (policy) interdependence with other societies. For example, non-governmental organizations can exert influence by forming societal coalitions or transnational societal networks that operate beyond state boundaries.[145] This is an important point because it allows us to examine the transnational dimension of NATO burden sharing. It also helps explain the variation and evolution of state preferences across national boundaries and can thus be seen as a causal mechanism between state preferences and state actions.

Fourth, the rise of democratic governments around the globe has led to a significant body of research showing that domestic politics and democratic forms of government are independent variables explaining the foreign policy behaviour of states. These findings show that domestic politics plays a much larger role in the foreign policy behaviour of states than realism admits. Thus, the richness of liberal political theory and the interplay of democratic governance, economic prosperity and integration, and the rule of law, which are used as explanatory variables, provide a causal explanation of state behaviour and how it changes. Liberal IR theory has also produced a multilayered approach to causal explanations of state actions and challenged the state-centric approach of realist scholarship. It recognizes that the exchange of ideas and preferences in the domestic political marketplace has the ability to change patterns of cooperation and conflict among states. It thus establishes causal relations between domestic and international politics.

Fifth, liberal IR theory is flexible enough in its research design to explain how states' goals and preferences change over time. In realist and institutionalist scholarship, these changes are attributed to systemic changes (i.e., distribution of power and information) rather than domestic ones. They are also believed to operate with a certain level of determinism, compelling states to act against other states in cases of power imbalances (i.e., appetite for balancing behaviour). Liberal IR

---

145 Keohane 1972, 1984, 1996; Keohane and Nye 1977.

theory, on the other hand, combined with a Weberian methodology is able to show that states are not automatically locked into determinism and that their foreign policy behaviour does not always follow rationalist thinking; it can also be driven by norms and values. Disarmament studies, for example, have shown that states do seek absolute gains and sign voluntary armament reduction treaties to reduce their military capabilities.

Why Not Other IR Theories?

In addition to examining the efficacy of liberal IR theory, it is helpful to briefly discuss liberalism's other theoretical competitors. This section will focus only on mainstream theories of IR, and a few points of comparison should suffice to prove the explanatory value of liberal IR theory in the study of NATO burden sharing.

The most popular competitor is, of course, the realist research program. Realists – in the most general terms – argue that states' foreign policy behaviour is determined by the configuration of their capabilities; in contrast, liberals hold that it is determined by the configuration of national state preferences. For realists, the variation in means matters the most, while for liberals it is the variation in ends. As discussed above, realists also do not stress the causal importance of state-society relations and apply very strong assumptions about state rationality; national preferences are fixed. In the liberal IR research program, they are flexible and open to variation.

Another powerful and competing research program is liberalism's sister program, neo-liberalism. It holds that the configuration of information and institutions, rather than state preferences, is the most important independent variable in explaining the foreign policy behaviour of states. Like realists, neo-institutionalists assume that state preferences are fixed or exogenously determined by the international system. In response, liberal IR theorists argue that unless the nature and extent of state preferences are known, a variation on them – or variation of state behaviour generally – is difficult to assess.

Constructivist theorists have become particularly known for their scholarship on the formation of social identity. While liberal IR theory does not have a distinct position on where the identity of social agents originates, constructivists (especially those with a systemic focus) argue that identities are formed in a reciprocal interstate socialization process.

In this area, constructivist theories of IR can complement liberal IR theory by establishing a correlation between identities and policy outcomes.[146] However, as leading liberal IR theorists contend, constructivist scholars fail to explain when these processes of socialization take place and which (and why) matter the most.[147]

Conclusion

In summary, liberal IR theory formulates two unique assumptions about world politics that give it superior explanatory powers for understanding the practice and preference formation of second-tier powers towards NATO's burden-sharing regime. First, by revealing the decision-making processes of states and thus eliminating any unitary assumptions of state actions, liberal IR theory holds that states represent social collectivities, which in turn shape state preferences. States represent societal preferences through institutions or collective actions, which consistently process the demands and interests of social groups; these groups are considered to be exogenous causes of the interests of states.[148] In other words, institutions process the interplay and exchange of the particularistic material and ideational interests of groups and actors in civil society.[149] They act like a transmission belt in the political exchange between society and the state and are exploited when they are perceived to exist (this is the bounded rationality assumption). The "ends" of this transmission process can be called "state preferences" – in Canada's case, the practice and behaviour of Atlantic burden sharing represent the basic national interests of Canadian society.

This preference formation process is not harmonious or balanced because social groups differ extensively in their capabilities and resources, membership, and representation. Under ideal conditions of data availability, the researcher is able to define which social actor (or groups of social actors) influences the preferences of states, and they do not follow any pre-assigned order or hierarchy; in fact, a range of preferences can operate alongside one another.

---

146 Checkel and Moravcsik (2001) reject constructivism as an IR theory because it does not produce testable research results.

147 Ibid., 230.

148 Moravcsik 2003, 161.

149 Ibid., 163.

The second key assumption of liberal IR theory is that states' preferences are influenced not only by their civil society but also by their (policy) interdependence with other societies.[150] Moreover, non-governmental organizations can exert influence by forming societal coalitions or transnational societal networks that operate beyond state boundaries.[151] This is a particularly important insight because it allows us to examine the transnational dimension of sharing collective burdens. It thus helps explain the variation and evolution of state preferences across national boundaries, and it functions as a causal mechanism between state preferences and state actions.

Moreover, liberal states are ontologically assumed to be rational social actors: they require a social purpose to become involved in international politics.[152] In other words, unless liberal states achieve a certain interdependence among their objectives, they are unlikely to become involved in transnational issues.[153] This suggests that we can hypothesize a degree of overlap in transnational preferences in the practice of NATO burden sharing. Also, while state preferences cross national boundaries, they naturally impose costs and/or benefits on other states and produce three possible negotiating outcomes: zero-sum-game preferences, overlapping preferences, and mixed preferences.[154] Moreover, a Weberian methodology, without abandoning the assumption of rationality, allows for interpretivist explanations of NATO burden-sharing practices.

An analysis of this interdependence of preferences is important for another reason. Liberal IR theorists define national power according to the degree of preference interdependence.[155] The more interdependent a state is, the more intense its preferences for a given outcome. A situation of asymmetrical bargaining, in which one state has stronger preferences than another, creates the possibility of bargaining power. The

---

150 Gourevitch (1978) has called this the "second-image-reversed" approach.
151 Keohane 1972, 1984, 1996; Keohane and Nye 1977.
152 Frieden 1999, 40.
153 In this sense, liberal IR theory rejects realist and institutionalist claims that a distribution of capabilities or information, respectively, causes states to behave in a certain way.
154 The scope of this book does not allow an extensive discussion of these outcomes; for details, see Martin 1992; Oye 1986; Snidal 1985.
155 For an early liberal discussion of this conceptualization, see Keohane and Nye 1977.

reverse, however, is true as well: the less a state wants something, the less important its national preferences are and thus the less power other states have over it.

Having said this, liberal IR theory joins its realist and institutionalist counterparts in assuming that states act under a condition of anarchy. But anarchy is not repetitive or cyclical.[156] States are rational and calculating entities that generally seek absolute over relative gains and form state preferences under conditions of anarchy.[157]

---

156 This latter assumption is not shared by realists or institutionalists; for a discussion, see Holsti 1985; Donnelly 1992; Gilpin 1986, 1981; Kennedy 1987; Waltz 1979.

157 This is a consistent assumption across all liberal theories; see Kant 1991, 46.

3 The Conceptual Puzzle of the "New World Order"

Introduction

This chapter provides a background analysis to contextualize some of the changes that occurred in the world order following the history-making events of November 1989 and that gave new meaning to NATO's public goods.[1] It will, first, carve out the distinctive features of the much celebrated "new world order" that President George H.W. Bush depicted in 1990 and, second, examine how that new world order was distinct from the "old" order of the Cold War. This raises important questions of continuity and change in pan-European security politics as well as alliance politics and the practice of burden sharing generally. The sea change caused by the end of the Cold War raised fundamental questions about what was new and what remained constant in the post–Cold War international order.

Against this backdrop, the chapter discusses the following questions: What has changed in our understanding of post–Cold War politics? What are the historical patterns of the new world order? Can the new order be better described as a period of disorder? What are its consistencies and inconsistencies? Was the complexity of the Cold War indeed replaced by the simplicity of the post–Cold War era, or did a

---

1 The objective is not to provide an extensive discussion of all political, economic, military, or socio-cultural changes that took place with the end of the Cold War but to highlight and discuss the most prevalent ones, those that had implications for the burden-sharing debate.

more benign Cold War era find a turbulent successor? And what are the impacts and consequences of these factors on order and stability in world politics in general and specifically as they relate to European security?[2]

These questions are central because the events surrounding the fall of the Berlin Wall and the subsequent peaceful social revolutions in CEE are celebrated in the scholarly literature as a significant turning point in world affairs.[3] Thus, another important aim of this chapter is to determine how decisive these forces of transformation were and what kind of new world order, if any, replaced the old one.

We follow Ian Clark's argument that the post–Cold War era can be conceptualized as a period of peacemaking.[4] The logic of this argument is simple: if the Cold War is indeed perceived as a form of war, the post–Cold War can be considered to be an era of peace. Ultimately, international orders are the product of peace settlements, but there remains a significant debate in the literature about when a peaceful settlement of the Cold War began. Marc Trachtenberg, for example, argued that much of the foundation for the post–Cold War peace order was laid during the Cold War, specifically in the period of détente in the 1960s.[5] Stanley Hoffman disagreed and held that the "world after the cold war will not resemble any world of the past."[6] He was joined by other analysts, who highlighted the historical significance of 1989 in shaping a new world order. For this group of analysts, it appeared that the idealist spirit of the interwar period had resurfaced; new scope and vigour could be given to international organizations as the guarantors of democratic rights, freedoms, and principles.

The term *new world order* was coined by President Bush, who foresaw a world of peace, stability, prosperity, justice, rights, and the rule of law. In an address to the UN General Assembly on 1 October 1990, he promised to share the "tasks and responsibilities within the international

---

2 It is, of course, accepted wisdom that much of the disorder of the 19th and 20th centuries was closely related to social, political, and economic changes taking place in continental Europe. For an excellent account of this piece of international history, see Judt 2005; Ferguson 2006.

3 Supporters of this argument are Cox, Booth, and Dunne 1999; Kaplan 2000; Knutsen 1999.

4 Clark 2001; for the limitations of this approach, see pp. 7–11.

5 Trachtenberg 1999.

6 Hoffmann 1998, 121–2.

community"[7] – that is, he made a new commitment to multilateralism rather than superpower politics. Speaking at the War College at Maxwell Air Force Base on 13 April 1991, he said he expected international affairs to be governed in the spirit and by the norms of partnership, cooperation, multilateralism, and human security and by "a set of principles that undergird our relations."[8] Soon after, the term "became operational" when UN coalition forces began the campaign for the liberation of Kuwait in Operation DESERT STORM on 2 August 1990. The quagmire of Cold War politics seemed to be overcome when the UN Security Council (including all five permanent members) endorsed the campaign.[9]

In a sense, though, as Anne-Marie Slaughter reminded us, *new world order* denotes "a system of global governance that institutionalizes cooperation and sufficiently contains conflicts such that all nations and their people may achieve greater peace and prosperity, improve their stewardship of the earth and reach minimum standards of human dignity."[10] Global order recognizes that the problems in world politics have become so complex, so diverse, and so multidimensional that no one state can find solutions to them. The normative impetus resulting from this insight is a recognition that these issues can be effectively solved only in cooperation with other states that are willing and able to help solve them.

At the same time, this increasingly convoluted and complex field of global studies has produced for states what Robert Keohane coined the "globalization paradox."[11] On the one hand, the effect of the globalization paradox is a governance dilemma for states, and international institutions in particular, because the forces of globalization have disaggregated the authority and responsibility of the state while at the same time calling for an increased role of governments on the national and regional level; the EU is a case in point. On the other hand, globalization has opened the door for small and middle powers to make their

---

7 United States Information Service 1991.

8 Ibid.

9 This issue will be discussed in more detail in ch. 4.

10 Slaughter 2004, 15. Yet to be fair, she used the term somewhat differently – namely, as a starting point to describe the extent to which states have become "disaggregated" and to which transnational actors, as well as horizontal and vertical networks, have gained increasing importance in the process of governing world politics.

11 Keohane 2001; for a similar argument, see Rodik 2011.

comparative advantage available in functional and issue-specific areas and thus to increase not only their international visibility but also their qualitative role in global politics and governance.[12]

Some pundits were quick to link this renewal of multilateralism to the success of liberalism in replacing Cold War ideological bickering;[13] the new era of geopolitical stability and cooperation, so the argument went, provided a triumph of liberalism over competing ideologies. As Hawthorn noted, "many expected that after the Cold War, there would be peace, order, increasing prosperity in expanding markets and the extension and eventual consolidation of civil and political rights. There would be a new world order, and it would in these ways be liberal."[14]

Aspects of liberalism also found their way into national security strategies, particularly those of the United States. It was not a coincidence that the 1995 national security strategy under President Bill Clinton was called "Engagement and Enlargement."[15] During his first term in office, his administration's domestic policy was shaped by economic considerations and priorities, and this was reflected in its foreign policy.[16] Liberalism in the form of engagement and enlargement was conjoined with the new international order through a democratization process and by extending Kant's "zone of peace." By spreading liberal democratic values abroad and making this one of the chief foreign policy goals of Western democracies,[17] Washington believed that stability, prosperity, and order could be brought to international politics.[18] Therefore, the pursuit of internal as well as external

---

12 It is interesting that at about the same time, scholars began to question the practice of governance in international politics. While that discussion goes beyond the scope of this study, it is noteworthy to point to a few key sources addressing this debate. See, e.g., Zürn 2003; Rosenau 1995; Hurrell 2011; Dingwerth and Pattberg 2006; Krahmann 2003; Finkelstein 1995; Ruggie 1992.

13 The list of supporters of this argument is rather long; see, e.g., Brown 1999; Fukuyama 1992.

14 Hawthorn 1999, 145.

15 President of the United States of America 1995.

16 See, e.g., Zyla 2007.

17 Indeed, many Western analysts believed that the world could be divided into zones of peace and zones of conflict or turmoil; see, e.g., Singer and Wildacsky 1993.

18 This is in line with Mueller's "obsolescence of war" thesis; by 1919, war was commonly viewed as barbaric, outdated, and an inefficient tool for managing transnational conflicts; see Mueller 1994.

democratic reforms became the guiding principle of America's new normative order.

Other scholars went even further and argued that the post–Cold War era had its origins in the pre-1945 world order.[19] One sign of continuity was the consistency of American power and its hegemonic ambitions in world politics.[20] After 1945, this position was often referred to as the "Washington consensus" or "Pax Americana." Following the Second World War, the United States shaped the outlook and mandate of international institutions such as NATO and the UN (in the area of security) and the Bretton Woods institutions (an umbrella term for international financial institutions such as the World Bank, the International Monetary Fund, and the General Agreement on Tariffs and Trade). Robert Jervis argued that the peace and liberal order achieved at the end of the war was "institutionalized" by American dominance rather than being an entirely new concept.[21] Nonetheless, these institutions remained active and alive in the post–Cold War era and witnessed American leadership.[22]

A more pessimistic group of scholars, however, warned that the new world order would hold not only benefits but also dangers.[23] They foresaw that the end of the bipolar structure of the international system and the rise of multipolar conditions would create a new set of great power rivalries and that a renewed balance of power[24] would replace the old order[25] that was in place at the beginning of the 20th century. It is noteworthy that Mearsheimer made extensive use of neorealist (offensive) and balance of power theory to argue that the end of bipolarity most likely held a disastrous forecast for the future of great-power peace and international institutions generally.

With regard to European security, fears of civic and ethnic nationalism and state-to-state rivalries led the pessimists to expect a break-up

---

19 Ikenberry 1996; Kegley 1991; Kegley and Raymond 1999; see also Cox, Booth, and Dunne 1999.
20 See, e.g., Cox 1995; Cox and Stokes 2008.
21 Jervis 1991/1992. For a critical view of how the liberal order is perceived from the "South" (less-developed countries), see Chubin 1995.
22 Zakaria 1998.
23 See Kirkpatrick 1989/1990; Kondracke 1990; Sloan 1990.
24 Mearsheimer 1990.
25 Skidelsky 1995.

rather than a unification of Europe.[26] They used the collapse of the Balkans in the early 1990s, which resulted in ethnic clashes, nationalistic confrontations, and mass atrocities, to show that democratic revolutions can turn ugly and pose threats to regional organizations (e.g., the EU). Samuel Huntington also cautioned against the optimistic view of the future of the world order by questioning the values of the democratic peace paradigm.[27] He argued that the end of the Cold War portended a return to the dangers of the past rather than to greater security: this period of transition did not imply an end to political, ideological, diplomatic, economic, technological, or military rivalries and competitions; indeed, it could lead to the end of the so-called Long Peace.

A third school questioned the existence of order in its entirety. Stephen Gill and Robert Cox argued that world order in 1990 was embedded in a Western structure of hegemonic power relations.[28] Others such as Andrew Hurrell constructed a normative argument of order by pointing to the inequalities it had created in the past;[29] it induced the development of a set of conflicting norms.[30] In security affairs, these critics charged, the current order – the immediate post–Cold War era – remained static and not emancipatory.[31] In short, they charged that the new spirit of multilateralism was at odds with America's hegemonic position in world politics: multilateralism was the simple expression of American dominance, not the proclaimed universalism of normative ideals.[32] An extension of this argument held that the new roles and functions of international institutions were nothing but instruments of American power and primacy.[33]

However, if we accept Trachtenberg's hypothesis that many of the features of the post–Cold War era were developed during the Cold

---

26 Kaplan 2000, xii. This argument is problematic to say the least because it reduces NATO's purpose to purely military functions. However, other studies have shown that it is held together and functional across many levels; see Pollack and Shaffer 2001, 5.

27 Huntington 1989, 7.

28 Cox and Sinclair 1996; Gill 1997.

29 Chubin 1995; Hurrell 1999.

30 Hoffmann 1998, 78.

31 Booth 1991.

32 Clark 2001, 175.

33 Cox and Sinclair 1996, 489.

War, then peacemaking, as Ian Clark argued, can be conceptualized as a process rather than a single historical event.[34] It sharpens our analytical mind to see the post–Cold War era as a continuity of the Cold War order. Thus, the misconception of the new world order rests with the distortion of time and events associated with it, seen on a longer historical continuum.[35] This notion was expressed by the Canadian government when Secretary of State for External Affairs Joe Clark stated that "we have been so impressed by the dramatic ending of the Cold War that we have failed to notice the substantial elements of continuity between the two periods. A richer historical perspective can be developed only by locating the period within a framework that spans the past sixty or so years."[36]

Ikenberry went even further, pointing to a historic continuum of the liberal world order that emerged in the interwar period rather than the immediate post–Cold War years.[37] Holsti also concluded that international institutions had not changed with the end of the Cold War.[38] In that sense, the new world order was in fact a refurbishment of the old order – or, as Clark argued, it was "repackaged."[39]

In spite of these disagreements about the novelty of the new world order, there is evidence that another form of order replaced the order of the Cold War.[40] For example, Germany's non-nuclear status in Europe remained a constant of its security policy.[41] The Federal Republic maintained its abstinence from the balance of power politics in Europe and continued to support and foster the project of European integration. In the old days of balance of power politics, Berlin would have most likely challenged the existing political order by either balancing or bandwagoning; now it did neither of these.

Clark bridged the two schools of thought by arguing that peace is best preserved by "power, exaction, imposition, and enforcement" in

---

34 Clark 2001, 5.
35 For a similar argument, see Hobsbawm 1992. In his mind, the evolving nationalism in south-eastern Europe in the 1990s was the "unfinished business" of 1919.
36 Clark 2001, 18.
37 Ikenberry 1996, 90.
38 Holsti 1999, 289.
39 Clark 2001, 220.
40 Hall and Paul 1999.
41 Trachtenberg 1999, 401; Dalgaard-Nielsen 2006.

combination with "legitimacy, consensus, acquiescence, and compliance."[42] In this new order, the United States occupied a pivotal "pole position"[43] and was at liberty to freely disperse its power resources among "old" countries such as Germany and France. In other words, it was a leading stakeholder of the new world order. This conjunction led Chris Brown to argue that it became difficult to distinguish between the new principles of liberal internationalism and American hegemony.[44]

Accounts of Continuity and Discontinuity

It is important to understand the continuities and discontinuities of the Cold War and post–Cold War eras and to explore the different meanings that power and security acquired in the order that existed between 1989 and 1999. In that period, power and security were defined on a multi- rather than a one-dimensional level. This has implications for our understanding of NATO as an international security actor as well as for its members because it gave national security policymakers a broader range of policy instruments in areas such as military defence, diplomacy, foreign aid, and economic interconnectedness. The Canadian government also benefited from this.[45] During the Cold War, national security politics was one-dimensional and considered "high" politics, while all other areas of politics were considered secondary concerns.[46]

However, especially in the context of NATO, national security politics failed to take into account or include in its analysis the political and economic affairs of a country at a micro level. Even those studies that factored in international cooperation focused on only one issue area.[47] As numerous studies have shown, the interplay and mix of these policies shape and affect the policymaking processes of states;[48] in the context of NATO, national security concerns can no longer be solved by national governments alone; they require coordination and cooperation among allies.

---

42 Clark 2001, 12, 22.
43 Heisbourg 1999, 5.
44 Brown 1999, 47.
45 McDougall 1991.
46 To be sure, this conceptualization of security is not unique to transatlantic affairs and includes countries like Japan; for a discussion, see Chapman, Drifte, and Gow 1982; Bobrow 1984.
47 Keohane 1984; Oye 1986.
48 See, e.g., Cooper 1987; Keohane 1984; Keohane and Nye 1975; Rosenau 1980.

Power and Resources of Power

There is near consensus among scholars of international affairs that power remained an integral component of international politics in the post–Cold War era.[49] There is less agreement, however, about whether the traditional resources of power, such as the size of a territory, military, and population, changed with the transformation processes of the late 1980s. The traditional components of nation-state power, according to Ray Cline, for example, were its critical mass (size and location), its population and natural resources, its economic capabilities, its military capabilities, and the strategic purpose of, and will to pursue, a national strategy.[50]

The power of a nation state can be understood in terms of its capacity to control or change the behaviour of other states. In this sense, power is relational. It can be contextualized as part of a relationship between two or more states and also comes with certain obligations and responsibilities.[51] Robert Dahl saw power as "the ability to shift the probability of outcomes."[52] David Baldwin asserted that "what functions as a power resource in one policy contingency framework may be irrelevant in another."[53] This was precisely the context in which power was exercised. Put differently, "power resources (or assets) in one policy contingency framework may not only lose their effectiveness in another context; they may actually become liabilities rather than assets."[54] This implies that it is difficult to characterize a nation state's power if the object of its power is unclear.

To be fair, the nature of power has been a long-standing issue in international politics – at least since the 1960s, when the effects of an evolving economic crisis as well as a "complex interdependence"[55] of states questioned traditional calculations of national power. An extension of these early arguments was that states' power resources changed as well. For example, in the agrarian economy of the 18th century, the size of a population was considered a critical power resource because a large citizenry would likely produce numerous military recruits; since

---

49 See, e.g., Art and Waltz 2004; Gaddis 2005.
50 Cline 1980, 1994.
51 See, e.g., Lake 2010.
52 Dahl 1957, 1969.
53 Baldwin 1979, 165.
54 Ibid., 166.
55 Keohane 1984; Keohane and Nye 1974, 1977.

1989, however, the size of a population has become a less valuable currency of international power.

Joseph Nye applied this same rationale to the United States in arguing that policymakers in Washington were faced with a "paradox" of US power[56] and that this preponderance of US power would ensure its hegemonic position in the years to come. At the same time, and in light of global interdependence, states were becoming increasingly dependent on the voice and input of other states to solve global problems. Thus, according to Nye, the United States needed to make use of its hard power – its military might – as well as its soft power – its foremost economic and cultural attractiveness in world politics.

Militarily, the United States enjoys what Barry Posen called the "command of the commons";[57] it was the most powerful state at sea, in space, and in the air. America, Posen charged, was not contested militarily and thus appeared to be the global military hegemon. "Command means that the United States gets vastly more military use out of the sea, space and air than others do; that it can credibly threaten to deny their use to others; and that others would lose a military contest for the commons if they attempted to deny them to the United States."[58] This unprecedented military capability allowed the United States to wage war against any aggressor at any time or to restrict access to military and economic assistance from like-minded states. In short, military, or hard power, capabilities allowed states to use coercive measures when necessary and achieve political objectives, either their own or those of an alliance. Military power was used as an expression of the national power and the test of a great power's strength in war.[59]

Nonetheless, Nye argued, unprecedented military capabilities were not sufficient to retain influence in international affairs in the 21st century. "Although force may sometimes play a role, traditional instruments of power are rarely sufficient to deal with the new dilemmas of world politics."[60] In the post-1989 world order, soft power capabilities became as important as, although not a substitute for, hard power. Soft power can be understood as the power of attraction. It is the ability of

---

56 Nye 2002.
57 Posen 2003.
58 Ibid., 8.
59 Nye 1990a, 154.
60 Ibid., 164.

states to entice other countries to voluntarily follow its course of action, build international coalitions, and successfully manage horizontal issues. Nye highlighted three sources of US soft power: its culture, its political values, and its foreign policies.[61] American popular music and films, for example, attract millions of people around the globe. Embedded in this global entertainment industry are Western cultural values and the American way of life. For example, the United States is the largest exporter of English-speaking television shows and movies; they are sold to broadcasting stations around the globe, including to non-Western states. In short, Hollywood is the personification of the American entertainment industry.

The recipe, then, for US foreign policy officials is to use America's soft power resources to persuade and attract, rather than coerce, other states and non-state actors. According to Nye, traditional conceptions of power, in which powerful states have large populations, territory, natural resources, economies, military forces, and political stability, have become obsolete in the post–Cold war era.[62] Rather, the new sources of state power are soft power resources. To be clear, governments have both hard power and soft power capabilities, but it is the latter that have become increasingly relevant in the post–Cold War era, replacing the traditional elements of national statecraft.

In the case of Canada, internal communications at the highest levels of government show that officials fully bought into the argument that soft power tools were to be assigned increased importance in international affairs. A fax sent by the Office of the Assistant Deputy Minister for Policy and Communication at National Defence Headquarters to the Department of Foreign Affairs and International Trade (DFAIT) noted that "in the future, the growth of 'soft power' resources abroad will likely play a greater role in national policy. Increasingly, foreign powers will be able to constrain national policymaking through control of information or the attractiveness of information-based cultures."[63]

---

61 Nye 2004.
62 For the traditional definition, see Cline 1975, 1980.
63 Tony Kellett, "Canada-2005 – Political/Military," fax to Tony Berger, DFAIT, 10 December 1996, 4, retrieved under the Access to Information Act, 10 April 2007, A-3, File No. 3947-01.

Diplomacy

While Fukuyama praised the "end of history,"[64] other analysts argued that it was not so much the triumph of an ideological struggle that was the feature of the end of the Cold War but rather multilateralism.[65] *Multilateralism* describes a social principle of international diplomacy. At its core is the "idea that if international cooperative regimes for the management of conflicts of interest are to be effective, they must represent a broad and sustainable consensus among the states of the international system."[66] Strong commitments to the pursuit of multilateral foreign policies, economic interdependence by means of a globalized economy, and a revival of and commitment to collective security are the key features of this new order. The new spirit of international politics, as noted earlier, is best captured by the dogmas of engagement and enlargement. It includes the voluntary commitment of nation states to a foreign policy that extends the liberal zone of peace, fosters economic prosperity and interdependency, and thus creates a sense of openness and community of states that share similar liberal norms and values.

In this sense, the liberal (market) norms and values of the 1990s as well as the confidence in neo-liberal economics became an integral part of the transformation processes in central Europe.[67] New forms of power such as negotiation and attraction were used to defend and export the zone of peace. Liberal internationalism advanced to become the accepted new norm of international politics and provided legitimacy for enforcing and defending the new liberal order. In other words, multilateralism was a form of interstate cooperation and conflict

---

64 Fukuyama 1989, 1992.

65 Morgan 1993, 345.

66 Iain McLean and Alistair McMillan, *The Concise Oxford Dictionary of Politics*, 3rd ed., 2014 online edition, s.v. "multilateralism," http://www.oxfordreference.com/view/10.1093/acref/9780199207800.001.0001/acref-9780199207800-e-854?rskey=eDhOh7&result=918.

67 Indeed, a high-profile conference with government officials noted in 1994, "Certainly we live in a world where the relationship between economic security and national security is seen to be intimate, with the result that economic self-interest is a principal influence on foreign policy, economic aid and economic sanctions important instruments of external relations, economic factors important determinants of defence policy and strategic activity without an economic content often perceived as devoid of purpose" (Chipman 1994).

management. It was also, as John Ruggie argued, a norm of international politics.[68]

Seen on the historical continuum, multilateralism, which Clark called the "cornerstone of the regulative settlement," can be seen as one of the constant variables of world politics since the 1930s.[69] Clark argued that multilateralism is "the principle formulated in the abstract that is universally applicable. In practice, it describes a code to govern substantive areas of international life."[70] In the area of international security affairs, multilateralism speaks to the fundamental principle by which states have "equal access to a common security umbrella."[71] This principle is universally applicable, non-exclusive, non-discriminatory, and indivisible;[72] it thus shows the character of constitutionality rather than hegemony.

This distinction is vital because it implies that states should not be discriminated against on the basis of their relative power capabilities or relative standing in the power hierarchy of international affairs. Seen from this perspective, the norm of multilateralism corresponds nicely with Ikenberry's thesis of the prevalence of the "old" liberal international order of the post–Second World War era. Hogan and Ruggie critically referred to this as the "internationalization" of American interests.[73] In short, the multilateralism that emerged after the Cold War encapsulated a set of fundamental ideas about how to conduct world diplomacy in the context of international institutions – specifically, international security institutions.

The new spirit of multilateralism was also noticed in international security institutions such as NATO and the UN. While the UN Security Council was to a large extent paralysed during the Cold War as a result of the zero-sum conditions of international diplomacy as well as superpower rivalries for influence in different parts of the world, scholars attested that with the events of 1989, the UN became a more viable international organization charged with collective action.[74] In fact,

---

68 Ruggie 1993a, 20.
69 Clark 2001, 167.
70 Ibid., 169.
71 Ruggie 1996, 22.
72 Clark 2001, 169.
73 Hogan 1987; Ruggie 1993a, 30.
74 Thakur 2006.

Security Council records show that its five permanent member states worked to put aside their ideological differences. Iraq's occupation of Kuwait in 1990 was a perfect test case in this regard. The UN was united in upholding the principles of collective security by mandating an international force to liberate Kuwait. This was seen as a commitment to enhanced multilateralism and international cooperation rather than competition.[75]

Even in Europe, the principles of multilateralism were regarded as the key ingredients for managing the security vacuum that emerged with the withdrawal of the Soviet Union from CEE. Furthermore, international security affairs after 1989 were managed by *interlocking institutions* – a set of overlapping international institutions in one or more policy fields.[76] Europe maintained a perspective of inclusiveness towards the liberated states of CEE after their meeting in Visegrad, Bosnia and Herzegovina, and in 1999, it allowed the Czech Republic, Hungary, and Poland to join an existing group of states that were committed to the principles and values of a liberal democracy. In this sense, multilateral institutions in Europe, such as NATO and the OSCE, functioned as a mechanism for stabilizing and managing the security needs of the "evolving" Eastern democracies.[77] Indeed, as Weber argued, these institutions enjoyed significant popularity rather than extinction.[78] Multilateralism, then, was the cornerstone of continuity in the new world order.

The practice of multilateralism also placed special emphasis on dialogue among states and non-state actors, and this resulted in greater cooperation, whereby states sought to communicate with each other, influence each other, and resolve conflicts through bargaining, either formal or informal.[79] In light of this renewed commitment to cooperation and dialogue, the UN began to address complex issues of transnational importance, such as drug trafficking, regional instabilities, national and ethnic conflicts, the spread of weapons of mass destruction, and terrorism. Indeed, the new international security agenda was filled with non-traditional security issues, including instabilities in the global trading and financial systems, the rise of nationalist

---

75 Cox, Booth, and Dunne 1999.

76 For the concept of *interlocking institutions* in general, see Cox 1997, 82–92. For an application of the concept to Canada, see McDougall et al. 1992.

77 This point will be examined in more detail in the following chapters.

78 Weber 1997.

79 Hamilton and Langhorne 1995.

tensions, and environmental pollution, that required the attention of international agents.[80] There was also a recognizable change in the tone of international diplomacy, which was driven less by narrow and ideologically coloured, dogmatic principles.

In terms of domestic or internal changes in diplomacy, after 1989 citizens began making increasing demands for a greater voice in formulating the national security policies of their states. If the spirit of multilateralism was to be extended horizontally, around the world, it should also be made available vertically, to all levels of society. Foreign policy, so public wisdom went, should be formulated in a process open to all citizens; the days of back-room negotiations in foreign ministries were over. Greater participation of citizens in the formulation of foreign policy would also ensure enhanced public control over the foreign policy decision-making machinery of government. Indeed, diplomacy in the new order took place in a public forum in which foreign ministers and government officials were regularly scrutinized by the media. Modern diplomacy underwent a process of transformation from a secret tool of statecraft to a more publicly controlled political space in which citizens and non-state actors were increasingly involved and able to exert influence over policymaking.[81]

Canadian officials were not sheltered from these international trends. During the 1993 federal election campaign, Lloyd Axworthy, a Liberal member of Parliament, publicly complained that Prime Minister Brian Mulroney's Progressive Conservative government was "unwilling to carry on a serious dialogue with the Canadian people on foreign policy issues."[82] At the centre of Axworthy's complaint was that the government rarely consulted the public, or Parliament, on important foreign policy issues, and this was leading to the unnecessary accumulation of a democratic deficit that distanced Canadians from their government officials. The "Red Book," the election platform of the Liberal Party, called for changes to this practice; the public should be engaged through round-tables and public meetings.[83] After being elected in 1993, the Liberals kept this election promise and held selective public hearings on foreign policy issues across the country.[84] According to Kim Nossal, the Red Book

80 Buzan and Waever 1993, 7.
81 For an extensive discussion, see, e.g., Nye 2005a, ch. 8; see also Barston 1988.
82 Axworthy 1992, 14.
83 Liberal Party of Canada 1993.
84 Draimin and Plewes 1995, 75.

would, in an effort to increase democratic participation in foreign policy, establish a National Forum on Canada's International Relations that would debate and discuss pertinent foreign policy issues.[85]

Nossal recognized two features of this democratization process in Canada's foreign policy, one external and one internal.[86] Externally, the Canadian government encouraged other states (e.g., those in CEE) to follow the Canadian example and adopt democratic ideals and practices. Internally, democratization referred to the "degree to which Canadian foreign policy itself is democratic."[87] Indicators of democracy, according to Nossal, were

> popular sovereignty, the political equality of all adult citizens, governance by the consent of the governed, which usually involved elections that must be free and fair; the existence of a set of political and civil rights and liberties, including the right of assembly, of free speech, of political organization, and of opposition to the regime; the rule of law, including a fair and independent judiciary and a range of judicial rights, among which the most important is equality before the law. We also seek evidence of equitable participation of all citizens, regardless of class, ethnicity, gender or other attributes, in the political life of the community.[88]

This "new" nature of diplomacy and formulation of Canada's foreign policy was rooted in the traditional liberal theory of the 18th century (as described in chapter 2), whereby a constant exchange takes place, on the one hand, between citizens and the foreign policy elites and, on the other, between the government and other nations.

Adaptation of Threat Perception(s) and Security Concerns

The transformation in diplomacy was in part induced by alterations in the structure of international threats. With the end of the Cold War, the Soviet Union was no longer the most ferocious threat to the Atlantic alliance. Subsequently, NATO reached out to CEE by offering friendship and cooperation rather than coercion. It engaged its former adversaries

---

85 Nossal 1995.
86 Ibid., 29.
87 Ibid.
88 Nossal 1995, 30.

politically and militarily through a combination of new institutions and programs, including the NACC and the PfP.[89] (These programs are discussed in detail in chapter 6.) These programs were implemented in response to a perceived security vacuum in CEE and the desire to foster democratic state building, and they were based on the mutually reinforcing pillars of dialogue, cooperation, and collective defence.[90] Yet regional instabilities and the rise of ethnic conflicts in Europe remained the primary security threat for the West, including Canada.[91]

The transformations in Europe also found reflections in the scholarly debate on the new security environment and the concept of security generally. Jessica Matthews, for example, posited that the end of the Cold War broadened the definition of national security from a one- to a multidimensional concept. It now encompassed "resource, environmental and demographic"[92] security concerns that posed security risks to states. Susan Strange put forward a similar argument, suggesting that in the post–Cold War era, security concerns had grown beyond territorial and strategic considerations towards a competitive economic one.[93]

This new definition had implications for studying alliances and security cooperation among allies. Concentrating exclusively on the military domain results in – at best – incomplete assessments of the shares of the collective burden. It is also misleading intellectually and theoretically because it is accepted knowledge that the Atlantic alliance has a significant and vibrant political as well as a transnational dimension to its operations and existence. Thus, any study of the behaviour of international organizations must take these transnational dimensions into account and assess the burdens incurred across the new security spectrum.

---

89 A more detailed discussion and examination of these institutions can be found in ch. 6.

90 As one aide to the secretary general put it, Manfred Wörner convinced NATO leaders that the window of opportunity to help shape the new democracies of CEE was very small (Jamie Shea, Deputy Assistant Secretary General for Emerging Security Challenges, interview by the author, NATO Headquarters, Brussels, 18 May 2007). For a detailed account of an evolving NATO in the 1990s, see, e.g., Kay 1998; Asmus 2002; Asmus, Kugler, and Larrabee 1993; Haglund 1996; Sloan 1989.

91 "Deputy Minister's Committee: Governance Paper," 25 March 1997, 3, retrieved under the Access to Information Act, 10 April 2007, A-3, File No. 3947-01.

92 Matthews 1989, 162.

93 Strange 1987a.

The debate over new definitions of national security affected the practice of NATO burden sharing. Scholars began to recognize that non-military problems put increasing limitations on state cooperation and that states included these non-military and domestic issues more and more in their national security calculations.[94] This supports the argument that the conventional measure for sharing alliance burdens in NATO (defence spending as a share of GDP) was severely limited to one policy area and thus holds significant conceptual and explanatory limitations. It also buttresses the methodology used in this study to separate civilian and military shares of the burden.

The changing discourse on security for assessing the NATO burden-sharing regime is also problematic in methodological terms. Above all, it dilutes the identification of a single dependent variable; it also establishes a causal relationship among the dependent and a number of possible other independent variables, thus going against the methodological rigour of a research design.

David Baldwin questioned these arguments by saying that with the end of the East-West conflict, "the dimensions of security have not changed ... but the substantive specifications of these dimensions that were appropriate during the Cold War are likely to differ from those appropriate for the 1990s."[95] Economic security,[96] environmental security,[97] and social and military security could be conceptualized as different forms of security, but they were not fundamentally different concepts of security itself. Nonetheless, scholars agreed that the definition of national security was too narrow and needed to be revisited. Issues such as environmental pollution, overuse of the world's oceans, and health epidemics posed increasing security risks for states but were not reflected in traditional concepts of security. As Baldwin stated, "recognizing that threats to national security or well being were not confined to the military realm, these proposals expand the notion of security threats to include such matters as human rights, the environment, economics, epidemics, crime, and social injustice."[98]

---

94 For an early discussion of this trend, see Flynn 1981; Sloan 1985a, 1985b.

95 Baldwin 1997, 23. This is consistent with Rosenau 1992.

96 For a discussion of economic security, see, e.g., Borrus et al. 1992; Crawford 1993; Kapstein 1992.

97 There are countless resources on this subject; a good overview is provided by Homer-Dixon 1994; Levy 1995.

98 Baldwin 1997, 26.

Internal Reforms and New Military Postures

The absence of a constant threat imposed internal and external transformation processes on NATO's armed forces. The alliance revised the structure of its forces and assigned them new roles and responsibilities. It called into question the existing doctrines of warfare as well as the necessities and installations of territorial defence. This, in part, was what the public was demanding from their governments by asking them to "cash in the peace dividend," although it would seriously reduce their defence budgets and the size of their armed forces. More fundamentally, the new international security system called into question NATO's raison d'être as a collective security organization,[99] which had been created in 1949 to contain the Soviet Union's expansionism and lust for power.[100] However, with the events following the fall of the Berlin Wall, governments and their defence ministries lost the rationale to justify rampantly growing defence budgets. According to the UN, total global military spending declined by 3.6% a year between 1987 and 1991, or from $995 billion to $767 billion,[101] resulting in significant savings for NATO taxpayers.

These external conditions compelled NATO's armed forces to adapt and transform themselves so that they could better respond to the demands posed by the new and evolving threats of intra-state conflicts, transnational border conflicts, and non-state actors such as terrorist organizations and nationalist movements.[102] Critics were quick to disagree with the list of threats. Gaddis, for example, argued that these "new" forms of nationalism were not a novel phenomenon in the history of international relations at all; they had simply resurfaced with the end of the Cold War, when the juggernaut of Cold War politics lost steam.[103] One might think, for example, of the old animosities between Hungary and Romania, or other nationalist sentiments in south-eastern Europe, where the forces of fragmentation resurfaced and competed with the forces of integration. The difficulty for defence planners, as Gaddis argued, was that "one can no longer plausibly point to a single

---

99 Mearsheimer 1994–95.
100 This, at least, was one of the interpretations of Cold War historians; see Gaddis 2005.
101 United Nations Development Programme 1994; see also Sivard 1996. All amounts are in US dollars unless otherwise stated.
102 Ignatieff 1998; see also Duffield 1998; Kaldor 1978.
103 Gaddis 1991, 105.

source of danger, as one could throughout most of that conflict [the Cold War], but dangers will still be there."[104]

The new security architecture in Europe also prompted NATO to review its future objectives and (military) roles in Europe and abroad. This reform process started with a strategic document published in 1991, which prepared the alliance for a greater role in peacekeeping, peace enforcement, and stabilization operations, particularly in the Balkans.[105] The alliance now recognized the need for flexible, rapidly mobile, and capable forces for both a highly uncertain new pan-European security environment and an era of failed and failing states.[106] The London Declaration of July 1990 acknowledged that "NATO will field smaller and restructured active forces. These forces will be highly mobile and versatile so that allied leaders will have maximum flexibility in deciding how to respond to a crisis. It will rely increasingly on multinational corps made up of national units."[107] The changes also spoke to the transformation of NATO's role from a Cold War defensive military alliance to a more political organization, one that placed increasing importance on political instruments rather than military deterrence while recognizing the relative decline of military power in international relations.[108]

The combination of a new strategy, political role playing, and new mandates of international crisis management demanded multinational rapid reaction force capabilities and replaced the need for large conventional military postures.[109] This emphasis on expeditionary forces can be seen in the levels of NATO's active duty personnel between 1990 and 2001, shown in table 3.1 below.

---

104 Ibid., 113.

105 North Atlantic Council, "The Alliance's New Strategic Concept: Agreed by the Heads of State and Government Participating in the Meeting of the North Atlantic Council," Rome, 7–8 November 1991.

106 See, e.g., Hauser and Kernic 2006; Mariano 2007. The Canadian government fully bought into this rationale in internal communications from the Office of the Assistant Deputy Minister (Policy & Communications) at DND; see Tony Kellett, "Canada-2005 – Political/Military," 4.

107 North Atlantic Council, "Declaration on a Transformed North Atlantic Alliance: Issued by the Heads of State and Government Participating in the Meeting of the North Atlantic Council ('The London Declaration')," London, 5–6 July 1990, para. 14(1).

108 See Garthoff 1992; see also Jervis 1992; May 1992.

109 Canada, Department of External Affairs 1991, 12.

The significance of this table is twofold. First, it shows that virtually all NATO allies, despite their rank on the scale of international power, downsized their armed forces by 30% to 50% during this time. This proves that second-tier powers like Canada did not unilaterally reduce their forces; countries across the alliance were downsizing as well. This is an important point because in 1994, Ottawa was accused by scholars and analysts alike of having abandoned NATO when it closed its two bases in Germany in an effort to achieve fiscal savings.[110] Geoffrey Bruce, for example, lamented that "Canada's influence in Europe has steadily, and understandably, diminished over the years and will continue to decline. ... In this context, the withdrawal of the Canadian forces from Europe has lasting costs. It is like a golfer who has disposed of his clubs but remains a member of the club."[111]

Second, compared to other second-tier powers such as Spain, the Netherlands, Belgium, and Norway, Canada made the fewest cuts. Thus, from a comparative perspective, Ottawa did not "underperform," and assigning Canada the label of "laggard" or "free rider" cannot be validated by the empirical evidence. Canada reduced its collective NATO commitments, but not more than other comparable allies, and, in fact, NATO's Secretary General, Manfred Wörner, explicitly approved this reduced Canadian commitment. In a speech given in Brussels in 1990, at a time when Canada was debating whether to pull out from Germany completely, he noted that "there is a clear desire to see the United States and Canada remain in Europe, of course with reduced forces, but remain nonetheless."[112]

---

110 Bland and Maloney 2004, 165; Keating 2002, 158. According to the International Institute for Strategic Studies (1992, 53), Canada's mechanized brigade consisted of 4,400 troops plus a 2,600-strong air division. Until France withdrew from NATO's integrated military structure in 1966, Canada had a military presence in Metz. In 1970, it reduced the size of its forces in Europe, most of which consisted of a mechanized brigade group in Lahr and a three-fighter squadron at Baden Soellingen. Canadian troops were stationed mainly in Germany's south.

111 Geoffrey F. Bruce, "NATO: New Life or Requiem?" *Ottawa Citizen*, 31 January 1996, A11.

112 Manfred Wörner, "Address Given to a Conference Sponsored by the United States Mission to NATO on the Future of the Atlantic Alliance" (Brussels, 19–21 September 1990).

Table 3.1 Active Duty Personnel, 1990–2001

Country	1990	1991	1992	1993	1994	1995	1996	1997	1998	1999	2000	2001	Total	Change (%)	Total (%)	Total (non-US) (%)	Rank
United States	2,181.0	2,115.0	1,919.0	1,815.0	1,715.0	1,620.0	1,575.0	1,539.0	1,505.0	1,486.0	1,483.0	1,482.0	2,0435.0	-32.0	35.2	n/a	1
Turkey	768.9	804.0	704.0	685.9	811.0	804.6	818.4	828.1	787.6	789.0	792.9	794.8	9,389.2	3.4	16.2	25.0	2
France	549.6	542.0	522.0	505.9	505.5	503.8	500.7	475.1	449.3	420.8	394.6	367.0	5,736.3	-33.2	9.9	15.3	3
Italy	493.1	473.0	471.0	450.2	435.6	435.4	430.6	419.4	402.2	390.9	381.3	373.7	5,156.4	-24.2	8.9	13.7	4
Germany	545.4	457.0	442.0	398.4	366.2	351.6	339.4	334.5	332.5	331.1	318.8	306.5	4,523.4	-43.8	7.8	12.0	5
United Kingdom	308.3	301.0	293.0	271.0	256.6	233.3	221.2	218.2	217.5	217.6	218.1	219.2	2,975.0	-28.9	5.1	7.9	6
Greece	201.4	205.0	208.0	212.7	205.5	213.3	211.6	205.6	202.0	203.8	205.0	210.8	2,484.7	4.7	4.3	6.6	7
Spain	262.7	246.0	198.0	204.2	212.9	209.7	202.8	196.6	189.1	155.2	144.0	134.0	2,355.2	-49.0	4.1	6.3	8
Portugal	87.5	86.0	80.0	68.4	69.1	77.7	73.3	71.9	71.4	70.5	67.7	70.4	893.9	-19.5	1.5	2.4	9
Netherlands	103.7	104.0	90.0	86.2	76.9	67.3	63.9	57.0	55.3	53.6	51.6	51.6	861.4	-50.2	1.5	2.3	10
Canada	87.1	86.0	82.0	76.4	74.6	69.7	66.0	61.3	60.3	59.6	58.8	59.4	841.2	-31.8	1.5	2.2	11
Belgium	106.3	101.0	79.0	69.6	52.5	46.6	46.1	45.1	43.2	42.1	41.6	41.2	714.3	-61.2	1.2	1.9	12
Poland	n/a	n/a	n/a	n/a	n/a	n/a	n/a	n/a	n/a	187.5	191.0	178.3	556.8	n/a	1.0	1.5	13
Norway	50.6	41.0	42.0	32.3	33.5	38.3	38.2	33.5	32.8	32.6	32.0	31.4	438.2	-37.9	0.8	1.2	14
Denmark	31.0	30.0	28.0	27.5	27.8	27.1	28.4	25.3	25.1	27.3	24.4	25.1	327.0	-19.0	0.6	0.9	15

Table 3.1 Active Duty Personnel, 1990–2001 (*cont.*)

Country	1990	1991	1992	1993	1994	1995	1996	1997	1998	1999	2000	2001	Total	Change (%)	Total (%)	Total (non-US) (%)	Rank
Czech Republic	n/a	n/a	n/a	n/a	n/a	n/a	n/a	n/a	n/a	54.4	51.8	48.7	154.9	n/a	0.3	0.4	16
Hungary	n/a	n/a	n/a	n/a	n/a	n/a	n/a	n/a	n/a	50.9	50.0	49.5	150.4	n/a	0.3	0.4	17
Luxembourg	1.3	1.0	1.0	1.3	1.3	1.3	1.4	1.4	1.4	1.4	1.4	1.4	15.6	7.7	0.0	0.0	18
Iceland*	0	0	0	0	0	0	0	0	0	0	0	0	0.0	0	0.0	0.0	19
Total	5,777.9	5,592.0	5,159.0	4,905.0	4,844.0	4,699.7	4,617.0	4,512.0	4,374.7	4,574.3	4,508.3	4,445.0	5,8009.0	–23	100	100	19
Total (non-US)	3,596.9	3,477.0	3,240.0	3,090.0	3,129.0	3,079.7	3,042.0	2,973.0	2,869.7	3,088.3	3,025.3	2,963.0	3,7574.0	–18	64.8	100	18
Average	361.1	349.5	322.4	306.6	302.8	293.7	288.6	282.0	273.4	240.8	237.3	233.9	3,053.0	n/a	5.3	5.6	n/a
Average (non-US)	239.8	231.8	216.0	206.0	208.6	205.3	202.8	198.2	191.3	171.6	168.1	164.6	2087.4	n/a	3.6	5.6	n/a

Sources: United States Department of Defense, *Report on Allied Contributions to the Common Defense* (Washington, DC, 2002); ranking compiled by the author.

* Iceland does not maintain military forces.

These NATO-wide reductions and restructuring of the armed forces was defended by the military establishment in Canada, which noted the following:

> Over the past few years, multilateral organizations have begun to employ impartial outside military forces in innovative ways to deal with regional instability. Such forces have provided disaster relief, helped in postwar reconstruction, ensured the protection of refugees, supervised fair elections, assisted nations to manage the transition to independence, and even protected ethnic minorities. ... The defence of Canada's sovereignty, our continued participation in collective security arrangements, and our aspiration to help resolve regional conflict, all call for the maintenance of flexible, capable armed forces. These forces will have to adapt to new domestic realities and new geostrategic conditions.[113]

What is noteworthy about table 3.1 is that between 1990 and 2001, Ottawa's cuts were relatively consistent with those made by its major allies. While at −31.8% they were extensive, they were not extraordinary when compared to other states with a similar or higher power status. Indeed, middle-power Canada reduced its armed forces to the same degree as, for example, France (−33.2%), the United Kingdom (−28.9%), and the United States (−32.0%), all of which had a higher power status. In fact, the table shows that all states cut their armed forces to a degree that was slightly above the NATO average.[114]

With these military transformations going on, NATO's military role became less important than its political functions, which had always been an integral part of the alliance but were less pronounced during the Cold War years. Then, the number of a nation's troops, amount of equipment, and level of defence spending according to its GDP combined to be a solid indicator of its commitment to NATO. In the

---

113 Canada, Department of National Defence 1992, 11.

114 From 1989 to 1993 Canada closed 15 bases, including the two in Germany, and 1,200 Canadian troops returned home by 1992. The government's rationale was purely economic, saving Canadian taxpayers nearly $1.2 billion a year, excluding the costs of training. Moreover, the decision to bring the forces home was made at a time of a large public debt. See, e.g., Canada 1989, 28; Rempel 1992, 232.

post–Cold War era, however, these parameters acquired new meanings.[115] Military size and capabilities were still considered a solid indicator of how much a NATO member shouldered allied burdens, but they had only limited explanatory value in the changing context of the post-Cold War era. The reason was simple: the alliance did not so much need military postures as flexible and highly mobile troops capable of completing a range of tasks, and these could be combat but also peace building and reconstruction. Moreover, NATO was increasingly becoming a political organization specializing in international crisis management. As one historian succinctly noted, "few wars ... are any longer decided on the battlefield. ... They are decided at the peace table."[116] Kalevi Holsti even went so far as to argue that wars had become deinstitutionalized – that is, not centrally controlled by "rules, regulations, etiquette, and armaments."[117]

While threat perceptions were adjusted to the new external security conditions, so were forms of military organization, and the modern military organizations of the Cold War were replaced with postmodern militaries.[118] Rather than preparing for large conventional threats, Mary Kaldor argued, NATO's armed forces should be trained to fight "new wars."[119] With the end of the Cold War, Western militaries updated their doctrines and concepts by introducing terms such as "operations other than war" and "stability operations" into their military vocabulary. The role of postmodern militaries now included separating belligerents, rebuilding war-torn societies, delivering food and medical supplies to refugees, and providing security for humanitarian and other non-governmental organizations. The new missions of postmodern forces were also a reflection of concerns for humans rather than states.[120]

---

115 This change in the notion of security was affirmed by NATO Secretary General Javier Solana. See North Atlantic Council, "Press Point of Mr. Javier Solana, NATO Secretary General, and Minister Igor Rodionov, Russian Defence Minister," Meeting in Defence Ministers Session, NATO HQ, Brussels, 18 December 1996.

116 Howard 1999, 130.

117 Holsti 1999, 304.

118 See Moskos, Williams, and Segal 2000. However, it is important to note that the concept of a modern and post-modern military is a theoretical construct that analyses the shift in military professionalism and organization after the end of the Cold War.

119 Kaldor 1978.

120 Martha Finnemore (2003) analyses the changing normative context of international interventions into sovereign states. She describes the role of humanitarian norms in shaping patterns of humanitarian interventions over 200 years.

Postmodern militaries were also affected by changes in conscription. Throughout the Cold War, nearly all Western militaries relied on conscription to increase their conventional forces, except for Britain, which turned to a voluntary army after 1963. The United States followed suit on 1 July 1973.[121] These Cold War militaries were equipped and trained to mobilize their forces to fight an excessive ground war with the Soviet Union on the fields of Western Europe by conventional and nuclear means. In turn, those large-scale conventional wars determined the size of the forces. As one analyst put it, "the power to destroy civilizations was the defining quality of the Cold War."[122] However, in the postmodern era of military organization, a smaller force was needed. The United States, for example, reduced its active duty force from 2.6 million soldiers during the Cold War to 1.4 million in 1999.[123] This in turn reduced demands for new recruits.

The most significant cuts in national defence spending were made by the United States, from an average of 5.2% between 1980 and 1984 to 3.7% between 1990 and 1995 (see table 3.2 below).[124] France, another major NATO ally (measured in terms of its GDP), cut its level of defence spending from an average of 4.0% between 1980 and 1985 to 3.4% between 1990 and 1995, then dropped it to an average of 3.0% from 1990 to 2001. The United Kingdom made similar cuts, from an average of 5.2% between 1980 and 1985, to 3.7% between 1990 and 1985, to 3.0% from 1990 to 2001. In actual dollars, the US defence budget was reduced from over $306 billion in the 1990 fiscal year to more than $278 billion in 1995.[125]

This increase in military spending also meant, according to Clark, that "some kind of de facto military specialization, or division of labour, has begun to appear."[126] As a result, most states in the post–Cold War order became less capable of engaging in fully fledged, large-scale operations.

This specialization among NATO's armed forces was eased by technological revolutions in warfare. The so-called Revolution in Military

---

121 See, e.g., Cowen 2006.
122 Moskos, Williams, and Segal 2000, 2.
123 Ibid., 18.; see also Clark 2004.
124 For greater detail, see, e.g., Lis and Selden 2003, 3; North Atlantic Treaty Organization 2003.
125 Ibid.
126 Clark 2001, 205.

Table 3.2 Defence Expenditures as a Percentage of GDP, 1990–2001

Country	1990	1991	1992	1993	1994	1995	1996	1997	1998	1999	2000	2001	Total ($)	Total (%)	Total (non-US) (%)	Difference (%)	Rank
Greece	4.66	4.26	4.46	4.42	4.43	4.42	4.49	4.57	4.80	4.84	4.87	4.60	54.82	11.80	13.11	-1.29	1
Turkey	3.53	3.76	3.88	3.93	4.05	4.25	4.14	4.10	4.38	5.39	5.99	4.90	52.30	11.26	12.51	38.81	2
United States	5.33	4.74	4.89	4.54	4.15	3.83	3.47	3.33	3.13	3.04	2.99	3.10	46.54	10.02	11.13	-41.84	3
United Kingdom	4.04	4.24	3.83	3.60	3.37	3.03	2.96	2.69	2.65	2.53	2.42	2.50	37.86	8.15	9.06	-38.12	4
France	3.56	3.56	3.41	3.41	3.34	3.11	2.99	2.94	2.77	2.72	2.66	2.50	36.95	7.95	8.84	-29.78	5
Portugal	2.79	2.73	2.67	2.59	2.49	2.57	2.39	2.36	2.19	2.23	2.21	2.10	29.31	6.31	7.01	-24.73	6
Norway	2.94	2.79	3.01	2.74	2.76	2.39	2.24	2.10	2.26	2.16	1.86	1.80	29.06	6.25	6.95	-38.78	7
Netherlands	2.62	2.50	2.46	2.26	2.14	2.03	1.90	1.82	1.75	1.78	1.63	1.60	24.49	5.27	5.86	-38.93	8
Italy	2.13	2.11	2.05	2.09	2.00	1.78	1.90	1.95	1.97	2.02	1.94	2.00	23.95	5.15	5.73	-6.10	9
Germany	2.82	2.30	2.13	1.95	1.78	1.70	1.64	1.57	1.54	1.54	1.49	1.50	21.96	4.73	5.25	-46.81	10
Denmark	2.05	2.06	2.00	1.99	1.86	1.80	1.69	1.67	1.64	1.60	1.52	1.60	21.47	4.62	5.14	-21.95	11
Belgium	2.42	2.35	1.87	1.78	1.73	1.65	1.58	1.51	1.46	1.45	1.43	1.30	20.54	4.42	4.91	-46.28	12
Canada	2.01	1.90	1.90	1.86	1.73	1.60	1.38	1.24	1.31	1.30	1.17	1.20	18.60	4.00	4.45	-40.30	13
Spain	1.84	1.72	1.57	1.73	1.54	1.55	1.42	1.37	1.29	1.26	1.27	1.20	17.76	3.82	4.25	-34.78	14
Luxembourg	1.08	1.15	1.17	1.05	1.13	1.05	0.78	0.77	0.78	0.75	0.72	0.80	11.23	2.42	2.69	-25.93	15
Czech Republic	n/a	n/a	n/a	n/a	n/a	n/a	n/a	n/a	n/a	2.24	2.30	2.10	6.65	1.43	1.59	n/a	16
Poland	n/a	n/a	n/a	n/a	n/a	n/a	n/a	n/a	n/a	2.04	1.99	2.00	6.03	1.30	1.44	n/a	17
Hungary	n/a	n/a	n/a	n/a	n/a	n/a	n/a	n/a	n/a	1.63	1.68	1.80	5.11	1.10	1.22	n/a	18
Iceland	0	0	0	0	0	0	0	0	0	0	0	0	0	0	0	0	19
Total	43.82	42.17	41.30	39.94	38.50	36.76	34.96	33.99	33.93	40.53	40.11	38.60	464.61	100.00	100.00	-11.91	19
Total (non-US)	38.49	37.43	36.41	35.40	34.35	32.93	31.49	30.66	30.80	37.50	37.12	35.50	418.07	89.98	88.87	-7.77	18
Average	2.74	2.64	2.58	2.50	2.41	2.30	2.18	2.12	2.12	2.13	2.11	2.03	25.81*	5.56*	5.26	-25.82	n/a
Average (non-US)	2.57	2.50	2.43	2.36	2.29	2.20	2.10	2.04	2.05	2.08	2.06	1.97	23.23*	5.00*	5.56	-23.14	n/a

Source: Official NATO data (2003).
*Cannot be calculated precisely because of enlargement in 1999 from 16 to 19 member states.

Affairs, whose tenets are that the application of technology changes the organization and conduct of modern warfare, helped NATO forces lower the costs of personnel and equipment. Military technology, as it became more readily available, replaced traditional military personnel.[127]

Partly for this reason, post-modern militaries abandoned the practice of military conscription almost collectively. Before NATO's enlargement in 1999, nine of the 16 member states had adopted a volunteer military, and only seven still employed conscripts.[128] The picture, however, changed with the first and second rounds of enlargement. In 2004, 16 of the 26 NATO member states still maintained conscription armies, and only 10 had switched to voluntary forces. (See table 3.3 below.) This development can be explained by the proportionally large number of post–Warsaw Pact countries with neither the financial resources to comprehensively restructure their militaries and adopt Western military structures[129] nor the political commitment to do so because of domestic political constraints.

Conclusion

We should now have a better understanding of the hidden and complex meanings of the new world order as well as an appreciation for some of the conceptual challenges of the transformation of order and security at the end of the Cold War. The importance of military power as a tool of statecraft declined after 1989, and new power resources became more prevalent (especially NATO's social role). This changed the nature and context of international politics and had implications for the burden-sharing debate. In turn, NATO's new force postures after 1989 allowed second-tier powers like Canada to restructure their armed forces using NATO directives to justify reduced spending on defence.

Unlike in the Cold War years, NATO's armed forces were expected to act more like diplomats than combatants. Moreover, with an absence of

---

127 Kluger 1999; Krepinevich 1994; van Creveld 1989. For an account regarding Canada, see Sloan 2002; Sokolsky 2001.

128 See, e.g., Moskos, Williams, and Segal 2000.

129 CEE countries had adopted comprehensive military reforms in order to make their military structures and operations more interoperable with those of Western states. This process took a long time because of constrained fiscal budgets.

Table 3.3 Conscription, 2004

Country	Conscription (yes/no)	Duration
Belgium	No	
Bulgaria	Yes	9 months
Canada	No	
Czech Republic	Yes	9–12 months
Denmark	Yes	10 months (later reduced to 4)
Estonia	Yes	8 months
France	No	
Germany	Yes	9 months
Greece	Yes	16–19 months*
Hungary	Yes	6 months
Iceland	No	
Italy	Yes	10 months
Latvia	Yes	12 months
Lithuania	Yes	12 months
Luxembourg	No	
Netherlands	No	
Norway	Yes	12 months
Poland	Yes	9 months
Portugal	Yes	4 months
Romania	Yes	12 months
Slovakia	Yes	4 months
Slovenia	No	
Spain	No	
Turkey	Yes	15 months
United Kingdom	No	
United States	No	

Source: International Institute for Strategic Studies, *Military Balance 2004/05* (London: IISS, 2005).
* Army: up to 16 months; navy and air force: up to 19 months.

threats to their own territorial security, second-tier powers like Canada were able to concentrate their foreign and defence policy efforts on supporting milieu goals – a liberal and multilateral international order in Europe shaped by liberal democratic norms and values – rather than fostering their own narrow national interests.[130] Territorial defence no longer required federal treasuries to release so much money, and multilateralism as a persistent principle of international affairs continued to appeal to governments because it allowed them to reduce their forces in Europe.

---

130 Clark 2001, 173.

PART II

Military Burdens

4 The "New" Wars in the Balkans and Iraq, Part I

Introduction

As noted in the introductory chapter, this book analyses a series of burden-sharing indicators. They are clustered (typologized) into military (or hard power) and civilian (soft power) burden-sharing indexes. The benefit of clustering variables is that it allows us to make a structured and focused comparison of the data and thus a systematic and cumulative analysis. The idea of creating typologies has a long history in the social sciences[1] because it enables the researcher to address complex sets of information and draw out similarities and differences from the indexes while avoiding oversimplification from the case study.[2] Alexander George and Andrew Bennett define typology theory as "a theory that specifies independent variables, delineates them into the categories for which the researcher will measure the cases and their outcomes, and provides not only hypotheses on how these variables operate individually, but also contingent generalizations on how and under what conditions they behave."[3]

Given the liberal theoretical paradigm that is used as the overall conceptual framework in this book, focusing on military burdens may sound surprising at first. However, recalling the discussions of liberal IR theory from chapter 2, liberal states are likely to use force under two

---

1 Elman 2005; George 1979; Lazarsfeld 1937.
2 See, e.g., Bailey 1994, 3–20.
3 George and Bennett 2005, 235.

conditions: first, against non-democratic states and, second, in defence of the liberal community of states should that community and its commonly held values be threatened by an external aggressor.

The analysis of military burdens is divided into two chapters. This chapter examines the civil and ethnic wars in the Persian Gulf and especially the Balkans in the early 1990s – specifically, Canada's military and security role in the liberation of Kuwait, the European Community Monitoring Mission (ECMM), and the United Nations Protection Force (UNPROFOR). The Balkan conflict was, so to speak, the "mother" of all ethnic conflicts that followed and thus justifies a detailed discussion and examination. Certainly, Canada's commitments to peace operations in south-eastern Europe were the most salient dimension of a decade-long commitment to European peace and security.

Gulf War I

The 1990s began with a collective security operation in the Persian Gulf. Operation DESERT STORM was a UN-sanctioned military operation seeking to liberate Kuwait from Iraqi occupation after Iraqi forces had invaded that country on 2 August 1990.[4] That same day, the UN Security Council discussed the matter, and the resulting Resolution 660 demanded the unconditional withdrawal of Iraqi troops.[5] Four days later, the Security Council passed another, more forceful resolution under Chapter VII of the UN charter and imposed economic sanctions against Iraq.[6] The military ground campaign started on 16 January 1991, after Iraq had failed to comply with UN demands for it to withdraw its troops.

Scholars have pointed out that with its decision to liberate Kuwait, the UN overcame nearly 50 years of paralysis, during which time the political and diplomatic stalemate of the Cold War had made any significant cooperation between the superpower blocs impossible.[7] The new collective security order of the post–Cold War era championed a

---

4 The literature on the Gulf War and the composition of Operation DESERT STORM is vast; however, a succinct overview is provided in Collins 1991. For a discussion of US forces returning to the United States rather than Germany, see Campbell and Johnson Ward 2003; for a greater analysis of the transformation of post-1989 forces, see Moskos, Williams, and Segal 2000.

5 UN, S/RES/660, 2 August 1990.

6 UN, S/RES/661, 6 August 1990.

7 Blechman 1998, 289.

more active UN, one that was committed to the principles of multilateralism and cooperation rather than conflict; and the UN's operation in the Gulf demonstrated its political willingness and capacity to enforce the multilateral norm of collective security to maintain international peace and security.[8]

Yet the pledges to multilateralism and the principles of collective security were made under unique historical conditions – that is, in a unique situational environment. The Soviet Union, for example, was preoccupied with domestic issues and showed relatively little interest in Middle East politics.[9] Also, Arab states were easily convinced by Iraq's blatant aggression to support the international campaign to liberate it. This support extended beyond financial support and included political as well as socio-economic assistance for the "coalition of the willing."

Operation DESERT STORM was a UN operation, but it affected NATO countries, as well as the alliance's force-planning divisions, in a number of ways. Turkey, for example, a NATO ally since 1952, needed to defend its common border with Iraq, and it officially received military assistance from NATO allies to do this. Patriot missiles were installed to address incoming missile threats, while NATO's Airborne Warning and Control Systems technology was deployed to monitor Turkish airspace. NATO's long-practised integrated command and control structure, coupled with common operational procedures, habits, techniques, and practices of cooperation, facilitated interoperability among the coalition forces as well as a rapid build-up in and deployment to the Gulf. NATO's Defence Planning Committee concluded, "We warmly welcome the success of the international coalition forces in the ... Gulf War. We note with satisfaction the effectiveness of the prompt action taken by the Alliance in deploying naval and air forces to its Southern region to deter any possible attacks on its members."[10]

The liberation of Kuwait would not have been achieved without the use of NATO's infrastructure. The Gulf War crisis also reaffirmed to allies that international security affairs continued to be a domain of disorder and instability rather than an idealized condition of international peace. It became accepted wisdom that even in the new world order,

---

8 Russett and Sutterlin 1991.

9 For the latest research on the end of the Cold War and the years that followed, see Brown 2009; Kotkin and Gross 2009.

10 NATO, "Final Communiqué of the Defence Planning Committee and Nuclear Planning Group," Brussels, 28–29 May 1991, art. 5.

violent conflicts were still likely and major and second-tier powers alike were affected by these forces of instability.

Canada was such a second-tier power, and it had an extensive record of contributing to international peace operations.[11] Like its NATO allies, it was upset by Iraq's violation of the basic principles of international law and sovereignty. The Gulf War also reaffirmed Ottawa's "old" strategic rationale that peace, order, stability, and prosperity in Europe remained important normative values for Canada, especially in cases where one of its NATO allies (in this case, Turkey) was threatened militarily by an external aggressor.[12] Indeed, Canada advocated the use of force against the regime of Saddam Hussein after sanctions did not bring results as quickly as hoped.[13]

In support of UN Security Council Resolution 661, Canada sent three warships, a supply vessel, a field hospital, a fighter jet squadron, and Special Forces personnel to the Gulf.[14] Canada also helped enforce the naval blockade against Iraq and dispatched 300 field engineers to the United Nations Iraqi/Kuwait Observer Mission.[15] A total of 6,600 Canadian Forces personnel were deployed in the Gulf operations for the duration of the conflict, which lasted from 2 August 1990 to 28 February 1991.[16] Moreover, Canada dispatched one ship and 250 support personnel to the Maritime Interception Force, which was deployed in the Red Sea in 1992 to support the post–Gulf War embargo against Iraq (Operation BARRIER).[17]

In 1992, both NATO and the Western European Union (WEU) began to monitor the Mediterranean Sea and enforce the sanctions (especially

---

11 See, e.g., Carroll 2009.

12 See, e.g., Canada, Department of External Affairs and International Trade Canada 1990, 2–3.

13 Hugh Winsor, "Foreign Policy: Has the One-Time Leader of the Pink Tories Turned into a Hawk or Is Joe Clark Just Putting the Best Face on Canada's Role in the Gulf Crisis? Joe Where?" *Globe and Mail*, 1990, D1.

14 See, e.g., Department of National Defence, "The Canadian Forces in the Gulf War (1990–1991)," backgrounder BG-97.017, 3 April 1997; see also Bland and Maloney 2004, 236–8.

15 Institute for Strategic Studies 1992, 53. Canada did not take part in Operation DESERT SHIELD or Operation DESERT STORM.

16 Department of National Defence, Policy Group, "Past Canadian Commitments to United Nations and Other Peace Support Operations," http://www.dnd.ca/admpol/content.asp?id=%7B4433D831-9230-4572-B297-CEA4F4C1DA3D%7D, accessed 1 June 2007.

17 Bland and Maloney 2004, 239–40.

the arms embargo) imposed against the Federal Republic of Yugoslavia.[18] The NATO mission, called Operation MARITIME MONITOR, and its WEU counterpart, Operation VIGILANCE, were merged on 8 June 1993 into Operation SHARP GUARD, which consisted of 20 ships.[19] This naval task force, supported by maritime patrol aircraft, was judged to be quite effective. Under the naval blockade and backed by the UN Security Council, Serbia was prohibited from importing or transporting crude oil, other petroleum products, and coal into Serbia or Montenegro. NATO/WEU vessels were authorized to inspect all ships destined for Serbia and deny them access, if necessary. NATO challenged a total of 74,000 ships, of which 6,000 were closely inspected at sea and 1,400 sent to a harbour for detailed inspection.[20]

Canada made naval contributions to the combined NATO/WEU mission from 1992 to 1995. For example, it sent two Aurora maritime patrol aircraft to monitor the Macedonian coastline, a helicopter-carrying frigate of the Halifax class with 210 seamen on board, and a fleet replenishment tanker.[21] In addition, Canadian naval officers served at the operational headquarters and headed up NATO's Standing Naval Force Atlantic.

The naval tonnage index is a useful way of measuring allied naval contributions. It is a static measure that aggregates fleet size, thus providing a more meaningful basis for comparison than simple tallies of ships. It tracks the number of specific vessels, such as aircraft carriers, submarines, naval cruisers, destroyers, frigates, larger corvettes, mine warfare ships and craft, and patrol ships for combat; it does not give any indication of how effective or how reliable these ships and their weapons are during an operation. Thus, it does not make any claims about combat effectiveness and should be considered only as a rough indicator of the overall naval potential of a state. Table 4.1 below shows naval tonnage by NATO country from 1990 to 2001.

---

18 UN, S/RES/ 752, 15 May 1992. Two weeks later, S/RES/ 757 (30 May 1992) attested that both parties to the conflict were not in compliance with the earlier Resolution 752.

19 For a detailed account of Canada's commitment to Sharp Guard, see Maloney 2000.

20 IFOR, "NATO/WEU Operation Sharp Guard," Final Factsheet, 2 October 1996.

21 Michael Chesson, "Canada-European Union Bulletin: Article on Canada and NATO," fax to Jacques Paquette, IDS, DFAIT, 5 July 1994, retrieved under the Access to Information Act, 10 April 2007, A-3, File No. 3947-01. Later, the Canadian contingent was augmented by the operational support ship HMCS Preserver; see Department of National Defence, "Operation Sharp Guard," backgrounder, 2 February 1996.

Table 4.1 Naval Tonnage, 1990–2001

Country	1990	1994	1995	1996	1997	1998	1999	2000	2001	Total	Total (%)	Total (non-US) (%)	Change	Average	Rank
United States	58.0	55.0	54.0	53.0	54.0	62.0	60.7	60.1	60.6	517.0	63.1	n/a	3.9	57.5	1
United Kingdom	11.0	11.0	11.0	11.0	11.0	9.1	9.3	9.3	9.2	90.7	11.1	29.7	–14.8	10.1	2
France	5.7	5.9	5.8	5.9	5.8	4.5	4.7	4.5	4.5	47.3	5.8	15.5	–21.1	5.3	3
Turkey	2.6	3.0	3.0	3.0	2.9	2.4	2.6	2.6	2.5	24.6	3.0	8.0	–3.8	2.7	4
Italy	2.1	2.8	2.7	2.8	2.9	2.6	2.6	2.7	2.6	23.8	2.9	7.8	23.8	2.6	5
Germany	3.0	2.6	2.6	2.7	2.8	2.2	2.2	2.4	2.3	22.8	2.8	7.5	–23.3	2.5	6
Spain	2.3	2.3	2.5	2.5	2.6	2.3	2.5	2.7	2.7	22.4	2.7	7.3	17.4	2.5	7
Canada	1.7	2.0	2.2	2.2	2.4	2.0	2.7	2.8	1.7	19.7	2.4	6.4	0	2.2	8
Greece	1.9	2.1	2.0	2.1	2.1	1.8	1.9	1.9	1.9	17.7	2.2	5.8	0	2.0	9
Netherlands	1.2	1.7	1.6	1.5	1.5	1.5	1.5	1.5	1.4	13.4	1.6	4.4	16.7	1.5	10
Portugal	0.7	0.7	0.6	0.7	0.7	0.6	0.6	0.6	0.6	5.8	0.7	1.9	–14.3	0.6	11
Denmark	0.4	0.6	0.6	0.7	0.7	0.5	0.5	0.4	0.5	4.9	0.6	1.6	25.0	0.5	12
Norway	0.6	0.7	0.7	0.8	0.5	0.4	0.4	0.4	0.4	4.9	0.6	1.6	–33.3	0.5	13
Belgium	0.3	0.3	0.2	0.2	0.3	0.2	0.2	0.2	0.2	2.1	0.3	0.7	–33.3	0.2	14
Poland	n/a	n/a	n/a	n/a	n/a	n/a	0.6	0.7	0.7	2.0	0.2	0.7	0.7	0.7	15
Czech Republic	n/a	n/a	n/a	n/a	n/a	n/a	n/a	n/a	n/a	0.0	0.0	0.0	0.0	0.0	16
Hungary	n/a	n/a	n/a	n/a	n/a	n/a	n/a	n/a	n/a	0.0	0.0	0.0	0.0	0.0	17
Iceland	0	0	0	0	0	0	0	0	0	0.0	0.0	0.0	0.0	0.0	18

Table 4.1 Naval Tonnage, 1990–2001 (cont.)

Country	1990	1994	1995	1996	1997	1998	1999	2000	2001	Total	Total (%)	Total (non-US) (%)	Change	Average	Rank
Luxembourg	n/a	0	n/a	n/a	n/a	n/a	n/a	n/a	n/a	0.0	0.0	0.0	0.0	0.0	19
Total	92.0	91.0	89.0	89.0	90.0	92.0	93.0	92.8	91.8	819.0	100	268.1	0.2	91.0	19
Total (non-US)	33.3	35.7	35.0	35.9	35.9	30.1	32.3	32.7	31.2	302.1	36.9	98.9	–6.3	33.6	18
Average	5.7	5.7	5.6	5.6	5.6	5.7	4.9	4.9	4.8	43.1	5.3	–*	–15.6	4.8	n/a
Average (non-US)	2.2	2.4	2.3	2.4	2.4	2.0	1.8	1.8	1.7	16.8	2.1	–*	–21.9	1.9	n/a

Source: United States Department of Defense, *Report on Allied Contributions to the Common Defense* (Washington, DC, 2002).
Note: The data excludes 1991, 1992, and 1993; these figures were not available when the data was being compiled.
*Cannot be calculated because the alliance grew from 16 member states to 19 in 1999.

As seen in table 4.1, Canada contributed 2.2% of the total naval tonnage on average from 1990 to 2001 (or 2.4% of the total); this is less than half of the total NATO average of 4.8%, yet above the average if the United States is considered in a separate category due to its supreme military capabilities. Overall, though, Canada ranked 8th out of the 19 countries. Thus, its rank as a percentage of total naval tonnage is consistent with its rank as a percentage of the NATO average.

The table also highlights the dominance of US naval power in the alliance. With 63.1% of total tonnage, the United States remained an unchallenged naval power in this time period. If, however, it were excluded from the calculation, Canada would be the 7th-largest naval power, shouldering 6.4% of the collective burden, far higher than the NATO average of 2.1%. Canada also ranked higher than comparable second-tier powers such as the Netherlands (at 10) and Denmark (at 12). Only Spain, with 2.7% (or 7.3% without the United States) performed slightly better.

European Community Monitoring Mission (ECMM)

Before 1989, the Federal Republic of Yugoslavia consisted of six republics: Bosnia and Herzegovina, Croatia, Macedonia, Montenegro, Serbia, and Slovenia. Serbia was itself made up of two autonomous provinces: Vojvodina and Kosovo. All of the people in the republics were ethnic Slavs, but they differed from each other by being associated with either the Croatian, Muslim, or Serbian communities. The federation was held together by the strong national leadership of President Josip Broz Tito, who, after July 1971, governed with a system of collective leadership and a regular rotation of senior government leaders. The new constitution of 1975 allowed the republics greater autonomy in the federation and limited federal power to deal with issues of national defence, foreign and security policy, and the single national market. With Tito's death in May 1980, however, this federal system of power sharing began to fall apart, and civil unrest and ethnic tensions began to break out among the various groups. Because of the rotating presidency, the executive was unable to agree on a new federal structure.

Yugoslavia began to further disintegrate in 1990, when Slovenia and Croatia held successful secession referendums on 25 June 1991. A referendum in Macedonia and Bosnia and Herzegovina in October 1990 had also supported secession from the federation. The case of Bosnia and Herzegovina is an important one because while both Bosnian Muslims and Bosnian Croats supported secession,[22] the Bosnian Serbs objected and were supported by Serbia. Declarations of independence by Slovenia and Croatia followed.

Six months earlier, on 22 December 1990, the Croatian government under Franco Tudjman had adopted a new constitution, which failed to recognize the large Serbian minority in Croatia. Violence had broken out in June 1991, when a faction of the Serbian community, supported by the Yugoslav People's Army (also known as the Yugoslav National Army, or JNA), opposed the declaration of independence. Tudjman's government also waged war against Bosnia and Herzegovina in an attempt to annex parts of that province to Croatia. This caused political tumults among ethnic Serbian-Croatians and in the central government. Serbian president Slobodan Milosevic responded by sending in troops in an attempt to restore order. In Slovenia, the battle between Slovenian forces and the JNA lasted 10 days, during which time Slovenian forces surrounded the JNA troops and cut off their supply lines.[23]

The initial responder to the conflict was expected to be the OSCE. It is a pan-European security organization with the reputation of an experienced confidence and security builder. It was anticipated that because the OSCE had a larger membership than NATO (ranging "from Vancouver to Vladivostok" and covering a large number of diverse countries, cultures, and contexts), it would be the better and more capable institution to broker a peace agreement first in Slovenia, then in Croatia and Bosnia and Herzegovina. The OSCE also had a track record of addressing the human dimension of international security affairs as well as promoting democracy and human rights.[24] However, in spite of its expertise and large membership, the OSCE delegated the responsibility for monitoring the withdrawal of JNA forces from Slovenia to the European Community (EC).[25]

---

22 United Nations 1996, 487.
23 Bennett 1995, 156–60.
24 Ibid., 2.
25 This was the precursor of the EU, which came into being with the Maastricht treaty in 1993.

Brussels, accepting this responsibility, commissioned a European peacekeeping force, the ECMM,[26] which attempted to broker and subsequently stabilize a ceasefire in Slovenia. But the conflict had grown out of control, not only causing regional instabilities but also threatening the stability of all of Western Europe;[27] Slovenia, the most northern republic, shared a territorial border with Austria and Italy, both members of the EC. The scale and intensity was something that Europe had not experienced since the Second World War. The European countries – ill prepared and still coping with the changes brought about by the end of the Cold War – were unable to manage an evolving large-scale civil war on their southern doorstep.[28] Indeed, the wars in the Gulf and the former Yugoslavia challenged the principle of multilateral cooperation among European member states.[29] The ECMM was relatively ineffective in managing and controlling the violence, but it was the predecessor of the much larger UNPROFOR.

One obstacle, however, remained. The condition of deploying the ECMM to Croatia and Slovenia was that either Canada or the United States, or both, would join the European force.[30] This speaks to Canada's reputation in crisis and conflict management and to the quality and professionalism of its peacekeepers. The government of Prime Minister Brian Mulroney accepted and deployed Canadian forces in concert with Czechoslovakia, Poland, and Sweden. This was a logical move for

---

26 The ECMM officially existed from 1991 until 2000. The EC imposed sanctions on Yugoslavia on 8 November 1991, cutting an aid package worth $1.5 billion, reimposing textile quotas, and ending preferential trade treatments. Canada followed suit one day later; it also ended its preferential trade treatments and imposed a system of discretionary export permits on all goods destined to Yugoslavia. See Paul Koring, "Sanctions Imposed on Yugoslavia: Canada Backs European Community Bid for UN-Sponsored Oil Embargo," *Globe and Mail*, 1991.

27 Slovenia, the most northern republic, shared a territorial border with Austria and Italy, both members of the EC.

28 Mann 2005, 352–427. The "never again" clause was particularly relevant for the German government and its decision(s) to send the German armed forces on a military mission outside the country. For historical reasons, the location of the Balkans was obviously difficult to justify. For a larger discussion, see, e.g., Elsässer and Fischer 1999, 161–251; Dalgaard-Nielsen 2006; Fischer 2007; Göttert 1993.

29 Salmon 1992.

30 Ibid.

Canada, considering its record of serving in nearly all UN peacekeeping operations since 1945.[31]

Canada sent nine military observers to the ECMM and one senior officer,[32] all of whom were tasked with monitoring the ceasefire agreement reached between Slovene forces and the JNA.[33] They were, however, not allowed to actively pursue or enforce the implementation of the ceasefire agreement.[34] The mission was primarily political rather than military, designed to help establish stability in the region. As one historian observed, in 1992 the objective of the ECMM was to monitor the "pink zones" in the Krajina, which were located in the border region between Croatia and Serbia.[35] These were the most contested zones and those in which proven practices of ethnic cleansing had taken place.

The ECMM had been created for human intelligence purposes – to collect political, military, demographic, geographical, and other human intelligence data, which was sent back to the respective countries for evaluation.[36] In 1992, however, its purpose shifted to one of addressing humanitarian issues by ensuring the availability of medical supplies, providing support for refugees, and supplying escorts for United Nations High Commission for Refugees (UNHCR) convoys.

The deployment of 50 soldiers to the ECMM cost the Canadian taxpayers more than $1 million per year. One factor that complicated the

---

31 For a detailed discussion of the history of Canada and UN peacekeeping, see, e.g., Beattie and Baxendale 2007; Bin 2007; Blanchette 2002; Jockel 1994; Legault and Tessier 1999; Maloney 2002.

32 Maloney 2002, 11. Even though the total numbers of troops to the ECMM fluctuated significantly, the Canadian commitment made up 5–10% of the total. In 1992, the number of ECMM personnel was close to 300, and Canada sent an average of 15 observers every six months. See also Bland and Maloney 2004, 230.

33 Maloney 1997, 13. It is important to note that this was only the initial task of the operation; it later expanded to several other states, including Albania, Bosnia and Herzegovina, the FYROM, the former Republic of Yugoslavia (Serbia + Montenegro), and Hungary. For a more detailed discussion, see Ishizuka 2004.

34 "OP BOLSTER: Canadian Contingent to the Monitoring Mission in Yugoslavia," Deputy Chief of Defence Staff Operation Order, November 1991, quoted in Bland and Maloney 2004, 230.

35 *Krajina* means "the frontier or borderland of a country with established military defence positions." It has been the location of battles for centuries.

36 Maloney 1997, 22.

mission, however, was a rotating European presidency, which changed every six months, confusing the chain of command as well as the line of political authority. Canadians worked under the authority of the Europeans, as one operational report sent to Ottawa noted.

> Canadians have a unique, high profile within the mission both as the only non-European member and through the appointments we hold. As we withdraw our forces from stationing in Europe, this mission provides continuing Canadian presence, and a degree of influence, in the European theatre within a European organization. As the mission expands its area of operation there have been other members of the CSCE [Conference on Security and Cooperation in Europe][37] who have discreetly attempted to join the ECMM for specific tasks. This approach has been discouraged both by the Mission and the host nations. Canada, therefore, has a foothold in an organization which ... will be the "flagship" for a continuing European mission to deal with the multitude of existing and future problems in the European area. ... Through our small contribution to the ECMM, Canada can reap significant benefits in a very cost effective manner.[38]

United Nations Protection Force (UNPROFOR)

The end of the Cold War unleashed a set of nationalist tensions in the Balkans that resulted in organized bloodshed, gross violations of human and humanitarian rights, thousands of internally displaced people, and genocide.[39] Serious fighting began in June 1991 between Croatia and Slovenia, which had unilaterally seceded from the loose federation of the Federal Republic of Yugoslavia. The federal presidency under Slobodan Milosevic, who was supported by the JNA, initially refused to agree to this. Meanwhile, Croatia also wanted to become independent but failed. The presidency was concerned about the large Serbian

---

37 The CSCE was the forerunner of the OSCE. For more information, see ch. 6, note 51.
38 "Op BOLSTER-Roto 2: Post Op Report," 24 September 1992, quoted in Maloney 1997, 36–7.
39 For a good overview, see Barany and Moser 2005; Hammond 2004. It is important to note that not only the Serbs were responsible for mass atrocities and acts of genocide but also other ethnic groups. For example, what some Croats did to the city of Mostar was perhaps comparable to the Serb shelling of Sarajevo; for a discussion, see Rudolph 2001; Thornberry 1996.

ethnic minority living in Croatia; if Croatia seceded, so the argument went, this minority would be disconnected from Serbia.

While the EC had attempted in 1990–91 to monitor borders, inter-ethnic relations, refugee traffic, and general security developments in the former Yugoslavia,[40] it was unsuccessful, and when the conflict turned violent in mid-1991, Belgium, France, and the United Kingdom internationalized the search for a solution by bringing the matter before the UN Security Council.[41] On 25 September 1991, the council passed Resolution 713, in which it urged the combatants to solve their disputes peacefully and abide by previously established ceasefire agreements. It also expressed the concern that "the continuation of this situation con-stitutes a threat to international peace and security" and called on all states to immediately implement a "general and complete embargo on all deliveries of weapons and military equipment to Yugoslavia."[42]

In an attempt to find a solution to the conflict, the UN secretary gen-eral's personal envoy to Yugoslavia, Cyrus Vance, hosted a peace con-ference at UN Headquarters in Geneva with the presidents of Serbia and Croatia. There the parties demanded a UN-led peacekeeping force that would be deployed to monitor the ceasefire agreement and be guided under Chapter VI of the UN charter. On 27 November 1991, the Security Council responded to this request in Resolution 721,[43] which established UNPROFOR.

This force operated from 1992 to 1995 and initially had four main objectives: to facilitate and provide security for the delivery of humani-tarian aid; to contain the conflict and protect certain safe zones (known as United Nations Protected Areas, or UNPAs), particularly those in eastern and western Slavonia and the Krajina; to establish a no-fly zone; and to negotiate ceasefires with the combatants.[44] Its first deploy-ment took place in Croatia[45] and was subsequently extended to Bosnia and Herzegovina and the Former Yugoslav Republic of Macedonia

---

40 The mission was financed by the EC and consisted of 75 field specialists. It was headquartered in Sarajevo, and its designated area included Bosnia and Herzegovina, Croatia, Serbia, Montenegro, and the Republic of Macedonia.
41 UN, S/23060, 23 September 1991.
42 UN, S/RES/ 713, 25 September 1991.
43 UN, S/RES/ 724, 21 November 1991.
44 See, e.g., "Fighting Escalates, UN Role in Question," *UN Chronicle* 32, no. 3 (1995).
45 Bennett 1995, 3.

(FYROM). It also held a mandate for the Federal Republic of Yugoslavia (Serbia and Montenegro).

The initial set-up of the operation resembled that of the UN's very first peacekeeping operation (the United Nations Emergency Force, established during the Suez Canal crisis of 1956), which had been a neutral force positioned between two conflicting parties. Consequently, guided by Chapter VI provisions of the UN charter, UNPROFOR was neither designed nor mandated to use any force that would force peace to develop. Canada was one of the few second-tier powers that immediately made troops and resources for that force available. Indeed, as one Canadian government official noted, the continuing imbalance in armaments, the economic disparities and inequalities, and the instability of constitutional and governmental structures were all identified as factors that justified a Canadian commitment.[46]

That Canada was a committed rather than a free-riding second-tier power can be established by the fact that Prime Minister Mulroney had sent a personal letter to UN Secretary General Javier Perez de Cuellar, calling on the Security Council to take action against a worsening humanitarian situation in Yugoslavia and to establish a much larger and effective peacekeeping presence on the ground.[47] Mulroney expressed frustration with the slow response of the EC, and later the UN, and their failure to recognize the seriousness and intensity of the ethnic conflict.[48] Barbara McDougall, Canada's secretary of state for external affairs, echoed this frustration in a speech to the UN General Assembly in 1992, saying that "recent events demonstrate that the use of force may be a necessary option, and we urge full consideration of the Secretary-General's view in this regard."[49]

While the Mulroney government preferred a Chapter VI mission, it did not rule out the possibility of an enforcement operation under Chapter VII of the UN charter, which could quickly contain the conflict using force, if necessary. Indeed, Canada was one of the first NATO

---

46 Canadian Joint Delegation to NATO, "APAG (Atlantic Policy Advisory Group) MTG with Cooperation Partners: European Security in Transition," telex YBGR 1092 to EXTOTT IDS (International Security and Defence Relations Divisions), DFAIT, 10, retrieved under the Access to Information Act, 10 April 2007, A-3, File No. 3947-01.

47 Gammer 2001, 81, 98–101.

48 Ibid., 98–101.

49 The Right Honourable Barbara McDougall, "Address to the Forty-Seventh Session of the United Nations Assembly," New York, 24 September 1992.

members to raise the issue of inefficiencies at the UN because it saw the collapse of Yugoslavia as a vital threat to the stability and security of Europe.[50] The greatest threat to Canada's national security was the revival of nationalist tensions in Europe, which might require Canadians to come to the rescue of Europe once again.

Despite the prime minister's personal interventions, Canadian policy initiatives did not gain much traction among the members of the Security Council. Nonetheless, the government maintained its position that UNPROFOR was too weak and ineffective to contain acts of ethnic violence, and it shifted its diplomatic pressure towards Washington in an attempt to lobby the United States to augment a failing UN force. It was well known among military strategists that only a large, well-equipped and logistically well-supported force could turn the tide,[51] but Washington had resisted such deployments because its peacekeeping experience in Somalia in 1992 had raised questions at home about the efficacy of US involvement in countries where it had no direct interest. (The Somalia disaster had resulted in the 1994 Presidential Decision Directive 25, which limited the scope and extent of US peacekeeping abroad).[52] In the end, however, the United States agreed to provide 25,000 troops to protect UN soldiers in the event that a complete pull-out of UN troops became necessary.

Although this was not the commitment it had asked for, Canada took a share of the responsibility. Ottawa sent the fifth-largest contingent to UNPROFOR, which it called Operation HARMONY. Canadian forces were deployed into Sector West and asked to observe the UNPAs in Croatia. According to Carol Off, they were deliberately placed in this sector because of their extensive experience in multinational peace operations.[53] Sector West was also one of the most dangerous sectors to operate in and shared a hostile front line.[54] The Canadian operation to UNPROFOR went through six rotations; the initial deployment

---

50 See, for example, McDougall et al. 1992; confirmed by a senior official, Privy Council Office, interview by the author, Ottawa, 12 June 2007.

51 MacInnis 1997, 147.

52 For a discussion of US contributions to UN peacekeeping operations, see MacKinnon 2000.

53 Off 2004, 66.

54 Ibid. The Canadians were placed in the contested territory between the Serbs and the Croats.

consisted of 1,139 personnel, later increased to 2,051.[55] (A large portion of these troops were drawn from the soon-to-be-phased-out 4 Canadian Mechanized Brigade in Germany.)[56] On the strategic level, Major-General Lewis MacKenzie served as chief of staff.

During its existence, from 1992 to 1995, UNPROFOR's objective was altered several times and extended to monitoring ceasefire agreements as well as JNA troop withdrawals – for example, from Sarajevo in Bosnia and Herzegovina. UNPROFOR also became responsible for the airport and the city of Sarajevo, where a large minority of Muslims resided.[57] Its task was to secure the airport, a 10-kilometre zone around it, and a transit corridor from the airport into the city of Sarajevo.[56]

Aside from monitoring the military campaign, the primary objective of Canadian diplomats was to ensure the safety of its peacekeepers when NATO ramped up its airstrikes against key targets in Serbia and Bosnia and to preserve the credibility of Western security institutions.[57] International diplomats demarcated a no-fly zone, to be enforced by NATO forces, as well as the UNPAs.[58] Deploying peacekeepers in these two areas of operation was met with great scepticism by some Canadian foreign policy officials, who feared that they would endanger the lives of Canadian soldiers.[59] Potential casualties were also worrisome for a government that in 1993 was in the midst of an election campaign:

---

55 Bland and Maloney 2004, 230. The two Canadian bases in Germany were closed in 1994. Despite the repatriation of its troops, Canada's commitment to NATO and thus the collective defence of Europe remained nearly unchanged. Ottawa continued to contribute (1) an infantry battalion group with pre-positioned equipment to serve in crisis or in war with the NATO Composite Force or the Allied Command Europe Mobile Force (Land) in Norway; (2) naval and air forces to NATO operations, including the Standing Naval Force Atlantic and the NATO Airborne Early Warning and Control Force; (3) a mechanized brigade group and two squadrons with up to 36 CF-18 aircraft based in Canada; (4) nearly 464 personnel to serve on NATO staff in Europe; (5) its participation in NATO's common funding programs; (6) an offer to train Allied forces on Canadian territory; and (7) resources to arms-control verification procedures in Europe. UN, Doc. S/24075, 6 June 1992, paras. 4, 6.

56 Ibid.

57 Canadian Joint Delegation to NATO, "APAG MTG with Cooperation Partners," 12.

58 A majority of Canadians (57.8%) supported such air strikes, according to a Gallup poll taken in September 1995.

59 Wright 2003, 203.

public opinion mattered a great deal, and politicians did not want to be perceived as neglecting the troops abroad.

From the outset, logistical support and supply for UNPROFOR was problematic. UN officials briefed the Canadians about the logistics of the operation, which was anticipated to be a collection of close to 40,000 troops from 39 countries. Among other things, each force-contributing state was told to bring along 15 armoured personnel carriers.[60] Major-General MacKenzie, however, found this number to be inadequate to carry out the task he had been given and asked his government to raise the number to 83.[61] He also demanded more ammunition, vehicles, and weapons than the UN officially allowed. According to Dawn Hewitt, the UN balked "at the Canadians' request, basically because it did not want to pay for it."[62] In the end, Ottawa agreed to shoulder the additional costs of shipping the extra equipment.[63]

The initial friction between the UN and the force-contributing states was the result of an inexperienced and understaffed UN engaged in international peacekeeping operations.[64] In particular, its bureaucracy underestimated UNPROFOR's tactical needs and attempted to micromanage the peacekeepers rather than provide a general framework within which they could operate.[65] Moreover, the peacekeepers themselves were faced with a new type of international peacekeeping operation. Throughout the Cold War, peacekeeping had been interpositional, whereby a military force was deployed to act as a buffer between combatants. Examples of such "classical peacekeeping" operations include the Suez Canal crisis and the conflict in Cyprus in 1964. After the Cold War ended, the business of peacekeeping, and thus the roles and tasks of the peacekeepers, was more complex, offering humanitarian assistance and rebuilding war-torn societies.[66] Indeed, the line between peacekeeping and peace enforcement became much

---

60 Hewitt 1998, 29.

61 Ibid.

62 Ibid.

63 MacKenzie 1993, 203.

64 *Report of the Secretary General Pursuant to General Assembly Resolution 53/55 (1998)* (New York: UN Secretariat, November 1999), para. 503.

65 For a larger discussion on the shortfalls and mismanagement of UNPROFOR, see Diehl 2008, 16, 161–2.

66 For a larger discussion of the different roles, see ibid., 1–27; for a more detailed account of UN peace operations, see, e.g., Paris 2004.

fuzzier, thereby putting a strain on the coherence as well as success of the operations. This, as one scholar noted, applied in particular to the case of UNPROFOR.

> The UNPROFOR mission in Bosnia had multiple missions with different characteristics: arms verification, humanitarian assistance, and some collective enforcement. The taxonomy suggests that some problems arise when a peace operation assumes functions that are fundamentally incompatible with one another in terms of their roles, attributes, and behaviors used in the classification. For example, intervention in support of democracy, in which peacekeepers assume primary-party roles in the conflict, may be difficult to achieve simultaneously with another mission that casts peacekeepers as third-party mediators.[67]

The trouble with UNPROFOR was that even though it was conceptualized as a peacemaking or peacekeeping operation, there was no peace to keep. While the combatants consented to the deployment of international peacekeepers, they showed no interest in meeting the conditions of the ceasefire or peace agreements. This posed great difficulties for the peacekeepers. It complicated their jobs because they became more than mediators in an escalating civil conflict; now they were active participants, tasked with preventing humanitarian disasters. The new range of tasks also increased the risks for the individual soldiers. In November 1994, for example, 55 Canadian troops under General Philippe Morillon were taken hostage near the city of Sarajevo in retaliation for NATO air strikes against Serbian forces.[68] The Serbs used the Canadians as human shields to deter further air strikes. This form of violence against international peacekeepers had not been anticipated when UNPROFOR was created.[69]

Bosnia and Herzegovina: Second Front for UNPROFOR

Bosnia and Herzegovina held a referendum on independence on 28 February 1992.[70] It was supported by an absolute majority of the

---

67   Diehl 2008, 16–17.
68   Wright 2003, 201.
69   Hewitt 1998, 38–41.
70   Bennett 1995, 186.

voters, 99.4%, and President Alija Izetbegovic declared the country in-dependent on 2 March 1992.[71] At the time, Bosnia and Herzegovina was the most ethnically diverse republic in the former Yugoslavia, with a population made up of 43.7% Muslims, 17.3% Croats, 31.4% Serbs, and 7.6% others.[72]

In January 1992, the government of the new Bosnia and Herzegovina asked the international community to pre-emptively deploy UN peace-keepers to prevent violence, and that year, UNPROFOR deployed a small contingent.[73] After recurring spirals of violence among Bosnian Serbs (who were supported as well as supplied by the JNA), Bosnian Croats, and Bosnian Muslims, both Washington and Moscow recognized the independence of Bosnia on 7 April 1992, hoping that formal recognition would help stabilize the entire Balkan region.[74] This hope, however, did not materialize. Violence resumed, particularly in the border region of Croatia and Bosnia as well as in Sarajevo. The city was strategically important because UNPROFOR was headquartered there.[75] The UN Security Council approved Bosnia and Herzegovina's request in Resolution 743 on 21 February 1992 and deployed more than 13,000 UN troops to Bosnia.

UNPROFOR's mandate in the initial phase included protecting hu-manitarian convoys; it was later amended to ensure order and security in the UNPAs. After a deadly mortar attack on the Sarajevo market-place on 5 February 1994, which killed 68 people, Canada's minister of foreign affairs lobbied France and the United Kingdom at a NATO

---

71 Boulden 1999, 77.
72 See, e.g., Shoup 1981, 156, table C-10. For a detailed discussion of this issue, see Burg and Shoup 1999, 16–61. Tim Judah (1997, 344), however, gives a different ethnic breakdown: 43.7% Muslims, 31.1% Serbs, 17.3% Croats, and 7.0% others.
73 After the massacres of Mostar, the UNPROFOR contingent was increased. For a detailed history, see United Nations, Department of Public Information 1996.
74 By 1994, NATO and the Soviet Union had also begun combined planning efforts. See Canadian Joint Delegation to NATO, "MC/PS 07 SEP-CMC Visit Russia and Former Yugoslavia," telex YBDR 6211 to EXTOTT IDS (International Security and Defence Relations Divisions), DFAIT, 7 September 1994, 2, retrieved under the Access to Information Act, 10 April 2007, A-3, File No. 3947-01.
75 Locating a headquarters at a distance from the actual operation, as occurred with UNPROFOR's first deployment in Croatia, turned out to be problematic. The UN's intention, however, was to send a stabilizing signal to the region. Locating the headquarters in Sarajevo became particularly dangerous when the city itself became a target of the violence.

meeting in Athens to make more troops available.[76] At the UN level, the secretary general called for an expansion of NATO air strikes after the violence reoccurred in other areas of the region, including the town of Gorazde. NATO issued a deadline for Bosnian Serb troops to withdraw their heavy weapons; this deadline was met, and further air strikes were averted. In 1993, the fighting increased once again. This time, Bosnian Serbs blocked a rotation of UN troops in Sarajevo and took control of the airport in Tuzla. Both cities were vital to the delivery of humanitarian aid, so based on Security Council Resolution 761 (29 June 1992),[77] the Canadian UNPROFOR contingent was tasked with reopening the Sarajevo airport and securing the city and the surrounding area.

According to Nicholas Gammer, nearly 10% of UNPROFOR troops, or 1,200, came from Canada.[78] Table 4.2 below shows Canada's contributions to the UNPROFOR operation as of the end of November 1994 and their rank relative to the other force-contributing countries.

The first part of table 4.2 lists the contributions made by NATO and non-NATO countries to UNPROFOR. It shows that Canada made the 5th-highest contribution of all 37 force-contributing states, with its contingents comprising 5.44% of the entire mission. This, seen in relative terms, can be interpreted as a significant contribution, especially in light of the fiscal constraints of the federal governments at the time. The Progressive Conservatives under Brian Mulroney and later the Liberals under Jean Chrétien were confronted with a situation that demanded budget cuts across all levels of government;[79] in fact, federal and provincial government deficits doubled from $33 billion in 1989–90 to $63.7 billion in 1992–93.[80]

The second part of the table lists the contributions made by NATO countries to UNPROFOR; they show that Canada ranked 3rd and only

---

76 Holbrooke 1998, 107.
77 Sloan 1998, 20.
78 Gammer 2001, 96.
79 See, e.g., Thomas J. Courchene, "Opening Statement to the House of Commons Standing Committee on Finance, 30 April 2002," http://www.irpp.org/miscpubs/archive/020501e.pdf, accessed 11 June 2008. For details, see Courchene 2002; also Thomas J. Courchene, "Balanced Budgets: A Canadian Fiscal Value" (paper prepared for the "Long-Term Budget Challenge: Public Finance and Fiscal Sustainability in the G7" conference, Washington, DC, 2–4 June 2005, http://www.irpp.org/events/archive/jun05/courchene.pdf, accessed 10 June 2008).
80 Courchene 2002.

Table 4.2 Personnel Contributions to UNPROFOR (Police, Troops, and Observers),
30 November 1994

NATO and Non-NATO Countries

Country	Police	Troops	Observers	Total	Total (%)	Rank
France	41	4,493	11	4,545	11.50	1
Jordan	71	3,367	48	3,486	8.82	2
United Kingdom	0	3,405	19	3,424	8.66	3
Pakistan	19	3,017	34	3,070	7.76	4
Canada	45	2,091	15	2,151	5.44	5
Netherlands	10	1,803	48	1,861	4.71	6
Russian Federation	36	1,464	22	1,522	3.85	7
Turkey	0	0	1,464	1,464	3.70	8
Bangladesh	40	1,235	43	1,318	3.33	9
Spain	0	1,267	19	1,286	3.25	10
Sweden	35	1,212	19	1,266	3.20	11
Poland	29	1,109	30	1,168	2.95	12
Ukraine	9	1,147	10	1,166	2.95	13
Kenya	50	967	47	1,064	2.69	14
Belgium	0	1,038	6	1,044	2.64	15
Czech Republic	0	971	37	1,008	2.55	16
Nepal	49	899	5	953	2.41	17
Norway	31	826	39	896	2.27	18
Argentina	23	854	5	882	2.23	19
United States	0	0	748	748	1.89	20
Slovak Republic	0	0	582	582	1.47	21
Finland	10	463	12	485	1.23	22
Egypt	0	427	27	454	1.15	23
Indonesia	15	220	29	264	0.67	24
New Zealand	0	249	9	258	0.65	25
Malaysia	26	1,550	27	1,603	4.05	26
Denmark	45	1,230	14	1,289	3.26	27
Nigeria	48	0	10	58	0.15	28
Portugal	·39	0	12	51	0.13	29
Brazil	6	0	34	40	0.10	30
Ghana	0	0	32	32	0.08	31

Table 4.2 Personnel Contributions to UNPROFOR (Police, Troops, and Observers), 30 November 1994 (*cont.*)

NATO and Non-NATO Countries (*cont.*)

Country	Police	Troops	Observers	Total	Total (%)	Rank
Lithuania	0	0	32	32	0.08	32
Ireland	20	0	9	29	0.07	33
Colombia	12	0	0	12	0.03	34
Switzerland	6	0	6	12	0.03	35
Tunisia	12	0	0	12	0.03	36
Venezuela	0	0	2	2	0.01	37
Total	727	35,304	3,506	39,537	100	37
Average	19.65	954.16	94.76	1,068.57	2.70	n/a

NATO Countries

Country	Police	Troops	Observers	Total	Total (%)	Rank
France	41	4,493	11	4,545	24.23	1
United Kingdom	0	3,405	19	3,424	18.25	2
Canada	45	2,091	15	2,151	11.47	3
Netherlands	10	1,803	48	1,861	9.92	4
Turkey	0	0	1,464	1,464	7.80	5
Spain	0	1,267	19	1,286	6.86	6
Belgium	0	1,038	6	1,044	5.57	7
Norway	31	826	39	896	4.78	8
United States	0	0	748	748	3.99	9
Denmark	45	1,230	14	1,289	6.87	10
Portugal	39	0	12	51	0.27	11
Total	211	16,153	2,395	18,759	100	11

Sources: United States Congressional Research Service, "Bosnia: US Military Operations," CRS Issue Brief for Congress, Order Code IB93056, 8 July 2003; United Nations, *The Blue Helmets: A Review of United Nations Peacekeeping* (New York: UN Department of Publication, 1996); LCol. Ross Fetterly, Finance Section, Department of National Defence (Canada), interview by the author, Ottawa, 2005. Totals and averages compiled by the author.

slightly behind the United Kingdom, conventionally considered a major power. Moreover, Canada's contribution is ranked ahead of other second-tier powers such as the Netherlands (at 4), Spain (at 6), and Norway (at 8). This table reveals Ottawa's strong belief in international peacekeeping operations and upholding regional security governance. It also provides strong empirical evidence to refute the notion that second-tier powers practised free riding,[81] while major powers became increasingly disinclined to support UN peacekeeping efforts.

Battle of the Medak Pocket

Canadian forces personnel were also caught up in a fierce battle around the Medak Pocket, where in September 1993 Croatian forces were in the process of ethnically cleansing Krajinan Serbs east of the town of Gospic. The Medak Pocket was an enclave that the Serbs of Croatia had claimed for themselves; they called it the Republic of the Serbian Krajina. In the initial phase of the operation, the region was monitored by French peacekeepers, but after two of their soldiers were shot dead, the French contingent left abruptly. Back at UNPROFOR headquarters, the commanding officer of all UN troops, French Lieutenant-General Jean Cot, singled out the Canadians as the UN's "swat-team, the only contingent of peacekeepers he could rely on."[82] He ordered the Canadian battle group from Sector West to split in half and take control of Sector South, where the Medak Pocket was located. This assignment speaks to the strong reputation of the Canadian Forces as effective peacekeepers.

The village of Medak was a strategic location for the Serbs because it allowed them to launch attacks on the Croatian headquarters in Gospic, a few kilometres away. When the Serbs took control of the city and the surrounding area in 1991, the Croats responded by murdering the Serbian elite, including the doctors, lawyers, and teachers in Gospic. The Canadians were essentially caught in the crossfire between Serbs and Croats and given the unenviable task of containing the violence.[83] Croatian forces advanced from the surrounding hills towards Medak,

---

81 Cohen 2004. For a similar argument, see Conference of Defence Associations Institute 2002; Granatstein 2004.
82 Off 2004, 13.
83 For a detailed description of the battle, see Hewitt 1998, 62–6.

which was being held by Serbian forces.[84] Their goal, as Carol Off described it, was not only to retake the Medak Pocket but also to eliminate the non-Croatian population.[85] The Canadian commanders knew that once the Croatian forces were on the move, their peacekeepers would not be able to stop them. In the end, though, no shots were fired, and the standoff dissolved.[86]

Srebrenica

Based on statistical data from 1991, the city of Srebrenica had a population of 37,000: 73% Bosnians and 25% Serbs.[87] In 1993, Bosnian Serb forces carried out violent assaults in eastern Bosnia, concentrating on Srebrenica. They ethnically cleansed two-thirds of Bosnia's territory,[88] especially the Muslim population, in an attempt to unite the Bosnian and Croatian enclaves of the Krajina. Srebrenica was harbouring more than 60,000 Muslim refugees, who began to flee the city when the Serbian forces advanced. Then UNPROFOR troops came under fire. The UN responded by passing UN Resolution 819, strongly condemning the violent attacks against UNPROFOR and restricting the Bosnian Serbs' freedom of movement. Srebrenica and the surrounding area were also treated as UNPAs, and more than 300 Canadian soldiers were deployed to the city to protect the Muslim population.[89]

The Canadian Forces (CF) effectively acted like a tripwire: if Serbian forces attacked them, the international community would perceive this as an act of aggression against the entire UNPROFOR operation. UN Resolution 824 declared the Bosnian Muslim–dominated towns of Tuzla, Zepa, Gorazde, and Bihac UNPAs, thus placing them under

---

84 The Medak Pocket was not part of a UNPA; it was part of the pink zones, areas from which Serbian forces refused to withdraw and over which the UN had no control.

85 Off 2004.

86 Hewitt 1998, 64.

87 UN General Assembly, *Report of the Secretary General Pursuant to General Assembly Resolution 53/35: Srebrenica Report (1998)* (New York: UN Secretariat), Section F. It describes in detail the events that led to the massacre in Srebrenica as well as its aftermath.

88 Ibid., 70.

89 Honig and Both 1997, 91.

international protection.[90] The areas around the towns were supposed to be free of weapons and ammunition,[91] and so the Milosevic regime in Belgrade was asked to stop supplying the Bosnian Serbs. Despite Resolution 824, compliance was entirely dependent on the parties to the conflict; no effective UNPROFOR control and enforcement mechanism was in place.

The situation in Srebrenica forced the United States to shift its strategic thinking. As Jane Boulden argued, "America's more forceful commitments and dual push for more air strikes and a diplomatic solution – brought the two streams of international response ... firmly together into one overall strategy and decision-making process for the first time."[92] The United States made it clear that if a peaceful settlement of the conflict was not possible, it would not hesitate to send in American troops to enforce peace. Again, NATO gave the Bosnian Serbs a specific list of demands as well as a deadline by which they were expected to comply. When none of these demands were met, NATO began an extensive air campaign (Operation DELIBERATE FORCE), while a team led by US diplomat Richard Holbrooke coordinated the diplomatic negotiations. The carrot-and-stick approach appeared to be successful: both parties agreed to recognize the existing borders of Bosnia and Herzegovina. A ceasefire agreement was signed on 5 October 1995, and the final peace accords were negotiated at the Wright-Patterson Air Force Base in Dayton, Ohio, on 21 October 1995.[93]

Conclusion

The UN's military experience, first in the Persian Gulf and later in the Balkans, marked the beginning of a historical collaboration between the UN and NATO. Following the Gulf War in 1990–91, the UN was tasked with managing the new world order and seeking solutions to other evolving conflicts, including those in Somalia, Haiti, and Rwanda. However, it was generally ill prepared to shoulder these

---

90 UN, S/RES 824 (1993), 6 May 1993.
91 For a detailed account of the massacre in Srebrenica and the role of the Dutch peacekeepers, see, e.g., Honig and Both 1997.
92 Boulden 1999, 90.
93 Among other things, the Dayton Agreement created the nation state of Bosnia and Herzegovina; see Holbrooke 1998.

demands. As one scholar succinctly put it, "From having done too little for too long, the UN apparatus was suddenly tasked to do too much
too soon. Its organizational, financial, and operational shortcomings
were seen exposed to full public view."[94] This history of mismanaged
order increased international disenchantment with the UN. Moreover,
because of these shortcomings, the UN increasingly "contracted out"
its peacekeeping operations to regional security organizations such as
NATO, which had superior military and planning capabilities and
was politically willing to take on this new generation of peacekeeping
operations.

Furthermore, it is noteworthy that the so-called Visegrad countries –
Poland, Hungary, and the Czech Republic, which later became full
members of NATO – participated in the war against Iraq in 1991.
Although their contributions were small and relatively insignificant
compared to the total NATO contribution, they represented a symbolic
commitment, underlining the intention to seek a closer relationship
with NATO and a growing acceptance of liberal democratic values.
Poland, for example, sent two hospital ships; the Czech Republic deployed its chemical decontamination unit, and Hungary recruited
37 volunteers.[95]

The empirical evidence presented in this chapter shows that Canada,
as a second-tier power, cannot be classified as a free rider or as a laggard in the UN-endorsed peace operations we have discussed. On the
contrary, the evidence shows that Canada was a committed and capable second-tier power. Ottawa believed strongly in the normative principles of international law and the sovereignty of states. It was the
situational environment – the violation of basic liberal democratic
principles of governance in international politics and threats against
humanity – that led Canada to send its soldiers into harm's way. The
deployments to the Balkans took place at a time when the country was
deep in debt, when withholding or postponing the deployment of
troops would have been an acceptable excuse not to participate. Yet
Canada's sense of external (social) responsibility to uphold the basic
public goods of international politics, including human and humanitarian rights, made it shoulder these military burdens at a time of national deficits.

---

94   Clark 2001, 201.
95   Simon 1993, 27.

Canada contributed considerable resources to the international (military) crisis-management activities of the Gulf War in 1991, the ECMM, and UNPROFOR. Of particular note is Canada's UNPROFOR mission, which demonstrated its commitment to international peace and security above and beyond its relative capabilities by making the largest single contribution to the mission efforts in Yugoslavia.[96] While "humanitarian missions like those in Bosnia clearly resonated back home,"[97] the government began to recognize that enforcing these values and norms would best be carried out by NATO, not the UN. These NATO-led missions in the Balkans are the focus of the next chapter.

---

96 McDougall 1992a, 12.
97 Mary Kurjata, "CPP0432-NATO Policy Planners: The Future of the Alliance," e-mail to Canadian Joint Delegation to NATO, 17 November 1997, retrieved under the Access to Information Act, 10 April 2007, A-3, File No. 3947-01.

5 The Balkans, Part II

When the call went out for further contributions,
Canada most definitely did not head for the washroom.[1]

Introduction

While the previous chapter discussed the share of the burden that
Canada as a second-tier power shouldered in the UNPROFOR opera-
tion in Bosnia and Herzegovina, Croatia, the Federal Republic of
Yugoslavia (Serbia and Montenegro), and FYROM, this chapter exam-
ines this practice in the missions that followed the peace agreement
concluded at Wright-Patterson Air Force Base in Dayton, Ohio, on 21
November 1995.[2] These missions were carried out under the leadership
of NATO and include the Implementation Force (IFOR), the Stabilization
Force (SFOR), and later, during the crisis in Kosovo, Operation ALLIED
FORCE and thereafter the Kosovo Force (KFOR).

As discussed in chapter 3, the liberal peace paradigm holds that
while liberal states are less prone to waging war than non-democratic
states, empirically they are willing to use force against non-democratic

---

1 Wright 2003, 195. Gerald Wright was special advisor to the secretary of state for
external affairs, 1992–3.
2 The Dayton peace agreement was signed in Paris on 14 December 1995. Based on a
Gallup poll conducted that month, 59.8% of Canadians favoured Canada contributing troops to IFOR.

states and external aggressors that threaten the democratic peace and their commonly held values, principles, and beliefs. These conditions applied especially to NATO's engagement in the Balkans. The alliance was seen as an institution of enforcement that was able to project and impose the will of the international community on the conflicting parties, to restore peace and order there, and, above all, to contain the civil wars and enforce human rights and security.

It is precisely in this context that supporting NATO's missions in the Balkans became a moral and strategic preference for Canada as a second-tier power. This chapter will show that the government of the day was driven by Arnold Wolfers' "external responsibility" and strongly pursued broader rather than narrowly defined national security interests. It is evident from studying NATO's operations in the 1990s that Canada pursued absolute rather than relative gains in its foreign policy practices and that its commitments to NATO were driven by the moral and normative principles of human rights and human security.

These ideational predispositions as well the specific situational context explain Canada's practice of sharing NATO's burdens, which, measured in relative terms, are disproportionately higher than collective action theorists have suggested. The empirical evidence, too, indicates that Canada did not practise free riding, that it in fact shared a disproportionately high proportion of the collective burden, especially when measured by the relative force share that it made available to the NATO missions. Thus, this chapter will establish that the *absolute* force share index commonly used to measure the extent of NATO burdens is outdated: instead, allied force contributions must be considered in *relative* terms – in relation to national force strength – and placed in the context in which the NATO burden sharing took place.

We will begin with a discussion of NATO's IFOR mission, proceed to the SFOR and KFOR operations, then conclude by looking at public opinion polls taken to measure Canadian attitudes towards those missions.

IFOR

IFOR was the first-ever peace-enforcement operation that NATO deployed, not only to the Balkans but also outside NATO territory. When NATO forces replaced the UN's unsuccessful peacekeeping operation (UNPROFOR), most of the allied forces simply exchanged their UN

arm patches for the NATO emblem. IFOR deployments were authorized by UN Security Council Resolution 1031 of 15 December 1995 and
remained in operation for one year. The nature of this peace-enforcement
mission allowed NATO troops to be heavily armed and able to use
force under Chapter VII of the UN charter; in other words, they were
mandated by the UN to use force beyond self-defence.

The official transfer of power from UNPROFOR to IFOR took place
on 20 December 1995, after the Dayton peace accord was ratified. Most
of the NATO member states, as well as some NATO partner countries
through the PfP program, participated in the mission. Of particular
note is that IFOR was augmented by a 2,200-strong Russian contingent
that became attached to the NATO forces. By early 1996, as shown in
table 5.1 below, more than 52,000[3] troops from 14 NATO states had
deployed their forces to the former Yugoslav republics to take part in
Operation JOINT ENDEAVOUR.[4] (They were joined by 10,000 troops
from 16 non-NATO countries.) IFOR was also augmented by a civil-
military cooperation (CIMIC) team, which consisted mainly of civilian
experts such as lawyers, judges, economists, health officials, and edu-
cators. Indeed, these augmentation capabilities can be seen as the pre-
decessors of the whole-of-government approach currently used by
NATO's ISAF mission in Afghanistan.[5]

While Canada had already shouldered a heavy burden in
UNPROFOR, earning it the reputation of a top-ranked second-tier
power, the government of Prime Minister Jean Chrétien remained committed to NATO and maintained the CF in the Balkans by participating
in IFOR.[6] The Canadian share consisted of a mechanized infantry company of 1,029 troops,[7] an engineer squadron, and national support and

---

3 The Dayton Accords had called for 60,000 troops to serve under NATO's IFOR
  command.
4 NATO, Regional Headquarters, Allied Forces Southern Europe Fact Sheet, 1 March
  1996.
5 Zyla 2010.
6 Velika Kladusa and Coralici were the two main locations at the northern tip of
  Bosnia near the border of Croatia (in the British Sector) where CF personnel were
  stationed.
7 This is the official Department of National Defence number (departmental officials,
  interviews by the author, Ottawa, June 2007). Other sources differ: Bland and
  Maloney (2004, 233): 1,047; Lenard J. Cohen (2003, 127): 1,035; *Military Balance*
  (1996/97): 1,024.

Table 5.1 Absolute Personnel Contributions to IFOR, 1995–6

Country	Number	Rank	Total (%)	Total (non-US) (%)	Power status
United States	18,400	1	35.2	n/a	Superpower
United Kingdom	10,500	2	20.1	31.1	Major power
France	7,500	3	14.4	22.2	Major power
Germany	4,000	4	7.7	11.8	Major power
Italy	2,200	5	4.2	6.5	Second-tier power
Netherlands	2,000	6	3.8	5.9	Second-tier power
Spain	1,400	7	2.7	4.1	Second-tier power
Turkey	1,300	8	2.5	3.8	Second-tier power
Canada	1,029	9	2.0	3.0	Second-tier power
Greece	1,000	10	1.9	3.0	Second-tier power
Portugal	900	11	1.7	2.7	Second-tier power
Denmark	807	12	1.5	2.4	Third-tier power
Norway	750	13	1.4	2.2	Third-tier power
Belgium	420	14	0.8	1.2	Third-tier power
Luxembourg	0	15	0	0	Third-tier power
Iceland	0	16	0	0	Third-tier power
Total	52,206	16	100	100	
Total (non-US)	33,806	15	64.8	100	
Average	3,263	n/a	6.3	6.7	
Average (non-US)	2,254	n/a	4.0	6.7	

Source: International Institute for Strategic Studies, *Military Balance 1996/97* (London: IISS, 1997).

command elements. As shown in table 5.1 above, this contribution was equivalent to an absolute share of the NATO burden of 2% (3% if the United States is not factored in), whereby the NATO average was 6.3% (and 4.0%, respectively).

Interpreting this *absolute* force share shows that Canada was rightly called a second-tier ally because it practised free riding in the alliance by receiving more benefits from the collective good in IFOR than it paid for. Moreover, the table reveals two other empirical findings. First, it shows that the United States shouldered more than 35% of the total force contributions and was thus the largest force-contributing ally by far. Second, it confirms conventional research findings on NATO burden sharing that the United Kingdom, France, and Germany acted according to their major-power status by sharing an extensive slice of the collective burden.

From a strategic perspective, the CF's mandate was limited and designed to uphold the military provisions negotiated in the Dayton Accords (as set out in Annex 1A). As noted above, IFOR troops were authorized to use force and take all military action necessary to ensure compliance with the ceasefire agreement and the peace accord generally.[8] They were asked, as Douglas MacGregor noted, "to prevent a resumption of ethnic cleansing and fighting, ... to formalize the creation of a Muslim-dominated multi-ethnic Republic of Bosnia-Herzegovina,"[9] and to provide basic humanitarian assistance. IFOR was tasked specifically with monitoring the border between Croatia and Bosnia and Herzegovina, their four-kilometre-wide zones of separation, and the transfer of land between the two. Its troops interpositioned themselves between the antagonists and physically separated them. IFOR also had responsibility for collecting heavy weaponry, demobilizing and disarming the remaining units of Bosnia and Herzegovina and Croatia, moving these weapons to controlled sites, and clearing out as many as possible of the 6 million landmines scattered around the area.[10] In the initial phase, IFOR also assisted UNPROFOR with a safe and speedy withdrawal of its forces.

Strategically, NATO troops sectioned Bosnia into three areas cutting across the previous front lines and conducted patrols in those areas later on. A British general based in Sarajevo had overall operational control of the sectors and reported to the commander of Allied Forces Southern Europe in Italy, who had ultimate responsibility for managing the military campaign.

---

8 This mandate was significantly different from that of UNPROFOR in that its soldiers were allowed to use military force only in self-defence. In addition, it has been noted in the literature that IFOR had only one mandate as opposed to the many that UNPROFOR was tasked with.

9 MacGregor 2001, 95.

10 Ailen McCabe, "Landmines, Refugees Pose Threat to Canadian Troops: Advance Party of Soldiers Is Setting Up Headquarters in a Small Bosnian Town That Lacks Water and Electricity," *Vancouver Sun*, 9 January 1996, A9.

Mandated by UN Security Council resolutions 981 and 1025, IFOR also ran an airlift operation into the city of Sarajevo.[11] The Canadian component, dubbed Operation AIR BRIDGE, contributed a crew of 48 soldiers as well as ground personnel and was fully backed by the House of Commons.[12] Together, the six countries that sent troops and made resources available to the operation delivered more than 176,000 tons of food, medicine, and supplies.[13] Operating out of NATO's air force bases in Italy, Canada flew 1,806 missions, France 2,133, Germany 1,279, the United Kingdom 1,902, and the United States 4,597,[14] for an overall average of 13.8 C-130 sorties per day.[15] Canada was the fourth-largest force contributor to the air bridge (in absolute terms); it carried almost as much of the burden as the United Kingdom[16] and more than Germany, both of which are considered major powers in the alliance.

In terms of the overall success of the IFOR mission, the strong presence of IFOR troops made a difference on the ground and forced both Serbs and Croats to comply with the Dayton peace agreement. They withdrew their heavy weapons and troops, and by 1996, IFOR had successfully brought an end to the violent hostilities in the former Yugoslavia. Its focus then shifted to patrolling the conflict areas, rebuilding the war-torn societies, and providing security for other international actors, such as the OSCE, which monitored elections, and the UNHCR, which helped refugees resettle in their country of origin. In other words, IFOR was responsible for enforcing the conditions of the military peace laid out in the Dayton peace accord, while a host of international agencies moved in to rebuild economic and social infrastructures and help resettle refugees.

As far as funding the IFOR mission goes, it is important to remember that NATO does not own military forces itself. Most operating expenses were paid for by those member states that agreed to send troops and make their military resources available. Very few things beyond command and control functions were paid for by NATO. Thus, while the

---

11 The airlift started on 3 July 1992 and ended on 9 January 1996; see, e.g., United Nations 1996, 500.
12 Canada, Parliament, House of Commons 1994, 3348.
13 Besides Canada, those nations included France, Germany, Italy, the United Kingdom, and the United States; see Wentz 1997.
14 United Nations 1996, 500.
15 Ibid.
16 For a critical assessment, see Graham 1998.

IFOR operation was financed by a complex matrix of national as well as limited communal NATO funding, the majority of that funding was shouldered by the member states themselves. The latter costs were taken from NATO's military budget and the NATO Security Investment Programme (its former infrastructure program). Indeed, member states shouldered all of the expenses for deploying their troops, including logistical costs – including Canada, in spite of domestic financial hardship.

However, as suggested in Part I of this book, this analysis of the absolute force deployments shows some significant explanatory limitations. Above all, it does not take into consideration the context of the time in which the practices of burden sharing took place. Against this backdrop, and viewing Canadian contributions in light of domestic fiscal austerity and the looming referendum on Quebec sovereignty, Ottawa's share of the burden of IFOR can be judged to be considerable. Despite facing an existential problem domestically, Canada's share of the burden was commensurate with that of a state with second-tier power status. Canada's attitudes and contributions were rooted in ideational predispositions and considerations for the security of human beings and an external responsibility to contribute to upholding international peace and security.

The absolute force share also does *not* discuss or highlight the overall benchmark against which these force deployments were made. I therefore suggest that to gain a more complete picture of the practice of Atlantic burden sharing in the IFOR operation, one must calculate the absolute force contributions made by the member states against their relative ability to send troops – that is, as a share of the size of its national armed forces. If, for example, country X maintains 80,000 personnel in the armed services, its contribution to IFOR must be seen as a share of those 80,000 forces; it cannot overcommit forces that are not available. Thus, the number of forces sent calculated as a percentage of forces available determines the relative ability of states to send troops on NATO deployments, and it produces a very different picture from the absolute force share index shown in table 5.1.

Table 5.2 below shows the contributions made by NATO member states to the IFOR operation calculated as a percentage of the total size of their national armed forces. It quickly reveals that unlike the conclusion drawn from table 5.1, the United States did *not* shoulder the largest share of the NATO burden in IFOR; it ranked 9th, putting it in the second-tier power category. The more interesting finding in table 5.2, however, is that those states that were labelled second-tier powers in

Table 5.2 Relative Personnel Contributions to IFOR, 1995–6

Country	Number	Total (%)	Total (non-US) (%)	Rank by absolute force share	Total national force size (%)	Rank by relative force share	Power status
United Kingdom	10,500	20.1	31.1	2	4.7	1	Superpower
Netherlands	2,000	3.8	5.9	6	3.1	2	Major power
Denmark	807	1.5	2.4	12	2.8	3	
Norway	750	1.4	2.2	13	2.0	4	
Canada	1,029	2.0	3.0	9	1.6	5	
France	7,500	14.4	22.2	3	1.5	6	Second-tier power
Portugal	900	1.7	2.7	11	1.2	7	
Germany	4,000	7.7	11.8	4	1.2	8	
United States	18,400	35.2	n/a	1	1.2	9	
Belgium	420	0.8	1.2	14	0.9	10	
Spain	1,400	2.7	4.1	7	0.7	11	Third-tier power
Italy	2,200	4.2	6.5	5	0.5	12	
Greece	1,000	1.9	3.0	10	0.5	13	
Turkey	1,300	2.5	3.8	8	0.2	14	
Iceland	0	0.0	0.0	15	0.0	15	
Luxembourg	0	0.0	0.0	16	0.0	16	
Total	52,206	100	100	16	22.1	16	
Total (non-US)	41,706	79.9	100	15	17.3	15	
Average	3,263	6.3	6.7	n/a	1.4	n/a	
Average (non-US)	2,780	5.0	6.7	n/a	1.2	n/a	

Sources: International Institute for Strategic Studies, *Military Balance 1996/97* (London: IISS, 1997); author's compilation.

table 5.1 show major-power status here because they shouldered a greater share of the collective NATO burden in relative terms than any otherwise major power shown in table 5.1. The only exception is the United Kingdom, which shouldered the largest share of the NATO burden in IFOR.

The Netherlands and Denmark were the top two contributors among the second-tier powers, deploying 3.1% and 2.8% of their national forces, respectively, to the IFOR campaign. Norway follows at 2.0%, then Canada with 1.6%. While these countries have second-tier power status by absolute force contribution, by relative force contribution they can actually be considered major powers in light of the fact that their contributions exceeded the NATO average of 1.4% (1.2% without including the United States).

How can we explain these empirical findings? In the case of Canada, qualitative content analysis of primary documents suggests that its major-power-like *relative* military contributions are the result of strong national preferences for the maintenance of peace, stability, order, and human security in the former republics of Yugoslavia. These preferences show a strong desire to enforce democratic values and principles, the rule of law, and freedom. For the second-tier states generally, this finding supports the earlier argument that their foreign policies were motivated by preferences for absolute rather than relative gains because they contributed more to the public good than they were expected to from Olson and Zeckhauser's collective action model.[17] Indeed, Canada's preferences can be interpreted as Ottawa demonstrating to its allies its commitment to what Arnold Wolfers' external responsibility – a conscious commitment to upholding milieu goals, such as the promotion of international economic, social, and political conditions – that states pursue above and beyond their narrowly defined security interests.[18]

What is interesting in our case study is that it both deviates from Wolfers' work and also builds on it. Wolfers assumed that only major powers or superpowers would be inclined to uphold milieu goals. But when we consider Canadian contributions to IFOR in *relative* terms (as in table 5.2), Canada stands out as a major power by showing strong preferences for practising foreign policy beyond narrowly defined national interests, regardless of whether it experiences a surplus of national

---

17 See the discussion in ch. 2.
18 Wolfers 1962, 73–7.

powers.[19] This, then, is the first indication that using the relative force share index as a benchmark, under special conditions (i.e., strong national preferences for external responsibility) second-tier powers can also experience an external responsibility and foster specific milieu goals.

To be sure, the conclusions to be drawn from table 5.2 for the Netherlands, Denmark, Norway, and Canada do not apply across the board to all otherwise second-tier or even third-tier powers. Reviewing the relative force contributions of Spain, Turkey, and Greece in table 5.2, for example, shows that their performance dropped to that of third-tier states; in relative terms, they were excessive NATO free riders and significantly out-benefited their relative cost contributions to IFOR. The worst Atlantic free riders in both relative and absolute terms were Iceland and Luxembourg – both of which made no force contributions at all. This inconsistency among second-tier powers supports the argument that they are far from homogeneous and should not be clustered into one analytical group. It also endorses the argument that studying the preference formations of individual NATO member states enables us to determine the ideational preferences of their foreign policy behaviour and establish causality between those preferences and Atlantic burden sharing.

SFOR

After one year in theatre and experiencing a much calmer security environment, IFOR was replaced by SFOR in December 1996. Also known as Operation JOINT GUARD, the new SFOR operation took its mandate from Security Council Resolution 1088 of 12 December 1996. Because it was a new, yet follow-on mission to IFOR,[20] allies were asked during the force-generation conferences to decide whether they would renew their force commitments and transfer them to SFOR, transfer a smaller number, or withdraw their IFOR forces altogether and not make any contributions to SFOR. In other words, member states were not expected to automatically pledge their forces to SFOR. This is an

---

19 It thus goes contrary to earlier findings in the literature that assert that states act primarily out of self-interest in peace operations; see, e.g., Neack 1995; Jakobsen 1996.

20 SFOR was a much smaller operation than IFOR; some analysts have suggested that this is a testimony to IFOR's success; see, e.g., David Bercuson, "Pull Our Soldiers out of Bosnia," *National Post*, 4 March 2003, A14.

important fact in assessing the SFOR operation and goes against what some analysts believed.

Examining the primary sources reveals that there was little or no hesitation among Canadian government officials to renew Canada's commitment and keep its forces forwardly deployed in the Balkans. At a ministerial meeting in 1997, government officials reiterated not only the importance of such a commitment but also the government's preference that NATO be in charge.[21] Gone were the days of Canada believing in the effectiveness of the UN for managing international conflicts.

Table 5.3 below shows the *absolute* force share of the countries that participated in the SFOR operation. A total of 6,443 CF personnel[22] helped stabilize the region under SFOR command from 1997 to 2001. They carried out essentially the same mandate as they did under IFOR – ensuring the civilian components of the Dayton peace agreement as well as supporting the international police task force. Canadian soldiers also helped provide humanitarian assistance, ensure the safe return of refugees and displaced people, and hunted down war criminals,[23] who were to be prosecuted under new and evolving governance structures on international criminal justice, especially the International Criminal Tribunal for the former Yugoslavia.

The absolute force share index in table 5.3 shows that the Canadian share of the burden was the second highest of any NATO second-tier power, accounting for 4.5% of the total NATO force (5.7% without the

---

21 Regional Security Section (DFAIT), "NAC Visit: Briefing Material on CDN Approaches to Current NATO Issues," telex IDR-0576, Regional Security Section (DFAIT) to Canadian missions in London, Bonn, Paris, The Hague, Copenhagen, Oslo, Brussels, Lisbon, Madrid, Rome, Ankara, Athens, Warsaw, Prague, Budapest, and Washington, 30 October 1997, retrieved under the Access to Information Act, 10 April 2007, A-3, File No. 3947-01.

22 These numbers are not identical to those found in the scholarly literature – e.g., Bland and Maloney (2004, 234): 1,327; Lenard J. Cohen (2003, 127): 1,800; senior officer, Finance Section, Department of National Defence, interview by the author, Ottawa, April 2007: 1,641.

23 In spite of frequent requests by the International War Crimes Tribunal, SFOR interpreted this mandate narrowly: that it would not explicitly hunt down and capture war criminals; it believed this was the job of international police forces. See Barbara McDougall, "The Dayton Peace Accord Needs Intensive Care," *Globe and Mail*, 9 May 1997, A23; Allan Thompson, "NATO Vows to Help Catch War Criminals," *Toronto Star*, 20 February 1996. Canada strongly and publicly opposed this narrow interpretation; see "NATO Approves Force for Bosnia," *Edmonton Journal*, 18 December 1996, A14.

United States); only Spain shouldered more of the burden. All other second-tier powers, including the Netherlands, Norway, and Denmark, contributed a far lower share. The NATO average is calculated at 5.3% (4.4% without the United States). It is debatable whether Spain and Canada should be ranked as lower-performing major powers or higher-performing second-tier powers and depends, of course, on where one sets the bar.

Table 5.3 confirms Olson and Zeckhauser's collective action problem by showing that conventional second-tier powers, when considering their absolute force share in SFOR, practised free riding. This includes Canada. What is noteworthy about this is that, excluding the United States, all NATO member states combined shared 78.8% of the total NATO burden; this should be interpreted as a high contribution of America's allies rather than an act of European free riding.

The Canadian deployment to SFOR was also known as Operation PALLADIUM. It consisted of an infantry battalion, reconnaissance squadron, engineer squadron, an administrative company, national support and command elements, and special force units.[24] In addition, Ottawa supplied NATO with a multinational divisional headquarters, which was shared on a rotational basis with the British and the Dutch,[25] and sent an air component under Operation BISON (February 1997 to February 1998), which served as part of NATO's Multinational Air Movement Detachment in Rimini, Italy. In addition, a 14-person Airlift Control Centre was sent there to provide intra-theatre movement for personnel and equipment in support of SFOR in Bosnia as well as pre-mission weather and intelligence briefings, flight planning and scheduling, passenger and freight handling, and aircraft servicing.[26] Moreover, six of Canada's CF-18 fighter aircraft, including 112 soldiers, served as part of Operation DELIBERATE GUARD, the air mission in support of SFOR. From August 1997 on, this operation provided tactical air support, including suppression of enemy air defences and electronic warfare, to the NATO forces on the ground.[27]

---

24 Bland and Maloney 2004, 234.
25 Zyla 2005.
26 Ibid.
27 Canada, Department of National Defence, Policy Group, "Past Canadian Commitments to United Nations and Other Peace Support Operations," http://www.dnd.ca/admpol/content.asp?id=%7B4433D831-9230-4572-B297-CEA4F4C1DA3D%7D, accessed 1 June 2007.

Table 5.3 Absolute Personnel Contributions to SFOR, 1997–2001

Country	1997–98		1998–99		1999–2000		2000–1		Total 1997–2001	Average	Rank	Totals and %, All Years		Power status
	No. of troops in Bosnia, Croatia	Total	No. of troops in Bosnia, FYROM	Total	No. of troops in Bosnia, Croatia	Total	No. of troops in Bosnia, SFOR	Total				Total force (%)	Total force (non-US) (%)	
United States	8,427; 701	9,128	7,400; 650	8,050	8,360; 150	8,510	4,600	4,600	30,288	7,572	1	21.3	n/a	Superpower
United Kingdom	3,610; 1,793	5,403	4,900	4,900	4,500	4,500	2,700; 3,500	6,200	21,003	5,250.8	2	14.8	18.7	
France	3,594; 52	3,646	3,300	3,300	3,000	3,000	3,200; 5,080	8,280	18,226	4,556.5	3	12.8	16.3	Major power
Germany	2,516; 87	2,603	2,600	2,600	2,738	2,738	2,369; 5,300	7,669	15,610	3,902.5	4	11.0	13.9	
Italy	1,812; 13	1,825	2,500	2,500	2,313	2,313	1,640; 6,400	8,040	14,678	3,669.5	5	10.3	13.1	
Spain	1,554; 1	1,555	1,600	1,600	1,600	1,600	1,600; 900	2,500	7,255	1,813.8	6	5.1	6.5	
Canada	982; 8	990	960; 1	961	1,380; 1,002	2,382	1,310; 800	2,110	6,443	1,610.8	7	4.5	5.7	Second-tier power
Turkey	1,488; 34	1,522	1,300	1,300	1,300	1,300	1,300; 950	2,250	6,372	1,593	8	4.5	5.7	
Netherlands	988; 71	1,059	1,220	1,220	1,220	1,220	1,267; 1,450	2,717	6,216	1,554	9	4.4	5.5	
Norway	579; 14	593	700; 43	743	700	700	125; 1,200	1,425	3,461	865.25	10	2.4	3.1	
Denmark	658; 4	662	600	600	630	630	425; 900	1,325	3,217	804.25	11	2.3	2.9	
Belgium	123; 12	135	550	550	550	550	550; 900	1,450	2,685	671.25	12	1.9	2.4	
Portugal	319; 1	320	350; 1	351	355	355	335; 340	675	1,701	425.25	13	1.2	1.5	

Table 5.3 Absolute Personnel Contributions to SFOR, 1997–2001 (cont.)

Country	1997–98 No. of troops in Bosnia, Croatia	Total	1998–99 No. of troops in Bosnia, FYROM	Total	1999–2000 No. of troops in Bosnia, Croatia	Total	2000–1 No. of troops in Bosnia, SFOR	Total	Totals and %, All Years Total 1997–2001	Average	Rank	Total force (%)	Total force (non-US) (%)	Power status
Poland	n/a	n/a	n/a	n/a	450	450	290; 763	1,053	1,503	375.75	14	1.1	1.3	
Greece	217; 1	218	250	250	250	250	250; 430	680	1,398	349.5	15	1.0	1.2	
Czech Republic	n/a	n/a	n/a	n/a	560; 1	561	560; 160	720	1,281	320.25	16	0.9	1.1	Third-tier power
Hungary	n/a	n/a	n/a	n/a	4; 310	314	4,310 (Croatia, 325)	639	953	238.25	17	0.7	0.9	
Luxembourg	22	22	25	25	23	23	23	23	93	23.25	18	0.1	0.1	
Iceland	0; 0	0	0	0	0	0	0	0	0	0	19	0.0	0.0	
Total	26,889; 2,792	29,681	–*	28,950	–*	31,396	–*	52,356	142,383	35,596	19	100.0	n/a	
Total (non-US)	18,462; 2,091	20,553	–*	20,900	–*	22,886	–*	47,756	112,095	28,024	18	78.7	100.0	
Average	1,415.2; 146.95	1,855.1	–*	1,809	–*	1,652	–*	2,756	7,494	1,873	n/a	5.3	5.6	
Average (non-US)	1,025.7; 116.2	1,370.2	–*	1,393.3	–*	1,271.4	–*	2,653.1	5,900	1,475	n/a	4.4	5.6	

Sources: International Institute for Strategic Studies, *Military Balance* (London: IISS, 1997 to 2001); United States Department of Defense, *Report on Allied Contributions to the Common Defense* (Washington, DC: Department of Defense, 2000), II-9; "CDA's Contribution to NATO," telex, NDHQ, D NATO POL, LHBF 2039, 17 December 1997, 2, Access to Information Act, 10 April 2007, A-3, File No. 3947–01.

n/a = The country did not participate in this mission.

* The figure cannot be provided; some countries did not break figures down by individual mission.

In sum, Canada's absolute force commitment to SFOR can be judged to be significant, especially when compared to other NATO allies holding similar power status. The extent of this commitment speaks for itself; but evidence is also found in the environment in which those operations took place – the shrinking economy, falling national budgets, high rates of unemployment, and the crisis in Quebec. In addition, almost all of Canada's army units rotated through Operation PALLADIUM.[28]

The discourse among Canadian government officials about the rationale for contributing troops to SFOR also shows strong normative elements. As was the case with IFOR, officials frequently noted the importance of Canada's external responsibility to ensure the rule of law and security of humans on the ground as well as to maintain peace, freedom, prosperity, stability, and order in the region – the threat to which had also threatened the foundation of the European integration project. These preferences provide an explicative understanding of the social action of deploying armed forces units into harm's way to serve as part of SFOR – that is, a strong national commitment and dedication to bringing peace and security to Bosnia and Herzegovina and Croatia and enforcing the human security provisions of the Dayton Accords.[29]

In addition to considering the *absolute* force share of NATO member states' ground force deployments to SFOR, we can achieve a more balanced view of their share of the burden by considering their *relative* share. We can calculate the member states' deployments to SFOR as a share of the total size of their armed forces by dividing their absolute force deployments by the total size of their armed forces. As noted in the IFOR section above, this relative perspective produces a far superior empirical analysis of NATO burden sharing because it takes into account the relative ability of states to send their armed forces on international peace missions. This relative force share is shown in table 5.4 below.

---

28 Bland and Maloney 2004, 234.

29 There is also evidence in the primary documents that Canada was motivated, in part, by preferences for introducing the former republics of Yugoslavia to capitalism. It indirectly hoped for economic benefits from building the peace. For a more detailed discussion on the economic interests of international peace builders, see Pugh 2001, 2003.

Table 5.4 Relative Personnel Contributions to SFOR, 1997–2001

Country	Number	Total available national force (%)	Rank by relative force share	Rank by absolute force share	Power status
Denmark	3,217	2.53	1	11	Superpower
Netherlands	6,216	2.31	2	9	
Canada	6,443	2.15	3	7	Major power
Norway	3,461	2.13	4	10	
United Kingdom	21,003	1.93	5	2	
Luxembourg	93	1.33	6	18	
Belgium	2,685	1.26	7	12	
Germany	15,610	0.96	8	4	Second-tier power
Spain	7,255	0.89	9	6	
France	18,226	0.87	10	3	
Czech Republic	1,281	0.83	11	16	
Italy	14,678	0.75	12	5	
Hungary	953	0.63	13	17	
Portugal	1,701	0.48	14	13	Third-tier power
United States	30,288	0.40	15	1	
Poland	1,503	0.27	16	14	
Turkey	6,372	0.16	17	8	
Greece	1,398	0.14	18	15	
Iceland	0	0	19	19	
Total	142,383	20.01	19		
Total (non-US)	11,2095	19.60	18		
Average	7,493.8	1.05	n/a		
Average (non-US)	5,900	1.03	n/a		

Sources: International Institute for Strategic Studies, *Military Balance* (London: IISS, 1997 to 2001); United States Department of Defense, *Report on Allied Contributions to the Common Defense* (Washington, DC: Department of Defense, 2000), II-9; "CDA's Contribution to NATO," telex, NDHQ, D NATO POL, LHBF 2039, 17 December 1997, 2, Access to Information Act, 10 April 2007, A-3, File No. 3947–01; author's compilation.

This table allows us to make a number of interesting and unexpected observations. First, the Netherlands, Canada, and Norway can be considered major powers when interpreting their SFOR contributions in relative terms. All three practised a burden-sharing behaviour that places them at the top of the major power cluster; the Netherlands ranks 2nd, Canada 3rd, and Norway 4th. Seen in tandem with the IFOR mission, this finding appears to be a consistent pattern of NATO's peace operations. Denmark outperformed any other country and was the largest relative force contributor to SFOR. Applying the conventional power status clustering of collective action theorists, this rightfully places it in the superpower category.

The difference in rank between the absolute and relative force contributions of the second-tier powers is significant across the alliance membership. To take Denmark again, it ranks 11th on the absolute force share index but 1st on the relative force share index. The same pattern can be observed for Norway: on the absolute force share index, it ranks 10th, while on the relative force share index, it ranks 4th. These findings suggest that the second-tier powers were driven in their burden-sharing practices by things other than relative gains or simple power politics. But an "under-evaluation" of burdens shared had significant implications for how supposedly second-tier powers were perceived as international actors and treated by other allies and states.

In the case of Canada, the relative force share index produces a similarly surprising result: on the absolute force share index, Canada ranks 7th, while on the relative force share index, it ranks 3rd. The extent of Canada's burden (2.15% of the total relative force share compared with a NATO average of 1.05%) can be interpreted as underlining Ottawa's strong commitment to NATO peace operations. From studying the Canadian discourse around its SFOR deployments, there is strong evidence that it wanted to pursue absolute rather than relative gains in SFOR. Strong national motives and preferences undoubtedly played a role in shaping Canadian foreign policy actions; one of the most apparent motives was a strong sense of external responsibility for bringing peace, freedom, and stability to the region.

Viewed in these terms, Canada was not a laggard or even a free rider, as assumed by collective action pundits. Rather, it was a leader in picking up the share of NATO's peace operations. In sharp contrast, the United States can actually be considered a free rider; it contributed only 0.4% of the relative force share of SFOR – ranking 15th and placing it in the third-tier power cluster – while it ranks first in absolute force share.

A similar downgrading can be observed for Germany, France, and Italy, which rank 8th, 10th, and 12th, respectively (and 4th, 3rd, and 5th in *absolute* force share). Based on the *relative* force share index, these countries are better described as second-tier rather than major powers. Indeed, in relative terms, all of these states were free riding on other NATO allies in that they shouldered a share of the collective burden that was smaller than the NATO average of 1.05%.

Operation ALLIED FORCE in Kosovo

In 1989, President Slobodan Milosevic came to power on the promise to reintegrate the ethnic Albanian-dominated province of Kosovo into Serbia.[30] Milan Kucan, himself a contender for the federal presidency, lost the election to Milosevic, who had secured half of the necessary eight votes in support of his view of how Yugoslavia should restructure itself politically after Tito's death.[31] Meanwhile, Kosovo's Serb minority felt discriminated against by the ethnic Albanian government. In 1998, some ethnic Albanians (nearly 90% of the total population of Kosovo) grouped together into the militant Kosovo Liberation Army (KLA) and began to attack Serbian police and Yugoslav army troops to protest Milosevic's clampdowns. Serbia responded with escalating violence and repression: it introduced martial law in Kosovo and replaced ethnic Albanian government officials with ethnic Serbs. It was in this environment that the conflict in Kosovo slowly but surely heated up to the point where violent conflicts erupted between the two ethnic groups in early 1999. It is estimated that the civil war between the KLA and Serb forces cost more than 2,500 lives and resulted in more than 400,000 refugees, most of whom fled to Western Europe and Albania.[32]

---

30 For an excellent overview and discussion of the Kosovo crisis, see Judah 2002, 2005–06. His numbers were taken from the early stages of the Kosovo crisis; the total can only be estimated.

31 Lampe 1996, 325. Kucan missed the votes of Bosnia and Herzegovina, Croatia, FYROM, and Slovenia.

32 United States, Library of Congress Congressional Research Service 2001, 2. NATO's numbers are even higher, listing the total number of refugees from Montenegro, FYROM, and Albania at 723.800, http://www.nato.int/pictures/1999/990520/b990520j.jpg, accessed 7 July 2009.

NATO acted as a peace broker throughout the ethnic conflict because the stakes were high for the alliance, especially after the failure of the negotiations at the Rambouillet peace talks in 1998–9. There were two reasons for this. First, because it had taken too long to stop acts of genocide and mass murder in Bosnia and Croatia in the early 1990s, it was now being called upon to move as quickly as possible before the conflict spiralled out of control. As some analysts suggested, if NATO were unable to stop the genocide in Kosovo in 1999 and defend its fundamental values of freedom, democracy, and the rule of law, it would most likely spell the end of the transatlantic alliance.[33] Second, NATO's international reputation as an effective crisis manager would be seriously damaged if the alliance failed to achieve this objective.[34] This is especially so since civil war was taking place in Europe right on the doorstep of some member states (e.g., Italy, Greece). Consequently, NATO's foremost goal was to stop a humanitarian crisis in Kosovo and address those forces that threatened to damage its cohesiveness and question its status.

NATO made initial attempts at the diplomatic level to convince the Milosevic regime to lay down its arms. When those efforts failed, and when the violence against ethnic Albanians escalated in March 1999, the alliance began the airstrikes it had long threatened to employ. While bombs were dropped against targets in Serbia and Kosovo, the so-called Group of Eight (G8) summit took place on 6 May 1999 in Petersberg Castle near Bonn, Germany. At that meeting, the heads of states and governments of the most powerful world economies demanded an immediate end to the civil war and violence against civilians, the withdrawal of all Yugoslav military and paramilitary forces from Kosovo, the deployment of UN peacekeepers, an interim

---

33 Before the NATO operation in Kosovo, British Prime Minister Tony Blair and French President Jacques Chirac met in the coastal town of St. Malo. They decided to create a European Security and Defence Identity (ESDI) to foster common defence in Europe. It would give the EU the capacity for autonomous (from NATO) action while being supported by credible military forces. The reaction of the United States was unequivocal: Secretary of State Madeleine Albright demanded that the new European forces should not duplicate, discriminate, or decouple from NATO; see Madeleine Korbel Albright, "The Right Balance Will Secure NATO's Future," *Financial Times*, 7 December 1998, 22. For a more detailed discussion of the transatlantic rift this caused as well as threats to the alliance, see Kaplan 2004, 124–6; Marsh 2006; United States Department of Defense 2000, 4; Gnesotto 2004, 42–5.

34 See, e.g., Shea 2002, 77–8; Roper 1999, 53–4.

administration led by the UN, the safe return of all refugees, and self-government for Kosovo.[35]

The endorsement of these demands by Russia, especially, was critical for two reasons. First, Russia was a permanent member of the UN Security Council and thus could veto any resolution on Kosovo. Second, Russia had strong historical ties to the Serbian leadership and continued to support it. The fact that Moscow actively pursued and enforced the demands of the G8 was seen as a major step towards forcing Milosevic to stop the violence. The rapprochement between NATO and Russia also helped to develop and ultimately institutionalize NATO-Russia relations through the NATO-Russia Council, which came into effect in 2002.

On diplomatic and military levels, Canada was one of the first countries to respond to the human rights violations – in fact, long before the ethnic conflict turned violent in 1999.[36] Its politicians were not, as some commentators suggested, "ventriloquists' dummies."[37] Endorsed by strong public opinion polls,[38] Canada's Kosovo mission was very much framed as enforcing an evolving human security agenda[39] that was transforming conventional definitions of state sovereignty and imposing new responsibilities on state leaders to ensure the security of their people. Ottawa worked hard in diplomatic circles, especially at the UN Security Council, to convince the other members to not only condemn the violence and disrespect for human rights but also lobby for a peace-enforcement operation that would stop the growing bloodshed in Kosovo.[40] Unfortunately, all efforts by Robert Fowler (then Canada's ambassador to the UN) to have the UN pass a resolution that endorsed

---

35 "G8 Foreign Ministers' Meetings: Statement by the Chairman on the Conclusion of the Meeting of the G8 Foreign Ministers on the Petersberg," 6 May 1999, http:// www.g8.utoronto.ca/foreign/fm990506.htm, accessed 18 August 2010.

36 DFAIT, "Axworthy to Visit Moscow and Former Yugoslavia," news release, 4 April 1996.

37 Watson 1999, 10. Others called Canada the "happy follower" (Nossal and Roussel 2001).

38 A number of polls spoke in favour of the government's actions. An Angus Reid poll conducted for the *Globe and Mail* and CTV on 11 April 1999 showed that 35% of Canadians were in favour of air strikes and 40% were in favour of sending ground troops. A separate Angus Reid poll (11 April 1999) showed that 61% of Canadians supported intervening in Kosovo with ground troops and believed that Canada should take part in that operation.

39 Heinbecker 1999, 2000, 2001, 2004.

40 DFAIT, "Axworthy Condemns Latest Violence in Kosovo and Calls for United Nations Action," news release, 7 August 1998. At that time, Canada was a non-permanent member of the UN Security Council.

such a peace operation were unsuccessful. In light of the escalating violence, the allies decided to disregard the opinion of the Security Council and launch a unilateral NATO air campaign without the blessing of the UN.

Against the backdrop of UN inaction and unwillingness to intervene in Kosovo, the January 1999 massacre in the village of Račak in southern Kosovo pushed the conflict to the top of Canada's foreign policy agenda, and both politicians and the public called for immediate action to save lives.[41] In a speech to the UN Security Council, Minister of Foreign Affairs Lloyd Axworthy pointed to the responsibility of the international community to stop mass atrocities from unfolding given the rising number of civilian deaths in Kosovo. "It is a state's prerogative and obligation to ensure the protection of all of its citizens, especially in times of armed conflict. This is a public good, but one that governments do not or cannot always provide."[42] Meanwhile, the UNHCR had reported that approximately 300,000 Kosovars had been displaced by the ongoing violence.[43]

It was therefore hardly surprising that Canadians were convinced of the need for military intervention. They supported their government's military participation in NATO's 78-day air campaign[44] in Kosovo to stop the ethnic conflict from escalating and bring the Milosevic regime back to order, thereby stabilizing the whole region. Canada participated with 18 CF-18 fighter-jets operating out of the NATO air base in Aviano, Italy – making it, in *absolute* military terms (shown in table 5.5 below), the eighth-largest contributor of fighter-jets to Operation ALLIED FORCE. It also shouldered the full logistical costs of the campaign and the expense of sustaining its ground forces in KFOR, deployed shortly after the air campaign ended.[45]

---

41 Heinbecker 1999, 541.

42 Lloyd Axworthy, "Notes for an Address of the Honourable Lloyd Axworthy, Minister of Foreign Affairs, to the United Nations Security Council," *DFAIT Statements and Speeches*, 12 February 1999, n.p.

43 UNHCR, "UNHCR Escorts Frightened Civilians to Safety, Ogata Renews Appeal for Cease-Fire in Kosovo," news release, 21 January 1999. The large number of refugees fleeing the conflict zone also began to affect the neighbouring FYROM.

44 According to an Angus Reid poll of 11 April 1999, 69% of Canadians supported Canada's participation in the air campaign.

45 The total cost of Canadian deployments in the Kosovo operation are unfortunately not yet available (LCol Ross Fetterly, Finance Section, Department of National Defence, interview by the author, Ottawa, 19 July 2007).

Table 5.5 Fighter-Jet Contributions to Operation ALLIED FORCE, 1999

Country	Number	Total (%)	Total (non-US) (%)	Rank	Power status
United States	731	69.09	n/a	1	Superpower
France	84	7.94	26.50	2	Major power
Italy	58	5.48	18.30	3	Major power
United Kingdom	39	3.69	12.30	4	Major power
Germany	33	3.12	10.41	5	Major power
Netherlands	22	2.08	6.94	6	Second-tier power
Turkey	21	1.98	6.62	7	Second-tier power
Canada	18	1.70	5.68	8	Second-tier power
Belgium	14	1.32	4.42	9	Second-tier power
Denmark	8	0.76	2.52	10	Third-tier power
Spain	7	0.66	2.21	11	Third-tier power
Norway	6	0.57	1.89	12	Third-tier power
Hungary	4	0.38	1.26	13	Third-tier power
Portugal	3	0.28	0.95	14	Third-tier power
Czech Republic	0	0	0	15	Third-tier power
Greece	0	0	0	16	Third-tier power
Iceland	0	0	0	17	Third-tier power
Luxembourg	0	0	0	18	Third-tier power
Poland	0	0	0	19	Third-tier power
Total	1,048	100	100	19	
Total (non-US)	317	30.91	100	18	
Average	55.6	5.21	5.56	n/a	
Average (non-US)	18.20	1.66	5.56	n/a	

Source: United States, Department of Defense, *Report to Congress: Kosovo/Operation Allied Force After-Action Report* (Washington, DC: Department of Defense, 31 January 2000).
Notes:
1. The data includes Hungary, the Czech Republic, and Poland, which officially joined NATO on 12 March 1999.
2. RAND provides somewhat different numbers. According to its analysis, Belgium contributed 12, Canada 18, Denmark 9, France 41, Germany 14, Italy 48, Netherlands 18, Norway 6, Portugal 3, Spain 6, Turkey 11, United Kingdom 36, and United States more than 700; see Peters et al. 2001, 19.
3. NATO also participated in Operation ALLIED FORCE by deploying 10 AWACS; however, they are not listed or used in the percentage calculations.

For methodological reasons, it is possible to consider only the absolute fighter-jet contributions that NATO members made to this operation. As the number and type of aircraft used among member states for such air operations vary considerably, and not every type of aircraft could be used in missions such as Allied Force, it is nearly impossible to accurately assess the relative contributions of each state.[46]

Two interesting findings emerge from table 5.5. The first is that the United States furnished nearly 70% of the fighter-jets for Operation ALLIED FORCE, whereas the other allies combined supplied only 31%. This underlines Washington's superpower status in the alliance, especially when the next largest contributor, France, supplied only 7.94%. Italy ranks third, with 5.48% of the fighter-jets, and the United Kingdom and Germany follow with 3.69% and 3.12%, respectively. America's supreme contribution to the operation is also in line with what collective action theorists would predict – that superpowers contribute more to the public good than they receive in benefits from it, while second-tier powers practise free riding. Moreover, the United States, France, Italy, the United Kingdom, and Germany carried 89.32% of the total allied burden. In other words, only four of America's 18 NATO allies made any substantial commitment to sharing the military burden in the Kosovo air campaign. The remaining 14 member states accounted for only 11% of the total burden.

The second interesting finding from table 5.5 is that with regard to the second-tier powers, the Netherlands once again shouldered a slightly higher share of the collective burden than Canada, contributing 2.08% to Canada's 1.70% of the fighter-jets, while the average of all 18 NATO member states (excluding the United States) was 1.66%. These two second-tier powers, therefore, cannot be considered Atlantic free riders or laggards because their force burden was consistent with the NATO average.

It is also interesting to place Canada's contribution in the context of the operation to determine its full extent. Its CF-18s were in high demand among NATO's commanding officers because they were among the few that were able to load and drop precision-guided munitions

---

46 The United States, e.g., owns by far the most advanced and diversified pool of fighter-jets, and it can therefore decide for tactical reasons which type of aircraft to deploy in an operation. In contrast, other NATO members own only one type of aircraft.

(PGMs), thereby allegedly limiting the potential for civilian casualties.[47] This reveals two things. First, Canadian pilots served on the front lines of the war. In fact, they flew nearly 2,600 hours, 678 of which were in combat missions, and dropped 532 regular and 361 laser-guided bombs on Serbian artillery positions[48] – all without losing any aircraft or pilots.[49] NATO flew close to 10,000 bombing missions from the start of Operation ALLIED FORCE on 24 March until it ended on 10 June 1999. The capability to carry PGMs day and night was a crucial asset and one frequently asked for by the American Joint Force Air Component Commander.[50]

Second, while 14 of the 19 NATO nations contributed aircraft to the operation, only eight flew combat missions; Canada was among them. As shown in table 5.6 below, CF pilots flew 2.1% of the total 38,441 NATO sorties (or 6.6% of the total sorties without the United States)[51] that helped to degrade and damage the military and security structure that President Milosevic had used to ethnically cleanse the Albanian majority in Kosovo.[52]

At first glance, this may seem to be a low percentage. However, seen in relative terms – that is, compared to Canada's equally ranked second-tier NATO allies – Canada's share of the contributions acquires a new meaning. Take, for example, Denmark, which flew only 1.3% of the total sorties; Norway, which flew 1.1%; or Spain, which flew 0.9% – all of these second-tier powers flew fewer sorties than Canada did. CF pilots flew 16 sorties per day, requiring 32 pilots; this, to put it into perspective, represented half of all available CF-18 combat-ready pilots.[53]

---

47 Bashow et al. 2000, 55.
48 Ibid.
49 Two US Apache helicopter pilots were killed in Operation ALLIED FORCE while on a training mission.
50 Colonel D.A. Davies, "The Campaign for Kosovo's Canada's Fighter Force in Action," 3 Feb 2000, 2, quoted in Bashow et al. 2000, 56. For a solid account of the US role in the air campaign, see Air Force Association 1999.
51 For additional numbers (which do not match those found in Coleman, the US Department of Defense, or Wesley Clark), see United States Congressional Research Service 2003, preface. Daalder and O'Hanlon (2000, 4), e.g., counted "nearly 40,000" sorties. Thus, the numbers must be treated with caution.
52 This is the line of argument presented in a prepared statement by William S. Cohen, secretary of defense, to the Senate Armed Services Committee, 15 April 1999.
53 Bashow et al. 2000, 60.

Table 5.6 Sorties, Operation ALLIED FORCE, 1999

Country	Number	Total (%)	Total (non-US) (%)	Rank	Power status
United States	26,266	68.33	n/a	1	Superpower
France	2,918	7.59	24.0	2	Major power
United Kingdom	2,112	5.49	17.3	3	
Netherlands	1,498	3.90	12.3	4	
Italy	1,306	3.40	10.7	5	
Canada	807	2.10	6.6	6	Second-tier power
Germany	768	2.00	6.3	7	
Belgium	730	1.90	6.0	8	
Denmark	499	1.30	4.1	9	
Turkey	461	1.20	3.8	10	Third-tier power
Norway	422	1.10	3.5	11	
Spain	346	0.90	2.8	12	
Hungary	154	0.40	1.3	13	
Portugal	154	0.40	1.3	14	
Czech Republic	0	0.00	0.00	15	
Greece	0	0.00	0.00	16	
Iceland	0	0.00	0.00	17	
Luxembourg	0	0.00	0.00	18	
Poland	0	0.00	0.00	19	
Total	38,441	100	100	19	
Total (non-US)	12,175	31.67	100	18	
Average	2,023	5.3	5.6	n/a	
Average (non-US)	676	5.6	5.6	n/a	

Sources: Katharina P. Coleman, *International Organisations and Peace Enforcement: The Politics of International Legitimacy* (Cambridge: Cambridge University Press, 2007), 203–4; United States, Department of Defense, *Report to Congress: Kosovo/Operation Allied Force After-Action Report* (Washington, DC: Department of Defense, 31 January, 2000), 77–9; Wesley Clark, "Report to NATO Secretary-General Robertson on Operation ALLIED FORCE Statistics" (unclassified NATO document SHJOC/J3AIR/0500/99, 6 January 2000).

When the United States is included in the calculations, Canada flew the 6th-highest number of sorties in Operation ALLIED FORCE, 5th when the United States is excluded. This contribution is also 1% higher than the NATO average of 5.6%. Thus, measured in relative rather than absolute terms, Canada stepped up to the plate. This is yet another example of a strong commitment by a second-tier power in international crisis management helping to enforce peace and security in Kosovo; it is not an indication of free riding.

On the diplomatic level, and while the air campaign was in full force, the alliance told the Milosevic regime that airstrikes would continue until the following conditions were met: (1) the halt of all military action and violence; (2) the withdrawal of the military, police, and paramilitary forces from Kosovo; (3) the acceptance of an international peace force; and (4) an unconditional and safe return of all refugees and displaced people.[54] To be sure, it was not NATO's objective to defeat the Serb-dominated Yugoslav armed forces or force a regime change in Belgrade; it was to force the Milosevic regime back to the negotiating table and allow an international peacekeeping force into Kosovo that would stop the violence from escalating.[55] The alliance did not demand independence for Kosovo but rather autonomy for its ethnic Albanian majority as well as respect for basic international rights and the freedom of its citizens. US President Bill Clinton described the overall aim of the Kosovo air campaign most succinctly.

> Our strikes have three objectives: First, to demonstrate the seriousness of NATO's opposition to aggression and its support for peace. Second, to deter President Milosevic from continuing and escalating his attacks on helpless civilians by imposing a price for those attacks. And, third, if necessary, to damage Serbia's capacity to wage war against Kosovo in the future by seriously diminishing its military capabilities.[56]

Canadian Prime Minister Jean Chrétien echoed this reasoning in a speech delivered to the House of Commons on 12 April 1999. In particular, he justified Canada's involvement in the NATO mission in

---

54 Statement of the North Atlantic Council, 12 April 1999.

55 Ibid., 2.

56 "Statement by the President on Kosovo," news release, 24 March 1999.

Kosovo by referring to its values, its national interests in a stable and secure Europe, and its obligations as a founding member of NATO.[57] Lloyd Axworthy expanded on the prime minister's justifications.

> NATO's actions are guided primarily by concern for the human rights and welfare of Kosovo's people. NATO's recourse to air strikes was precipitated by evidence that the regime of repression by the Serb government was on the rise and accelerating. ... NATO did not provoke this tragedy – it responded to it. And the decision to act was not motivated by a military threat to Alliance territory, but by an affront to Alliance values and belief – perhaps more explicit in some capitals than others – that human security matters. Alliance members could not turn away from the humanitarian crisis taking place on NATO's European doorstep. That is why Canadian pilots are part of the effort, why we are providing humanitarian relief and why we are offering sanctuary to 5,000 refugees.[58]

In short, Canada saw the new NATO as a tool for promoting non-material security issues such as human security and upholding its external responsibility to contribute to world peace and security.[59] At the same time, primary document analysis reveals that the seemingly unstoppable conflict in the Balkans and the response of the international community through the UN had reinforced the view among Canadian foreign policy officials that when it came to security interests, NATO was the more effective and politically willing institution than the UN. Canada had simply lost faith in the UN and its agencies.[60] Moreover, Canada was willing to use force to stop the violence long before other states advocated it. Indeed, "the Canadian government would not have been unhappy had NATO embraced a more robust ground troops option earlier in the conflict, even though Ottawa did not follow the path of former British prime minister Tony Blair, who openly campaigned

---

57 Canada, Parliament, House of Commons, 12 April 1999. See also http://www.parl .gc.ca/HousePublications/Publication.aspx?Language=E&Mode=1&DocId=2332912 &File=0#LINK29, accessed 20 August 2014.
58 Axworthy 1999.
59 This is an issue that will be discussed in detail in the next chapter. For a detailed discussion of the human security agenda, see Booth 2005; Human Security Centre 2005; Kay 2006; MacFarlane and Khong 2006; McRae 2001.
60 For a soldier's perspective, see Hillier 2009; MacKenzie 1996.

for the use of ground troops."[61] Thus, it was not surprising that nearly 90% of Canada's deployments to peace operations took place under the auspices of NATO.[62]

One of the negative side effects of the Kosovo war was that it produced a large number of refugees. Ivo Daalder and Michael O'Hanlon calculated that the Milosevic regime had removed 1.3 million people from their homes while pushing another 800,000 or so out of the province of Kosovo;[63] up to 10,000 died during the conflict.[64] In turn, those refugees who returned to Kosovo at the end of the air campaign, nearly 1 million people,[65] indicated that overall, and within limits, the air campaign had been successful.[66] A total of 78% of Canadians polled voiced strong support for allowing those refugees to come to Canada.[67]

KFOR

With the termination of the air campaign on 10 June 1999 and following the examples of the IFOR and SFOR missions, the international community decided to assemble a considerable ground force to enforce the Kosovo peace agreement, and it began to deploy forces to southern Serbia on 12 June 1999. KFOR, also called Operation JOINT GUARDIAN, received its mandate from UN Resolution 1244 of 10 June 1999 as well as the Military-Technical Agreement reached among NATO, the Federal Republic of Yugoslavia, and Serbia. Like IFOR and SFOR, KFOR was a Chapter VII peace enforcement operation, and its

---

61 Nossal and Roussel 2001, 183.
62 Haglund 2001; see also MacKenzie 1996.
63 Daalder and O'Hanlon 2000, vii.
64 Ibid., 3.
65 The literature on the displaced people of Kosovo is vast, and the number of refugees remains imprecise. A good account of the refugee flows, however, can be found in Judah 2002, 240–54.
66 Nonetheless, NATO missed its initial goal of preventing a humanitarian disaster or genocide: its air campaign did not stop Serb operations against ethnic Albanians. This debate on the effectiveness of the air campaign has not come to an end, and no definitive answer has been commonly accepted in the literature. Another criticism was NATO's handling of the campaign, specifically that the "war by committee" – that is, the collective decision making on tactical decisions – hampered the daily operations on the ground. For a more detailed discussion, see Clark 2001.
67 Angus Reid Poll for the *Globe and Mail* and CTV, 11 April 1999.

forces were authorized to use coercive means, if necessary, to implement the Rambouillet peace accord.

Among the primary objectives of KFOR was demining the province of Kosovo and ensuring the safety of all ethnic minorities, including Serbs, Bosniaks, Roma, Turks, and Albanians, which comprised nearly 90% of the total ethnic population of Kosovo.[68] A successful element of the KFOR contingent was a CIMIC cell, which was designed to help establish a close working relationship between NATO forces and the local population and functioned as a nation-building unit. Its task was to assist with building and repairing roads, bridges, and mountain passes as well as providing humanitarian aid.[69] The Canadian contingent consisted of an infantry battle group, a reconnaissance squadron, eight helicopters, and an engineer contingent. Its role was to take part in the demilitarization of the KLA and transform it into the Kosovo Protection Corps, a civilian organization responsible for coordinating civil emergency responses.

Table 5.7 below lists the absolute force share contributed by NATO countries to KFOR between 1999 and 2001.

Two things are worth noting about the data presented here. First, the United States' absolute force contribution to allied operations once again underlines its supreme power status in the alliance; no other NATO member state contributed more forces to KFOR than the Americans. From the inception of KFOR until 2001, the United States deployed 16,000 troops, equal to 15.7% of the total force. France ranks second, slightly behind the Americans, deploying 15,380 troops and contributing 15.1% of the total NATO force, while Germany, Italy, and the United Kingdom contributed 14.7%, 14.5%, and 9.4%, respectively. Interpreting this data confirms the hypothesis put forward by collective action theorists: superpower America contributed the most to the collective good and benefited disproportionately less. The major powers' contributions also exceeded their received benefits.

The second interesting finding is that while Canada clearly ranks in the second-tier power cluster, shouldering just 4.3%[70] of the absolute

---

68 United States Congressional Research Service 2003, 1.

69 Reinhardt 2000, 17.

70 The numbers are identical in Bland and Maloney and Lenard J. Cohen as well as from DND, while the *Military Balance* (1999 to 2002) lists the Canadian contribution at 800. The calculations in table 5.7 use the DND numbers.

Table 5.7 Absolute Personnel Contributions to KFOR, 1999–2001

Country	1999	2000	2001	Total	Rank	Total (%)	Total (non-US) (%)	Power status
United States	5,500	5,400	5,100	16,000	1	15.7	n/a	Superpower
France	5,080	5,100	5,200	15,380	2	15.1	17.8	
Germany	5,300	5,100	4,600	15,000	3	14.7	17.4	Major power
Italy	6,400	4,200	4,200	14,800	4	14.5	17.2	
United Kingdom	3,500	3,900	2200	9,600	5	9.4	11.1	
Canada	1,450	1,450	1,450	4,350	6	4.3	5.0	
Netherlands	1,450	1,450	1,450	4,350	7	4.3	5.0	
Greece	430	1,700	1,700	3,830	8	3.7	4.4	Second-tier power
Spain	900	1,300	1,300	3,500	9	3.4	4.1	
Norway	1,200	980	980	3,160	10	3.1	3.7	
Turkey	950	940	940	2,830	11	2.8	3.3	
Belgium	900	800	800	2,500	12	2.4	2.9	
Denmark	900	900	540	2,340	13	2.3	2.7	
Poland	763	532	574	1,869	14	1.8	2.2	
Hungary	325	325	325	975	15	1.0	1.1	
Portugal	340	313	313	966	16	0.9	1.1	Third-tier power
Czech Republic	160	175	400	735	17	0.7	0.9	
Iceland	0	0	0	0	18	0.0	0.0	
Luxembourg	Some	Some	Some	Some	19	Some	Some	
Total	35,548	34,565	32,072	102,185	19	100	n/a	
Total (non-US)	30,048	29,165	26,972	86,185	18	84.3	100.00	
Average	1,870.95	1,819.21	1,688.00	5,378.16	n/a	5.26	n/a	
Average (non-US)	1,669.33	1,620.28	1,498.44	4,788.06	n/a	5.55	5.55	

Source: Author's compilation.

KFOR force share, its burden sharing was the greatest of any other second-tier power. Norway, for example, contributed 3.1% of the slightly
more than 102,185 troop burden, while Denmark shouldered only 2.3%.
Because these states contributed less than NATO's average of 5.26%,
they can rightly be considered free riders because their contributions to
the allied good were lower than the collective benefit they received
from it.

As was the case with IFOR and SFOR, absolute force share is commonly used to assess the share of the collective burden that allies shouldered in IFOR, but the relative force share of a member state's
contribution arguably provides a more accurate and contextual index.
The relative force share index for KFOR in 1999 (presented in table 5.8
below) measures the contributions of the member states according to
their ability to their national forces on peacekeeping operations.

The relative force share index assumes that governments can deploy
only as many forces as they have at their disposal, measured by the
size of their armed forces. What is interesting to observe from table 5.8
is that contrary to the hypothesis posed by NATO collective action
theorists, and in relative terms, superpower America *cannot* be considered a supreme burden sharer but rather a laggard and indeed a free
rider. The United States sent only 1.1% of its military forces to serve in
KFOR, placing it in the third-tier power category. It gained a net benefit from the alliance's collective public good, deriving more benefit
from the collective good than it paid for. The superpower of old became a third-tier power.

Another interesting conclusion that we can draw from table 5.8 is that
states that were formerly considered second- or even third-tier powers
now place in the major power cluster. Norway, for example, ranks 10th
on the absolute force share index but 1st in relative terms; Denmark
ranks 13th on the absolute force share index but 2nd on the relative
index. Canada is the 6th-highest absolute force contributor but ranks
4th on the relative scale, deploying 7.3% of its armed forces to KFOR.

These findings point to two things. First, the commonly used absolute burden-sharing indexes are inaccurate because they show no relation to the relative abilities of states to contribute forces to a collective
cause. Second, by shouldering a significantly higher share of the collective NATO burden, otherwise second-tier powers like Canada appear
to be driven in their foreign and defence policies by absolute rather
than relative gains. Indeed, based on the Canadian government's discourse about the KFOR mission, officials were driven in their policy

Table 5.8 Relative Personnel Contributions to KFOR, 1999–2001

Country	Number	Total available national force (%)	Rank	Power status
Norway	1,200	9.7	1	Major power
Denmark	900	8.6	2	
Netherlands	1,450	8.1	3	
Canada	1,450	7.3	4	
Belgium	900	5.9	5	
Germany	5,300	4.5	6	Second-tier power
United Kingdom	3,500	4.4	7	
Italy	6,400	3.8	8	
France	5,080	3.7	9	
Turkey	950	3.6	10	
Spain	900	2.3	11	
Hungary	325	1.9	12	Third-tier power
Greece	430	1.9	13	
Portugal	340	1.4	14	
Czech Republic	160	1.4	15	
United States	5,500	1.1	16	
Poland	763	1.0	17	
Iceland	0	0.0	18	
Luxembourg	Some	0.0	19	
Total	35,548	70.4	19	
Total (non-US)	34,348	69.4	18	
Average	1,871	3.7	n/a	
Average (non-US)	1,633	3.9	n/a	

Source: Author's compilation.

decisions by normative questions of human rights and security as well as a self-identified external responsibility to act in support of those normative and value predispositions.[71] In relative terms, Ottawa contributed more to NATO's collective good than it received benefits from it; it was neither a free rider nor an Atlantic laggard.

A third interesting conclusion to be drawn from table 5.8 is that former major powers such as Germany, the United Kingdom, Italy, and France ranked considerably lower and are now clustered in the second-tier power rather than the major power group.

Table 5.9 below offers a detailed breakdown of the absolute expenses that NATO allies incurred in the operations in Kosovo in 1999. However, the numbers should be viewed with caution because member states calculated the costs of their national contributions in a variety of ways, and these non-uniform accounting practices made it difficult to make an accurate and objective comparison. For example, some countries grouped their Kosovo-related costs according to the nature of the operation (military or humanitarian); others listed only the costs of particular operations.[72] Despite these methodological difficulties, the table shows that Canada was the largest contributor among its second-tier power peers; it shouldered 7.1% of the total costs, not far behind Germany, and more than France, which is considered a major power.

Despite a lack of comparable methodological practices by NATO allies, table 5.9 provides a rough picture of how much each contributing state spent throughout the course of the Kosovo campaign. Considering the distribution of the costs, it is surprising that the United States, once again, is the supreme burden-sharing nation and also that Canada as a second-tier power ranks third. This implies two things: first, collective action theorists are wrong in hypothesizing about the free-riding behaviour of NATO allies. Indeed, as this table shows, second-tier states excel in their burden-sharing practices rather than practising free riding. Second, these practices in themselves in their specific contexts provide a strong indication that Canada was driven by absolute rather than relative gains during the Kosovo crisis; it did not practise

---

71 This moral predisposition was widely shared among Canadians; 93% of them believed that Canada had a moral obligation to assist victims of human rights violations, Angus Reid poll for the *Globe and Mail* and CTV, 11 April 1999.

72 United States Congressional Research Service 2000.

Table 5.9 Expenditures on Operation ALLIED FORCE, Operation JOINT GUARDIAN, and Humanitarian Assistance (Millions of US Dollars), 1999

Country	Allied Force	Joint Guardian	Humanitarian assistance	Total ($)	Total (%)	Total (non-US) (%)	Rank
United States	1,775.7	1,050.2	5,005.0	7,830.9	66.8	n/a	1
Germany	26.2	192.0	743.0	961.2	8.2	24.7	2
Canada	397.6	429.8	n/a	827.4	7.1	21.2	3
France	203.2	192.0	239.0	643.2	5.5	16.5	4
Norway	19.1	94.9	262.1	376.1	3.2	9.7	5
Italy	n/a	n/a	329.6	329.6	2.8	8.5	6
Denmark	7.4	46.2	133.6	187.2	1.6	4.8	7
United Kingdom	n/a	n/a	45.0	136.0	1.2	3.5	8
Netherlands	n/a	n/a	n/a	107.5	0.9	2.8	9
Spain	23.0	57.3	9.18	89.5	0.8	2.3	10
Turkey	26.0	30.0	14.6	70.6	0.6	1.8	11
Portugal	6.0	44.9	0.7	51.6	0.4	1.3	12
Greece	n/a	40.0	10.0	50.0	0.4	1.3	13
Czech Republic	n/a	15.5	14.6	30.1	0.3	0.8	14
Hungary	n/a	18.7	2.7	21.4	0.2	0.5	15
Poland	n/a	9.6	2.9	12.5	0.1	0.3	16
Belgium	n/a	n/a	n/a	n/a	n/a	n/a	17
Iceland	0	0	n/a	0	0	0	18
Luxembourg	0	0	7.32	7.32	0.1	0	19
Total	2,484.2	2,221.1	6,819.3	11,724.8	100	n/a	19
Total (non-US)	708.5	1,170.9	1,814.3	3,893.9	33.2	100	18
Average	130.7	116.9	358.9	617.1	5.3	n/a	n/a
Average (non-US)	39.4	65.1	100.8	216.3	1.8	5.6	n/a

Sources: Canada, Department of Defence (Access to Information Request, Ref.# A-2009–00150/Team 5–5, 10 April 2007); Carl Ek, *NATO Burdensharing and Kosovo: A Preliminary Report*, Report for Congress RL30398 (Washington, DC: Congressional Research Service, 3 January 2000).

or pursue narrowly defined national interests. As stated above, it is evident from studying the government's discourse that officials strongly espoused Canadian engagements in the context of human rights and security, the rule of law, and the promotion of democracy.

Public Opinion

Liberal IR theory attributes a strong role to individual citizens and groups within the state in the foreign policymaking process. By taking a bottom-up approach and opening up the "black box" of foreign policy decision-making processes, liberal scholars hold that the external actions of a government are held to account by constituents in a given polity. One way in which this occurs is in public opinion polls, which are a strong, yet informal yardstick for gaining access to the preference formation of governments and determining the mood of citizens on a particular policy issue.

With the strong support of the Canadian public, it was hardly surprising that the Chrétien government sent ground troops to the Balkans under the framework of the UN and NATO. Such strong support provided reassurance and justification for the government to intervene there in spite of dire fiscal cutbacks and a looming recession.[73] For example, at the height of the massacres in Srebrenica in 1995, the Canadian International Development Agency found that 75% of Canadians supported the government's preference for enhancing international peace and security as well as enforcing human and humanitarian rights in the former republics of Yugoslavia through NATO.[74] The public also wanted Canadian politicians to stop the violations of human rights and killings of civilians, especially in Sarajevo and Srebrenica.[75]

It seems an oxymoron that while support for these missions was strong, domestic polls indicated that only 16% of Canadians supported spending on the military, whereas 73% supported increasing federal

---

73 Jeff Sallot, "Canada's Tone Turning Dovish," *Globe and Mail*, 20 May 1999, A16.

74 Canadian International Development Agency 1995, 12.

75 See Compass/Southam/IISS survey, quoted in Martin and Fortmann 2001, 45, note 11.

monetary transfers to the provincial governments, followed by spending on youth employment measures (66%) and health care (64%).[76] These numbers imply that Canadians supported the mission of the armed forces to the Balkans but did not think that increased spending on the armed forces was required to carry out the job and did not support active procurement programs, such as replacing aging CF equipment.

Above all, NATO was popular among Canadians, and their support for Canada's role in the alliance was remarkably high. In 1999, for example, 32% believed that Canada should place a very high priority on its role in NATO; 41% believed it should be high.[77] Thus, 73% of Canadians actively supported Canada's role in NATO. When the Kosovo crisis was heating up in 1998, 67% of Canadians believed that NATO was very relevant in the new security environment; only 35% considered it to be an outdated organization that was not able to cope with the new geopolitical realities of the post–Cold War era.[78] In the wake of the Kosovo campaign, media commentators tried to sell the war as the "right thing to do."[79] Nearly 80% of Canadians supported the rationale of the government and believed that NATO air strikes were sufficiently justified; 57% were also in favour of sending ground troops. As many as 57% of Canadians also supported the decision to send armed forces into Kosovo. The total support among Canadians for NATO's actions in Kosovo was close to 80%.[80] Such strong support was echoed in the House of Commons, where Parliament expressed "its profound dismay and sorrow concerning the atrocities being suffered by the civilian population in Kosovo and ... [call] on the Government of

---

76 Edward Greenspon, "How We'd Spend Our Federal Surplus," *Globe and Mail*, 14 February 1998.

77 Department of National Defence, "Les Canadiens et la défense: les Canadiens appuient les FC au Kosovo," news release, June 1999.

78 The numbers are rounded up. See the Compass/Southam/IISS survey quoted in Martin and Fortmann 2001, 45, n. 11. This number was almost identical to the official numbers provided by the government, which stated that support for NATO membership among Canadians was somewhere between 60% and 70%; see Canadian International Development Agency 1995, 12.

79 Indeed, all of Canada's major newspapers, including the *Globe and Mail*, the *National Post*, and *La Presse*, as well as all political parties, supported Canada's active participation in this humanitarian intervention.

80 Both numbers were taken from a poll for the *National Post*, 11 April 1999, 1, quoted in Martin and Fortmann 2001, 50.

the Federal Republic of Yugoslavia and the parties involved in this inhumane confrontation to put down arms immediately and start negotiating a solution."[81] However, these polls by no means infer that the Kosovo campaign was without its critics.[82]

Conclusion

To sum up, calculating the absolute force share of allies participating in an operation excludes consideration of relative force share, a contextual perspective that provides much deeper analytical insights into determining distributive justice among participating allies. The findings set out in this chapter are consistent with those of chapter 4, and they demonstrate that, in relative terms, Canada shouldered a significant and adequate burden of UN crisis management and exceeded the expectations of collective action theorists. Canada was not an Atlantic free rider, nor did it play free-riding politics; in fact, it can be considered a major rather than a second-tier power.

The premise of this chapter was slightly different from that of chapter 4 in that it showed how the Dayton Accords transferred responsibility for international crisis management from the UN to NATO. However, the nature and extent of Canadian burdens did not change; second-tier power Canada maintained its military commitments to NATO's crisis-management operations in the Balkans. It stepped up to the plate when NATO called and maintained its troops, logistics, and resources in Europe even as the fiscal situation at home was dire. Moreover, the government's policy preferences for military engagements in the Balkans in the 1990s reveal a self-imposed normative predisposition towards an external responsibility, a conscious commitment to upholding milieu goals, such as the promotion of international economic, social, and political conditions.

It is evident from the archival material available on the IFOR, SFOR, and KFOR missions (including Operation ALLIED FORCE) that

---

81 Canada, Parliament, House of Commons, *Debates*, 8583.

82 For a detailed discussion, see Martin and Brawley 2001. A different group of critics charged that the objective of the alliance should not be achieved through air campaigns only. For details, see Cooper 2001, 84. For a similar view comparing the air campaign during the Gulf War 1990-1, OP Deliberate Force (1995), and OP Allied Force (1999), see Forage 2002.

Canada's preference for armed intervention in the Balkans was consistent throughout the 1990s and based on the normative values of defending the NATO community as well as enforcing basic human and humanitarian rights, including the security of humans. Taken together, this provided the context in which Canadian burden-sharing practices took place. Put another way, Canada carried an unexpectedly large share of the UN's burden in the Balkans, and it upheld that level of commitment as part of NATO. Measured against its relative capability to send troops on international peace operations, Canada was the fifth-largest force-contributing ally to IFOR (out of 16 NATO states), the third largest to SFOR (out of 19), and fourth largest to KFOR (out of 19). Moreover, Canada was the eighth-largest contributor to Operation ALLIED FORCE in terms of numbers of aircraft supplied (out of 19 NATO states) and flew the sixth-largest number of sorties in that operation. Of all 19 NATO allies, Canada was the third-largest contributor to the combination of Operation ALLIED FORCE, Operation JOINT GUARDIAN, and general humanitarian assistance provided in 1999. Taking these figures into consideration as well as the context of the action itself, Canada cannot be judged a free rider.

PART III

Civilian Burdens

6 The NATO of Canada's Dreams: Practising Civilian Burden Sharing, Part I

The East is turning to the West. Our political approach of co-operation instead of confrontation, as set out in the Harmel Report, is gaining increasing acceptance. Our ideas are on the advance. Democracy, human rights, pluralism. You need to read Gorbachev's speech to the United Nations to see how far concepts which we have fostered for two decades have penetrated the Soviet vocabulary. Our initiatives are determining the course of political events.[1]

To answer the question I posed at the outset, this is an Alliance for a vision of peace, security and prosperity.[2]

Introduction

With the enactment of *glasnost* and *perestroika* in May 1988, Russian President Mikhail Gorbachev put his country on a path of rapprochement with the West. The alliance, taken by surprise by the sudden geopolitical revolutions in Europe, slowly recognized the extent of these new policies and responded in kind by extending a "hand of friendship."[3] This gesture of sociability and kindness was a German-Canadian initiative based on ideas put forward by the foreign ministers of those

---

1 Manfred Wörner, "Stability in Europe – NATO's Way Forward" (address to the Annual Meeting of the World Economics Forum, Davos, Switzerland, 1 February 1989, n.p.).
2 Manfred Wörner, "NATO and a New European Order" (address to the Italian Senate, Rome, 19 April 1990, n.p.).
3 McDougall et al. 1992, 4.

two countries, Hans Dietrich Genscher and Joe Clark,[4] who noted that "we welcome the decision of the London Summit to propose a joint declaration between the member states of NATO and the Warsaw Treaty Organization (WTO), extending the hand of friendship. We also support the invitation to President Gorbachev to address the North Atlantic Council, and welcome the establishment of regular diplomatic liaison between NATO and the embassies of WTO member states in Brussels, including the briefing of these embassies after major NATO meetings."[5]

In more general terms, the events surrounding the fall of the Berlin Wall put in motion tremendous geopolitical transformations that affected not only individual states, but also European security institutions like NATO and the EU, and thus their practices. The alliance embraced the new friendships as well as the political and economic instability that resulted from the breakup of the Warsaw Pact and the lack of governance structures to manage these new circumstances. The allies were fully aware of the significant socio-economic and political difficulties that societies from CEE were confronted with. In a telephone call to US President George H.W. Bush, Helmut Kohl, the German chancellor at the time, stressed the urgency of the socio-economic situation of the former Warsaw Pact. "The problems [Gorbachev] faces are enormous – nationalities, the food supply situation – and I do not see a light at the end of the tunnel yet."[6] Indeed, the Soviet Union and the other former members of the Warsaw Pact faced a significant economic downturn in the early 1990s.[7] A report by NATO's Political Committee concluded that Russia's economic growth was shrinking at the rate of 1.5% per year.[8] Its total budget deficit had reached some $160 billion, or 9% of its gross national product,[9] and its share of world trade had

---

4 Ibid.

5 Clark 1990.

6 Helmut Kohl, "Memorandum 1180 of Telephone Call from Helmut Kohl to President Bush" (Washington, DC, 13 February 1990), 1.

7 The possibility of sending $20 billion in emergency aid was discussed at the G7 Summit in Houston, Texas, in 1990; see Paul Koring, "Alliance Sings Seductive Song 'Come to NATO,' U.S. President Croons to His Soviet Counterpart," *Globe and Mail*, 1990, A8.

8 Manfred Wörner, "Address Given at the 35th Annual Session of the North Atlantic Assembly" (Rome, 9 October 1989).

9 Ibid.

dwindled to 4%, so low that its supply of basic foodstuffs had dropped to a minimum.

Other CEE countries were equally affected, particularly Poland. In another conversation with the US president, Kohl promised, "I will do all I can to support the new [Polish] government, especially in the economic area. With the EC, I intend to give assistance in human resources. This seems to be the problem, if I may put it bluntly: there is a lot of good will and many good ideas, but the Poles do not know how to put them into practice."[10] In a bilateral meeting between Germany and Poland, Kohl indirectly reiterated this point and urged Polish officials to introduce a market-oriented economy. He also lobbied his colleagues from other European capitals to make more humanitarian and development assistance available.[11] When the promised help did not arrive, Kohl grumbled to his US counterpart about his EU colleagues, "My feeling is that our Western friends and partners should be doing more. There is a difference between words and deeds."[12]

While these conversations took place in private, Kohl's views were widely shared among the allies. NATO Secretary General Manfred Wörner remarked that "the East is turning to the West for help, inspiration and expertise. We cannot sit passively on the sidelines and watch a human tragedy unfold. It is our humanitarian duty to help all peoples who aspire to our values."[13] Undeniably, the prevalent perception among the NATO allies was that the future security of CEE depended on economic development as well as a reliable security framework and governance institutions. This assessment and the subsequent decisions by individual member states to provide assistance to CEE were consistent with the theoretical discussions on the liberal peace paradigm, discussed in chapter 3. The existing security community (NATO) chose not only to maintain and expand that community but also to actively export its value and belief systems to the new

---

10 Helmut Kohl, "Memorandum 8520 of Telephone Call from Helmut Kohl to President Bush" (Washington, DC, 23 October 1989), 1–2.

11 See, e.g., Hacke 1997, 364–7; Sloan 2005, 145–80. The most explicit analysis is provided in Baker and DeFrank 1995, 231.

12 Helmut Kohl, "Memorandum 8520 of Telephone Call from Helmut Kohl to President Bush," 2.

13 Manfred Wörner, "The Future of the Alliance" (speech at Istanbul University, Istanbul, 18 September 1989).

regions of CEE based on its collective ideational, political, economic, and institutional preferences.[14]

For the alliance, it was a mutually constitutive process of international socialization,[15] and the promising and evolving CEE democracies responded by showing their willingness to learn the norms of liberal democracy,[16] including respect for human and humanitarian rights and security, democracy, the rule of law, and freedom. Following liberal IR theory, in the absence of such communal interests, neither NATO nor the CEE states would have engaged in this outreach process. For NATO, this strategy was an easy sell. Above all, the democratization of states on NATO's eastern border enhanced the security needs of existing members (e.g., Germany). It also helped export NATO's normative predispositions and practices of governance to evolving democracies, and this in turn was expected to produce stable relations and order in the new Europe.

It is against this backdrop that this chapter examines NATO's early transformation from an "old" to a "new" alliance. It traces the developments that led to the social actions of civilian burden sharing, such as building internal outreach institutions. Transformation can be conceived as a practice of burden sharing because it was the NATO member states that developed the new ontological perspectives on European security and incorporated them into their national security policies. The chapter will not set out a history of all events[17] or account for all developments, but it will examine the preference formations of second-tier power Canada to share collective civilian burdens in the aftermath of the transformation process. These transformations began with NATO's pivotal Turnberry Meeting (7–8 June 1990) and reached their first peak when the alliance invited the Czech Republic, Hungary, and Poland to join it in 1999.

We will begin with a brief synopsis of the exogenous forces at play after the fall of the Berlin Wall, including the Canadian government's discourses and preferences for how to respond to and manage these

---

14 The literature examining this aspect of NATO transformation is extensive; see, e.g., Schimmelpfennig 2003.

15 For one of the first works on the role of international organizations in socialization processes, see Johnston 2001.

16 See, e.g., Gheciu 2005b.

17 This has been done elsewhere; see, e.g., Asmus 2002, 2003; Asmus, Kugler, and Larrabee 1993; Stanley R. Sloan 2002, 2005.

forces. This is followed by a brief discussion of the concepts of inter-locking institutions and cooperative security; the Turnberry sum-mit; the creation of new security regimes such as the North Atlantic Cooperation Council, the Partnership for Peace program, and the Euro-Atlantic Partnership Council; and the enlargement of NATO.

The "New" NATO?

After the fall of the Berlin Wall, NATO Secretary General Wörner[18] took the historic opportunity to unilaterally prescribe new roles and respon-sibilities for the alliance. His ideas for a political NATO – which essen-tially recommended cooperation with rather than containment of the East – injected new life into an aging Euro-Atlantic security institution. In many ways, these ideas were not novel or groundbreaking, but rath-er a repackaging of the 1967 Harmel Report. Wörner charged that this was the time for NATO not to reduce its mandate but rather to push itself to the next level by taking on new commitments and responsi-bilities in European security governance. This would include actively shaping the insecurities unfolding in CEE and engaging in crisis-management operations inside and outside NATO territory. As a result, at a meeting of NATO foreign ministers in June 1992, the alliance agreed to assume peacekeeping operations on a case-by-case basis and under the auspices of the Conference on Security and Co-operation in Europe (CSCE).[19] In a speech in Brussels, Wörner noted,

> I am experiencing the fortieth anniversary of NATO rather like the man-
> ager of a successful football team which has just won the league title. His
> initial instinct is to celebrate the season's glories. But instead his mind is
> inevitably on the team's promotion to the higher division. How will the
> team cope with the new, more demanding environment where not only

18 He was probably one of the most visionary secretaries general NATO has ever had;
   see Hendrickson 2006. This view was also expressed by a senior NATO official in
   interviews by the author, NATO Headquarters, Brussels, 9 May 2007. See also Kay
   1998, 1, 60–74.
19 The CSCE was established in 1973 and became the OSCE on 1 January 1995. It has
   a formal Secretariat, Senior Council, Parliamentary Assembly, Conflict Prevention
   Centre, and Office for Free Elections. Since the Lisbon Declaration was published in
   1996, it has affirmed the universal and indivisible nature of security on the European
   continent.

the rewards, but also the challenges, are so much greater? Such is life. The more successful we are, the more new tasks we find ourselves taking on.[20]

This new role of the alliance as a crisis-management institution was identified at its Turnberry Meeting in June 1990, which was a prelude to the London Summit taking place a month later. NATO's political leadership officially adopted the "hand of friendship"[21] idea and settled on a carefully drafted statement, noting, "If we want to be able to meet the challenge of change, we have to change ourselves. We are equipping the Alliance for its role as a partner in stability and progress."[22] It was also at Turnberry that NATO first discussed cooperation and dialogue as new elements of its political posture.[23] The Heads of State and Government noted that

> the Alliance has done much to bring about the new Europe. ... We need to keep standing together, to extend the long peace we have enjoyed these past four decades. Yet our Alliance must be even more an agent of change. It can help build the structures of a more united continent, supporting security and stability with the strength of our shared faith in democracy, the rights of the individual, and the peaceful resolution of disputes.[24]

This vision was based on the assumption, as a Canadian government official interpreted them, that "economic development is critical to democratic development, which is essential for stability."[25] This understanding was echoed at the highest political level. Deputy Minister of Foreign Affairs Gordon Smith maintained that "NATO, while a

---

20 Manfred Wörner, "The Future Tasks of the Alliance" (speech to the Quadrangular Forum, Brussels, 1 April 1989).

21 Gilbert Lewthwaite, "NATO Welcomes Warsaw Pact Security Plan," *Ottawa Citizen*, 9 June 1990, A10.

22 Manfred Wörner, "Opening Remarks at the Ministerial Meeting of the North Atlantic Council" (Turnberry, 7–8 June 1990).

23 Ibid.

24 Heads of State and Government Participating in the Meeting of the North Atlantic Council, "London Declaration on a Transformed North Atlantic Alliance," London, 5–6 July 1990.

25 Michael Chesson, "Canada-European Union Bulletin: Article on Canada and NATO, fax to Jacques Paquette, IDS, DFAIT, 5 July 1994, 2, retrieved under the Access to Information Act, 10 April 2007, A-3, File No. 3947-01.

common security organization, has long recognized that its strength depended on the health of the economies of its member states."[26]

Given the diffusion of its Cold War roles, responsibilities, and functions as a security institution in Europe, and with the turn of the security tide in Europe, it was justifiable to question NATO's raison d'être.[27] Indeed, the prevalence of the principle of collective defence in Europe was no longer naturally assured at the end of the Cold War. NATO's principal threat had disappeared, and each member state had, theoretically, the option of renouncing its membership. Moreover, one might argue that NATO had fulfilled its primary objective, which was, in the words of Lord Ismay, "to keep the Russians out, the Germans down and the Americans in."[28] However, in spite of the geopolitical turmoil and insecurity that 1989 had brought, the alliance stood together.[29] None of its constituent parts renounced their membership in 1989 or at any time after that. This endorsement gave the institution a strong backbone for the future.

For Canada, withdrawal from NATO was never an option, even though some critics had accused the government of contemplating it when it closed Canada's two forward operating bases in Germany.[30] On the contrary, the government conveyed to its allies in private that its NATO commitments were to be understood in the larger context of European security and prosperity rather than in a narrow military sense – that is, Article 5. Indeed, in 1991, government officials stated that "as a result of this change in CEE there has been an extraordinary realignment of political and economic interests. Countries such as Czechoslovakia, Hungary and Poland are looking to the European

---

26 Gordon Smith, "Managing EU-NATO Relations" (address to the 36th IISS Annual Conference, Vancouver, 8–11 September 1994, 1, retrieved under the Access to Information Act, 10 April 2007, A-3, File No. 3947-01).

27 One may even go so far as to argue that it has been the victim of its own success. Many books have been written about the question of the existence of NATO after the end of the Cold War; see, e.g., Carpenter 1995; Carpenter and Conry 2001; Cohen, Moens, and Sens 2003; Eyal 1997; Gordon 1997.

28 One might also add "the French happy." Lord Ismay was the first secretary general of NATO, 1949–57.

29 Some analysts had suggested that since its objective in 1949 was to develop a preponderant power against an expansionist and power-hungry Soviet Union, now that it had made friends with its former enemy, it no longer had a raison d'être; see Mearsheimer 1990, 1994-95.

30 Bland and Maloney 2004, 165.

Community, North America and Japan as the locomotives to pull them toward a new era of democratic polity and economic prosperity."[31]

Canadian bureaucrats recommended to their political masters that Canada engage these states politically and use this newly gained political space to foster economic relations. Secretary of State for External Affairs Barbara McDougall noted, "Economic and social progress, as well as confirmation and consolidation of democratic processes, are essential for longer term peace and security in the CSCE region."[32] In other words, Ottawa's preference was to help stabilize the European continent politically and create a zone of peace that was prosperous and free from aggression and hostility. Canada's preferences were defined as "the survival of the nation state as a distinct entity; the maintenance of democracy and freedom; economic prosperity; and the physical safety of Canadians."[33] As McDougall explained in a speech to the Universal Speaker's Group in Toronto, "Commercial credits ... are a key element in our assistance because they induce and reward economic change, foster private sector relationships and have a number of multiplier effects – including the stimulation of direct trade with Canada."[34]

Officials probably did not realize this, but these policy preferences reflect a strong, yet unspoken endorsement of Schumpeterian (liberal) economic principles, while the policy of promoting democratic values to CEE can be seen as a means to an end – namely, to stop violent conflicts from evolving in Europe. In political terms, the policy preferences were informed by the principles of engagement and enlargement: political engagement while cultivating greater economic relations.[35] In her Toronto speech, McDougall recapped Canada's preferences.

Many Canadians probably do not recognize the innovative nature and magnitude of our assistance efforts to date, nor the leadership we have shown to other Western countries in the rationale and mechanisms for our assistance. ... Canada has provided and is providing assistance to Eastern

---

31 Ibid., 1.
32 Barbara McDougall, "Europe Needs New Security Framework," *Province* (Vancouver), 1991, 29.
33 Canada, Department of External Affairs 1991, 4.
34 Barbara McDougall, "Canada, NATO, and Eastern Europe: The Challenge" (speech to the Universal Speakers' Group, Toronto, 16 April 1992).
35 See, e.g., Keohane and Nye 1977; Slaughter 1997, 2004.

Europe worth about $4.5 billion through a creative mix of debt relief, balance of payments support, currency stabilization, commercial credits, technical assistance, humanitarian aid, and business incentives.[36]

To be sure, the Canadian government's preference for helping CEE states transform their governments, economies, and societies was not only good for peace and security in CEE; it would also benefit Canadian business at home at a time of an economic recession. This pursuit of gains was beneficial for those states that received them and those, like Canada, who exported them. The new and evolving markets in CEE held the prospect of new economic prosperity for Canadians.[37] This prosperity would contribute to order, stability, and cost-effectiveness at home and free up political energy and resources to address the more prevalent structural security issues in Europe.

NATO officials also recognized that those preferences were entirely reciprocal, as Secretary General Wörner noted in a speech in Brussels.

In its quest for growth, the East will need to import our values as much as our technology. It must also find ways to integrate its economies into the international trading system through participation in our Western economic and financial institutions. We will therefore have more influence over the domestic evolution of these societies than we have enjoyed over the past.[38]

Translated into IR theory language, what Wörner was referring to was consistent with one of the basic tenets of classical liberal IR theory: that democracies do not wage war against one another because the stakes for their interdependent economies, societies, and political networks are too high and too costly. In other words, liberal IR scholars would completely agree with the secretary general that helping

---

36 McDougall, "Canada, NATO, and Eastern Europe."
37 See, e.g., Canada, Department of External Affairs and International Trade 1990, 2. See also Regional Security Section (DFAIT), "NAC Visit: Briefing Material on CDN Approaches to Current NATO Issues," telex IDR-0576, Regional Security Section (DFAIT) to Canadian missions in London, Bonn, Paris, The Hague, Copenhagen, Oslo, Brussels, Lisbon, Madrid, Rome, Ankara, Athens, Warsaw, Prague, Budapest, and Washington, 30 October 1997, retrieved under the Access to Information Act, 10 April 2007, A-3, File No. 3947-01.
38 Manfred Wörner, "The Future Tasks of the Alliance," n.p.

transform CEE states into prosperous and stable democracies would bring a lasting peace to Europe.

This policy of extending the zone of peace – expanding the Western zone to the East while assuming that the East wished to seek a closer partnership with the West – was easy to sell to domestic constituents in Canada, especially at a time of redeeming peace dividends and slashing federal budgets. Hence, NATO's policy of engagement and enlargement was a relatively inexpensive (political and fiscal) option for Canadian foreign policymakers to pursue.

This new political, social, and cultural affinity with Europe, as Kim Nossal noted, did not suddenly occur when the Cold War ended. It has been embedded in Canada's self-perception and political practice since the 1770s.[39] Canada has long shared ties with CEE in terms of family, nationality, commercial interests, and political-cultural interdependence. This Euro-centric predisposition did not abruptly change at the end of the Cold War, but remained active in spite of Canada's increasingly multicultural character and immigration flows from Asia. For example, in the 1970s, 82% of the population was of European decent (mostly British, French, German, and Italian), but even in 1991, only half this number, 41% of all immigrants, came from Europe.[40] These numbers disprove the perception that new immigrants to Canada have diluted the country's image and perception as a European nation. As the authors of the study noted, "The hypothesis that immigration affected the outlook of the Canadian public on Europe as a focus of foreign policy may also be intuitively attractive, but it does not seem to stand up under closer scrutiny."[41]

Particularly among the younger generation of immigrants, support for Canada's involvement in European security was significant. Indeed, they were more likely to support Canada's military engagements in the Balkans than any other segment of Canadian society.[42] In fact, in light of the pre-eminence of the domestic environment in the early 1990s, none of Canada's ethnic minorities opposed Canada's Eurocentric foreign policy – or the enlargement of NATO into CEE, for that matter.

---

39 Nossal 1992.
40 Buteux, Fortmann, and Martin 1996, 155–6.
41 Ibid., 159.
42 Ibid.

Based on this historically derived interpretation and responsibility as well as its culturally inclined disposition, the government decided to preserve its foreign policy preferences in the new and evolving Europe. It was Canada's secretary of state for external affairs, Joe Clark, who initially outlined these interests by stating that

> Canadian interests in Europe are real, contemporary and compelling. Our primary interest is peace. Two world wars this century have left thousands of Canadian graves in Europe, teaching us that security at home has no meaning without security in Europe. Politically, the values that have triumphed in Europe are our values too.[43]

An internal government report provided a more detailed and precise account of Canada's foreign policy preferences in the new NATO:

> respect for and defence of sovereignty; military defence; peaceful resolution of conflicts; arms control and disarmament; effective international institutions; stability in the international trade and financial systems; economic competitiveness; growth of free market principles; economic growth in developing countries; expansion of Canada's international trade; orderly procedures for the international movement of persons (immigrants, refugees); democratic development and respect for human rights; environmental protection; detection and prevention of crime, including narcotics trafficking; prevention of terrorist activities; respect for international law; protection of marine resources.[44]

It is against this backdrop that Canada argued that "the constancy of our commitment was firm, as attested to by our contributions to NATO, the OSCE, and to UN peacekeeping within the European continent."[45] Above all, those preferences provided the rationale for Canada's multidimensional contributions to the maintenance of stability and order in times of fundamental socio-political change in Europe. In so doing, it helped maintain and transform a transatlantic security community,[46]

---

43 Clark 1990, n.p.
44 Canada 1991, 11.
45 Ibid., 15. The military dimension has been discussed in the previous two chapters.
46 Ross 1998–99, 120.

which (according to liberal IR theorists) is the foremost duty of any state in a given community.

At the same time that this geopolitical euphoria was unfolding, Canada reminded its citizens of the threat of transatlantic complacency, noting that a healthy relationship with the new Europe required careful attention and the commitment of all NATO member states. Secretary of State for External Affairs Joe Clark wrote,

> Nostalgia is not a basis for policy. Our interests in Europe are real, contemporary and compelling. ... Powerful new economic and political forces are at work, forces over which Canada has limited influence. A European role will not be bestowed upon us because we decide it is in our interest. It must be earned. That requires imagination and realism and hard work.[47]

This reminder is consistent with the liberal IR research paradigm that complacency threatens to overcome peaceful security communities.

Interlocking Institutions and the Spirit of Democratic Peace in Europe

Another concept used in the new NATO was that of *interlocking institutions*, and it echoed the liberal ontological predispositions of international politics. Classical liberal theorists like Immanuel Kant held that international institutions and "cosmopolitan international law" were two key ingredients of a perpetual peace. Modern liberal IR theorists, especially neo-liberals, have used this insight in a more rigorous and mostly positivist research program to "test" this hypothesis, and they have found that international organizations can facilitate cooperation among states by reducing transaction costs and increasing the flow of information among their members.[48]

If there were no such institutions to enforce commonly held rules, norms, and values and ensure international order, the greatest danger to NATO and thus Canada would be a renationalization of European

---

47 Canada, Department of External Affairs and International Trade 1990, 2.

48 This is a shortened version of a much more extensive theoretical account of neo-liberal IR theory; for an elaboration of this argument, see, e.g., Keohane, 1988, 1989a; Keohane and Nye, 1977.

societies,[49] a situation that would heat up the new political environment.[50] Against such prospects, strengthening existing international institutions was a logical and viable option for Canadian policymakers; they recognized Canada's power status in international politics, which did not allow it as a second-tier power to have a large military capability or project its preferences unilaterally upon other states. Therefore, Canada depended on international institutions and also need to practise multilateralism within them.[51]

From the outset, the CSCE rather than NATO seemed to be the "natural fit" as the organization responsible for managing the evolving insecurities in CEE, especially in the area of arms control, and addressing minority issues and questions of territorial borders. Its large membership of more than 34 European, North American, and Asian countries gave it broad international legitimacy. Canada had set up an intergovernmental security task force to discuss the geopolitical challenges resulting from the fall of the Berlin Wall, and it strongly endorsed this view. "NATO may gradually become less central to European security. The new type of conflict may increasingly be managed within the CSCE or a strictly European context. NATO may become the locus for the management of whatever strategic threats remain."[52]

This suggests that Canada viewed the CSCE as a rising and complementary institution to NATO and as a "true instrument of cooperative security, one that would supplement deterrence with assurance."[53] Secretary of State for External Affairs Barbara McDougall put the preference this way: "Cooperative security is to be constructed by putting into place many different international instruments and institutions which, although they function separately, contribute to overall security."[54]

---

49 Keohane 1989a, 5.
50 Karkoszka 1997, 2.
51 For a discussion of the meaning of *multilateralism*, see Keohane 1990; Martin 1992, 1993; Ruggie 1993b.
52 Task Force on Canadian Security Policy (IFBS), *Europe and Canadian Security*, retrieved under the Access to Information Act, 10 April 2007, A-3, File No. 3947-01, 3.
53 Clark 1990, n.p.
54 McDougall 1992a, 222–5. On another occasion, she wrote (see "Europe Needs New Security Framework"), "An enhanced CSCE is one of the key elements of Canada's approach to the 'new Europe.'"

The concept of *cooperative security* was based on the assumption that institutionalized regulative mechanisms would be able to mitigate the uncertainties that resulted, for example, from border disputes or other exogenous threats and that former adversaries would recognize the virtue of discussing divergent interests and problems without using threats.[55] It was designed as a preventative concept, one based on the principles of dialogue and outreach, to address security concerns before they developed into violent trans-border conflicts.[56] It was also based on the recognition that in the so-called new Europe, no single organization or country could guarantee European security. In short, it denoted cooperation rather than conflict or confrontation. Canada's preference for CSCE had one other aspect: with NATO in possible decline, the CSCE would give Canada the best possible and continuous access to Europe.[57]

A network of interlocking institutions and relationships, neither competitive nor mutually exclusive but functionalist in that they were assigned a specific task rather than a range of tasks, constituted a comprehensive and logical framework in which the alliance could operate.[58] In 1994, Canada's diplomats in Brussels noted, "The concept of mutually reinforcing institutions continues to have validity."[59] In

---

55 Stares and Steinbruner 1992, 222–5. The Canadian government was one of the architects of the cooperative security concept. In a report, the government praised itself. "In the absence of true common security, a comprehensive, flexible and evolutionary 'cooperative security' concept and approaches appear more realistic. Such a 'cooperative security' concept would envisage countries (including, as in the European instance, former adversaries) joining voluntarily in a variety of institutions, organizations and agreements which, taken together, cover a variety of issues that impinge on security, such as arms control, trade, the environment and human rights" (Canada, Department of External Affairs 1991, 8).

56 For a larger discussion, see Gottfried 1989; Carter, Perry, and Steinbruner 1992; Stares and Steinbruner 1992; de Nooy 1996; NATO Defence College 1997.

57 John Hay, "Who Will Talk Sense into the U.S. Government If NATO Enters Semi-Retirement?" *Ottawa Citizen*, 9 July 1990, A7.

58 North Atlantic Council, Meeting in Ministerial Session, "Partnership with the Countries of Central and Eastern Europe," statement issued in Copenhagen, 6–7 June, 1991. However, the concept failed in Yugoslavia, where "interlocking" resulted in institutional bickering.

59 See, e.g., Canadian Joint Delegation to NATO, "APAG (Atlantic Policy Advisory Group) MTG with Cooperation Partners: European Security in Transition," telex YBGR 1092 to EXTOTT IDS (International Security and Defence Relations Divisions, DFAIT), 5 May 1994, 3, retrieved under the Access to Information Act, 10 April 2007, A-3, File No. 3947-01.

addition, a network of institutions would function as an early warning mechanism, identifying emerging conflicts and instabilities and enabling countries to respond to them.[60]

However, the lack of enforcement capabilities that would give the CSCE the powers and tools to govern effectively turned out to be its primary deficiency.[61] And for a second-tier power like Canada, the proliferation of international organizations that aspired to manage European security issues would have sharply increased the burden on its national resources. Paying membership dues for more organizations than necessary would be not only redundant but also economically imprudent at a time of depleted budgets at home. Recall that in 1992–93, Canada's federal deficit had reached $41 billion ($65.8 billion for the federal and provincial governments combined).[62] At the same time, its defence spending had shrunk from $12 billion in 1993–94 to $9.2 billion in 1998–99.[63] This represented a reduction of nearly 23% in nominal terms and more than 30% in purchasing power.[64] The proportion of the defence budget allocated to capital investments had fallen to 20% and for new equipment to 15%.

To address these deficits, the government demanded fiscal austerity from its employees and institutions, and it cut back on social programs and benefits. Finding additional money to send to yet another security institution in Europe was simply not feasible or politically astute. As a result, it made sense for Ottawa to buttress traditional and already functioning security institutions like NATO. Moreover, the CSCE was a

---

60 It is not the objective of this book to describe the nature or structure of this network, so it does not offer a network analysis approach of European security governance.

61 This is an interesting phenomenon for future research projects. Classical liberal IR theory and liberal institutionalism in particular hold that international institutions would facilitate cooperation rather than conflict by improving flows of information. However, these theorists were silent on explaining why one international institution was preferred over another based on the argument that it held weak enforcement tools to effectively govern.

62 For a detailed list of federal and provincial deficits, see Courchene 2002. It is worth pointing out that there were virtually no disagreements among scholars or experts about the existence of the recession.

63 To be fair, membership dues were taken not only from the DND budget but also from DFAIT.

64 Department of Defence, "CDA's Contribution to NATO," telex LHBF 2038 to D NATO POL, 17 December 1997, 3, retrieved under the Access to Information Act, 10 April 2007, A-3, File No. 3947-01.

"talking shop"[65] – a forum where decisions regarding security and defence issues in Europe were made without being legally binding or enforced. This assessment was widely shared by government officials, who expressed their reservations more diplomatically.

> The CSCE has lacked the institutional framework now required for effective and ongoing cooperation and confidence-building. It must therefore develop the tools to perform those tasks. Canada believes that continuing political direction from the highest level is required on a regular basis.[66]

Unlike the membership of NATO, CSCE members did not share a common value or belief system; they were not a close political community that could act collectively. The CSCE thus remained a forum for states to play political games and further their national interests.[67] There was also the problem of Russia. Officials pointed out diplomatically that while the Russian government had attempted to strengthen the CSCE in 1994, it was increasingly evident that its primary goal was to place the CSCE at the top of the hierarchy of European security institutions as a key element of a pan-European security system that would confer on the major powers (including Russia) a special responsibility for governing global security.[68]

Given all of these deficiencies of the CSCE, Canada placed its political emphasis on NATO as the organization that was in the best position to manage the geopolitical instability in CEE.[69] As the Canadian delegation to NATO reminded its political masters in Ottawa, the alliance also uniquely combined military assets and effectiveness that distinguished it from other institutions. And it remained essential for managing European insecurity, particularly for

> providing stability and security in a world where there are new security challenges; helping to manage crisis, under a UN/CSCE mandate; avoiding any re-nationalization of defence policies, fragmentation or a return

---

65 See, e.g., Letourneau and Hebert 1999, 114.
66 Clark 1990, n.p.
67 Gheciu 2008.
68 See Meeting of the Atlantic Policy Advisory Group, 4–8 September 1994, retrieved under the Access to Information Act, 10 April 2007, A-3, File No. 3947-01.
69 See, e.g., Canadian Joint Delegation to NATO, "APAG MTG with Cooperation Partners," 3.

to old power politics and opposing alliances in Europe; maintaining the trans-Atlantic link; increasing cooperation with its partners and opening the way for new members; helping control conventional weapons and international extremism/terrorism; helping to ensure effective implementation of and full compliance with arms control obligations ... ; providing the military instruments needed to support successful diplomatic efforts to resolve crisis; serving as a forum to harmonize policies among allies; helping in collective crisis management and assisting global efforts to protect security.[70]

Canadian diplomatic officials also maintained that in order to strengthen NATO, Canada should support the suggestion to create the European Security and Defence Identity (ESDI) inside NATO as well as the Western European Union (WEU).[71] While ESDI was of limited relevance to Canada, being excluded from any WEU-led operation[72] under the NATO framework would severely impinge on Canadian interests and should be rejected.[73] Instead, Canada preferred to bind the WEU somehow into the NATO framework.

London Summit

The London Summit (5–6 July 1990) officially recognized the end of the political division in Europe, and Soviet President Mikhail Gorbachev was invited to address the North Atlantic Council (NAC).[74] The Soviet Union and its satellite states were no longer listed as NATO's foremost

---

70 Canadian Joint Delegation to NATO, "APAG MTG with Cooperation Partners," 16.
71 DG POL OPS noted in "European Command Arrangements," fax to Canadian Joint Delegation to NATO, 29 January 1997, retrieved under the Access to Information Act, 10 April 2007, A-3, File No. 3947-01, "This is consistent with our overall position that while ESDI is a matter for the Europeans to implement themselves, we do not wish to see Canadian interests adversely affected by decisions taken in ESDI deliberations." It went on: "ESDI is of limited relevance to us ... and is not [an organization] in which Canada can or should become deeply engaged." Thus, Ottawa instructed Canadian officials to quash any expectations by ESDI of Canadian financing. For a good discussion of ESDI and the WEU, see, e.g., Græger 1999; Hoffmann 1992; NATO Defence College 1997; Schürr 2003.
72 The WEU was the military arm of the EU.
73 DG POL OPS, "European Command Arrangements."
74 The NAC is the highest political decision-making body of the alliance.

enemy.[75] This readjusted threat perception, however, was not to be mistaken for a lack of concern about the security vacuum that was created by the withdrawal of the Soviet Union from CEE. Canadian diplomatic officials were at the forefront of the negotiations to manage this vacuum, reminding their allies of Canada's preference that NATO's Article 5 obligations should remain strong and that the alliance should continue to uphold its nuclear force shield for deterrence purposes.[76]

The London Summit also endorsed a new approach for NATO's conventional forces: they should have greater flexibility, adaptability, and mobility and should establish multinational rapid reaction forces.[77] This decision to have fewer conventional but more flexible forces distilled down to the member states, who were asked to endorse this new force posture. Member states would need to make extensive reforms in their force postures, doctrines, and strategic planning and agree to take on new missions, such as peacekeeping and crisis management.[78] An internal Canadian government report had concluded months before that "new European security arrangements are likely to involve an increased attention to peacekeeping, peace monitoring and verification functions. Canada should be ready to reconfigure some Canadian Forces for such duties."[79] Indeed, NATO's new direction dovetailed with Canada's historical preference for international peace and crisis-management operations.

The military leadership at National Defence Headquarters in Ottawa – given the dire fiscal situation – was receptive to the force adaptations demanded by NATO. It responded that the CF were eager to develop

---

75 It also invited the Soviet Union, Bulgaria, Hungary, Poland, and Romania to establish regular diplomatic liaison offices at NATO Headquarters.

76 The allies did, however, agree to cut their sub-strategic nuclear weapons up to 80% to acknowledge the reduced threat levels.

77 This fact is highlighted in many NATO declarations; see, e.g., Defense Planning Committee and Nuclear Planning Group, "Final Communiqué," Brussels, 28–29 May 1991, art. 8; London Summit Declaration, 5–6 July 1990; see also Maccloskey 1967; Moskos, Williams, and Segal 2000b.

78 For example, NATO agreed to get rid of its nuclear-tipped artillery shells in Europe in return for a reciprocal arrangement by the Soviet Union, and member states pledged to use nuclear weapons only as a last resort to reassure the Soviet Union that NATO did not pose a threat.

79 Task Force on Canadian Security Policy (IFBS), *Europe and Canadian Security*, 10.

"general-purpose combat capable armed forces, ... ready to deploy anywhere in the world in defence of Canada's interests."[80] Thus, Canada fully supported the proposed high-readiness force structures and promised to implement them at home. Unlike most of its European allies, it understood that a high-intensity combat capability was essential if, as a second-tier power, it wanted to remain interoperable with its American and Western European allies "over serious military threats to the allies' common security interests."[81] Indeed, as a group of analysts attested, Canada was one of the first NATO member states to successfully transform its armed forces from a traditional to a postmodern military. "Among the Anglo-American nations ... Canada has probably moved earliest and farthest from a traditional military model. The armed forces themselves have been increasingly democratized, liberalized, and civilianized."[82]

At the NATO level, however, military transformation could not be effective without reforming the political organization and structures that governed its armed forces, including decision-making procedures, and streamlining the command and control infrastructure. These restructuring efforts, following Canada's lead, were to be motivated by the principles of military effectiveness and economies of scale.[83]

In sum, the London Summit laid the groundwork for an extensive transformation within NATO while reassuring partner countries[84] that it would remain a defensive alliance with no offensive intentions. On this latter point, the US secretary of defence raised the concern that the

---

80 de Chastelain 1992, 8.

81 Ross 1995, 724–5.

82 Moskos, Williams, and Segal 2000a, 9.

83 This is a point made by government officials in various internal government documents throughout the 1990s; see, e.g., Regional Security Section (IDR), DFAIT, "NATO Command Structure: Bilateral Fallout," telex YBGR 9447 to Canadian Joint Delegation to NATO, 23 December 1996, 1, retrieved under the Access to Information Act, 10 April 2007, A-3, File No. 3947-01; DG POL OPS, "Road to Madrid: Military Guidance."

84 At the time (1990), NATO consisted of 16 countries (Belgium, Canada, Denmark, France, Germany, Greece, Iceland, Italy, Luxembourg, Netherlands, Norway, Portugal, Spain, Turkey, United Kingdom, and United States). States from CEE who showed either an interest in working with NATO or intentions of applying for membership were considered partners. Today, countries as far afield as Australia, New Zealand, Japan, and others are NATO partner countries.

Soviets were still sending about $6 billion to Cuba every year and that Soviet missiles continued to be aimed at America.[85]

Following the London Declaration, Secretary General Wörner visited Moscow (13 to 17 July 1990). This official visit of the highest-ranking official of the Western military alliance to the headquarters of its former enemy was a significant symbolic gesture. It was indicative of the new political NATO and the pivotal role of the secretary general in it.[86] Wörner praised the new role of the alliance and the symbolic meaning of extending friendship to states from CEE by remarking that "the political role and function of NATO is increasing in importance. Something that was occasionally lost sight of during the Cold War is acknowledged again: NATO is a political Alliance, a community of the destinies and values of the free world."[87] He was referring to Article 2 of the Washington Treaty.

Article 2

The new political character of NATO was by no means a novelty for the alliance – or Canada. Article 2, the so-called Canadian article, states,

> The Parties will contribute toward the further development of peaceful and friendly international relations by strengthening their free institutions, by bringing about a better understanding of the principles upon which these institutions are founded, and by promoting conditions of stability and well-being. They will seek to eliminate conflict in their international economic policies and will encourage economic collaboration between any or all of them.[88]

In 1949, Canada had lobbied NATO's founding members to include this explicitly political reference in the treaty[89] because it recognized that it was a politically and economically weaker member and thus had little economic influence over prosperity in Europe, especially when there were no international financial institutions governing

---

85 Dalton Camp, "Invest the Peace Dividend: Buy Cuba," *Toronto Star*, 25 July 1990, A25.

86 In the view of some NATO officials, he became one of the most successful secretaries general the alliance has ever had (NATO official, interview by the author, NATO Headquarters, Brussels, 24 May 2007). For an excellent comparison of NATO secretaries general, see Hendrickson, 2006.

87 Manfred Wörner, "Address to the Konrad Adenauer Stiftung," Brussels, 7 July 1989.

88 NATO, *The North Atlantic Treaty* (Washington, DC, 1949), art. 2.

89 For an extensive historical discussion, see, e.g., Chapnick 2005, 2007.

transatlantic commerce. For Canada, NATO was not only a military alliance but also a springboard for enhanced economic cooperation with Europe; it was a wider security community with the potential for institutionalizing transatlantic commerce.

In the early 1950s, however, this commercial potential of NATO lost significance with the Korean War (1950–3) and the military issues that preoccupied the political decision makers in Brussels at that time. The Canadian article lost further ground with the rise of the European Economic Community in the late 1950s as well as the formation of the Organisation for Economic Co-operation and Development (OECD) in 1961. These institutions assumed responsibility for economic integration in Europe and beyond, making Article 2 redundant.

With the fall of the Berlin Wall, however, the alliance regained political momentum as a community of like-minded states,[90] and Article 2 became useful again by providing NATO with a new raison d'être in the post–Cold War era. This was especially true for Canada, which embraced NATO as a military organization as much as an allied community guaranteeing political exchanges and discussions on international peace and security. Canadian government officials considered NATO to be an instrument of stability and peacekeeping, while maintaining Article 5 as a collective deterrent for potential aggressors.[91]

North Atlantic Cooperation Council (NACC)

The NACC was the first institutionalization of the spirit of cooperative security infecting NATO in the early 1990s. In an attempt to manage the new and evolving threats from Eastern Europe, a decision was made at the NATO summit meeting in Rome (7–8 November 1991)[92] to engage in cooperative security practices and create a new international regime.[93]

---

90 Deutsch 1957.
91 Sens 1995, 697.
92 The inaugural meeting took place on 20 December 1991. The following countries were members: Belgium, Canada, Denmark, France, Germany, Greece, Iceland, Italy, Luxembourg, Netherlands, Norway, Portugal, Spain, Turkey, United Kingdom, and United States as members of NATO and Bulgaria, Czech Republic, Estonia, Hungary, Latvia, Lithuania, Poland, Romania, Slav Federal Republic, and one representative of the Soviet Union as countries from CEE.
93 Such a regime is defined as "a set of implicit or explicit principles, norms, rules, and decision making procedures around which actors' expectations converge in a given area of international relations" (Krasner 1983, 2).

The idea of the NACC had first been floated in 1991 by Prime Minister Brian Mulroney[94] and was part of a larger Canadian-US effort[95] to facilitate interlocking institutions – referring to an overlap of institutions in terms of membership and scope –with the goal of preserving peace and order in Europe, establishing formal diplomatic ties with former Warsaw Pact countries, and cooperating with them on defence and security issues. An important reason for this outreach, according to the prime minister, was "to make sure that [states from CEE] don't feel that they have to resort to huge defence buildups themselves."[96]

A small group of states and diplomats became key players in the negotiations that led to the establishment of the NACC regime on 20 December 1991; the Canadian ambassador to NATO was one of them.[97] When Britain and France voiced their resistance to an associate membership of CEE states in NATO (primarily for security reasons),[98] James Karl Bartleman, Canada's chief diplomat in Brussels, negotiated for some kind of NATO membership for these countries under the auspices of the NACC.[99] Those efforts were fully consistent with the agenda of his political masters in Ottawa, who, as noted above, wanted

---

94 A high-level NATO official told Canadian journalists in Brussels that Mulroney's proposal to broaden relations with CEE states was not only considered the most "liberal" of any member state but also "very revolutionary" (Dave Todd, "PM Wants NATO Ties Extended to the East," *Calgary Herald*, 6 November 1991, A3). The prime minister made a similar statement on the future of NATO at a convocation speech at Stanford University a few months earlier, in which he said that NATO "association could be extended eventually to former adversaries, where they want it, once they had fully and irreversibly embraced the transatlantic democratic values we share" (Office of the Prime Minister, "Notes for an address by Prime Minister Brian Mulroney on the Occasion of the Centennial Anniversary Convocation, Stanford University, California, 29 September 1991"). The proposal initially ran into opposition from the French and the British, who wanted to avoid the impression that a "cooperative relationship" implied extending Article 5 to CEE.

95 Todd, "PM Wants NATO Ties Extended to the East."

96 Ibid.

97 Three members of NATO's International Staff, interviews by the author, Brussels, April and May 2007.

98 Todd, "PM Wants NATO Ties Extended to the East."

99 Senior Canadian official and one member of the International Staff, interview by the author, NATO Headquarters, Brussels, 20 May 2007. CEE states did not formally enjoy the collective security protections of Article 5; nonetheless, it was accepted wisdom that in the event of unexpected external aggression or a hostile invasion, NATO would not stand idly by its new partner countries.

NATO to become more political and less military. Secretary of State for External Affairs Barbara McDougall, for example, noted rather unenthusiastically that "it is only natural in these circumstances for NATO to assume a more political role, a role which would reflect both the new European reality and a declining military mission."[100]

The NACC was part of the new NATO; membership was voluntary, inclusive rather than exclusive, and open to new members. While the alliance stated publicly that it was "determined to work towards a new, lasting order of peace in Europe,"[101] the NACC's primary function was to provide transparency among its members through institutionalized meetings and to establish working relations with states of the former Warsaw Pact. It created a forum for political consultation on issues such as military defence planning, arms control, crisis management, civil-military relations, and force structure,[102] but only for states that showed a willingness to cooperate and become democracies. The NACC also facilitated debates on economic, political, and social issues,[103] thereby providing a forum for discussions on civil-military relations, reform of the armed forces, and the defence industries. It was a loose partnership

---

100 Canada, Department of External Affairs and International Trade 1990, 3.

101 North Atlantic Council, "North Atlantic Cooperation Council Statement on Dialogue, Partnership and Cooperation," news release M-NACC-1[91]111, art. 2.

102 See, e.g., NATO Parliamentary Assembly, "Report: NATO Enlargement" (International Secretariat, October 2001), art. 3. The negotiations for the Treaty on Conventional Armed Forces in Europe as well as Russian troop withdrawals are often cited as examples of where the NACC process had a practical and important impact.

103 Despite these rather positive elements, some analysts saw the NACC through critical eyes. It could not give each partner country the opportunity to develop an individual relationship with NATO, leading some critics, such as Jonathan Eyal (1997, 701), to argue that it was only a gigantic talking shop, similar to the OSCE, and produced no real results or significant decisions. Moreover, the NACC operated on a scarcity of resources and failed to solve security problems among its partners. Canada noted that "achieving C/EE's goals had been revealed as more difficult than originally thought, which has produced uncertainty. Overall, while there has been progress in dealing with challenges, no risks have been fully eliminated and new variants have emerged"; see Canadian Joint Delegation to NATO, "APAG MTG with Cooperation Partners," 2–5. The NACC was also perceived by some partner states as unsuccessful in developing a community of security and having too much of a bilateral relationship with NATO and CEE partners.

between NATO and CEE without locking its members into legally binding agreements or extending the collective defence clause.[104] It was the "first bridge NATO constructed over Europe's old divide"[105] and one that Canada regarded highly.[106]

The NACC's primary objective was to promote understanding and governance on questions of stability and security in Europe. By providing a political forum for mutual exchange and debate, it would allow information to be circulated and issues debated among the members. This new political culture was expected to promote mutual respect and thus increase the prospects for cooperation.[107] An internal Canadian government report praised the success of the new institution, saying that the NACC brought "countries closer together, had contributed to a new openness, had created a new philosophy of international relations through cooperation, had helped to overcome the division of Europe and had created new habits, new rules of behaviour and new transparency. It had contributed to confidence building and had helped defuse a crisis while projecting democratic values to partner countries."[108]

Partnership for Peace (PfP) Program

The design of NATO's PfP program was outlined by US Secretary of Defense Les Aspin in Travemünde, Germany, in October 1993, and the plan was formally accepted on 10 January 1994 during the NATO summit in Brussels. The PfP was created as a forum in which NATO would provide "practical" – meaning more individually targeted – answers to specific policy concerns raised by CEE states to help them adjust to NATO standards and priorities. It would address issues of

---

104 This is also why Canada favoured a NATO enlargement over an EU expansion: an EU expansion was most likely to take a decade or longer because of the extensive requirements of the *aquis communautaire*, its large regulation framework.

105 United States, Department of State, "Statement to North Atlantic Cooperation Council: Statement by Secretary of State Warren Christopher" (Brussels, 11 December 1996).

106 Documents sent from the Canadian Joint Delegation to NATO are consistent in stating that the NACC has "contributed in a number of important ways to an improvement in stability and security in Europe"; see Canadian Joint Delegation to NATO, "APAG MTG with Cooperation Partners."

107 Some scholars have described this phenomenon as the evolution of a behavioural norm; see Finnemore 1996; Katzenstein 1996.

108 Canadian Joint Delegation to NATO, "APAG MTG with Cooperation Partners," 5.

internal stability and progress that the NACC was unable to provide for individual partner states.[109] To this end, a Partnership Coordination Cell[110] was established at Supreme Headquarters Allied Powers Europe (SHAPE) in Mons, Belgium, that stressed transparency among PfP members as one of its highest principles. Through joint planning, training, and exercises, it helped strengthen their ability to participate in NATO's new peace operations.[111]

The PfP's primary goal was to transform the societies and institutions of member countries into modern democracies and help them adjust to the new socio-economic, political, and security challenges they were facing.[112] This process implied an expansion as well as an intensification of political and military cooperation among its members, and it helped build mutual confidence.[113] In their final communiqué, the Heads of States and Government noted,

> We ... are committed to enhancing security and stability in the whole of Europe. We therefore wish to strengthen ties with the democratic states to our East. We reaffirm that the Alliance, as provided for in Article 10 of the Washington Treaty, remains open to the membership of other European states in a position to further the principles of the Treaty and to contribute to the security of the North Atlantic area. ... We have today launched an immediate and practical program that will transform the relationship between NATO and participating states. This new program

---

109 It was recognized that these internal frictions could lead to external conflict, including frictions between neighbouring states, over attempts to re-establish regional hegemony, the proliferation of weapons of mass destruction and their delivery systems, disproportionate transfers of conventional arms, cross-border terrorism, pollution, migration and criminality, and establishing democratic culture and institutions.

110 For a greater discussion about its role, see Lange 1995.

111 Members of the PfP program as of 2007 were Albania, Armenia, Austria, Azerbaijan, Belarus, Bosnia and Herzegovina, Bulgaria, Croatia, Czech Republic, Estonia, Finland, FYROM, Georgia, Hungary, Ireland, Kazakhstan, Kyrghyz Republic, Latvia, Lithuania, Moldova, Montenegro, Poland, Romania, Russia, Serbia, Slovakia, Slovenia, Sweden, Switzerland, Tajikistan, Turkmenistan, Ukraine, and Uzbekistan. But the PfP was not without its critics.

112 White House, "National Security Directive 23," Washington, DC, 22 September 1989.

113 The PfP also bridged the gap between states that held membership in the OSCE but not the NACC (and vice versa).

goes beyond dialogue and cooperation to forge a real partnership – a Partnership for Peace.[114]

The PfP operated under the authority of the NAC but within the framework of the NACC. In this sense, it was consistent with the concept of cooperative security. It was a soft power tool of post-1989 diplomacy, designed to manage a diverse group of states while encouraging its own members to "tame their élan, go back to their capitals and acquire some knowledge of government."[115]

Ottawa committed itself to actively help build and foster the PfP.[116] For example, under the PfP umbrella, it invited officers from CEE to Canada to receive intensive language training and take courses in peace-support operations, civil-military relations, the legal framework of modern peacekeeping, and questions of military standardization.[117] The Canadian Peacekeeping Centre in Cornwallis, a former CF base, functioned as the host institution for teaching these soft power skills.

As a second-tier power, Canada's interest in the PfP was to establish bilateral defence relationships with CEE states and raise its profile in the region. Its key objective was to "increase the opportunities for additional political consultation with CEE partners"[118] as well as to explore economic opportunities in the new Europe. The principle of self-determination was the bedrock of this outreach process. Indeed, the PfP was high politics for second-tier power Canada. It clearly held the prospect of mutual gains by providing (1) transparency and democratic control of the armed forces of CEE states, (2) a network of military and defence-related issues,[119] (3) cooperation between CEE states

---

114 NAC, "Partnership for Peace: Invitation," Press Communiqué M-1[94]2, issued by the Heads of State and Government participating in the Meeting of the North Atlantic Council, NATO Headquarters, Brussels, 10–11 January 1994.

115 Eyal 1997, 697.

116 See, e.g., Scott 1990.

117 Canadian Joint Delegation to NATO, "PfP Activities [blacked out] Canada – IPP," fax YBDR 2645 to NDHQ – D NATO POL, 24 February 1997, 5, retrieved under the Access to Information Act, 10 April 2007, A-3, File No. 3947-01.

118 DG POL OPS, "European Command Arrangements."

119 Hanna Suchocka (presentation, IISS 36th Annual Conference, Vancouver, 8–11 September 1994), prime minister of Poland 1992–3, noted, for example, that Poland would accept German troops on Polish territory only within the framework of NATO; to have them within the uncertain framework of the PfP was less attractive.

and NATO, and (4) confidence-building measures across Europe. Internal government documents revealed that other governments also appreciated the "breathing space" it provided, especially on the increasingly contentious issue of NATO enlargement.[120]

However, the trouble with the PfP, as Canadian diplomats quickly realized,[121] was that the more successful it (and the NACC) became, the more pressing was the question of if and when to extend invitations for formal membership to associate members, to which the alliance up to this point did not extend a security guarantee under Article 5.

Politically, the PfP socialized its members by introducing them to the basic principles of a liberal democracy, including a strong commitment to upholding the values of a liberal democracy. That is to say, they were introduced to the normative elements of the liberal democratic principles of governance in international affairs. Before being considered for the program, PfP members had to fulfil the obligations set out in the UN charter and abide by the principles of the UN's Universal Declaration of Human Rights. For example, members had to speak and act in favour of refraining from the threat or use of force against the territorial integrity of other states or minorities.[122] Conditions for PfP membership also obliged CEE states to refrain from challenging existing borders in Europe and to actively commit themselves to the peaceful settlement of internal as well as external disputes.

Euro-Atlantic Partnership Council (EAPC)

The EAPC officially replaced the NACC. Launched in 1997, and first presented by US Secretary of State Warren Christopher in a speech in Stuttgart, Germany, on 6 September 1996, it was designed to bring an institutional relationship of consultation and cooperation on political

---

120 Canadian Joint Delegation to NATO, "APAG (Atlantic Policy Advisory Group) MTG 94: NATO and Euro-Atlantic Security," telex YBGR 1185 to EXTOTT IDS (International Security and Defence Relations Divisions, DFAIT), 12 September 1994, 2, retrieved under the Access to Information Act, 10 April 2007, A-3, File No. 3947-01.

121 Ibid., 7.

122 NAC, "Partnership for Peace: Framework Document," annex to M-1[94]2, issued by the Heads of State and Government participating in the Meeting of the North Atlantic Council, NATO Headquarters, Brussels, 10–11 January 1994.

and security issues to the satellite states of the former Warsaw Pact countries.[123]

The first issue on the agenda of the new EAPC was to develop an action plan that would outline areas in which member states were able to increase their consultation and cooperation over questions like the conflict in Bosnia and Herzegovina, the crisis in Kosovo, problems of international terrorism, and the proliferation of weapons of mass destruction. The first NATO communiqué on the EAPC noted,

> We are determined to raise to a qualitatively new level our political and military cooperation with our Partners, building upon the success of the North Atlantic Cooperation Council (NACC) and the Partnership for Peace (PfP). ... The EAPC, in replacing the NACC, will unite the positive experience of NACC and PfP by providing the overarching framework for political and security-related consultations and for enhanced cooperation under PfP, whose basic elements will remain valid.[124]

As an allied institution providing a political forum for long-term political consultation and cooperation beyond the PfP, the EACP enabled members to debate policy issues and problems in greater detail, including the proliferation of weapons of mass destruction, international terrorism, defence planning, budgeting, strategy, oversight, and civil-military relations.

Canada and the Enlargement of the New NATO

With the new security institutions – the NACC, PfP, and EAPC – in place, NATO was faced with the prospect of enlarging the alliance into CEE, a prospect that created some controversy. In September 1990, CEE states themselves voiced strong aspirations for membership, especially Poland, Hungary, and the Czech Republic. They had formed a

---

123   It brought together 49 NATO partner countries. As of January 2007, the following countries were members of the EAPC: all current NATO member states plus Albania, Armenia, Austria, Azerbaijan, Belarus, Bosnia Herzegovina, Croatia, Finland, FYROM, Georgia, Ireland, Kazakhstan, Kyrgyz Republic, Moldova, Montenegro, Russia, Serbia, Sweden, Switzerland, Tajikistan, Turkmenistan, Ukraine, Uzbekistan.

124   NAC, "Final Communiqué," Ministerial Meeting of the North Atlantic Council, Sintra, Portugal, 29 May 1997, art. 2.

small and informal alliance in Visegrad, Hungary, to increase cooperation among themselves and with Western Europe in particular. The Americans strongly supported such a plan.[125] One month later, on 30 November 1990, this trilateral alliance resulted in an agreement called Pro Memoria, which allowed for the liberalization of trade, greater transparency and openness of administration, and national force planning among all three states.[126]

The nature of the enlargement debate was highly complex and diverse; so was the scholarship that followed. Once allies had decided to invite certain states to become members, these aspirant states were obliged to fully subscribe to NATO's liberal democratic values.[127] Indeed, some analysts saw these values and principles as the driving forces of enlargement. In a comprehensive study, Timothy Edmunds, for example, argued that NATO's enlargement had a huge impact on Eastern Europe.[128] Enlargement, he charged, contributed to the democratization of CEE by providing an associate and possibly a full partnership through the PfP program. It also offered technical assistance to aspirant member states, reinforced existing democratic rules and norms, and accentuated NATO's new role as a political organization.[129]

For example, as a precondition for associate membership, NATO stipulated[130] that each aspirant state reform its domestic institutions and show a strong commitment to democratic forms of government, liberal

---

125 Olivia Ward, "NATO's Door Creaks Open: At a Summit Starting Tomorrow, the Alliance Is Expected to Welcome at Least Three New Members from Eastern Europe, but the Debate over Expansion Continues," *Toronto Star*, 7 July 1997, A13.

126 Spero 1992.

127 They were required to contribute to NATO's eight new functions: (1) contribute militarily to NATO's collective defence posture by allowing their forces to be assigned to NATO missions, (2) bring their national command structures up to NATO standard to become interoperable with it (in turn, NATO had to determine whether new command posts in Eastern Europe would be required), (3) actively participate in NATO training and exercises, (4) actively subscribe to the strategic concept of deterrence, (5) as a prerequisite for the success of NATO's collective defence structure, allow NATO forces to be deployed to CEE, (6) share intelligence information with NATO allies, (7) contribute financially to enlargement, and (8) undertake all measures necessary to speed up the process of becoming interoperable with NATO forces; see North Atlantic Treaty Organization 1995, ch. 5A, art. 70.

128 See also Gheciu 2005b.

129 Edmunds 2003, 151; Schimmelpfennig 1999.

130 The Geneva Centre for the Democratic Control of Armed Forces has done some far-reaching work in this area; see, e.g., Born and Arbatov 2003.

market economies, civilian control of the armed forces, a transparent civil bureaucracy, peaceful resolution of territorial or ethnic conflicts, and respect for human rights as set out in the UN's Universal Declaration of Human Rights.[131] Now NATO was imposing non-negotiable components of the democratization process: parliamentary oversight of the armed forces in CEE, a functioning and effective legislative branch empowered to autonomously investigate and govern the armed forces of CEE states, restructuring processes for the armed forces, and turning the page on managing civil-military relations.

These were the political preconditions for full NATO membership. The alliance was striving to foster a comprehensive reform of CEE's socio-economic and political institutions,[132] calculating that domestic reforms would extend to other policy areas such as security and defence. On the military side, aspirant states were assessed for their ability to contribute to NATO's collective defence commitments – that is, Article 5 operations – and for how their membership could enhance security and stability in the Euro-Atlantic area.

Canada's role in and contribution to NATO's enlargement process is best understood in qualitative rather than quantitative terms. Above all, one needs to consider the context in which its preferences for or against enlargement were made. First, while the debate on NATO enlargement was going on, Canada went through three federal election campaigns – in 1993, 1997, and 2001. The first two, in particular, absorbed all of the government's attention, while the country's economic performance, high inflation rates, and questions of national unity dominated national debates. The Chrétien government undertook an extensive information campaign to explain these domestic political difficulties to Canada's NATO allies. In one initiative, it invited the NAC to hold a ministerial session in Ottawa in October 1997. During a luncheon with their NATO counterparts, officials from the Department of Finance and from Intergovernmental Affairs stressed that while Canada remained

---

131 Simon 1993, 32.
132 Critics, however, argued that this reform process could be better guided and enforced by an enlargement of the EU because it would provide an evolutionary perspective that would be more stabilizing than if both organizations conducted their expansion separately. By linking NATO expansion to EU enlargement, the former could adopt a more leisurely approach. This was discussed at a meeting of the Atlantic Policy Advisory Group, 4–8 September 1994, retrieved under the Access to Information Act, 10 April 2007, A-3, File No. 3947-01.

committed to Atlantic solidarity, it was battling a national deficit and political instability at home.

During this time, Canadian officials maintained that the government was taking decisive and effective measures to address this situation.[133] In addition to the closed-door sessions it was holding with NATO's foreign and defence ministers, the government organized a luncheon for foreign media representatives to explain the overall economic situation in Canada, its progress in reducing the deficit, and the challenges that remained. While this was clearly a public relations campaign and somewhat unprecedented in the alliance, its chief objective was to put a spin on the public discourse on Canada among its allies and correct its image of being an Atlantic free rider.

The peaceful unification of Europe and the question of enlarging the alliance came at the right time for Canada. Archival evidence suggests that Ottawa made it clear to its allies that Canada remained a strong supporter of NATO enlargement. Government officials reiterated the position, especially behind closed doors, that Canada saw NATO both as a collective defence organization and as a political forum to closely integrate like-minded countries on both sides of the Atlantic.[134] It favoured an inclusive approach to enlargement,[135] but stressed that "the decision on which among them are to be invited to join NATO will have to be made in advance and known in advance; it is not acceptable to expose Heads of Government of aspiring countries to an 'Academy Awards' situation."[136]

Indeed, Canada favoured a far larger first round of enlargement. In addition to welcoming Poland, Hungary, and the Czech Republic to the alliance in 1999,[137] Ottawa supported the invitation of Slovenia,

133 "NAC Visit: Briefing Material on CDN Approaches to Current NATO Issues," telex IDR-0576, Regional Security Section (DFAIT) to Canadian missions in London, Bonn, Paris, The Hague, Copenhagen, Oslo, Brussels, Lisbon, Madrid, Rome, Ankara, Athens, Warsaw, Prague, Budapest, and Washington, 30 October 1997, retrieved under the Access to Information Act, 10 April 2007, A-3, File No. 3947-01.

134 Ibid.

135 Mary Kurjata, "CPP0432-NATO Policy Planners: The Future of the Alliance," e-mail to Canadian Joint Delegation to NATO, 17 November 1997, retrieved under the Access to Information Act, 10 April 2007, A-3, File No. 3947-01.

136 Ibid.

137 Lloyd Axworthy, "Letter to Minister of Foreign Affairs, Italian Republic," 28 May 1997.

Romania,[138] and Macedonia as new members.[139] It thus sided with the Europeans on this question. Prime Minister Chrétien himself made this preference known to his NATO colleagues at the summit meeting in Madrid in 1997,[140] while other government officials stressed the point that membership should remain open and that the alliance must make this clear at the Madrid summit.[141]

Canada's unequivocal support for an enlarged alliance, however, had a dimension of self-interest. Its experience in the Balkans had taught it that no international organization other than NATO – not the OSCE, EU, or WEU – could enforce peace and maintain order in Europe. The failure of UNPROFOR in Bosnia and Herzegovina and in Croatia was a case in point. Moreover, NATO gave credibility and fostered respect because it was the only functioning and effective multilateral alliance and one of which Canada was a member.[142] Furthermore, the policy of engagement and enlargement was easy to sell at home, especially in light of the referendum on the separation of Quebec from Canada.[143]

---

138 While Canada was not entirely convinced about Romania's readiness for NATO membership, it unofficially supported its candidacy based on justifications of shared cultural and linguistic ties as well as the rationale that the domestic tensions between ethnic Hungarians living in Romania would be more manageable if both Romania and Hungary were admitted to the alliance at the same time.

139 Lloyd Axworthy, "Statement by Canadian Minister of Foreign Affairs the Honourable Lloyd Axworthy" (address to the North Atlantic Council Special Ministerial Meeting, Brussels, 18 February 1997). See also Axworthy, "Letter to Minister of Foreign Affairs"; Eyal 1997, 708.

140 Alan Freeman, "Soviet Bear Now More Like a Hamster: Question of Respect Dominates Talks," *Globe and Mail*, 22 February 1997. During the summit, Chrétien accused the United States of pursuing NATO enlargement for domestic purposes, and Freeman writes that an open microphone caught him saying, "It's not reasons of state. It's all done for short-term political reasons, to win elections. Take the quarrel over whether to admit the Baltic states. That has nothing to do with world security. It's because in Chicago, Mayor Daley controls lots of votes for the nomination." In reality, however, Chrétien acted like US president Clinton and was equally concerned about domestic politics; see Naim, 1997–98, 37.

141 Axworthy, "Statement by Canadian Minister of Foreign Affairs."

142 Buteux 1994.

143 In 1995, a slight majority of Quebec residents voted against separation, and the referendum was lost. For a more detailed discussion, see Cardin 1990; Gauvin 1994; Simard 1987; Young 1999.

The "single greatest challenge"[144] arising from the sovereignty issue was the capacity of the federal government to sustain national unity in the face of new and developing centrifugal forces. Only a united Canada, noted Secretary of State for External Affairs Barbara McDougall, could make a significant contribution to international prosperity, peace, and security.[145] Thus, insisting on NATO's principles of solving minority issues peacefully and demanding respect for sovereignty in CEE was not the "away game"[146] for Canadian foreign policy officials; it was the "home game," affecting issues central to Canadian society.

Moreover, Canada's historical affinity with Europe predisposed it to maintaining an interest in European security issues. Diaspora Canadians had family connections to Poland, Hungary, the Czech Republic, and the Baltic states. Internal government figures estimated that 10 million Canadians[147] maintained family links to CEE, shared their cultural values, and spoke their languages. McDougall's predecessor, Joe Clark, had noted in 1990,

The remarkable events in Central and Eastern Europe are intensely personal for millions of Canadians whose roots are there. Many have ties of language and family. Some were forced to flee by the very regimes that have now collapsed. Most have family or friends whose hopes were thwarted, or lives diminished, by those old regimes, but who have the prospect now of building new lives and new societies in old homelands. Virtually no other nation possesses the web of intense personal connections to Eastern and Central Europe which we have in Canada. That gives Canadians a special interest, and a special capacity, in helping those societies become prosperous and free.[148]

---

144 Tony Kellett, "Canada-2005 – Political/Military," fax to Tony Berger, DFAIT, 10 December 1996, 14, retrieved under the Access to Information Act, 10 April 2007, A-3, File No. 3947-01.
145 Quoted in Randy Newell, "Canada Can Make a Contribution Only If United," *Windsor Star*, 11 December 1991, C10.
146 This term, although used in a different context, is borrowed from Sokolsky 2004a.
147 "NAC Visit: Briefing Material on CDN Approaches to Current NATO Issues," telex IDR-0576, Regional Security Section (DFAIT) to Canadian missions in London, Bonn, Paris, The Hague, Copenhagen, Oslo, Brussels, Lisbon, Madrid, Rome, Ankara, Athens, Warsaw, Prague, Budapest, and Washington, 30 October 1997, retrieved under the Access to Information Act, 10 April 2007, A-3, File No. 3947-01.
148 Canada, Department of External Affairs and International Trade 1990, 1.

These cultural affinities gave Canada a cooperative advantage in the new NATO and a strong motivation to support it. Canada (and the United States) saw enlargement of the alliance as a potential instrument of democratization.[149] This motivation was different from that of NATO's European members, who viewed the new NATO, and especially its enlargement, through the lens of historical ethnic conflict in Europe rather than ethnic diasporas.[150]

The Russian Factor

Apart from its consideration for regional stability and order in Eastern Europe, Canada was one of the first NATO allies to be concerned about the future and stability of Russia.[151] Its large military arsenal and extensive stockpiles of nuclear weapons were particularly troubling. Moreover, even though the former Soviet Union's geographical sphere of influence had diminished significantly with the breakup of the Warsaw Pact, the threats posed by the resulting security environment did not vanish;[152] they only changed in scope, scale, and extent. A task force on Canadian security policy actually warned fellow NATO countries that "the Soviet Union will remain, despite unilateral and negotiated force reductions, a major continental military power. As well, Soviet nuclear capabilities will continue to be a match for USA strategic forces and, retargeted, could threaten all Europe."[153]

NATO's general predicament was its inability to predict Russian reactions to an enlarged alliance. Because Canadian diplomats believed that Russia lacked a historical frame of reference, they predicted that a

---

149 Ibid.
150 Mary Kurjata, "CPP0432-NATO Policy Planners."
151 Yet in 1996 that threat was downgraded considerably. An internal memo from the Office of the Assistant Deputy Minister (Policy & Communications) at DND noted that in 2005, "Russia will not have fully recovered its military strength and will not be a threat to most of its neighbours" (Tony Kellett, "Canada-2005 – Political/Military," 2.
152 In addition to the external insecurities, the Soviet Union also faced struggles within its republics: dissident republics opposed the central government, Communist hardliners mocked the party leadership, and general reformers were against the government; see John Gray, "One Germany: There Is Little That Mikhail Gorbachev Can Do to Stop the Unification Blitzkrieg – Soviet Leader on the Sidelines," *Globe and Mail*, 30 June 1990, D3.
153 Task Force on Canadian Security Policy (IFBS), *Europe and Canadian Security*, 4.

number of unexpected political configurations were likely to occur, including "the persistence of Soviet-style reflexes; an archaic, ineffective, and still largely centralized economy; a generally underdeveloped and wasteful energy sector; a complex and unpredictable internal political dynamic in which the military was a force to be reckoned with; the absence of a multilateral security mechanism capable of meeting Russia's interests; and serious instabilities in neighbouring regions."[154] Canadian officials in Brussels privately pointed to the absence of any coherent, defining political idea or structures of governance in Russia, which would foment domestic problems. They warned that the process of NATO "enlargement cannot be held hostage to negotiations with Russia."[155]

Officially, the Canadian position was more ambiguous. On the one hand, the deputy minister of foreign affairs noted that "investing in Russia's future is clearly in our interest, and insurance payments are not a waste, if they facilitate security."[156] On the other hand, Minister of Foreign Affairs Lloyd Axworthy charged that "the onus is on the Russians to persuade us that they have really changed."[157] Official government policy preferred to integrate Russia into the international community as much as possible while fostering more openness and political reforms there.[158] Cables sent from Canada's delegation to NATO reiterated that the alliance's relationship with Russia should be substantive[159] and suggested that Russia should join the PfP.[160] It is apparent that Canada preferred apolitical engagement with Russia to military provocations,[161] which risked, as Canadian diplomats warned their political masters in Ottawa, that country "embarking on a path of self-isolation."[162]

---

154 Canadian Joint Delegation to NATO, "APAG MTG 94," 12.
155 Axworthy, "Statement by Canadian Minister of Foreign Affairs."
156 Task Force on Canadian Security Policy (IFBS), *Europe and Canadian Security*, 4; also quoted in Smith 1994, 6.
157 Quoted in Axworthy, "Statement by Canadian Minister of Foreign Affairs."
158 Canadian Joint Delegation to NATO, "APAG MTG 94," 2.
159 DG POL OPS, "European Command Arrangements."
160 Canadian Joint Delegation to NATO, "APAG MTG with Cooperation Partners," 13.
161 For example, by building new command posts or stationing nuclear weapons in CEE, suggested in DG POL OPS, "European Command Arrangements."
162 Canadian Joint Delegation to NATO, "APAG MTG with Cooperation Partners," 13.

Conclusion

The purpose of this chapter was to situate Canada's foreign policy preference formation in the context of the new NATO and thus show the qualitative extent of what this book calls the civilian burden that Canada shared. Examining the organization's transformation and ideational development from an old to a new alliance provided the context for analysing the social actions of civilian burden sharing, such as building outreach institutions, and allowed an examination of Canada's preference formation for practising civilian burden sharing.

While the seminal summit meetings in London (1990) and Rome (1992) reaffirmed NATO as the permanent transatlantic link between North America and Europe, transatlantic solidarity remained the cornerstone for safeguarding its values and principles. NATO also chose to embark on an extensive process of engagement and enlargement, politically engaging former enemies of the Warsaw Pact while enlarging economic ties with newly independent states from CEE. These practices, as Francis Fukuyama reminds us, showed a strong correlation between economic development and a stable and prosperous democracy.[163] The London and Rome summits took place in this liberal democratic environment and created a new political atmosphere for practising cooperative security rather than deterrence.

NATO's development from a military to a more political alliance was entirely consistent with historically derived objectives, manifested in Article 2 of the Washington Treaty of 1949. They were also consistent with Canada's preference[164] for a strong, political NATO that would help democratize CEE states and engage them economically, a view that matches the ontological assumptions held by classical liberal IR scholars. The new NATO would open up new CEE markets to Canada, helping to both pacify the evolving democracies and alleviate Canada's deficit. As a result, it was understandable that Canada should develop strong preferences for strengthening its international relations with CEE states while promoting national unity at home and abroad. NATO's new directions were easy to sell to Canadians and thus likely to gain domestic support, especially as they were relatively inexpensive for a country that was struggling to repay its debt.

---

163 Fukuyama 1992, 83–4.
164 Mary Kurjata, "CPP0432-NATO Policy Planners."

With NATO receptive to new friendships with CEE states (and vice versa), new internal institutions like the NACC, PfP, and EAPC were set up to facilitate the outreach process. They helped socialize aspirant member states and extend the partnership arrangements to eventual full membership.

Canada's preference as a second-tier power was to ensure that its domestic house was in order and that it returned to international prosperity and competitiveness. This policy of fiscal restraint and restructuring was popular among its citizens, which also explains the fact that there was no significant domestic resistance to an evolving new NATO. NATO's new role gave Canada a new lease on life in the post–Cold War international order. At the same time, and consistent with classical liberal IR theory, Canada supported the creation of new institutions to facilitate the outreach process, and to export NATO's norms and values to CEE. Nonetheless, as government records show, Canadian officials were not idealistic about the security situation in CEE, and they repeatedly warned their NATO colleagues that even though Russia lacked a coherent political vision and could not be trusted entirely, the alliance should not close the door on it for good.

7 Sharing the Civilian Burden, Part II

All valid contributions to the common prosperity must be credited. Most welcome should be those contributions that make effective use of each donor's limited capabilities.[1]

Introduction

While chapters 4 and 5 focused on the military share of the burden that NATO incurred in the new world order, this chapter turns to the civilian dimension of the debate. It broadens the discussion of Atlantic burden sharing by introducing what I call civilian, or soft power, indicators, which can be found at the intersection of military and civilian indicators and which address questions of distributive justice in NATO's civilian burden-sharing regime. These are novel indexes; they have not yet been discussed in the literature.[2]

Moreover, the chapter contextualizes these civilian indicators in the new security environment in Europe, which assigned new meanings to them. This contextualization helps us understand the burden-sharing practices of Canada as one of NATO's second-tier powers. Above all, the situational context of Canada's practices of NATO burden sharing – that is the circumstances in which Canada's burden sharing took place – need to be considered in order to understand the value-rational and instrumentally rational motivations and preferences that led to it

---

1 Sullivan 1985, 93.
2 The closest discussion is Boyer, 1993.

sharing the Atlantic burden in the first place. The qualitative content analysis of archival material shows that Canadian burden-sharing practices were influenced by having a national sense of external responsibility – the normative duty to promote better international economic, social, and political conditions while abstaining from pursuing narrowly defined national interests.[3]

The chapter starts with a brief discussion of soft military indicators, such as contributions to NATO peacekeeping, modernization and rapid reaction forces. This is followed by a discussion of hard civilian indicators: the economic aid and foreign assistance given to CEE states and NATO's common budgets.

Soft Military Indicators

UN Peacekeeping Personnel

The Cold War increased the relative instability of the international system, resulting in an increase in intra-state conflicts. This demanded exponentially more peacekeepers to serve in places like Haiti, Slovenia, Somalia, and Rwanda.[4] As noted in chapter 3, the end of the Cold War generated a sense of activism at the UN, which drove it to try to manage conflicts around the world. The role of the Security Council in international security governance was expected to be strengthened by this collective political will, and the operation to liberate Kuwait after the Iraqi invasion was the first test case of this new approach, even though it was executed by a coalition of forces led by the United States.[5] The liberation of Kuwait was followed by serious UN engagements in the Balkans as well as in parts of Africa and Asia.[6]

Armed with these new tasks, mandates, and political will, the UN set about redefining its role and functions in a post–Cold War security order. This included reforming its organizational principles, governance structures, and practices. A report commissioned by the UN Security Council and prepared by then secretary general Boutros

---

3 Wolfers 1962, 73–7.
4 See, e.g., Bellamy, Williams, and Griffin 2004; Boutros-Ghali 1992, 1995.
5 Cox, Booth, and Dunne 1999.
6 See, e.g., Boulden 2001, 2003. One may recall especially the UN's operations in Somalia, Congo, East Timor, and Haiti.

Boutros-Ghali in 1992 provided guidance for this evolving reform process. *An Agenda for Peace* redefined the UN's relationship with other international security institutions referred to in the UN Charter, Chapter VIII. One of these organizations was NATO.

The report recommended exploring the question of how these security institutions were to relate to the UN and advocated closer collaboration among them. "Regional action as a matter of decentralization, delegation, and cooperation with the United Nations could not only lighten the burden of the [UN Security Council] but also contribute to a deeper sense of participation, consensus and democratization in international affairs. ... Today a new sense exists that they have contributions to make."[7] Against the background of an increasingly overwhelmed and dysfunctional organization, *An Agenda for Peace* provided the conceptual framework for "contracting out"[8] peacekeeping responsibilities to security actors like NATO – one example of the new roles it prescribed for the UN in international security governance.

Above all, peacekeepers from around the world were seen as tools for managing new and evolving conflicts and pockets of regional instability. While the report discussed in great detail the individual contributions of NATO allies to UN peacekeeping operations in the Balkans, including those in Bosnia and Herzegovina, Croatia, and Kosovo, it did not discuss the increasing demands for UN peacekeepers generally. This increase is tracked in table 7.1 below, which shows the absolute personnel contributions – peacekeepers, military observers, and international police forces – of NATO member states to major peace operations, both UN and non-UN, from 1994 to 2001.

This table indicates that Canada was the 6th-highest-ranking NATO member state to these missions by *absolute* force, shouldering 5.96% of the total. It thus practised burden sharing above and beyond the NATO average of 5.3% (4.6% without the United States) and can consequently not be considered an Atlantic free rider. Spain and the Netherlands, on the other hand, also considered second-tier powers in the alliance, rank far behind Canada, contributing 4.3% and 3.7% of the *absolute* force, respectively. What is even more noteworthy is that Canada was the highest-ranking second-tier power by absolute force

---

7 Boutros-Ghali 1992, 64–5. For a more detailed description of the division of labour between the UN and NATO, see Boutros-Ghali 1995.

8 Thakur 2006, 52.

share, outperforming all other second-tier powers, including Spain, the Netherlands, and Norway. Norway, for example, shouldered only roughly 60% of Canada's contribution, while Denmark contributed slightly more than 36%.

This shows that despite the accepted wisdom of collective action theorists, in terms of *absolute* personnel contributions to UN peace-keeping operations Canada cannot be accused of being a NATO free rider. Quite the contrary: the empirical evidence in table 7.1 shows that Canada lived up to its reputation as a second-tier power and practised burden sharing above the NATO average. To use the language of the collective action theorists, it benefited less from its investments in contributions of personnel to major multinational peace operations than it paid for them. This suggests that given the domestic situation, discussed in previous chapters, the government was driven in its actions by absolute rather than relative national interests, which were informed by normative predispositions that can best be understood as an external responsibility to promote milieu goals – namely, enforcing human and humanitarian rights through international organizations; establishing the rule of law; and promoting democracy, economic order, and stability.

However, as noted in previous chapters, the absolute force contributions of the member states must be weighed against the total strength of their armed forces. This calculation produces the *relative* ability of member states to contribute to the public good, shown in the "Total of national force (%)" column. And it shows that with the exception of the United Kingdom, second-tier powers were the top force contributors, deploying a comparatively higher share of their armed forces to peace operations. Moreover, the top two relative force contributors of NATO's second-tier powers were Norway (2nd) and Canada (3rd). They sent 3.5% and 3.0%, respectively, of their armed forces personnel to peace operations and thus outperformed major powers such as France and Germany (both 1.0%), Italy (0.9%), and even the United States (0.4%). Thus, we can say that normally second-tier powers are more accurately labelled major powers.

Regardless of whether one considers the absolute or relative force share that Canada made available to multinational peace operations between 1994 and 2001, it ranked above the NATO average. As noted above, it shouldered 6.6% (7.2% without the United States) of the absolute force, above the NATO average of 5.3% (4.6% without the US), and 3.0% of the relative force share, well above the NATO average of 1.45%.

Table 7.1 Absolute Personnel Contributions to Major Multinational Peace Operations, 1994–2001

Country	1994	1995	1996	1997	1998	1999	2000	2001	Total	Rank by absolute force share	Total of national force (%)	Rank by relative force share	Power status
United Kingdom	3,820	437	415	459	416	7,390	5,430	5,317	23,684	5	5.3	1	Super-power
Norway	1,692	995	726	708	153	1,338	1,244	1,236	8,092	9	3.5	2	
Canada	2,811	956	1,034	889	297	3,394	2,006	1,784	13,171	6	3.0	3	Major power
Denmark	1,366	273	126	126	116	551	1,288	969	4,815	15	2.6	4	
Netherlands	1,889	230	97	93	169	2,639	1,569	1,478	8,164	8	2.0	5	
Belgium	1,054	682	845	146	11	331	1,011	1,039	5,119	14	1.6	6	
Portugal	264	274	411	474	155	1,357	1,674	1,528	6,137	11	1.2	7	
Hungary	n/a	n/a	n/a	n/a	n/a	386	641	632	1,659	16	1.1	8	
Czech Republic	n/a	n/a	n/a	n/a	n/a	519	831	231	1,581	17	1.1	9	Second-tier power
France	5,149	494	503	474	664	8,218	8,577	8,546	32,265	2	1.0	10	
Germany	15	29	172	190	190	7,636	8,124	7,494	23,850	4	1.0	11	
Poland	n/a	n/a	n/a	n/a	n/a	1,268	2,168	1,884	5,320	13	1.0	12	
Italy	278	78	76	97	194	8,547	8,504	7,954	25,728	3	0.9	13	
Spain	1,358	22	46	56	71	2,454	2,725	2,716	9,448	7	0.8	14	
Luxembourg	0	0	0	0	0	0	26	23	49	18	0.5	15	
Greece	13	12	18	13	12	1,436	2,043	2,175	5,722	12	0.4	16	Third-tier power
United States	963	2,449	700	637	583	11,948	11,138	9,567	37,985	1	0.4	17	
Turkey	1,473	17	40	42	42	1,671	2,361	2,144	7,790	10	0.1	18	
Iceland	0	0	0	0	0	0	0	0	0	19	0.0	19	

Table 7.1 Absolute Personnel Contributions to Major Multinational Peace Operations, 1994–2001 (cont.)

Country	1994	1995	1996	1997	1998	1999	2000	2001	Total	Rank by absolute force share	Total of national force (%)	Rank by relative force share	Power status
Total	22,145	6,948	5,209	4,404	3,073	61,083	61,360	56,717	220,939	19	27.5	19	
Total (non-US)	21,182	4,499	4,509	3,767	2,490	49,135	50,222	47,150	403,893	18	27.1	18	
Average	1,384.1	434.3	325.6	275.3	192.1	3,214.9	3,229.5	2,985.1	11,628.4	n/a	1.45	n/a	
Average (non-US)	1,412.1	299.9	300.6	251.1	166.0	2,729.7	2,790.1	2,619.4	22,438.5	n/a	1.51	n/a	

Source: United States Department of Defense, Report on Allied Contributions to the Common Defense (Washington, DC: Department of Defense, 1995 to 2001); International Institute for Strategic Studies, Military Balance (London: IISS, 1990 to 2001).

Notes:

1. Yearly data rounded; "Total (%)" calculated before rounding.
2. Data for 1995–8 reflects forces contributed only to NATO operations; data for 1999–2001 also includes forces committed to operations not under UN auspices.
3. Data not provided for Hungary, Czech Republic, or Poland before their admission to NATO in 1999.

This empirical discovery leads to two inferences. First, it disproves the assumptions of collective action theorists that second-tier states are inclined to practise Atlantic free riding; states like Norway and Canada show a burden-sharing practice that places them squarely in the major power category. This suggests that common classifications (and generalizations) of super-, major, second-tier, and third-tier powers currently used in public as well as academic discourse need serious reconsideration. Second, in contrast to France, Germany, and Italy (the conventional major powers) and the United States (the superpower), second-tier states must have assigned higher national preferences to sending their forces to take part in these multinational peace operations. It suggests that they held stronger national predispositions towards their normatively informed external responsibility to make their forces available.

Financial Contributions of NATO States to UN Peacekeeping Operations

This increase in commitment to multinational peace operations is also reflected in NATO member states' financial contributions to UN peacekeeping operations. This dimension of the argument is shown in table 7.2 below.

Table 7.2 shows that Canada was the 6th-largest financial contributor to UN peacekeeping missions, followed by Spain and the Netherlands. More important, however, it shows that Canada was the highest-ranking second-tier power in the alliance; only major powers such as the United States, Germany, France, and the United Kingdom ranked higher. This finding is consistent with expectations held by collective action theorists. With 4.5% of the total cost share, Ottawa ranked slightly below the NATO average of 5.3%. However, if the United States is excluded from this calculation because of its superpower status, Canada ranks significantly above the NATO average of 3.0%.

Again, it is important to put Canada's financial contributions into a comparative perspective and, in this instance, into the context of its general economic well-being and the domestic instability caused by the threat to national unity. It is clear from table 7.2 that Canada's financial contribution took a sharp nosedive in 1996 and remained at very low levels until 2000: compared to 1994, it had shrunk by 75.96% in 1999, but rose by 163.1% in 2000. This is an impressive increase from which we can infer the government's strong preferences towards UN peace operations.

Defence Expenditures Allocated to Modernization

The geopolitical events surrounding the end of the Cold War, on top of NATO's new strategic concept, its resulting new force postures, and its decision to accept three new member states in 1999 (the Czech Republic, Hungary, and Poland), placed significant demands on its organizational abilities to meet the new security challenges of the post–Cold War world as well as its looming enlargement. New capabilities and significant upgrades in the areas of command, control, communications, intelligence, strategic mobility and sustainability, theatre missile defence, and nuclear and biological force protection were either in particularly high demand or required a major technical overhaul. As a result, the alliance undertook a significant and extensive process of organizational modernization during the 1990s to overcome outdated Cold War governance and management structures as well as strategic thinking.

However, such transformation processes cost money, and they can be considered to be practices of burden sharing. Thus, defence expenditures directed at modernization can provide a general indicator of allied burden sharing in the civilian domain. Table 7.3 below outlines the percentage of national defence spending allocated by NATO countries to modernization of major equipment, including equipment used in research and development,[9] thereby providing an indication of how and in which areas governments spent their precious defence dollars.[10]

The table shows that while Canada's modernization investments were above the NATO average in 1990 and from 1995 to 1998, they fell below that average between 1998 and 2000 and represented a 24% decline in total NATO modernization investments from 1990 to 2001 (46% between 1995 and 1999). This may seem to be a surprisingly high number at first, but it actually is not. Compared with the average of all NATO states from 1990 to 2001, Canada's investments in collective infrastructure projects sat at 5.7%, slightly above the NATO average of 5.3%. Nonetheless, examined over the 1990s, Canada still spent the 8th-highest amount on NATO's modernization programs and was the 4th-highest-ranking second-tier power.

---

9 The statistical information for this indicator is partially derived from NATO's annual *Defence Planning Questionnaire*.

10 The baseline for this modernization indicator, however, remains the states' defence budgets.

Table 7.2 Financial Contributions to UN Peace Operations (Millions of Constant US Dollars at 2001 Exchange Rates)

Country	1994	1995	1996	1997	1998	1999	2000	2001	Total ($)	Total (%)	Total (non-US) (%)	Rank	Power status
United States	1,128.9	453.8	303.9	319.8	218.7	225.2	513.6	1,365.5	4,529.4	46.5	n/a	1	Super-power
Germany	216.9	195.5	89.0	74.5	66.1	59.0	209.3	298.9	1,209.2	12.4	23.2	2	Major power
United Kingdom	218.9	221.1	96.3	63.1	47.3	43.9	126.4	212.1	1,029.1	10.6	19.8	3	
France	130.0	230.5	81.2	59.2	57.8	35.9	111.0	186.7	892.3	9.2	17.2	4	
Italy	135.7	129.3	50.2	52.1	40.5	39.2	105.8	147.9	700.7	7.2	13.5	5	
Canada	98.6	94.9	37.4	29.2	23.7	21.4	56.3	73.4	434.9	4.5	8.4	6	Second-tier power
Spain	75.2	56.3	36.6	21.0	17.4	20.3	21.8	52.5	301.1	3.1	5.8	7	
Netherlands	40.3	38.3	15.8	13.9	12.4	11.8	31.6	51.3	215.4	2.2	4.1	8	
Belgium	30.4	15.5	17.6	10.5	8.0	7.4	19.1	32.6	141.1	1.5	2.7	9	
Denmark	18.7	17.5	7.3	6.4	5.0	4.8	14.5	22.7	96.9	1.0	1.9	10	
Norway	20.7	16.9	6.5	5.8	5.4	4.8	13.2	20.6	93.9	1.0	1.8	11	
Greece	2.0	1.9	1.1	1.7	1.8	2.4	3.5	12.0	26.4	0.3	0.5	12	

Table 7.2 Financial Contributions to UN Peace Operations (Millions of Constant US Dollars at 2001 Exchange Rates) (cont.)

Country	1994	1995	1996	1997	1998	1999	2000	2001	Total ($)	Total (%)	Total (non-US) (%)	Rank	Power status
Portugal	1.5	1.6	1.4	1.5	0.5	2.4	0.7	12.4	22.0	0.2	0.4	13	Third-tier power
Poland	n/a	n/a	n/a	n/a	n/a	5.5	3.4	0.8	9.7	0.1	0.2	14	
Luxembourg	1.6	1.6	0.6	0.5	0.5	0.4	1.4	2.5	9.1	0.1	0.2	15	
Czech Republic	n/a	n/a	n/a	n/a	n/a	0.9	2.1	3.9	6.9	0.1	0.1	16	
Turkey	0.4	0.6	0.8	0	0.8	1.3	1.8	1.1	6.8	0.1	0.1	17	
Iceland	0.8	0.7	0.4	0.6	0.3	0.1	0.7	0.7	4.3	0.0	0.1	18	
Hungary	n/a	n/a	n/a	n/a	n/a	0.2	0.4	1.1	1.7	0.0	0.0	19	
Total	2,120.6	1,476.0	746.1	659.8	506.2	486.9	1,236.6	2,498.7	9,730.9	100	100	19	
Total (non-US)	991.7	1,022.2	442.2	340.0	287.5	261.7	723.0	1,133.2	5,201.5	53.5	n/a	18	
Average	111.6	77.7	39.3	34.7	26.6	25.6	65.1	131.5	512.2	5.3	5.6	n/a	
Average (non-US)	55.1	56.8	24.6	18.9	16.0	14.5	40.2	63.0	289.0	3.0	5.6	n/a	

Source: United States Department of Defense, *Report on Allied Contributions* to the Common Defense (Washington, DC: Department of Defense, various years).

Table 7.3 Percentage of Defence Expenditures Allocated to Modernization, 1990–2001

Country	1990	1995	1996	1997	1998	1999	2000	2001	Change over period (%)	Total ($)	Total (%)	Total (non-US) (%)	Rank	Power status
United States	37.1	30.8	30.2	29.3	29.0	28.2	25.0	25.1	-32.4	234.7	11.0	n/a	1	Super power
Turkey	20.0	29.7	30.9	27.1	20.8	25.6	28.3	36.7	84.1	219.1	10.3	11.5	2	Major power
United Kingdom	18.3	24.0	26.1	26.9	28.5	28.9	27.6	29.0	58.6	209.3	9.8	11.0	3	
Norway	22.8	25.4	25.2	24.6	25.0	22.6	20.1	24.0	5.3	189.7	8.9	10.0	4	
Greece	21.4	20.0	21.4	19.4	20.7	19.5	17.9	15.1	-29.5	155.4	7.3	8.2	5	Second-tier power
Netherlands	18.7	17.2	20.3	17.7	16.1	17.7	17.7	18.1	-3.4	143.5	6.7	6.7	6	
France	n/a	23.7	n/a	22.0	19.4	19.4	18.9	19.9	n/a	123.3	5.8	109.6	7	
Canada	20.1	20.9	17.6	14.9	10.7	9.6	13.8	15.2	-24.0	122.8	5.7	6.5	8	
Italy	17.5	15.0	14.3	11.4	12.4	11.7	14.3	12.4	-29.1	109.0	5.1	5.1	9	
Denmark	14.9	12.5	12.5	13.7	14.4	11.4	14.8	14.2	-4.5	108.4	5.1	96.4	10	
Spain	12.8	14.4	14.1	14.2	12.6	12.1	13.7	13.8	7.6	107.7	5.0	5.0	11	
Germany	16.6	11.9	11.6	11.3	13.2	13.6	14.0	13.5	-18.8	105.7	4.9	94.0	12	

Table 7.3 Percentage of Defence Expenditures Allocated to Modernization, 1990–2001 (cont.)

Country	1990	1995	1996	1997	1998	1999	2000	2001	Change over period (%)	Total ($)	Total (%)	Total (non-US) (%)	Rank	Power status
Czech Republic	n/a	n/a	10.6	n/a	n/a	18.9	23.9	21.2	n/a	74.6	3.5	3.9	13	Third-tier power
Portugal	10.3	5.9	6.3	8.2	3.9	4.5	6.4	6.3	-38.8	51.8	2.4	2.7	14	
Hungary	n/a	n/a	7.7	n/a	n/a	21.1	12.4	10.5	n/a	51.7	2.4	2.7	15	
Belgium	7.9	5.4	5.3	6.2	5.9	6.5	5.8	5.4	-30.9	48.4	2.3	2.5	16	
Luxembourg	3.2	2.4	4.1	3.5	6.5	5.0	4.6	16.3	401.9	45.6	2.1	2.4	17	
Poland	n/a	n/a	7.4	n/a	n/a	11.1	9.0	9.2	n/a	36.7	1.7	1.9	18	
Iceland	0.0	0.0	0.0	0.0	0.0	0.0	0.0	0.0	0.0	0.0	0.0	0.0	19	
Total	241.6	259.2	265.6	250.4	239.1	287.4	288.2	305.9	346.1	2,137.4	100	100	19	
Total (non-US)	204.5	228.4	235.4	221.1	210.1	259.2	263.2	280.8	378.5	1,902.7	89.0	n/a	18	
Average	15.1	13.6	14.8	13.2	12.6	15.1	15.2	16.1	18.2	112.5	5.3	21.1	n/a	
Average (non-US)	13.6	15.2	13.8	14.7	14.0	14.4	14.6	15.6	21.0	105.7	4.9	21.1	n/a	

Source: United States Department of Defense, *Report on Allied Contributions to the Common Defense* (Washington, DC: Department of Defense, 2000).
Note: The data for 1991 to 1994 is not publicly available.

Canada also shared a burden that was higher than the NATO average, making it a net contributor to NATO's modernization programs rather than an Atlantic free rider. It paid more for providing the public good than it did to receive benefits from it. Moreover, it shared more of its modernization investments than comparable allies with equal or similar power status, such as Denmark (10th), Spain (11th), and even major powers like Italy (9th) and Germany (12th). All these other second-tier powers benefited more from NATO's modernization investments than they contributed. They can thus be considered free riders. Only second-tier powers such as Norway (4th) and the Netherlands (6th) outperformed Canada.

This leaves us with the question of how to interpret Canadian burden-sharing practices in the civilian domain of NATO modernization. The reductions in the Canadian share began in 1997, a time when the federal deficit hung like the sword of Damocles over all government expenditures and policies. In fiscal year 1992–93, Canada's federal deficit reached $41 billion ($65.8 billion for the federal government and the provinces combined) and $42 billion ($62.2 billion combined) in 1994–95.[11] But it took until 1996 for the effects of budget cuts to be reflected in the official NATO data sets. This is why the full extent of Canadian reductions in modernization investments did not show up in NATO's budgets until fiscal year 1998–99.

Seeing the Canadian share in NATO's modernization regime in this context helps, on the one hand, to explain the reductions that took place in the mid-1990s. On the other hand, I suggest that Canada's share remained significantly high for a state that was so deeply in debt. This allows for the interpretation that at the height of NATO's first round of transformation decisions and processes, in fiscal year 1989–90, Canada had a strong preference for investing in the civilian aspects of NATO's transformation. This national predisposition is echoed in the investments made for collective infrastructure projects (see next section). It also suggests that government officials placed greater emphasis on boosting NATO's non-military domain than overhauling its military technology and equipment.

---

11 Courchene 2002.

Defence Expenditures Allocated to Infrastructure

Virtually since its inception, NATO has provided the infrastructure it needs based on a commonly agreed formula. Its infrastructure projects finance cooperative military enterprises that are of collective benefit to the alliance, and they are aimed at satisfying the military needs and requirements determined by its military arm, SHAPE. Thus, a project is eligible for collective funding only if it provides common benefits to all member states and only if all states are able to use the resulting infrastructure. Examples of collectively funded projects include communication installations, feasibility studies, pollution clean-up, television and radio stations, storage facilities, ports, radar installations, and airfields. This suggests that infrastructure investments are essential components for alliance preparedness – both militarily and politically.

Given the nature and purpose of the alliance, the debate about financing collective infrastructure projects is inherently political and rests on the definition of the term *eligibility*. Eligibility refers to the principle that NATO common funding should occur only when funding for a particular infrastructure project cannot be reasonably expected from the host nation of an operation. For example, NATO's collective infrastructure was an integral component of maintaining stability and freedom in Europe during the Cold War by providing its armed forces with the tools they needed to ensure the collective defence of NATO territory, and it focused mainly on military installations in Europe, such as airfields, naval ports, and air defence battery systems. The end of confrontations in 1989, however, transformed the scope and extent of proposed projects. Above all, given its new mandate of crisis management, NATO needed to update its existing technology, including communications and information systems as well as the systems necessary for crisis response and expeditionary operations – all of which need maintenance and thus continuous investment.

Examining the percentage of Canada's defence expenditures allocated to infrastructure in table 7.4 below suggests an increase in commitment rather than free riding. Canada ranked 7th in the 1990s, shouldering 6.9% of NATO's total infrastructure investments (7.1% if the United States is not counted), well above the NATO average of 5.3%. Surprisingly, the United States, with the single largest economy of the alliance, ranked only 11th, thus benefiting proportionately more from NATO's infrastructure investments than it contributed. This is an example of the United States practising free riding on its allies rather

Table 7.4 Percentage of Total Defence Expenditures Allocated to Infrastructure, 1990–2001

Country	1990	1991	1992	1993	1994	1995	1996	1997	1998	1999	2000	2001	Total ($)	Total (%)	Total (non-US)	Rank	Power status
Norway	9.8	9.5	9.8	8.2	8.8	6.7	6.9	5.9	6.9	5.2	5.0	5.0	87.7	13.1	13.6	1	Major powers
Luxembourg	7.0	14.8	10.6	11.8	9.4	5.5	1.7	4.7	4.5	6.7	4.9	2.0	83.6	12.5	12.9	2	
United Kingdom	5.1	4.4	2.9	6.8	8.8	5.5	5.8	5.2	4.6	5.1	4.3	1.7	60.2	9.0	9.3	3	
Germany	5.9	4.9	4.5	4.6	4.7	4.6	5.0	4.8	4.6	5.1	4.9	4.7	58.3	8.7	9.0	4	
Netherlands	5.9	6.2	5.8	4.6	4.1	3.1	4.4	4.5	3.7	3.7	4.3	4.5	54.8	8.2	8.5	5	
Turkey	3.2	2.8	3.5	2.9	2.6	2.5	3.0	4.2	6.1	8.5	7.2	5.7	52.2	7.8	8.1	6	
Canada	3.9	3.4	3.1	3.1	2.5	2.4	4.1	3.4	5.1	5.4	5.3	4.1	45.8	6.9	7.1	7	Second-tier powers
Belgium	3.6	2.8	5.2	2.9	2.6	3.9	4.5	4.0	3.4	3.6	1.9	3.1	41.5	6.2	6.4	8	
Denmark	3.4	4.3	3.7	2.5	2.7	2.6	2.4	2.3	1.8	2.0	1.4	2.7	31.8	4.7	4.9	9	
Greece	2.1	1.7	2.4	2.6	0.6	1.9	1.5	2.1	2.1	2.1	1.8	2.0	22.9	3.4	3.5	10	
United States	1.7	1.2	1.4	1.6	1.7	2.4	2.5	2.2	2.2	2.0	1.7	1.7	22.3	3.3	3.5	11	
France	n/a	n/a	n/a	n/a	n/a	n/a	n/a	4.0	3.9	4.4	4.5	4.6	21.4	3.2	3.3	12	
Portugal	3.4	3.4	5.3	n/a	0.7	1.6	1.3	1.2	0.6	0.6	1.5	1.1	19.2	2.9	3.0	13	Third-tier powers
Italy	2.8	2.3	2.7	2.5	1.9	1.1	0.8	0.8	0.8	0.8	1.2	1.0	18.7	2.8	2.9	14	
Spain	2.3	1.6	1.0	0.9	0.9	0.7	0.7	0.7	0.8	1.8	1.7	2.5	15.6	2.3	2.4	15	
Czech Republic	n/a	n/a	n/a	n/a	n/a	n/a	n/a	n/a	n/a	7.1	3.3	4.6	15.0	2.2	2.3	16	
Hungary	n/a	n/a	n/a	n/a	n/a	n/a	n/a	n/a	n/a	4.0	2.9	5.7	12.6	1.9	2.0	17	
Poland	n/a	n/a	n/a	n/a	n/a	n/a	n/a	n/a	n/a	1.4	1.9	1.8	5.1	0.8	0.8	18	
Iceland	0	0	0	0	0	0	0	0	0	0	0	0	0	0	0	19	

Table 7.4 Percentage of Total Defence Expenditures Allocated to Infrastructure, 1990–2001 (cont.)

Country	1990	1991	1992	1993	1994	1995	1996	1997	1998	1999	2000	2001	Total ($)	Total (%)	Total (non-US)	Rank	Power status
Total	60.1	63.3	61.9	53.5	52	44.5	44.6	50	51.1	69.5	59.7	58.5	669.0	100	100	19	
Total (non-US)	58.4	62.1	60.5	51.9	50.3	42.1	42.1	47.8	48.9	67.5	58	56.8	646.0	97.0	96.5	18	
Average	4.0	4.2	4.1	3.6	3.5	3.0	3.0	3.1	3.2	3.7	3.1	3.1	35.2	5.3	5.3	n/a	
Average (non-US)	3.2	3.5	3.4	2.9	2.8	2.3	2.3	2.7	2.7	3.8	3.2	3.2	35.9	5.4	5.4	n/a	

Source: NATO defence expenditures, 1990–2001.

than the other way around. With the exception of the United Kingdom
and Germany, this also holds true for other major powers; for example,
France and Italy shouldered only 3.2% and 2.8%, respectively, of collective infrastructure investments.

In particular, the Canadian share rose from 3.9% in 1990 to 5.3% a
decade later. This suggests that Canada assigned a particularly important meaning to collective infrastructure projects, deeming them to be a
critical component of a civilian transformation of the alliance.[12] This
preference continued to be strong throughout the years of fiscal restraint (1992 to 1995), when Canada's percentage of collective infrastructure investments show a downward curve of close to 40%. In 1994
and 1995, for example, Ottawa spent only 2.5% and 2.4%, respectively,
of its total defence expenditures on collective infrastructure projects,
meaning that the government was conscious of Canada's overall financial situation and adjusted its financial commitments accordingly. Yet
compared to the indicators discussed above, these reductions in infrastructure were less extensive; by 1996, this trend was reversed, and
Canadian investments in collective infrastructures rose to 4.1%.

Indeed, when NATO was in need of new infrastructure investments
on the eve of enlargement in 1999, Canada had increased its share to
5.4% – an increase of 104% from 1994 – while voicing a strong preference for infrastructure investments in communication installations to
facilitate greater interoperability among new and old member states.[13]

One other point that Canada raised with its allies, as discussed in
chapter 6, was questions of how to distribute the costs of NATO enlargement among the allies. Canada had a strong preference for an all-
inclusive first round of enlargement – inviting not just the Czech
Republic, Hungary, and Poland into the alliance but also Slovenia,
Romania, and Macedonia. It was accepted wisdom in Brussels that
once it had been decided which countries would be invited to join, their
national military and political infrastructures would require significant investments and upgrading,[14] but one question that was hotly debated among the allies was who should pay for these infrastructure
investments. Table 7.4 indicates that for the most crucial period of

---

12 This can be confirmed in Barbara McDougall, "Canada, NATO, and Eastern Europe:
    The Challenge" (speech to the Universal Speakers' Group, Toronto, 16 April 1992).
13 DG POL OPS, "European Command Arrangements." fax to Canadian Joint
    Delegation to NATO, 29 January 1997, retrieved under the Access to Information
    Act, 10 April 2007, A-3, File No. 3947-01.
14 Ibid.

managing NATO enlargement (between 1998 and 2000), Canada shouldered one of the highest shares of all NATO allies.

Contributions to Rapid Reaction Forces

With the UNPROFOR mission dissolving in 1995, the focus of burden sharing shifted from the UN to NATO. As discussed in chapter 4, with the political, economic, and military landscape in continental Europe in flux and adjusting to the new geopolitical realities, NATO underwent a significant and extensive process of transformation. During the Cold War, the level of burden sharing among NATO allies had been determined by how many forces or how much military equipment and technology a country was able to put towards achieving a collective objective, despite the fact that those commitments may have been made mostly on paper. Contingency plans had been drawn up whereby member states pledged troops up to a negotiated ceiling while not being pressed politically to actually deploy them. In light of the changing security environment in Europe, however, these burden-sharing benchmarks were called into question.

An alternative indicator for measuring the contributions of the allies to the collective defence, I suggest, is their contributions to NATO's rapid reaction forces. These are military forces that maintain a high level of readiness, flexibility, and mobility. They can deploy on short notice to remote and dangerous theatres of operation, function despite a lack of pre-established lines of communication and host-nation support, and engage effectively in multinational formations in hostile environments at division and even corps level. These units can be considered NATO's tactical crisis manager; they carry out the new out-of-area crisis-management operations envisioned during the transformation process of the early 1990s.[15]

When NATO gave itself a new mandate with its 1991 Strategic Concept (which in the broadest political terms provided a justification for its enduring purpose and future tasks in the area of global security governance), these high-readiness forces were the practical manifestation of NATO's forward operating capability. They can thus be deemed a suitable indicator for assessing a degree of distributive justice among the allies as well as their preferences. Given the new security environment in Europe as well as NATO's ongoing organizational transformation in the 1990s and the resulting rapid response force concept, the

---

15 For a more detailed discussion, see, e.g., Cornish 2004; Garnett 2003; Giarra 2009.

extent of allied contributions to NATO's rapid response units provides an alternative indicator of Atlantic burden sharing, one that can be placed at the intersection of the military and civilian domains.

By the 1990s, NATO's rapid response units included multinational command structures and formations such as the Allied Command Europe Mobile Force (Land), or AMF(L), the Allied Rapid Reaction Corps for ground forces, and the Immediate and Rapid Reaction Forces (Air). The AMF(L) consisted of 5,000 troops and was supplied by 14 participating countries; Ottawa earmarked an infantry battalion group and two maritime patrol aircraft. NATO also maintained standing naval units – for example, the Standing Naval Force Atlantic (SNFA), which consisted of between six and ten destroyers as well as two frigates, a logistics ship, one submarine, and one F-18 squadron of 15 aircraft. Canada, Germany, the Netherlands, the United Kingdom, and the United States all earmarked one ship permanently to these naval rapid reaction forces.[16]

It took NATO until the Prague Summit of 2002 to fully realize the creation of an amalgamated force. The NATO Response Force (NRF) was a fully joint and multinational force – a central crisis-response mechanism without the separate land, maritime, and air elements of the AMF(L) and SNFA. It was activated in 2006 with a full strength of 25,000 personnel[17] and could deploy with five days' notice and sustain itself for operations lasting 30 days, longer if resupply was guaranteed.

Table 7.5 below shows the member states' contributions to NATO's rapid reaction forces for 1998 in both absolute and relative terms (as a share of NATO GDP, or the combined total GDP of all member states).[18] As is the case with other indexes in this book, the absolute contributions of member states provide only half of the picture; they do not show how each state's share is weighed against its relative ability to contribute. The "Rank by GDP" column does just that.

---

16 National Defence Headquarters, "CDA's Contribution to NATO," telex LHBF 2039 to D NATO POL, 17 December 1997, 2, retrieved under the Access to Information Act, 10 April 2007, A-3, File No. 3947-01. Canada was also the fourth-largest contributor to NATO's AWACS program.

17 I thank Scott Davy for his assistance with this paragraph.

18 Data is provided only for 1998 due to NATO access restrictions; however, it shows the distribution of the relative burden. Because NRF units are highly mobile and flexible, national force contributions are top secret. Canada's numbers for other years, e.g., remain classified.

Table 7.5 Financial Contributions to NATO's Rapid Reaction Forces, 1998 (Millions of US Dollars)

Country	Land force	Naval force	Air force	Total ($)	Rank	Total (%)	Total (non-US) (%)	Share of NATO GDP (%)	Rank by GDP	Power status
United States	7.4	21.6	49.0	78.0	1	26.0	n/a	48.6	1	Super power
Germany	7.4	5.2	10.2	22.8	5	7.6	10.3	12.7	2	Major power
France*	18.6	10.3	0	28.9	3	9.6	13.0	8.5	3	
United Kingdom	20.0	14.7	13.2	47.9	2	16.0	21.6	8.1	4	
Italy	13.6	8.6	2.9	25.1	4	8.4	11.3	7.0	5	
Canada	0.7	3.4	1.5	5.6	13	1.9	2.5	3.5	6	Second-tier power
Spain	7.6	3.4	3.1	14.1	9	4.7	6.4	3.3	7	
Netherlands	2.2	6.9	5.6	14.7	8	4.9	6.6	2.2	8	
Belgium	3.0	1.7	3.7	8.4	10	2.8	3.8	1.5	9	Third-tier power
Turkey	6.7	7.8	6.2	20.7	6	6.9	9.3	1.2	10	
Denmark	2.3	3.4	1.2	6.9	11	2.3	3.1	1.0	11	
Norway	0.7	4.3	0.8	5.8	12	1.9	2.6	0.9	12	
Greece	7.4	7.8	0.8	16.0	7	5.3	7.2	0.7	13	
Portugal	2.3	0.9	1.7	4.9	14	1.6	2.2	0.6	14	
Luxembourg	0.2	0	0	0.2	15	0.1	0.1	0.1	15	
Iceland	0	0	0	0	16	0.0	0.0	0.0	16	
Total	100.0	100.0	100.0	300.0	16	100.0	100.0	100.0	15	
Total (non-US)	92.6	78.4	51.0	222	15	74.0	100.0	51.4	n/a	
Average	6.3	6.3	6.2	18.8	n/a	6.3	6.3	6.3	n/a	
Average (non-US)	6.2	5.2	3.4	14.7	n/a	4.9	6.3	3.4	n/a	

Source: United States Congressional Budget Office, 2001.
* France maintained its reaction forces separate from NATO in the 1990s.

In absolute terms, Canada ranked 13th out of the 16 member states with its 1.9% share of NATO's rapid reaction forces. However, in relative terms, it was the 6th-largest contributor and the largest in the cluster of second-tier powers. Comparable second-tier powers like the Netherlands, Denmark, and Norway shared less of the burden than Canada did, and their practice of burden sharing conforms to the expectations of collective action theorists regarding free riding.

Ottawa's Financial Costs of Burden Sharing

The costs of international peace operations in the 1990s, particularly those carried out under the leadership of NATO, were significant and extensive. While the alliance provided the political guidance and governance for those missions, it was the member states themselves that had to pay the costs. Under NATO's formula, they paid all of the costs of an operation except those that were of collective interest – e.g., command and control structures necessary to run a collective operation.

This practice and financial management of operations deviates from that of the UN, which reimburses a significant proportion of the contributing member states under a specific formula and according to the number of soldiers deployed and the states' relative ability to pay. The formula is revised each year by the General Assembly's Committee on Contributions, taking into account factors such as total national income, per capita income, and economic dislocations.[19] The UN's cost-sharing models are designed to defray operational costs such as deploying troops into theatre, sustaining them, and providing general logistical support.

Table 7.6 below shows the Canadian share of UN and NATO operations in the Balkans between 1991 and 2001. The total financial commitment was $3.074 billion, including Canada's contributions to the Kosovo crisis in 1999 and the subsequent ground force deployments under KFOR.[20] Focusing only on NATO operations (using the numbers available), Ottawa spent $203.3 million for the IFOR operation, $1.507 billion for SFOR, $515.9 million for KFOR, and $3.760 billion for all operations combined.

---

19 Mingst and Karns 2000, 39–42.
20 As mentioned earlier, the data has not yet been released (LCol Ross Fetterly, Department of National Defence, Finance Department, interview by the author, Ottawa, 19 July 2007).

Table 7.6 CF Deployments to the Balkans and Total Cost, 1991–2001
(Millions of Canadian Dollars)

Designation	Personnel	Full Cost	Incremental Cost*
UNPROFOR – CANBAT I (Croatia)	860	530,300	203,200
UNPROFOR – CANBAT II (Bosnia)	826	626,100	248,100
UNPROFOR – Others (Bosnia and Croatia)	340	125,100	39,100
UNHCR AIRLIFT – Operation AIR BRIDGE (Sarajevo airlift)	48	75,200	15,200
ECMM (Yugoslavia) – Operation BOLSTER	48	0	0
United Nations Committee of Experts – Operation JUSTICE (former Yugoslavia)	7	2,000	0.020
Operation DENY FLIGHT (former Yugoslavia)	13	2,000	0.011
IFOR (NATO) – Operation ALLIANCE (Balkans)	1,029	203,300	52,700
SFOR (NATO) – Operation PALLADIUM (Bosnia)	1,641	1,507,400	489,100
KFOR (NATO)		515,900	
European Union Force in Bosnia-Herzegovina – Operation BRONZE/BOREAS	83	0	0
UNMIBH – Operation NOBLE (Bosnia-Herzegovina Mine Action Center)	4	2,500	900
Total by fiscal year	4,899	3,073,900	1,048,300

Source: Canada, Department of National Defence, Finance Section, June 2007.
* Additional costs incurred during deployment.

Defence economists distinguish between the full and the incremental costs of an operation. The former is defined as the sum of all costs – variable and fixed, direct and indirect, cash and non-cash – incurred by a government for a specific period of time. Incremental costs are defined as additional costs that arise from resources added or reallocated – for example, as a result of supplying a force being deployed. Thus, incremental costs are the *additional* costs incurred by deploying that force.[21] To put the numbers in table 7.6 into perspective, Canada shouldered 21.46% of the total burden that the United Nations incurred for its operations in the Balkans.[22]

To be fair, however, the empirical data in the table needs to be treated with extreme caution. For example, the United Nations lists the total costs that it incurred for its peacekeeping missions – UNPROFOR (I and II), UNCRO, UNPREDEP, and UNPF-HQ – at $4,616,725,556.[23] Comparing this data with the total amount spent by Canada for the same time period is difficult primarily because Canadian accounting practices are very different from those used by the UN. Still, if one follows official government documents to obtain a very rough estimation of its contribution, Canada spent a total of $1.361 billion for those operations.[24]

Another problem with assessing the UN data is that its accounting practices are not publicly accessible so that it is not clear, for example, whether the monthly stipends allocated to UN peacekeepers were factored into the UN's total costs. So the question remains whether the UN treats these amounts as costs or stipends. If they are considered stipends, the funds are reimbursed to the countries, thereby reducing the UN's costs. If they are considered costs, the Canadian contribution would certainly be smaller than 21.46%. It is also not clear whether the UN's numbers are raw numbers or adjusted for inflation. Because of

---

21 Salaries for soldiers and civilian support personnel, e.g., are considered full costs. I thank Ugurhan Berkok for his comments here.

22 For a detailed breakdown of the costs and troop contributions, see ch. 5.

23 This is the official number estimated for the entire operation by the UN's Department of Public Information, http://www.un.org/Depts/dpko/dpko/co_mission/unprof_p.htm, accessed 20 June 2007.

24 Department of National Defence, Finance Section, June 2007. In 1996, the exchange rate for the Canadian dollar against the US dollar was 0.7280; thus, the total amount is US$99,095.4 billion.

this lack of detail, it is assumed here that the numbers are not inflated and that they reflect the total costs for UN peacekeeping.

Nonetheless, and in spite of the confusion arising from the UN's accounting practices, the statistics provided here can be treated as an indication that second-tier power Canada shouldered a significant burden of the costs of UN operations in the Balkans. The contribution is even greater in light of the government's significant spending cuts in the early 1990s.

Canadians also paid a heavy human price for their commitments to the Balkans. Twenty Canadian soldiers lost their lives in the former Yugoslavia,[25] 9.4% of the total UNPROFOR death toll of 213 soldiers: six military observers, 198 other military personnel, three civilian police officers, three international civilian staff, and three local staff.[26] In addition, many returning troops suffered from physical and emotional distress. While measuring these human costs in relation to the physical costs of troop deployments is nearly impossible, it does give meaning to the social actions of enforcing peace and security in the Balkans on the one hand and practising Atlantic burden sharing on the other.

Hard Civilian Indicators

The ongoing transformation in European security affairs in the 1990s, especially the wars in the Balkans, demanded extensive investments above and beyond military means to govern the aftermath of the civil wars. These non-military, or civilian, resources were used to rebuild and maintain peace, order, and good government in the region. Against this backdrop, this section will examine the following hard civilian indicators of Atlantic burden sharing: foreign aid and assistance, especially the economic aid provided to CEE states, and NATO's common budgets.[27]

---

25 Veterans Affairs Canada, "Canadian Forces in the Balkans," http://www.vac-acc
   .gc.ca/youth/sub.cfm?source=history/canadianforces/factsheets/balkans, accessed
   1 April 2008.
26 UN Department of Public Information, "Former Yugoslavia – UNPROFOR,"
   31 August 1996, htttp://www.un.org/Depts/dpko/dpko/co_mission/unprof_p
   .htm, accessed 6 July 2009.
27 These indexes are not very well known and have not been discussed before in the
   literature; see Boyer 1993, 81.

Foreign Aid and Assistance

Foreign aid, broadly speaking, is the transfer of capital from industrial countries to developing countries by means of official development assistance (ODA) for the purpose of promoting economic development and overcoming global poverty.[28] For example, ODA has been used to help pay for particular community, health, and commercial projects as well as the general socio-economic development of a particular state or region.[29]

Scholars in the field of international development often date the origins of foreign assistance programs to the Marshall Plan, which sent large amounts of financial resources from the United States to rebuild Western Europe in the aftermath of the Second World War[30] and was particularly designed to provide socio-economic assistance. Since 1961, ODA has become formalized with the creation of the OECD's Development Assistance Committee (DAC), which defines the term as a financial program that is "primarily intended to promote economic development, if at least 25 percent of the program consists of grants (gifts), and if loans are extended at below-market interest rates."[31]

In this discussion of hard civilian burden-sharing indexes, we will examine two: the broader and more general index of NATO states' foreign assistance[32] to the world's less developed states and the more specific index of economic aid made available to CEE states. We will start with the latter.

---

28 Gerald Hallowell, *The Oxford Companion to Canadian History*, 2004 online edition, s.v. "foreign aid," http://www.oxfordreference.com/view/10.1093/acref/9780195415599.001.0001/acref-9780195415599-e-580?rskey=bPTz84&result=579.

29 Chris Park, *A Dictionary of Environment and Conservation*, 2012 online edition, s.v. "official development assistance," http://www.oxfordreference.com/view/10.1093/acref/9780198609957.001.0001/acref-9780198609957-e-5607?rskey=Rqz7SV&result=5612.

30 For further discussion, see Anderson 1999; Sogge 2002.

31 Joel Krieger, ed., *The Oxford Companion to Politics of the World*, 2nd ed., 2004 online edition, s.v. "foreign aid," http://www.oxfordreference.com/view/10.1093/acref/9780195117394.001.0001/acref-9780195117394-e-0255?rskey=G0t6r0&result=255.

32 Foreign assistance is understood as the sum of both bilateral aid provided by one state to another as well as that given by one state to an international regime (e.g., the African Development Bank, World Bank, or supranational organizations like the EU). These institutions, in turn, take responsibility for distributing the money according to institutionally agreed principles and practices. In this sense, the amount of foreign assistance is an important aspect of burden-sharing practices, and it indicates the importance that states assign to global peace and stability as well as to long-term investments in human resources development, technical assistance, financial infrastructure improvement, and general poverty reduction.

Most of the ODA sent to CEE was allocated by member states on a bilateral basis (not as part of any collective NATO effort), and member states sent their contributions as part of a wider foreign aid campaign for CEE; NATO undertook no effort to become an active participant. Thus, the level of foreign aid sent to former Warsaw Pact states is a justified index for examining the practice of NATO burden sharing and questions of distributive justice. This index is shown in table 7.7 below.

In general terms, ODA has both public and private benefits. It promotes political stability, as well as Western values and beliefs, in those countries that receive it, and this in turn is believed to enhance Western and thus NATO's security.[33] All of these are public benefits. Economic aid contributes to the economic stability of the trading regime and access to markets by promoting growth and stability, and this is expected to reduce economic instability and insecurity. Gaining access to new markets can be considered a private benefit.

Table 7.7 below outlines the absolute ODA as well as the loans (including credits) provided by NATO members to CEE from 1991 to 1997. It shows that second-tier powers clearly ranked ahead of major powers;[34] Canada, for example, was the 4th-highest-ranking NATO donor at 6.7% of the absolute share.[35] Only two other second-tier powers made more economic assistance available: Denmark, with an absolute share of 16.1%, and Norway, with 11.6%.[36]

These findings are interesting because they suggest that second-tier powers tend, more than major powers, to invest their precious tax dollars in ODA regimes; except for Germany and France, it was mainly the second-tier powers that shared the biggest burden. At the same time, the table disproves the assertion made by Stanley Sloan that European countries, especially, shoulder a larger foreign aid burden because of

---

33 See, e.g., Boyer 1993, 66; Wedel 1998.
34 This study confirms earlier but not meticulously comprehensive findings by Boyer 1993, 72.
35 In the first three months of its SFOR deployment in 1996, Canada spent $15 million on humanitarian assistance, rebuilding Bosnia's shattered education and health care institutions and promoting democracy and freedom of the press. Canada also named Michael Berry special coordinator for reconstruction of the former Yugoslavia; see Allan Thompson, "New Rules Apply in Bosnia Mission: Canadians Join NATO Troops as 'Peace Enforcers,'" *Toronto Star*, 6 January 1996, A6.
36 For this chapter, it was decided to take the total amount of aid provided from 1990 to 2001 as a benchmark in order to avoid distortions caused by yearly volatilities and currency fluctuations.

Table 7.7 Economic Aid to CEE Countries per Million Dollars of GDP, Selected Years, 1991–7

Country	ODA	Loans	Total ($)	Total (%)	Total (non-US) (%)	Rank	Power status
Germany	1,078.1	51.5	1,129.6	30.3	32.4	1	Superpower
Denmark	490.3	108.6	598.9	16.1	17.2	2	Major power
Norway	416.0	16.0	432.0	11.6	12.4	3	
Canada	251.0	0.0	251.0	6.7	7.2	4	Second-tier power
United States	225.4	19.2	244.6	6.6	n/a	5	
France	213.4	5.6	219.0	5.9	6.3	6	
Belgium	159.8	58.0	217.8	5.8	6.2	7	
Netherlands	184.1	33.2	217.3	5.8	6.2	8	
Luxembourg	194.7	0.0	194.7	5.2	5.6	9	
Italy	98.4	11.1	109.5	2.9	3.1	10	Third-tier power
United Kingdom	106.5	0.0	106.5	2.9	3.1	11	
Spain	3.4	4.3	7.7	0.2	0.2	12	
Portugal	1.3	0.0	1.3	0.0	0.0	13	
Turkey	0.0	0.0	0.0	0.0	0.0	14	
Greece	0.0	0.0	0.0	0.0	0.0	15	
Iceland	n/a	n/a	0.0	0.0	0.0	16	
Total	3,422.4	307.5	3,729.9	100.0	100.0	16	
Total (non-US)	3,197.0	288.3	3,485.3	93.4	100.0	15	
Average	213.9	19.2	233.1	6.3	6.3	n/a	
Average (non-US)	213.1	19.2	232.4	6.2	6.3	n/a	

Sources: United States Congressional Budget Office, 2001; author's compilation.
Note: Numbers are rounded up; percentages and rank are calculated individually.

their colonial past:[37] none of the member states had had a colonial relationship with any of the CEE states.

The high share of foreign aid shouldered by the second-tier powers is best understood by examining the context in which their decisions were made. As we have seen, the transformation of the European security environment and the new world order, in particular, challenged old paradigms of international security affairs, including the values and prerequisites attached to a country's own national security affairs. It dovetailed nicely with the structural predispositions of international security affairs, in which soft power, not hard power, resources were becoming the new currency of international politics.[38]

Second-tier powers such as Canada seem to have understood best that CEE states undergoing an extensive process of democratization and transition did not need large conventional forces, excessive military equipment, or technology as much as they needed investment in their socio-economic and governance infrastructure.[39] As numerous studies have shown, this ODA fostered advancement in these areas as well as the development of normative values such as the rule of law.[40] It also resonated well with theoretical propositions of the democratic peace theory. Thus, second-tier powers felt an external responsibility to share a bigger slice of the collective NATO burden in the form of ODA and that they took on that responsibility in the heavily sought-after civilian domain of fostering socio-economic development.[41]

---

37 Sloan 1985a, 1985b.

38 Nye 2004, 2005b, 2008.

39 For a discussion of the importance of national institutions in war-torn societies, see, e.g., Paris 2004.

40 Norms are commonly understood as "intersubjective beliefs about the social and natural world that define actors, their situations, and the possibilities of action" (Wendt, 1995, 73–4) or as "social facts, which define standards of appropriate behaviour and express actor's identities" (Katzenstein 1996, 19). Constructivists have generally debunked the construction of national identities and interests as not being externally determined, as asserted by rational choice theorists, but socially constructed. Their epistemological claim is that societies shape the identities, interests, and capacities of individuals, thereby challenging the epistemological individualism and autonomy of the rationalist scholarship.

41 Inferred from Michael Chesson, "Canada-European Union Bulletin: Article on Canada and NATO, fax to Jacques Paquette, IDS, DFAIT, 5 July 1994, retrieved under the Access to Information Act, 10 April 2007, A-3, File No. 3947-01.

Furthermore, this external responsibility seems to be consistent with second-tier powers' practices of foreign assistance. Table 7.8 below suggests that second-tier powers like the Netherlands and Canada contributed a much greater amount to NATO states' foreign aid regime than they benefited from it. From 1990 to 2001, the total amount of foreign assistance distributed by NATO member states was more than $560 billion. Canada shouldered $26.6 billion of this, or 4.7%, ranking slightly below the NATO average of $29.5 billion, or 5.3%. If the United States is not factored in (its superpower status places it in a completely different league of assessment),[42] the NATO average drops to $22.8 billion, or 4.1%, almost $4 billion less than Canada's contribution. When the United States is factored in, Canada ranks as the 7th-largest foreign aid donor country out of 19 NATO members; if not, it ranks 6th out of 18.

Table 7.8 also shows that for 1996, the size of the Canadian foreign aid budget was reduced by 16.7%, when the Canadian government was running high deficits. In spite of these cuts, however, the government maintained its share of foreign assistance at a relatively stable level of approximately $2 billion per year.

This situation was not unique to Canada. Other second-tier powers such as Spain, Belgium, and Portugal showed a similar downward trend in their foreign aid contributions. On the one hand, this may support Stanley Sloan's argument that nations that have colonial histories appear to be more efficient aid donors than states that do not. This, he argues, is a result of the cultural, linguistic, and historical ties that the colonial power had with the colony.[43] Yet a conclusive causal relationship between the two factors cannot be drawn from this table; the argument does not seem to be fully convincing, and Canada seems to be the "odd man out" in this explanation because it does not have a colonial history; it was a colony itself.

NATO Common Budgets

Considering NATO's common budgets as a civilian indicator of Atlantic burden sharing is an interesting, and probably the most important, part

---

42 I made this argument earlier too. The United States spent close to US$150 billion on foreign assistance between 1990 and 2001. This is 46.12% more than Germany, the second-highest contributor.

43 Sloan 1985b, 87–9.

of this indicator because the history of NATO's commonly funded budgets and its fair distribution among its allies is as old as the alliance itself. The common budgets are based on the principle of economies of scale, whereby each country can reduce its costs of providing defence and security by pooling its assets with other countries – for example, through alliances.

Since NATO was inaugurated in 1949, it was divided about how to equally distribute its costs; in fact, this is probably one of the most significant consistencies in its history. For example, at its meeting on 17 December 1951, the Payment and Progress Sub-Committee of the Special Committee on Infrastructure agreed to invite rather than compel NATO members to pay their share of the collective bill of over 5 billion francs.[44] The breakdown of the costs at the high point of the Cold War in the 1950s left the United States with 48.1% of the total bill, France with 21.52%, the United Kingdom with 17.72%, Canada with 4.43%, the Netherlands with 2.91%, and Belgium and Luxembourg with 5.32% each.[45] It was also agreed that because the economies of Belgium and Luxembourg were so weak following the Second World War and they could not afford additional international expenditures, they could postpone their payments until a later date.

This brief history demonstrates that common funding issues can be one of the oldest and thus most effective means of measuring allied responsibilities. While today's common budgets are much more sophisticated and complex, they nonetheless remain one of the most politically contested and sensitive issues of the alliance. And it is precisely because of this that they function so well as a civilian indicator of allied burden sharing.

NATO operates on three distinct budgets: the so-called civil budget, the military budget, and the NATO Security Investment Programme (NSIP). These three budgets finance the allied facilities, structures, and programs needed to allow political consultation and joint decision-making to take place. In other words, these three budgets make NATO work. However, whenever NATO takes on military missions or other

---

44 The exact amount was 5,112,000,000 francs; see NATO Document AC.4(PP)-D/1, OR.ENG, 18 December 1951. The amount was in francs because NATO was headquartered in Paris at the time.

45 Ibid.

Table 7.8 Foreign Assistance (Millions of Constant US dollars), 1990–2001

Country	1990	1991	1992	1993	1994	1995	1996	1997	1998	1999	2000	2001	Total ($)	Total (%)	Total (non-US) (%)	Change over period (%)	Rank	Power Status
United States	13,761	14,765	13,600	12,160	12,915	8,827	12,100	10,071	12,191	13,228	12,724	13,326	149,668	26.7	n/a	-3.2	1	Super-power
Germany	9,425	12,100	12,385	10,849	10,370	11,536	6,541	5,465	5,247	5,457	5,759	7,289	102,423	18.3	24.9	-22.7	2	Major power
France	8,716	9,562	6,546	9,839	10,150	9,069	6,161	5,854	5,596	5,660	5,860	7,161	90,174	16.1	21.9	-17.8	3	
United Kingdom	2,999	3,515	3,359	3,423	3,585	3,466	3,911	3,835	4,200	3,737	5,058	5,605	46,693	8.3	11.4	86.9	4	
Netherlands	3,159	3,245	3,245	3,237	2,906	3,377	2,648	2,723	2,921	2,981	3,621	4,495	38,558	6.9	9.4	42.3	5	
Italy	3,571	3,644	4,134	3,725	3,260	2,067	2,239	1,342	2,229	1,728	1,836	2,518	32,293	5.8	7.9	-29.5	6	
Canada	2,324	2,457	2,581	2,413	2,395	2,366	1,971	2,204	2,007	1,991	1,958	1,939	26,606	4.7	6.5	-16.6	7	
Denmark	1,410	1,523	1,622	1,777	1,676	1,676	1,869	1,623	1,664	1,719	1,914	2,340	20,813	3.7	5.1	66.0	8	Second-tier power
Spain	1,065	1,384	1,544	1,470	1,681	1,539	1,098	1,137	1,265	1,281	1,256	2,367	17,087	3.0	4.2	122.3	9	
Norway	1,296	1,285	1,376	1,245	1,379	1,311	1,317	1,401	1,518	1,503	1,346	1,751	16,728	3.0	4.1	35.1	10	
Belgium	1,155	1,399	1,149	1,056	909	1,086	753	718	829	756	916	1,247	11,064	2.0	2.7	8.0	11	
Portugal	225	308	345	310	394	294	201	251	260	285	312	397	3,582	0.6	0.9	76.4	12	
Turkey	1	183	300	404	92	117	135	119	114	196	133	87	1,881	0.3	0.5	8600.0	13	
Greece	7	95	124	88	129	184	152	158	174	184	248	283	1,826	0.3	0.4	3942.9	14	Third-tier power
Luxembourg	36	64	51	72	79	74	67	87	102	109	130	189	1,060	0.2	0.3	425.0	15	
Poland	n/a*	n/a*	n/a*	n/a*	n/a*	n/a*	n/a*	n/a*	28	38	43	47	156	0.0	0.0	n/a	16	
Czech Republic	n/a*	n/a*	n/a*	n/a*	n/a*	n/a*	n/a*	n/a*	n/a*	16	21	50	87	0.0	0.0	n/a	17	
Hungary	n/a*	n/a*	n/a*	n/a*	n/a*	n/a*	n/a*	n/a*	n/a*	n/a*	n/a*	n/a*	n/a	n/a	n/a	n/a*	18	
Iceland	n/a	n/a	n/a	n/a	n/a	n/a	n/a	n/a	n/a	n/a	n/a	n/a	n/a	n/a	n/a	n/a	19	

Table 7.8 Foreign Assistance (Millions of Constant US dollars), 1990–2001 (cont.)

Country	1990	1991	1992	1993	1994	1995	1996	1997	1998	1999	2000	2001	Total ($)	Total (%)	Total (non-US) (%)	Change over period (%)	Rank	Power Status
Total	49,150	55,529	52,361	52,068	51,011	46,989	41,163	36,988	40,345	40,869	43,135	51,091	560,699	100.0	100.0	13315.1	n/a	
Total (non-US)	35,389	40,764	38,761	39,908	38,096	38,162	29,063	26,917	28,154	27,641	30,411	37,765	411,031	73.3	100.0	13318.2	n/a	
Average	3,072	3,471	3,273	3,254	3,188	2,937	2,573	2,312	2,522	2,151	2,270	2,689	29,510	5.3	5.3	700.8	n/a	
Average (non-US)	2,359	2,718	2,584	2,661	2,540	2,544	1,938	1,794	1,877	1,536	1,690	2,098	22,835	4.1	5.6	739.9	n/a	

Source: United States Department of Defense, *Report on Allied Contributions to the Common Defense* (Washington, DC: Department of Defense, 1997–2002).

Notes:

1. Total foreign assistance includes net distributions of ODA and official aid to developing countries and territories and those in transition (e.g., CEE, new dependent states of the former Soviet Union).

2. The numbers for 1990 to 1995 are based on 1996 exchange rates. Beginning in 1996, they are based on the exchange rate for the corresponding year.

* Net aid recipient.

collective projects, each member state is financially responsible for its own troops, including their logistical and transportation needs.[46]

Yet with the fall of the Berlin Wall and NATO's decision to reach out to CEE and respond to the new peacekeeping demands in the Balkans, a new debate surfaced about the amount and scope of NATO's common budgets. It was initiated by the second-tier powers, including Canada,[47] who felt disadvantaged by the existing burden-sharing regime. Especially with regard to the common infrastructure program, Canada maintained its position that allied infrastructure projects must satisfy a common NATO security requirement and emphasize the crisis-management and flexibility aspect of collective deployments. Government officials argued that "the bottom line is that any new project which is likely to require common funding must follow the budget review process; be measured against other projects; and should not lead to any ceiling increase."[48] A project should also serve a particular need for NATO's command and rapid reaction forces.[49] While the NAC's initial resistance was steadfast, Canada's argument prevailed.[50]

In NATO's civil budget, by far the biggest item is operating and maintaining its Headquarters in Brussels as well as the joint military

---

46 The only common assets that NATO owns are its AWACS.

47 Canadian Joint Delegation to NATO, "NATO Senior Resource Board-In Difficult Waters," telex YBDR 7039 to National Defence Headquarters ADM, 20 June 1994, retrieved under the Access to Information Act, 10 April 2007, A-3, File No. 3947-01. Indeed, Canada wanted NATO to review the "current responsibilities, authorities, scope and effectiveness" of the Senior Resource Board; see International Security and Defence Relations Division, Department of External Affairs, "NATO Resource Board," telex to Canadian Joint Delegation to NATO, 23 June 1994, retrieved under the Access to Information Act, 10 April 2007, A-3, File No. 3947-01. "The Senior Resource Board (SRB) is a subsidiary body of the North Atlantic Council (NAC) and the Defence Planning Committee (DPC), which have given the Board a lead policy and planning role in all military resource areas" (NATO Handbook 1994). It was created by the NAC in May 1993 to provide high-level resource management in NATO and tasked with reviewing the rationalization of NATO resource management to provide the NAC with greater flexibility in light of declining resources and expanding activities.

48 DG POL OPS, "European Command Arrangements."

49 International Security and Defence Relations Division, Department of External Affairs, "NATO Infrastructure Program," telex IDS 267 to Canadian Embassy in Bonn, 23 June 1994, retrieved under the Access to Information Act, 10 April 2007, A-3, File No. 3947-01. Indeed, Canada believed that a fundamental review of all NATO budgets was an urgent necessity.

50 Ibid.

command posts in various countries across Europe, such as the Allied Command Operations near Mons, Belgium, and the Allied Air Component Command in Ramstein, Germany.[51] The budget was approximately US$161 million in 1999 and, as NATO documents show, has not changed much since 1955.[52] It pays the salaries and benefits of the International Staff at Headquarters as well as of all support staff. The International Staff functions as the support body for the alliance and makes the organization work on a day-to-day basis. It manages the numerous internal committees and helps implement the political guidelines set by the NAC. The civil budget also pays the costs of running the Private Office of the Secretary General, staff salaries and benefits, and travel, communications, and utilities expenses.

NATO's military budget is by far the largest of the three (US$496 million in 1999), accounting for 44.4% of the total.[53] It is determined by the Defence Planning Committee based on an annual, collectively negotiated formula. It finances NATO's command infrastructure, including the operational headquarters at SHAPE in Mons, and AWACS, based in Geilenkirchen, Germany. (But soldiers operating in these units are paid by the member states rather than the alliance.) Before France rejoined NATO's integrated military structure in 2009, the total military costs were divided among 26 rather than 27 member states.

NATO's third operating budget is NSIP. Formerly known as the Infrastructure Fund, its name as well as its overall objectives were changed in 1993 to reflect the alliance's response to the post–Cold war security environment. The NSIP budget (US$458 million in 1999)[54] provides collective financing for NATO's support functions, such as command and control infrastructure, communications, logistics, the maintenance of training installations, and storage facilities for equipment, fuel, and ammunitions. For example, NSIP has helped finance American storage facilities in Europe and naval ports in Halifax, Nova Scotia.[55]

---

51 On 12 June 2003, NATO defence ministers agreed to a new command structure for the alliance. At the strategic level, only one command post – Allied Command Operations – holds operational responsibilities; it replaced the old Allied Command Europe and Allied Command Atlantic. At the tactical level, six joint force component commands as well as a new transformation common post in Norfolk, Virginia, were created; see, e.g., Institute for National Strategic Studies, National Defense University 1997.
52 Lis and Selden 2003, 25.
53 Ibid., xv.
54 Ibid.
55 Ek 2006.

In the early days of the successful PfP program, the NSIP budget was also used to provide assistance to PfP countries. This was a preference that Canada had strongly pushed for, with government officials arguing that it should be considered for "PfP operations, exercises, training, interoperability or communications."[56] It is not clear what rationale was behind this strong stance, but it can be reasonably expected that domestic political factors played a significant role. If funding for certain PfP initiatives came from NATO's operating budget, no additional monies had to be sent by the member states. In difficult fiscal times, this was good politics for Canada. It is thus hardly surprising that Ottawa had such strong preferences for this option, which rested on the principle that only an economically healthy Canada could be sufficiently committed to the alliance.[57]

Table 7.9 below shows the contributions of NATO members to the three common NATO budgets from 1997 to 2003. Data for 1990 to 1996 remain classified, except Canada's,[58] although even that data is of very limited use because it does not provide a comparative (or even relative) perspective on Canadian burden sharing. However, comparative data is available for 1997 to 2003.

As the table shows, Canada was the 6th-highest-ranking contributor (5th when the United States is not counted in) to NATO's common budgets in this period, spending $509.2 million[59] and outperforming all other second-tier powers. The Netherlands, for example, trails Canada

---

56 DG POL OPS, "European Command Arrangements."

57 Regional Security Section (DFAIT), "NAC Visit: Briefing Material on CDN Approaches to Current NATO Issues," telex IDR-0576 to Canadian missions in London, Bonn, Paris, The Hague, Copenhagen, Oslo, Brussels, Lisbon, Madrid, Rome, Ankara, Athens, Warsaw, Prague, Budapest, and Washington, 30 October 1997, retrieved under the Access to Information Act, 10 April 2007, A-3, File No. 3947-01.

58 Canadian payments to the military budget and NSIP combined were $160,416 (1989–90), $172,506 (1990–91), $188,081 (1991–92), $160,644 (1992–93), $158,032 (1993–94), $169,073 (1994–95), $170,608 (1995–96), and $114,462 (1996–97), averaging 5.5% between 1989 and 2008. Payments to the civil budget were made by DFAIT (Access to Information Request A-2009-00109/Team 5 C-1, 1 June 2009).

59 While the NATO budgets were being reviewed in 1994, the Canadian delegation to NATO received instructions from Ottawa to keep the Canadian cost share as low as possible; see J.C. Hunter, [blacked out], "Participation in NATO Infrastructure Program," fax YBDR 7036, 3 June 1994, retrieved under the Access to Information Act, 10 April 2007, A-3, File No. 3947-01. This is consistent with the Chrétien government's preoccupation with domestic politics, especially the financial crisis and the resulting cuts to social benefits. Canada sought a reduction of 1% of its contributions to the common budget, while being the largest per capita net contributor.

at 7, Spain at 9, and Denmark at 10. But all second-tier powers are similar in their relative cost share – that is, their contributions to the common budgets relative to their GDP. This number is particularly disproportionate in the case of Canada, which, even though it ranks 6th in total spending, ranks 13th in relation to its GDP.

Moreover, in 1997 and 1998, Canada's share of the common budgets was close to 12% higher than that of France, which is considered a major power. We can infer two things from this empirical finding. First, it suggests that the defence expenditures relative to GDP appear to be highly inaccurate in assessing the share of the collective burden contributed by the member states. Second, it suggests that in line with other indexes discussed in this chapter, second-tier powers had significantly different burden-sharing preferences than the major powers like the United States or the United Kingdom in the sense that they placed a high importance on civilian areas. Indeed, second-tier member states seemed to have very strong preferences for pursuing non-military collective objectives.

Contributions to NATO's common budgets can be better explained in the context of the time. At the Madrid Summit in 1997, the alliance unanimously agreed to enlarge by 1999 and invite the Czech Republic, Hungary, and Poland to join. The enlarged alliance required new organizational structures and procedures, especially in infrastructure and communications, to allow the new member states to fully access and participate in alliance politics and decision-making processes. For example, when the expansion was agreed on, NATO's eastern border grew longer and required additional resources to effectively monitor and protect it. Moreover, outdated technical infrastructure in CEE such as command, control, and communications equipment and technology needed to be upgraded to NATO standards because inferior Russian military technology had dominated CEE defence markets for decades. These upgrades would make the Czech, Hungarian, and Polish forces fully interoperable with NATO forces and allow NATO to effectively extend the Article 5 provisions to the new member states.[60]

There are two explanations for why NATO's common budgets shrank between 1997 and 2003 by an average of 25.84%.[61] First, the Czech

---

60 For further details and discussion, see Anthony 1994; Kiss 1997; Michta 1999.

61 One empirical exception to this is 1999, when the common budget contributions increased slightly. This can be explained by the preparation for and conduct of the Kosovo war and the high costs of Operation ALLIED HARMONY. For example, the NATO air base in Aviano, Italy, where most of the fighter jets operated from, received partial NATO funding.

Table 7.9 Contributions to NATO's Common Budgets, 1997–2003 (Millions of US Dollars)

Country	1997	1998	1999	2000	2001	2002	2003	Total ($)	Total (%)	Total (non-US) (%)	Change over period (%)	Average over period	Rank	Defence spending as share of GDP*	Power status
United States	472.9	453.2	281.1	281.0	299.0	340.9	510.7	2,638.8	27.0	n/a	-36.8	357.4	1	3	Superpower
Germany	362.9	300.9	218.5	223.8	242.7	268.6	385.1	2,002.5	20.5	28.1	-33.1	269.8	2	11	Major power
United Kingdom	222.3	193.7	172.8	164.0	173.3	200.2	226.9	1,353.2	13.9	19.0	-22.0	185.2	3	6	
Italy	120.1	101.0	78.3	83.4	88.4	103.6	136.7	711.5	7.3	10.0	-26.4	94.2	4	5	
France	88.5	77.6	88.3	77.3	74.8	111.8	124.7	643.0	6.6	9.0	-15.5	81.3	5	4	
Canada	100.8	83.6	53.7	53.0	51.2	64.9	102.0	509.2	5.2	7.1	-49.2	68.5	6	13	
Netherlands	65.4	54.1	44.9	43.2	47.2	52.1	69.2	376.1	3.8	5.3	-27.8	51.0	7	9	Second-tier power
Belgium	61.2	50.6	41.0	40.7	44.4	48.9	64.7	351.5	3.6	4.9	-27.5	47.6	8	12	
Spain	12.1	13.2	31.6	36.0	44.0	51.3	68.6	256.8	2.6	3.6	263.6	27.4	9	14	
Denmark	42.3	34.4	28.5	28.7	31.3	34.8	44.4	244.4	2.5	3.4	-26.0	33.0	10	10	
Norway	33.1	26.2	21.4	23.0	25.3	27.8	35.1	191.9	2.0	2.7	-23.6	25.8	11	7	
Poland	n/a	n/a	14.8	24.2	31.2	37.4	14.9	122.5	1.3	1.7	n/a	14.0	12	17	
Turkey	23.4	22.2	16.0	15.9	16.9	19.6	27.2	141.2	1.4	2.0	-27.8	18.9	13	2	
Greece	10.4	9.2	6.9	7.8	8.3	10.0	12.5	65.1	0.7	0.9	-20.2	8.5	14	1	Third-tier power
Czech Republic	n/a	n/a	5.4	8.8	11.3	13.6	15.2	54.3	0.6	0.8	n/a	5.1	16	18	
Portugal	8.7	8.2	6.0	5.9	6.4	7.4	10.5	53.1	0.5	0.7	-26.4	7.0	17	8	
Hungary	n/a	n/a	3.8	6.4	8.2	9.8	11.0	39.2	0.4	0.5	n/a	3.7	15	19	
Luxembourg	2.4	1.6	1.5	1.6	1.7	1.9	2.5	13.2	0.1	0.2	-29.2	1.8	18	15	
Iceland	0.4	0.4	0.3	0.3	0.3	0.3	0.4	2.4	0	0	-25.0	0.3	19	16	

Table 7.9 Contributions to NATO's Common Budgets, 1997–2003 (Millions of US Dollars) (cont.)

Country	1997	1998	1999	2000	2001	2002	2003	Total ($)	Total (%)	Total (non-US) (%)	Change over period (%)	Average over period	Rank	Defence spending as share of GDP*	Power status
Total	1,626.9	1,430.1	1,114.8	1,125.0	1,205.9	1,404.9	1,862.3	9,769.9	100.0	100.0	-152.9	1,300.5	19	19.0	
Total (non-US)	1,154.0	976.9	833.7	844.0	906.9	1,064.0	1,351.6	7,131.1	73.0	100.0	-116.1	943.1	18	18.0	
Average	101.7	89.4	58.7	59.2	63.5	73.9	98.0	514.2	5.3	5.3	-8.0	68.4	n/a	n/a	
Average (non-US)	76.9	65.1	46.3	46.9	50.4	59.1	75.1	396.2	4.1	5.6	-6.5	52.4	n/a	n/a	

Source: United States Department of Defense, *Report on Allied Contributions to the Common Defense* (Washington, DC: Department of Defense, 1997 to 2002); International Institute for Strategic Studies, *Military Balance* (London: IISS, 1998 to 2004); public accounts of Canada, fiscal years 1989 to 2001–3 (Access to Information Request A-2009–00109/Team 5-C1, Department of National Defence).

Republic, Hungary, and Poland, now part of the integrated military structure, were asked to carry their share of the common costs; this allowed the burdens for the existing members to shrink. Second, during the process of enlargement, NATO transformed its armed services and took increasing advantage of the so-called revolution in military affairs (RMA). This helped streamline command and control functions as well as the bureaucracy (both military and civilian) at Headquarters and at various command posts.[62] The RMA also cut down on the cost of equipment, personnel, and military capabilities.

Conclusion

This chapter analysed Canada's soft military and hard civilian contributions to allied security, such as personnel and infrastructure expenditures, NATO's rapid reaction forces, and NATO's common budgets. It showed that the benchmarks for burden sharing that were commonly used during the Cold War, such as the level of defence spending relative to a country's GDP, had become inaccurate and mostly obsolete at the beginning of the post–Cold War era, when NATO transformed from a military to a political organization. What mattered to NATO now was not so much "boots on the ground" as political and diplomatic commitments. Thus, while the soft power tools and resources of its member states mattered increasingly more, they were not reflected in the burden-sharing debate or in the commonly used burden-sharing indexes. For second-tier power Canada, for example, the measure of its defence spending in NATO could not be reduced to the level of its GDP or the size of its armed forces.

This chapter developed new and more accurate benchmarks for measuring national contributions to NATO; they are alternative reference points in a fundamentally transformed security environment. These new benchmarks are a country's contribution to NATO's rapid response forces, its level of aid to CEE and countries around the world for humanitarian and economic purposes, and its contribution to NATO's common budgets.

Partly out of humanitarian concerns, Canada took the initiative and set up three programs worth $30 million to assist Poland and Hungary,[63]

---

62 For a good discussion, see Stanley R. Sloan 2002; Sokolsky 2001.
63 Clark 1990, n.p.

sent $12 million in emergency food aid,[64] and supported a training program for Polish farmers in livestock and farm management.[65] In 1991, it also became a founding member of the European Bank for Reconstruction and Development, which was set up to assist with private sector initiatives and infrastructure projects down to the local level.[66] These initiatives demonstrate that Canada believed in the role and function of international institutions as moderators and facilitators for cooperation rather than an anarchical international system. It believed that progress and cooperation were possible. Guided by liberal international values, Canada was a strong supporter of matters that required increasingly soft rather than hard power resources and burden-sharing practices. For example, by embracing the collective need for rapid reaction forces with flexible response capabilities, Ottawa strengthened NATO's infrastructure, the development of the NRF, and NATO's common budgets. It also invested proportionally more than equally ranked second-tier powers in economic aid to CEE states as well as general foreign assistance.

In sum, the notion of a free-riding second-tier power Canada is not sustainable when compared to the empirical data provided in this chapter. Indeed, its practices of Atlantic burden sharing in the civilian domain confirm its external responsibility to provide sustainable governance, peace, and stability in CEE in particular and European security generally.

---

64 Canada, Department of External Affairs and International Trade, 1990, 9.
65 Clark 1990, n.p.
66 Karns and Mingst 2004, 398, 401–2.

8 Conclusion

Broadly speaking, this book has examined the practice of sharing the NATO burden in the 1990s, with a particular emphasis on Canada. Sharing is conceptualized not as a predetermined outcome of state behaviour, but as a dynamic process of national preference formations for certain state actions. Indeed, sharing the burden of an international institution can be regarded as such an action directed towards a specific set of social purposes at the national and international levels. This process necessitates contextualizing the behaviour of the individual social actions of states in the emerging new world order following the Cold War.

The preceding chapters looked at the practice of sharing transatlantic burdens in the 1990s by focusing on the preference formations of NATO's so-called second-tier powers for sharing Atlantic burdens, drawing on liberal IR theory as the theoretical framework, a Weberian epistemology, and using Canada as a case study. These second-tier powers were also an integral part of the discussion about the new regional order in Europe.

Contrary to conventional wisdom espoused by collective action theorists, second-tier powers were not Atlantic free riders but rather committed allies who enforced NATO's new public good of crisis management. Second-tier powers made an essential (albeit not easily quantifiable) contribution to upholding that good. This contribution must be interpreted in the larger situational context of an evolving security environment in Europe, national societal predispositions (or preferences) towards an evolving Europe, and transatlantic security and international organizations in general.

In contrast to realist and liberal institutionalist ontologies, liberal IR theory contends that states are not unitary actors in world politics but rather highly decentralized and fragmented entities. They are composed of different societal groupings and actors, all of which are expected to have competing preferences on policy issues. Actors are assumed to have a social purpose and preferences for outcomes (i.e., wealth, peace), which lead them to pursue strategies – that is, means to achieve ends.[1] To be sure, preferences (or interests) are analytically different from strategies or strategic settings of foreign policy. Actors also rank their preferences and outcomes in a given environment.

Methodologically, it is thus imperative that we analyse whether it is preferences or the situational environment that is causally responsible for the behavioural outcomes of states. Actors might rank their preferences and form strategies to achieve them contingent on the environment in which they are embedded.[2] An exchange of these societal interests and exogenous externalities determines which of these preferences is most likely to influence the policymaking process. In other words, the national preferences of second-tier powers are *causally* independent of political strategies pursued by other actors in the political marketplace.

In our case study, Canada showed a strong propensity to share significant parts of the collective NATO burden in spite of domestic and societal limitations. It had a strong preference for remaining an active and committed agent rather than an Atlantic free rider. Its foreign policy actions in Europe were driven by ideational, commercial, and institutional preferences as well as normative values of enforcing human and humanitarian rights and freedoms. This book has shown the significant analytical limitations of existing works on Atlantic burden sharing that stress security threats or risk of alliance abandonment as the causes of states sharing a collective burden.[3] This study found no supporting evidence for either hypothesis.

---

1 Frieden 1999, 45. These preferences may not be directly observable but can be investigated empirically.

2 This is a long-debated issue in IR. For a discussion, see, e.g., Bueno de Mesquita and Lalman 1992b; Levy 1990–91.

3 See Bennett, Lepgold, and Unger 1994; Snyder 1997; Walt 1987; Kupchan 1988; for the Canadian context, see Zyla 2011.

Methodologically, studying the social actions of sharing Atlantic burdens is a meaningful inductive research strategy because it reveals the societal predispositions (or preferences) that lead to state actions (i.e., sharing collective NATO burdens) in the first place. In this sense, studying patterns of national state preferences allows a bottom-up analysis of collective action behaviour whereby the demands and preferences of individuals and groups are analysed *before* policymaking or policy outcomes.

It is precisely these domestic predispositions that liberal IR theory as the theoretical framework, coupled with a Weberian epistemology bridging instrumental and value rationality, helped explain. Liberal IR theory espouses unique and multi-causal hypotheses that enable us to make more accurate explanations and understanding of collective action behaviour than theories stressing variations in relative capabilities (realism) or participation in international organization (neo-liberalism). It allows us to gain access to the formation and patterns of Canada's national preferences towards NATO burden sharing and enables us to examine whether particular types of state preferences and their variations – individual rights (ideational liberals), commercial interests (commercial liberals), domestic institutions (republican liberals), or an interplay of all three – determined its foreign policy behaviour in the 1990s.

Above all, state preferences are derived from domestic and transnational pressures. Liberal IR theory thus overcomes the rigid assumptions of its competitors (realist and neo-institutionalist accounts) that state preferences remain static and stable over time. By treating the issue of order as a dynamic process and linking discussions of violence to other elements of that order (as opposed to upholding the static view that "war is war is war"), we see that violence is symptomatic of changes in other social spheres. In other words, those changes are not simply structural constants determined or produced by the anarchic system, as suggested by some IR theories.[4] Both material *and* non-material or social interests, motivations, and values are important variables for explaining the foreign policy behaviour of states. This book has shown that second-tier powers practised NATO burden sharing not as a result of a cost-benefit analysis, but out of a combination of material and non-material preferences (e.g., ethics, external responsibility) in their foreign policy decisions. In doing so, they helped transform NATO from a purely military to a political alliance and maintain peace and order in Europe.

---

4 See Kaldor 1999, ch. 2, 3.

Against this backdrop, it was the objective and purpose of this study to examine how second-tier powers' national preferences can help explain their behaviour in the alliance's burden-sharing regime in the 1990s. It introduced a clustering of military and civilian burden-sharing indexes to increase the explanatory value of the burden-sharing debate. This form of clustering holds great promise for more accurately determining the civilian and military share of the NATO pie.

Summary of Empirical Evidence

Part I of this book looked at existing theories of collective action in the literature on NATO burden sharing and IR in general. It then formulated eight theoretical and conceptual shortfalls and four methodological ones that are evident in existing studies on NATO burden sharing, and it demonstrated their unsuitability to explain the burden-sharing behaviour of second-tier powers in the post–Cold War era. To be forthright methodologically, I was, in fact, able to formulate this criticism after consulting the empirical material on NATO burden sharing and before starting the analysis. In other words, I employed a dialectical approach between theory and empirical material that allowed me to uncover flaws in the literature and the (rationalist) theories.

The empirical data also suggested that existing studies on burden sharing were ill-equipped to explain the behaviour of second-tier powers in the post–Cold War era, and it pointed me towards liberal IR theory as a more suitable theoretical framework, one able to provide a new perspective on NATO burden sharing. I recognize that this is not a stringent deductive research strategy in the formal sense of "testing" existing (liberal) theories, as is perhaps practice in rationalist research designs in IR. However, it enabled me to engage early with the data and formulate a more precise critique of existing theoretical accounts of collective action theory.

This book had two objectives: first, to produce empirical evidence that would demonstrate that Canada was not an Atlantic free rider; and second, to show how second-tier powers' national preferences explained their motivations and behaviour in the NATO burden-sharing regime in the 1990s. The empirical evidence was presented in Part II. Chapter 3 analysed some of the changes resulting in the new world order, while Chapter 4 discussed the share of the military burden that Canada shouldered, ranging from its contribution to the first Gulf War in 1990 and the ECMM in 1991 to the Kosovo campaign in 1999. The initial mandate of the CF in UNPROFOR was to monitor and demilitarize UNPAs in Croatia, and, in so doing, they encountered some of the most difficult operational situations posed by the mission. They were witness to the massacres in Srebrenica in 1993, taken hostage in Sarajevo in 1994, and confronted with direct combat in the battle of the Medak Pocket[5] – helping to keep the peace where there was no peace to keep.

Canada sent 2,151 soldiers (5.44% of the total UN force) to serve under UNPROFOR, ranking 5th overall.[6] (If non-NATO states are excluded, Canada ranked 3rd, shouldering 11.47% of the total.) In view of the domestic situation (context) – the curtailing of the federal budget in the early 1990s, rising threats to national unity precipitated by the referendum on the independence of Quebec, and a genuine concern for human rights violations – Canada's preference was to support the UN mission in the former Yugoslavia (UNPROFOR) by sending forces and making other, non-military resources available. Weighed against Canada's relative capabilities as well as the situational context in which these deployment decisions were made, its contributions can be considered noteworthy. They certainly do not lend credence to the hypothesis of a free-riding Canada, as suggested by some.[7]

Chapter 5 described the failure of the UN mission in the Balkans to secure peace and order in the former Yugoslavia. Following the signing of the Dayton Accords in December 1995, UNPROFOR was replaced with IFOR, a NATO peace enforcement mission. The litmus test of the alliance, then, was the recruitment of national troop contributions to help enforce the Dayton Agreement. Canada was part of the IFOR operation and maintained its existing UN expeditionary forces in theatre to support the NATO-led crisis-management and conflict-prevention operations. It sent 1,029 troops (2.0% of the absolute force share), ranking 9th out of the 16 NATO countries. While this contribution was slightly below the alliance average, Canada was the 5th-largest contributor in relative terms, sending 1.6% of its national force compared to the NATO average of 1.4%. It was also the 4th-largest force contributor to Operation AIR BRIDGE, which provided the city of Sarajevo with humanitarian aid.

However, as suggested in Part I, such absolute force deployments have significant explanatory limitations because they do not take into

---

5 See Off 2004.
6 This is well out of proportion to its population as the ninth largest of all NATO allies.
7 See, e.g., Cohen 2004; Conference of Defence Associations Institute 2002; Granatstein 2004; Nossal 1998–99.

account the context in which those practices of burden sharing take place or highlight the overall benchmark against which those force deployments were made. I therefore argue that to gain a fuller picture of the practice of Atlantic burden sharing in the IFOR operation, one must weigh the *absolute* force contributions made by the member states against their relative ability to send troops. In other words, those national force contributions to IFOR must be calculated (and interpreted) as a share of size of the national armed forces. This *relative* perspective produces a far superior empirical analysis of the practice of NATO burden sharing because it takes into account the relative ability of states to send their armed forces on international peace missions.

The most interesting result of this exercise is that in relative terms, the United States did *not* shoulder the largest share of the NATO burden in IFOR; the United Kingdom did. The United States ranked only 9th, placing it in the second-tier power category. Moreover, those states that were usually considered second-tier powers (e.g., Canada and the Netherlands) had major-power status because they shouldered a higher share of the collective NATO burden in relative terms than any otherwise major power (the sole exception being the United Kingdom). Canada was the 5th-largest force contributor and can therefore be considered a major contributor to the IFOR operation.

One year later, SFOR succeeded IFOR, and Canada once again maintained its forces in theatre. From 1997 to 2001, it sent 6,443 soldiers to SFOR, 4.5% of the absolute force share (5.7% without the United States), above the NATO average of 5.3%, and making it the 7th-largest NATO-contributing country out of the 16 (19 countries as of 1999). To truly comprehend the magnitude of this burden, we must recognize that all of Canada's army units rotated through the operation. Also, studying primary documents on the government's decision-making processes makes it clear that Canada's force contributions were driven by strong preferences for enforcing human rights and alleviating human insecurity, for staying allied, and for enforcing the Dayton Accords and evolving norms of human security.[8] In sum, Canada's *absolute* force commitments to SFOR were significant, especially when compared to

---

8 Indeed, NATO was an effective and dynamic alliance in the 1990s. CEE considered it a prestigious club of liberal states that appeared to provide a cost-effective defence against external aggression. While this paradigm undoubtedly appealed to CEE, it had been the cornerstone of Canada's foreign policy since it joined the alliance. Above all, NATO's outreach and enlargement processes suggested to Canadian officials that an expanding club of states "indicates that membership remains worthwhile" (Hartley and Sandler 1999, 666).

other NATO allies holding similar power status. The empirical findings do *not* support the free-riding hypothesis put forward by collective action theorists.

An even more balanced assessment of Canada's share of the SFOR operation comes from considering its contribution in relative terms. Following this analysis, Canada (and other second-tier states like Norway and the Netherlands) was a major power. The extent of Canada's burden, 2.15% of the total compared with a NATO average of 1.05%, places it 3rd in the ranking. The Canadian practice of burden sharing epitomized Ottawa's commitment to NATO peace operations and suggests that things other than relative gains or simple power politics informed its preferences for burden sharing. There is strong evidence that Canada pursued absolute rather than relative gains, including showcasing a strong sense of external responsibility for bringing peace, freedom, and stability to the region.

In 1999, when ethnic Albanians and a Serb minority engaged in ethnic cleansing in Kosovo, Canada responded once again to NATO's call for troops, a commitment to enforce human rights, and a response to human security needs. From 1999 to 2001, Ottawa deployed 1,450 troops each year to the KFOR operation (4.3% of the total NATO force, 5.0% without the United States), making it the 6th-largest absolute force contributor out of the 19 nations. But in relative force share, Canada ranked 4th, with 7.3% of its armed forces deployed to KFOR. An equally interesting observation obtained from the relative force share index is that contrary to the hypothesis posed by collective action theorists, America was not a supreme burden sharer but rather a laggard and a true free-rider: it sent only 1.1% of its military forces to serve in KFOR, placing it in the third-tier power category.

As a second-tier power, Canada shouldered a disproportionate burden of Operation ALLIED FORCE, the 78-day air campaign, flying 6.6% of the total sorties (calculated without the United States; the NATO average was 5.6%). Taking the ground and air campaign together, it was the 3rd-largest NATO force-contributing nation. Yet again, this was a significant contribution (in relative terms) by a second-tier NATO country and is more accurately interpreted as an indicator of commitment rather than free riding or, worse, irrelevance.

Part III of this book examined the civilian indicators of Atlantic burden sharing and Canada's preference formation for sharing those burdens. It contextualized Canada's position vis-à-vis the debates surrounding the political transformation of the alliance, including questions

Table 8.1 Canadian Participation in the Balkans, 1991–2001

Mission	Time period	Approximate maximum size (all countries)	Maximum Canadian contribution	Description	Absolute rank	Relative rank
ECMM	1991	75	9 military observers; 1 senior officer	Monitor cease-fire reached between Slovenia and JNA	5–10% of total	n/a
UNPROFOR	1992–6	39,537;750 civilian and police force	2,151;45 civilian and police force	UN Protection Force Bosnia, Croatia (UNCRO), Macedonia	5 out of 37	n/a
IFOR	1996–7	52,206	1,029	NATO-led Implementation Force Bosnia-Herzegovina	9 out of 16	5 out of 16
SFOR	1997–2001	30,000–35,000 per year	1,000–2,500	NATO-led Stabilization Force Bosnia-Herzegovina	7 out of 19	3 out of 19
UNPREDEP	1995–2001	1,100	2	UN Preventive Deployment Force (FYROM)	n/a	n/a
UNMOP	1996–2001	27	1	UN Mission of Observers in Prevlaka (Croatia)	n/a	n/a
UNMIBH	1996–2001	5;2,057 civilian and police force	1;30 civilian and police force	UN Mission in Bosnia and Herzegovina	n/a	n/a
UNMACBiH	1996–7	72	6	UN Mine Action Center Bosnia-Herzegovina	n/a	n/a
KFOR	1999–2001	35,000	4,350	NATO-led Kosovo Force	6 out of 19	4 out of 19
UNMIK	1999–2001	4,366 police	86 RCMP	UN Interim Administration Mission in Kosovo	n/a	

Sources: Cohen 2003, 127; relative force contributions compiled by author.
n/a: Not calculated for this table.

of new membership, enlargement, and the establishment of new political regimes, such as the PfP program and the EAPC.

Chapter 6 provided an explicative understanding[9] of Canadians' thinking about and preferences for their county's actions in the alliance. It examined material and ideational preferences (norms, values, and identity) affecting Canada's foreign policy behaviour and attempted to attribute meaning to a particular set of its social actions in the new world order. The fall of the Berlin Wall and the extensive transformation processes of societies in CEE following the peaceful revolutions of 1989 delineated this historical context and, consistent with the hypothesis put forward by liberal IR theory, revealed the government's strong preferences for economic development as well as stable and prosperous liberal democracies.

Canada was not only a strong supporter of defending the liberal peace in Europe. It also held strong preferences for extending the liberal community of states to CEE by putting in place a structured economic, political, and military outreach process that promised new relationships as well as access to new export markets. In so doing, Ottawa helped keep the peace not only in Europe but also at home. It was a relatively inexpensive preference for a government to adopt as it faced a deep recession, cash-strapped federal departments forced to cut back on programs and priorities, a strong secessionist movement, the resulting political crisis on the federal level, and its armed forces in disarray after the Somalia mission in 1994.

While pursuing these preferences of restraint – dubbed "pinchpenny diplomacy"[10] by some – engaging in the new Europe was a viable option for Canadian officials, and this civilian-oriented foreign policy priority appeared to put Canada's economic house in order. It is therefore not surprising that – partly out of necessity, partly out of strong ideational predispositions – Canada became a strong advocate for a political alliance that increasingly emphasized and made use of its soft rather than hard power resources.[11] It was also not surprising that Canada's foreign policy elite as well as a majority of Canadians strongly supported building a new NATO and its new outreach regimes (e.g., the PfP program).

---

9 See Bloomfield and Nossal 2007.

10 Nossal 1998–99.

11 See also John Gray, "One Germany: There Is Little That Mikhail Gorbachev Can Do to Stop the Unification Blitzkrieg: Soviet Leader on the Sidelines," *Globe and Mail*, 30 June 1990.

A more politically oriented alliance was a dream that Canada had argued for in the negotiations leading up to passing Article 2 of the Washington Treaty, now commonly known as the Canadian article.

Chapter 7 focused on soft power resources and how they related to NATO's burden-sharing regime. It introduced a set of alternative soft military burden-sharing indexes, such as UN peacekeeping personnel, amount of defence expenditures allocated to modernization and infrastructure, and contributions to NATO's rapid reaction force. The contributions of NATO countries in these categories are summarized in table 8.2 below.

This table shows that Canada was not a laggard but rather a committed transatlantic ally that shouldered its burden according to its relative capabilities. Compared to most other second-tier powers, Canada outperformed its peers, scoring higher in relative contributions. Two other second-tier powers, Norway and the Netherlands, shouldered more, but it is inaccurate to classify them as second- or even third-tier powers; they are major powers when it comes to NATO's soft military burdens.

The second part of Chapter 7 analysed the hard civilian indicators of Atlantic burden sharing – foreign economic assistance to CEE, foreign aid, and NATO's common budgets. These three indexes as well as the ranking of NATO states are summarized in table 8.3 below. It shows that Canada shouldered a significant share of NATO's collective soft power responsibilities; indeed, it outperformed its peers in the soft power cluster, providing yet more support for viewing it as a major second-tier power.

The empirical analysis suggests that relative to its abilities and weighted against the arithmetic median of all NATO allies, Canada bore its fair share of NATO's soft *and* hard military burdens. In fact, the data indicates that Canada was a committed and reliable second-tier NATO power and that NATO continued to be one of the basic pillars (or preferences) of its national security policy and its international foreign policy engagements. Canada's track record testifies to its reliability and proportionality in taking on its burden-sharing responsibilities and practices. This conclusion does not stem from political or ideological preferences for military actions but is borne out in examining all of Canada's practices of burden sharing in the 1990s.[12]

---

12 These findings provide an interesting basis for future testing on, for example, NATO's ISAF mission and the air campaign in Libya, which were beyond the scope of this study.

Table 8.2 Ranking by Soft Military Indicator

Country	Contribution to peacekeeping personnel	Expenditures on modernization	Expenditures on infrastructure	Contribution to rapid reaction force
United Kingdom	5	3	3	2
United States	1	1	11	1
France	2	6	12	3
Germany	4	11	4	5
Turkey	10	2	6	6
Norway	9	4	1	12
Netherlands	8	7	5	8
Italy	3	10	14	4
Canada	6	8	7	13
Greece	12	5	10	7
Spain	7	12	15	9
Denmark	15	9	9	11
Czech Republic	17	13	16	n/a
Belgium	14	16	8	10
Hungary	16	15	17	n/a
Poland	13	18	18	n/a
Portugal	11	14	13	14
Luxembourg	19	17	2	15
Iceland	18	19	19	16
Total	19	19	19	19

Source: author's compilation.

Table 8.3 Ranking by Hard Civilian Indicator

Country	UN Peace Fund	Economic Aid to CEE, 1991–7	Foreign Assistance 1990–2001	NATO Common Budgets, 1997–2003
Belgium	9	10	11	8
Canada	3	3	7	6
Czech Republic	0	n/a	17	15
Denmark	7	1	8	10
France	0	4	3	5
Germany	0	5	2	2
Greece	0	15	14	14
Hungary	0	n/a	18	17
Iceland	0	16	19	19
Italy	1	11	6	4
Luxembourg	8	6	15	18
Netherlands	6	9	5	7
Norway	4	2	10	11
Poland	0	n/a	16	12
Portugal	0	13	12	16
Spain	5	12	9	9
Turkey	0	14	13	13
United Kingdom	2	8	4	3
United States	0	7	1	1
Total	9	16	19	19

Source: author's compilation.

It was therefore hardly surprising that future "coalitions of the willing" after 9/11, including NATO's campaigns in Afghanistan and, more recently, Libya, called on Canada to participate. Prospective partners assessed coalition alternatives in those crises and looked to Canada as a reliable partner. Pundits who suggest that Canada was "declining" or "sleeping" in the 1990s are mistaken, as this book has shown. Why else would NATO appoint a Canadian general commander of its armed forces in Libya or allow Canada to become one of the largest resource providers to the ISAF mission in Afghanistan? And if one calculates the NATO states' relative contributions to ISAF, Canada emerges as the second-largest force contributor (after the United Kingdom at 5.41%), deploying 4.31% of its national armed forces personnel.[13] The real free riders are Greece (at 0.05%), Turkey (0.35%), Portugal (0.61%), and France (1.06%).[14]

Canada was able to make such contributions because of its strong preference for retaining an expeditionary force. This policy was laid out in its 1994 Defence White Paper and ran contrary to public recommendations to cash in the so-called peace dividend and axe those capabilities. In conjunction with strong societal preferences for preventing genocide and mass murder resulting from the conflicts in the Balkans, and recognizing a responsibility to contribute to UN-sanctioned peace operations, Canada retained an expeditionary force to deploy a battalion-sized battle group to IFOR and SFOR, which at the time were NATO's most salient out-of-area operations. Second-tier power Canada even increased its share of SFOR, originally a much smaller force than its predecessor IFOR. It also shouldered a significant burden in the Kosovo conflict in 1999.

Strategically, politically, and materially, Canada deployed military forces and expend resources when called upon by its allies.[15] It was at the forefront of shaping NATO's new political role, advocating a comprehensive approach to enlarging the alliance. In large part, it achieved this by pushing for a thorough reform of NATO's civilian and military structures and by actively supporting effective partnerships with non-NATO states, most notably Russia and the Ukraine.

---

13 The United States follows, with 3.95% of its total force deployed to Afghanistan, then the Netherlands (3.64%), Estonia (3.37%), Latvia (2.96%), and the Czech Republic (2.93%).

14 Admittedly, this calculation does not take into account the US troop surge in 2009. The argument is more fully developed in Kammel and Zyla 2011; see also Zyla 2011.

15 See Zyla and Sokolsky 2010, 246.

Table 8.4 Minor and Major NATO Operations, 1991–2002

Time period	Designation	Country/region	Purpose
Jan. 1991– Mar. 1991	Operation SOUTHERN GUARD	Turkey	Protect Turkey from Iraqi missiles
June 1992– Mar. 1993	Operation MARITIME MONITOR/MARITIME GUARD	Balkans, Adriatic Sea	Implement and monitor UN weapons embargo
April 1994– Dec. 1995	Operation DENY FLIGHT	Balkans	Implement UN no-fly zone, protect UN peacekeepers
Dec. 1995– Dec. 1996	Implementation Force (IFOR)	Croatia	Implementation of Dayton Accords
Dec. 1996– Dec. 2004	Stabilization Force (SFOR)	Bosnia and Herzegovina	Peace enforcement
Dec. 1998– Mar. 1999	Kosovo Verification Mission	FYROM	Control of Kosovo airspace
Mar. 1999– June 1999	Operation ALLIED FORCE	Former Yugoslavia	Prevention of human catastrophes in Kosovo
April 1999– Aug. 1999	Albania Force (AFOR)	Albania	Humanitarian assistance as part of Kosovo conflict
June 1999– present	Kosovo Force (KFOR)	Kosovo/FYROM	Implementation of Kosovo peace agreement
Aug. 1999– Nov. 1999	Operation ESSENTIAL HARVEST	FYROM	Disarming of Macedonian forces, support of UN observers, stabilization of Macedonia
Sept. 2001– Dec. 2001	Operation AMBER FOX	FYROM	Disarming of Macedonian forces, support of UN observers, stabilization of Macedonia
Oct. 2001– May 2002	Operation EAGLE ASSIST	North America	Control of North American airspace

Source: author's compilation.

Theoretical Implications

The empirical findings summarized above demonstrate that the commonly held ontological assumptions of rationalist collective action theory and its sister IR theories (e.g., hegemonic stability theory and power transition theory) do not have sufficient explanatory power in contemporary world politics to explain NATO's burden-sharing practice at the end of the Cold War. Those theoretical presumptions and ontological predispositions do not fully account for the human nature of states or the ethics of national statecraft – or for the fact that states form their preferences before the consideration of politics.

Rationalist scholarship on NATO burden sharing posits an ontology in which states are assumed to be unitary actors in world politics, actors who lack a conscience and an independent mind. Thus, social groupings that struggle to achieve influence in the governing processes of the state and push their interests forward have no analytical standing in that ontology and are considered irrelevant. National preferences (or interests) are predetermined by the international structure and remain static in spite of changing environments and circumstances. State leaders are thus considered to be prisoners of the international structure, whose activities are dictated by the structural predispositions produced by the state system.

As stated above, I did not follow a deductive research strategy of testing existing theories of Atlantic burden sharing. Rather, I took those theories as a starting point to uncover flaws in the scholarship and develop a new perspective on the practice of burden sharing. After an initial engagement with the empirical material, I discovered that existing theories do not allow me to fully exploit the richness of the material or to interpret it to its fullest extent;[16] on the other hand, the empirical material suggested that liberal IR theory holds greater explanatory power and provides more conceptually parsimonious insights into the practice of burden sharing than theoretical accounts stressing variations in relative capabilities, while at the same time maintaining rationality assumptions.

The research began by establishing that the international context changed with the end of the Cold War. It demonstrated that Canada was

---

16 For details, see the methodological, theoretical, and conceptual critique of existing theories of Atlantic burden sharing in ch. 2.

a second-tier power and that the old paradigms – first, that the major powers contribute more to providing the public good while second-tier states practise free riding, and second, that the scope and extent of military capabilities determine the position of states in the hierarchy of international politics – have significant explanatory deficiencies, as exemplified by Canada's foreign policy behaviour in NATO in the 1990s.

In addition, the traditional currency of international politics – state power and relative capabilities – was given new meaning at the end of the Cold War, one now defined by new roles, responsibilities, and self-perceptions for national armed forces and international security institutions. The new order also required a readjustment of governance practices, including the formulation and execution of national security policies, which required capabilities and resources much different from those that preceded them (i.e., soft power). First and foremost, this broad call for a transformation of national security policies was largely the product of a change in societal predispositions and preferences of NATO member states towards questions of national security that rested on the dictum of cashing in on the peace dividend.

Liberal IR theory based on a Weberian epistemology helps gain access to these domestic predispositions, and they in turn explain how national preferences affected Canada's behaviour during this period. It can be conceived of as a domestic theory of international politics according to which the human nature, institutions, and their interactions merit the lion's share of the analysis. States are recognized as highly decentralized and fragmented entities rather than unitary actors. Ontologically, the theory bridges the artificial divide between domestic and international politics by situating the relationship between the state and society at the centre of the analysis, and it relaxes the rationality assumptions of conventional liberal IR theory. As stated earlier, the objective of liberal IR theory is to determine whether the foreign policies of the state are shaped by individual rights, commercial interests, or domestic institutions or by an interaction of all three. In the theoretical discussions in chapter 2, these streams were clustered into ideational liberals, early commercial liberals, and republican liberals.

The empirical data assessment of both civilian and military burden sharing suggests that Canada shouldered a fair share of the NATO burden, and this seriously problematizes the view of Canadians as free riders. Nonetheless, and despite the power of the statistical data, the empirical evidence alone only partially explains why Canada shouldered the burden to the extent that it did. Here is where national preferences provide the crucial causal link to how political, economic, and social predispositions and changes affect state behaviour. The observed burden of the alliance is mostly the outcome of decisions made by governments, most notably whether to contribute their precious national resources to an international organization, but there is also the question of fairness in NATO's burden-sharing regime, of distributive justice. This normative dimension of the burden-sharing debate could not be fully discussed due to space constraints. The next section summarizes the empirical findings on how Canada's national preferences causally affected its behaviour in NATO in the 1990s.

Identity and Nature of Social Orders (Ideational Liberals)

As discussed in chapter 2, ideational liberals examine the nature of actors and states in international politics. They hold that individuals or organized groups in society – not unitary state interests – articulate national preferences for foreign policy behaviour. Their actions are guided normatively by values of human rights, including the right and duty to ensure the survival of the state as well as the safety of citizens inside sovereign states (human security). In line with the writings of John Locke, ideational liberal theorists maintain that it is the primary responsibility of the state to ensure the life, liberty, and property of its subjects and to promote individual rights and freedoms.[17] Above all, a liberal state is founded on principles that safeguard peaceful relations among states – most notably, individual rights, equality before the law, free speech, private property, and elected representation. These principles also provide the context in which the benefits of laissez-faire commerce can be enjoyed.

Thus, normatively speaking, aggressive authoritarian leaders and totalitarian forms of government threaten the peaceful relations of states and can lead to wars. A democratically legitimized government is judged to be superior to authoritarian or autocratic systems. In a democracy, the rights of the executive are regarded as an extension of the rights and duties of the individual. This does not make the state an actor per se, but rather a representative institution of civil society entrusted with the task of enforcing the rights conferred on it by society. Should an external aggressor ever threaten to infringe upon those rights, individuals, and thus the state, are morally allowed to defend them, by

17 Locke 1988.

force if necessary, because violators of these rights ought to be punished to deter future violations. This insight helps explain Canada's felt responsibility to CEE and its preference for civilian and military engagement in those states.

The Lockean state system remains in a condition of peace unless laws are broken or until such time as the physical integrity, and thus the survival, of the state is threatened. Lockean states seek to avoid threats of war and instead pursue opportunities for improved regulation through, for example, international treaties and agreements, which provide reliable frameworks and a degree of order. This point of view, as Michael Doyle noted, considers international law and order as quasi-public goods rather than competing concepts; it also helps explain Canada's actions in the new Europe.

The state of peace, as classical thinkers such as Locke and Bentham remind us, is corrupted by misjudgements, misinformation, and uncertainty. As discussed in chapter 6, it is precisely these fears of misjudgment, misinformation, and uncertainty in the new Europe that shaped Canada's preferences to become involved in the future of the CEE states. Canada was particularly concerned about the security vacuum and the effects of the withdrawal of the Soviet Union on regional order and stability in CEE – for example, that the former Soviet republics could provide a breeding ground for national and ethnic tensions in and among members of the former Warsaw Pact and thereby destabilize Eastern Europe.[18] European nationalism was a well-known concept and experience in Canadian history, and the government preferred to actively support CEE through international organizations, chiefly NATO. Canada's preference was for an institutionalized approach that would channel collective efforts through the Atlantic alliance, creating new regimes inside NATO that would manage threats of insecurity and disorder and foster cooperation among former enemies.[19] Against this backdrop, Ottawa helped to shape the new political mandate of NATO.

The normative principles enshrined in individual rights, equality before the law, free speech, private property, and elected representation were in their infancy in the former Warsaw Pact states in 1989. Following

---

18 In this sense, liberal values are consistent with those held by realists; see Hasenclever, Mayer, and Rittberger 1997, 107.

19 In strict liberal IR theory terms, these institutions, coupled with the engagement of CEE polities across various levels, also established the regulative character of the liberal peace and thus surmounted the most prevalent danger that authoritarian states posed to that peace.

liberal IR ontology, it was the duty of fellow liberal democratic states to nourish the development and application of those liberal democratic principles and actively support the emerging democracies, particularly Poland, the Czech Republic, and Hungary. And, in fact, Canada perceived these states as evolving democracies that required help. Actors sought to adhere to these normative predispositions and fulfil the obligations encapsulated in the role, identity, and membership in a liberal political community of states.[20] (Rational) public goods theory cannot provide meaningful insights into the normative preferences of the member states because it categorically excludes the domestic context in foreign policymaking.

By engaging CEE through NATO, Canadian foreign policymakers received solid domestic support, as gauged by public opinion. Consequently, there was no variance between the external actions of the government and the societal predispositions and preferences towards those actions. The public polling data presented in chapter 6 shows major support for the promotion and extension of those rights and freedoms to CEE states. Moreover, these preferences for engaging former enemies and eventually enlarging the alliance were consistent with promoting the values of human rights, freedom, property, and respect. In so doing, the Canadian government joined other like-minded liberal democratic states in a dual-track approach: deterring potential aggressors by increasing the attractiveness of the alliance. Aggressors were unstable, fragile states in the CEE region and bore incalculable risks for NATO's strategic planners. Meanwhile, the context of the new world order and the spirit of progress, as well as the evolving democracies in CEE, created the opportunity for NATO to enforce those rights and freedoms by peaceful means and engage those states politically rather than militarily.

This power of attraction was not to be underestimated and held some currency in European security governance. According to the head of NATO's Partnership for Peace Section, the alliance was unable to process the vast number of applications to the PfP program in a reasonable time; the demand for membership simply exceeded the supply.[21]

---

20 This is also known as the "logic of appropriateness," which refers to an action involving an identity or role that is matched with the obligations that come with that identity in a specific situation. For example, good international citizenship has become an intrinsic component of Western nation states; see March and Olsen 1995.
21 Head of NATO's PfP section, interview by the author, Brussels, 20 May 2007.

While critics may not be fully convinced by the empirical analysis regarding Canada's commitment to NATO in the 1990s, Ottawa's pref- erences for sharing Atlantic burdens were in line with classical liberal thinking on international politics – that a government's primary duty is to ensure the survival of the state, including its economic and societal safety. This was the case with Canada, as we have seen. By 1995, Canada was facing the possibility of Quebec separation, a crisis that threatened to undermine government business, including its foreign relations. Thus, it was both explainable and understandable that the govern- ment's foremost efforts and energy were spent on ensuring the survival of the country. This crisis also brought home what Canada stood for in NATO – ensuring, protecting, and nourishing the life, liberty, and prop- erty of human beings. Ottawa was at the forefront of the call for peace- ful management of nationalist tensions in CEE.

Commerce and Cross-Border Transactions (Early Commercial Liberals)

Commercial liberals posit that a market-oriented economy creates con- ditions of peace, which is to say that market forces hold pacifying pow- ers. They establish a causal nexus between market forces and peace because war among states weakens the economic output of a state and diminishes its working force. Thus, according to Adam Smith, states have three responsibilities: to protect society from external aggression, to protect members of society from injustice, and to maintain public institutions that ensure the free flow of goods and services. Schumpeter extended Smith's arguments by holding that a combination of a free market economy *and* a functioning democratic system are the founda- tions of liberal peace. He makes liberal peace the structured outcome of capitalist democracies.

As the empirical analysis reveals, there is strong evidence that Canada's foreign policy behaviour in NATO in the 1990s was driven, at least in part, by economic preferences. To be sure, employing domestic values and institutions of liberal democratic behaviour (ideational lib- erals) did not occur without self-interest. That interest (or preference) was commercial. The underdeveloped economies of CEE, especially their infrastructure and investment markets, held significant potential for Canadian exporters of goods and services. This was a particularly promising perspective during periods of recession at home. Exploring new foreign markets resonated not only with liberal economic thinking but also with the country's foremost policy preference – overcoming the economic recession at home. To that end, DFAIT created a Team Canada section that centralized the country's efforts to explore the markets in CEE. Canada also expressed interest in promoting a rules-based system of governance in trade, energy, and financial services in CEE and enforcing existing legislation governing those services.

The politics of commercial liberals was relatively inexpensive considering the potential return for Canadian business. Following Schumpeterian logic, investors were assured that their trade relations with CEE states were relatively secure and protected by the evolving domestic governance institutions there. Those institutions acquired increasing powers to provide the regulative framework governing transnational business relations by updating their oversight mechanisms and implementing legislation protecting transnational commerce. Nonetheless, these commercial interests were mutual. On the one hand, they provided economic opportunities for Western states to do business in CEE; on the other hand, they allowed CEE states to gain access to Western markets and increase their living standards. Thus, commercial liberals' hypothesis that increasing trade produces transnational stability remained a very strong preference for Canada in the context of the new Europe.

Representation and Cosmopolitanism (Republican Liberals)

Immanuel Kant noted that a perpetual peace is possible only when liberal states interact with other liberal democracies. The perpetual peace is a metaphorical treaty signed by liberal republics, establishing peace by means of a "pacific federation" – a combination of a republican form of representation, respect for human rights, and social and economic (or transnational) interdependence. According to Kant, a democratic state has a duty to pursue a liberal peace. By instituting reliable international law, collective security, and transnational hospitality, republics create the conditions for peace and ameliorate anarchy, uncertainty, and the security dilemma.[22] Expanding those conditions creates the potential for a perpetual, or lasting, peace. Kant's contribution to liberal IR theory is a stark reminder that we cannot study domestic and international politics separately.

---

22 In contrast to competing realist and liberal institutionalist theories, the condition of anarchy is not repetitive or cyclical. See Donnelly 1992; Gilpin 1981, 1986; Holsti 1985; Kennedy 1987.

But the reverse is true also. While liberal democracies create incentives for a separate peace among themselves, historical records reveal, as Michael Doyle has shown, that they act aggressively against non-liberal states. In this sense, Kant's constitutional democracies remain in a state of war with non-republics because they feel threatened by them. Once a full transition to liberal democratic forms of government is established – that is, a combination of republican representation, liberal values of democracy, and transnational interdependence – a democratic or perpetual peace will be achieved.

Based on liberal IR ontology, liberal states have a positive duty to defend other members of the community of states and rescue individuals who live under conditions of regime oppression. This insight is particularly pertinent to the case study discussed in this book. It is accepted knowledge in the literature on the Cold War that members of the Warsaw Pact were subjected to totalitarian rather than democratic forms of governance. With the fall of the Berlin Wall and the ensuing attempts by the Czech Republic, Hungary, and Poland to transform their societies into liberal democracies, the values of a liberal democracy acquired new meaning for them. Because of their shared values, liberal (NATO) states felt obliged to assist these countries in their transition efforts and lay out steps towards their membership in the NATO community. In other words, NATO members felt an obligation to assist transitioning societies to become functioning democracies and help expand the liberal community of states. Such practice is in line with liberal IR ontology, and this embedded social collectivity provided internal prescriptions for a socially defined norm (how to defend the liberal security community), notwithstanding the uncertain utility for the members of the collectivity.[23]

Once again, these are precisely the efforts that NATO (i.e., the liberal community of states) undertook; it built new institutions to foster transnational engagement (e.g., the NACC, PfP, and EAPC), which ultimately gave full membership to some CEE states. Efforts to democratize states in NATO's immediate geographical area had positive internal

---

23 Elias 1982. It is this political institutionalization of distinct political rules, practices, and actions that shapes the logic of the external actions of states; see Huntington 1965. Nonetheless, the logic of appropriateness is not a theory of action in itself. Rather, it helps describe the outcome of social dynamics in a community or group of social actors. It is also deterministic in the sense that it holds that social actors pursue their actions according to a set of rules.

and external effects on other states and reassured other members of the need to use the alliance as a vehicle for identifying common interests and thus strengthening its internal coherence. Canada's duty as an active member of the liberal community of states was to export the values of liberal democracy to CEE, and this became both a moral and a strategic imperative.

By actively shaping and engaging the CEE states, Canada worked to address the pre-eminent danger confronting all liberal states – namely, the complacency to preserve the basic conditions of their community in times of international turmoil. The end of the Cold War created a situation of insecurity on many levels, and addressing potential security issues was a necessary preference for Canada as part of the liberal security community. In this sense, the liberal peace was strengthened, not weakened.

Burden-Sharing Indexes and Their Analysis

This book has also looked at the resilience and validity of the commonly used GDP/level of defence spending index as a benchmark for determining the fair share of the burden that NATO member states shouldered during the 1990s. NATO has employed this form of measurement since 1949 in spite of societal and system-wide changes in international affairs. This study, however, went beyond applying this historically accepted GDP index and provided additional cross-level analysis of burden-sharing indexes clustered around hard and soft power indicators. It assumed that only by using a large number of indexes could a researcher empirically evaluate a nation's share of the burden, that in fact, the greater the number of indexes used in an empirical study, the more capable the researcher would be of determining objectively and most precisely the exact share of the burden. This research design allowed us to refute the hypothesis of free riding put forward by collective action theorists.

The empirical analysis demonstrated three things. First, it showed that the commonly held assumption that second-tier powers like Canada engaged in Atlantic free-riding behaviour does not withstand empirical analysis of NATO in the immediate post–Cold War era. Canada shouldered significant civilian and military burdens, as has been demonstrated throughout this book. This practice is explained by the domestic preference formation in the Canadian political system to pursue absolute gains rather than purely zero-sum games; I also suggested that the norm of "external responsibility" (see further discussion below) was a driving force in this regard.

Second, these empirical findings suggest that NATO's current burden-sharing indexes are imprecise at best and deceiving at worst. This has significant implications for the resulting political discourse and may lead to unfair discrimination against certain countries. Third, there is the argument of specialization, that the practice of burden sharing should be viewed holistically and across policy fields.[24] States hold comparative advantages over other states in certain policy fields, and these fields are linked (and issues traded) when it comes time to negotiate sharing the collective alliance burden. As a result, their share of the burden varies according to national specialization (or comparative advantage).[25] To be sure, this is an argument transcended from the field of international political economy into the study of alliances.[26]

However, this study did not find conclusive evidence to either support or refute such hypotheses. On the one hand, one might argue that the number of burden-sharing indexes used in this study support the comparative advantage argument because especially second- and third-tier NATO powers appear to outperform the major powers in taking on their share of the civilian burdens. On the other hand, there is no empirical evidence that any forms of this comparative advantage discourse have occurred between Canada and its allies or even that trade-offs (or side payments) have been discussed. Thus, the comparative advantage hypothesis is inconclusive.

Finally (and this is more of a sidebar to the discussions about the civilian burden-sharing indexes) there does not seem to be any empirical evidence to support Stanley Sloan's thesis that NATO states that previously maintained colonies are better foreign aid donors than states that did not.[27] Here, again, Canada is a case in point because it

---

24 The argument of specialization is drawn from the field of international political economy; see, e.g., Ricardo 1817. See also ch. 2 for a more detailed discussion. For a discussion of trading public goods, see Connolly 1970, 1972; Loehr 1973; Kiesling 1974.
25 Most recently, NATO adopted the new terminology of "smart defence" to encourage specialization; see Rasmussen 2011; Henius and McDonald 2012.
26 For details, see, e.g., Ricardo 1817 and ch. 2. For a discussion on trading public goods, see Connolly, 1970, 1972; Loehr 1973; Kiesling 1974.
27 Sloan 1985b, 85–7.

does not have a colonial history but ranks at the top when it comes to foreign aid donations.

Yet, as noted earlier, while the empirical analysis could show that second-tier powers like Canada did not engage in Atlantic free riding, the empirical data was unable to sufficiently explain *why* states contributed to the collective burden-sharing regime to the extent observed in the empirical material. It is here that this study offered a fresh epistemological approach (that of explanatory understanding) to the burden-sharing debate by attempting to explain social actions from the context in which they took place. In so doing, it attempted to overcome the divisive positivist and interpretive epistemologies in the domain of institutional burden sharing.[28]

To borrow from Max Weber's *Economy and Society*,[29] a lumberjack may cut wood in his backyard. However, questions investigating why he cut the wood without situating his actions in the relevant social context remain largely unanswered. His social actions, for example, could be induced by rational calculations, motivational factors, or emotions. In the case study provided in this book, it is precisely the change of meaning that Canadian societal groups assigned to values of national security, collective defence, diplomacy, and national statecraft that ought to be factored into the analysis to explain the level of burden that Canada as a second-tier power shared.

While the debate between *erklären* ("explaining") and *verstehen* ("understanding") in the social sciences is an old one,[30] the mainstream IR literature tends to favour the middle-ground approach; so does this book. At the core of this meta-theoretical debate is the distinction in the social sciences between "positivist" and "post-positivist" approaches.[31] The middle-ground approach holds that the two approaches can be

---

28 By positivism, I relate to the view that the task of the social sciences is to show causality and thus logical coherence among issues. These "if-then" generalizations are then tested systematically against empirical evidence; see King, Keohane, and Verba 1994. On the construction of causality, see Elster 1989.

29 Weber 1968.

30 See Hollis and Smith 1990. Some analysts have argued that this division in the history of ideas should be overcome; see Haglund 2011, 502.

31 This is a simplification of the vast literature and its meta-theoretical streams, but it serves the purpose for the present argument; see Ashley 1986; Smith and Owens 2005; Walker 1993, 1995.

considered only in combination with – not in isolation from – one another.[32] Let us revisit that debate in the history of ideas.

The debate is best captured by Martin Hollis and Steve Smith in their seminal book, *Explaining and Understanding in International Relations*. Hollis is closely associated with the former, Smith with the latter. On the one side are the post-positivists, who argue for a structuralist reading of IR theory, which treats individuals as a given material reality, and attempt to deconstruct any meta-narrative. On the other side of the debate are positivists, who advocate a Galilean approach to causal explanations in the social sciences, maintaining that an objective reality (or laws) exists in the social sciences that can be observed and measured.

While these are two extreme positions along the positivist–post-positivist spectrum of epistemological assumptions, the more moderate versions of these meta-theories provide a rich epistemological middle ground[33] that rests on the assumption that theories of international politics always contain both subjective and objective elements.[34] The subjective dimension is grounded in the belief that non-material issues such as values and norms shape our social lives and allow an *understanding* of our social actions, while the objective element speaks to an agreement about our knowledge of the causality of social reality and allows for an *objective explanation* of social facts.[35] This study of NATO's second-tier powers has provided this mutual ground and explained what makes it a novel contribution to the literature on NATO burden sharing.

Relevance of This Study for Other Theoretical Debates in IR

In addition to the issues on NATO burden sharing raised above, this book relates to some of the most hotly debated issues in IR. Five of them are presented below, making specific reference to Canada. While they by no means represent the full extent of current theoretical issues and debates in the field, they are the most prevalent.

---

32 See Sørensen 1998, 87.
33 Various scholars have demonstrated the benefit of such a middle-ground approach; see, e.g., Keohane 1998; Ruggie 1998; Waever 1996. For a rather sceptical view, see Tickner 1998.
34 See Nicholson 2000.
35 See Weber 1947.

First, the empirical findings show that liberal states do not always act in a cooperative spirit with other states. This point relates to the dualism between cooperation and conflict in international politics, a problem that has preoccupied the academic literature for decades.[36] While the democratic peace paradigm comes close to, as one analyst noted, an empirical law in IR,[37] it does *not* apply to states that are in transition from authoritarian to democratic forms of government.[38] Following the logic of liberal IR theory, one would expect liberal states to be hostile to evolving democracies.

This (empirical) hypothesis could be only partially confirmed by this study. Chapter 6 showed that Canadian foreign policymakers were publicly supportive of political and economic engagement with CEE states in light of Russia's domestic instability,[39] but inside the alliance and behind closed doors, they took a hard line against Russia, arguing that the alliance should not be taken hostage because of Russian concerns over NATO's possible enlargement to the east.[40] It is clear that Canadian government officials assigned considerable diplomatic weight to the position that the Kremlin lacked a coherent, defining political idea that would allow the Soviet Union to facilitate the resolution of its domestic and international conflicts and that the regime could not be trusted. Owing to the lack of trust and the large number of domestic issues (an archaic, ineffective, and still largely centralized economy; an underdeveloped and wasteful energy sector; and a complex and unpredictable internal political dynamic),[41] Canada maintained that the political processes surrounding questions of NATO enlargement should

---

36 This refers to the "neo-neo debate" between neo-realist and neo-liberal IR theorists; see Keohane 1986.

37 Levy 1989; see also Ray 1988.

38 Mansfield and Snyder 1995a, 1995b.

39 Tony Kellett, "Canada-2005 – Political/Military," fax to Tony Berger, DFAIT, 10 December 1996, 2, retrieved under the Access to Information Act, 10 April 2007, A-3, File No. 3947-01.

40 Lloyd Axworthy, Statement by the Canadian Minister of Foreign Affairs, the Honourable Lloyd Axworthy, to the North Atlantic Council, Special Ministerial Meeting, Brussels, 18 February 1997.

41 Canadian Joint Delegation to NATO, "APAG (Atlantic Policy Advisory Group) MTG 94: NATO and Euro-Atlantic Security," telex YBGR 1092 to EXTOTT IDS (International Security and Defence Relations Divisions, DFAIT), 12 September May 1994, 12, retrieved under the Access to Information Act, 10 April 2007, A-3, File No. 3947-01.

be addressed in consultation with Russia. At the same time, further confrontation with Russia was anticipated.

This reflects Canada's inherent distrust of other non-democratic states as, in the case of Russia, they were unable to permanently act in a cooperative manner. This foreign policy behaviour resonates with a long-held belief in liberal IR scholarship that war is always a possibility. At the same time, it highlights the importance of domestic perceptions and preferences on this issue. However, it is clear from the empirical discussion that Canada did not pursue its policies based on idealist national preferences or blindly buy into the democratic peace paradigm. It was quite aware of the public's concerns that the fall of the Berlin Wall could cause conflict in Europe rather than improve cooperation and that maintaining peace required significant efforts and investments on the part of Canadians.

Second, while this book used Canada as a case study and as a representative second-tier power, its findings also inform the debate on the general role of states in international affairs. In this way, it contributes to the so-called agent-structure debate,[42] and it does so by advancing three arguments. First, when stakes are high – in this case, the regional security of south-eastern Europe as well as transnational respect for human and humanitarian rights – the role of states grows rather than diminishes. States are more reluctant to delegate authority and decisions to international organizations, preferring instead to control and manage issues in their respective capitals. At the same time, second-tier-power Canada recognized the importance of certain norms, rules, and values (e.g., human security, human rights) that needed to be enforced.

Juxtaposed to this, sovereign states are generally inclined to retain as much sovereignty over their armed forces as possible, especially given that organizations like NATO do not have standing forces. Above all, they launch, participate in, and maintain international peace operations. This implies that states, rather than international organizations, are peace enforcers[43] and that organizations like NATO cannot force member states to share collective burdens. That decision remains the prerogative of the

---

42 For an excellent overview and discussion of this debate, see Wight 2006. Here the study also intersects with the literature on global governance; see, e.g., Zürn 1998; Lake 2010; Hurd 1999; Strange 1995.

43 For a similar argument, see Claude 1966.

members, and thus the ability of international organizations to promote burden-sharing practices is limited. It is therefore understandable that states look less favourably on transferring command and control of their armed forces to an international organization.

Finally, since the share of the Atlantic burden is largely monetary, national governments have an inherent interest in retaining control over spending. Here the Canadian case is a prime example because Canada not only unilaterally withdrew its NATO forces from Europe in 1994, but also slashed its financial commitments to NATO.

The third hotly debated IR topic addressed in this book is that the liberal IR research paradigm and its reference to the values of democracy, rule of law, and freedom hold significant explanatory power for ascertaining why liberal democratic states were less confrontational towards the CEE states. While former members of the Warsaw Pact were just beginning to run democratic systems of government at the end of the Cold War,[44] NATO's perception of these newly evolving regimes was cooperative and engaging, not confrontational; this is as one would expect given that progress towards democratic forms of government was measurable and thus the perceived level of threat calculable.[45] The case study demonstrated that Canada did *not* perceive states from CEE as a threat but rather as potential allies and friends. This book thus confirms that a combination of material and non-material interests (e.g., values, norms, identities, and the like) played a role in the preference formation of states and thus provides an extension of Andrew Moravcsik's liberal research program.

Furthermore, this book partly supports an important element of that research program by finding that some allies perceived non-democratic states as well as states transitioning to democratic forms of government as threats. Canada did not perceive the CEE states as genuine threats, but rather as agents of regional change that required its assistance and help.[46] It felt a sense of external responsibility, which in itself suggests a preference for value rather than instrumentally rational foreign policy preferences. As discussed in the Introduction, the notion of external

---

44 See Keating, Hughes, and European Forum 2003; Krieger-Boden, Morgenroth, and Petrakos 2007; Parker 2008; Seidelmann 2002; Simon 1993.

45 Asmus 2002.

46 It did, however, internally perceive Russia as a continuous threat to the alliance, even though it engaged with it publicly.

responsibility goes back to the writings of Arnold Wolfers, who argued that it was associated only with great powers because their power resources allow them to act beyond narrowly defined national interests. This book has demonstrated, however, that second-tier powers can also hold an external responsibility by devoting their resources to alliances above and beyond their relative capabilities. Above all, this constitutes not rational but altruistic foreign policy behaviour.

While this book did not analyse the factors (material or non-material) that led to the peaceful perception of CEE states, it raised this issue tangentially in its theoretical discussions and to some extent in chapter 6. However, this is where the liberal IR research program reaches its analytical limitations;[47] structure-centred constructivist theories of the liberal peace seem to be better positioned to examine the "why" and "what" of this perception. This points us to the possibility of combining liberal IR theory with that of constructivism to expand the explanatory power of IR theories by allowing for multi-causal explanations.[48]

As Ernst Czempiel and his associates remind us, constructivist peace scholars posit that democratic norms facilitate the resolution of conflicts in a peaceful manner.[49] Constructivist scholars add a causal link by arguing that democracies not only perceive other democracies as being peaceful but also interact with them.[50] In other words, a process of social interaction and learning takes place, and democracies need to recognize that transition process. In this way, constructivist theories, understood as meta-theories of international politics, complement classical liberal IR theory and offer new ontological insights. They can also explain why the contributions of second-tier powers were constructed in such a disparaging way for much of the 20th century and why they persisted for so long. Liberal IR theorists can only point to the fact that mutual perception exists. Put another way, they point towards the outcome of social actions rather than making generalizations as to how these perceptions were shaped. The findings of this study suggest that this is a fruitful avenue for future burden-sharing studies.[51]

---

47 Andrew Moravcsik's defence that it does not matter to liberals where this perception comes from is not totally convincing analytically.

48 See Checkel 2010.

49 See, e.g., Czempiel 1986; Doyle 1983a; Risse-Kappen 1995b; Russett 1993.

50 See Risse-Kappen 1995b, 508.

51 It has been discussed to some extent in Gheciu 2005b; see also Schimmelpfennig 2003.

The fourth important topic addressed by this book is brought out in the Canadian case study, which showed that change in international affairs is possible without relying on military capabilities, relative power resources, or the distribution of these resources in a structured international system of states as explanatory variables. It also showed the power of liberal IR theory to explain change in international politics. Liberal IR theory is progressive in the sense that a constant change of societal predispositions can produce a new set of state preferences. Realist theorists, on the other hand, have a hard time explaining the existence of international cooperation and considering domestic politics as viable independent variables capable of explaining change in international politics, including the foreign policy behaviour of states.[52] For them, change is the result of a variation in the distribution of relative capabilities.

Liberal IR theorists assert that the power of ideas rather than power per se can explain historical change.[53] Power in this sense is more diffuse and less tangible; this is why soft power resources grew increasingly important in the 1990s.[54] The power of ideas is not conditioned by the anarchical nature of international politics, structural predispositions, ahistorical facts, or natural conditions. While liberal IR theorists agree with realists that states act under conditions of anarchy, they disagree on the nature of that anarchy.

The fifth point ties into the previous argument. While realists hold that the conduct of international politics is a zero-sum game,[55] liberal IR theorists contend that it is a positive-sum game in a separate zone of peace among fellow liberal states.[56] This zone of peace is governed by a community of states, the values of liberal democracies, and an exchange of liberal ideas – all of which help to mitigate the effects of anarchy. A failure to inform or trust fellow liberal states within that community can disrupt the liberal peace and undermine cooperation.[57]

---

52 This description is admittedly simplistic, but it is useful in this line of argument.
53 Moravcsik 1997, 535; see also Hall 1997; Reus-Smit 2001.
54 See Nye 1990a.
55 See Grieco 1988. Robert Jervis (2003) criticizes this point by arguing that relative gains in the realist sense were never the only thing that mattered.
56 See Doyle 2008, 59.
57 It has been pointed out that the differences between neo-liberalism and neo-realism, especially, are a reflection of the issues they study. While neo-liberals concentrate mainly on international political economy, realists are preoccupied with questions of security and war. Moreover, neo-liberal scholars focus on questions of efficiency, while realists analyse the distribution of capabilities.

It is here that this study makes a contribution, showing when, why, and how second-tier powers like Canada, under certain conditions, pursued absolute rather than relative gains in its burden-sharing decisions.[58] These conditions include relative status in international politics, embeddedness within a liberal community, and unique historical predispositions at the domestic level. This book shows that states do not necessarily act rationally by following a strict cost-benefit analysis. They are influenced by their national preferences, societal norms and values, and their reputation,[59] all of which may or may not resonate with rationality assumptions.

This does not imply that the distribution of those gains inside the zone of peace must be equal among all states. This insight is consistent with liberal institutionalist scholarship, which distinguishes between problems of a distributional nature and those concerning relative gains.[60] As demonstrated in this book, the importance of relative gains is conditional; it is not *whether* relative gains are important, but rather "under what conditions such distributional conflicts are severe."[61] Duncan Snidal goes even further and holds that concerns for relative gains "can be criticized as a misspecification of an argument that could be better expressed in absolute gains terms" – that is, as a "trade-off between short-term absolute gains (i.e., immediate payoffs from cooperation) and long-term absolute gains (i.e., long-term security and order)."[62]

In the case of second-tier power Canada, given its domestic preferences for fiscal austerity and societal disputes over the status of Quebec in the Canadian federation, contributing to regional security governance in the Balkans was clearly the result of pursuing an absolute gain

---

58 Jervis (2003, 286) has asserted that neorealist scholars do not see more cooperation than realist scholars but hold that there is much more unrealized and potential cooperation.

59 See Schimmelpfennig 1999.

60 Keck 1993, 56.

61 Keohane and Martin 1995, 44–5. Other liberals hold that the competition among societal actors for interests, institutions, and information automatically creates winners and losers because only the strongest ideas and interests are successful. That is to say, their internal struggle shapes their possibilities and nature. In turn, cooperation among states is not affected by perceptions of fear and threat, but rather is the result of distributional consequences of domestic units. In other words, "rather than the struggle for state survival taking priority, the struggle for internal power and compromise dominates foreign policy making" (Milner 1997, 9–10, 14).

62 Snidal 1991, 704.

given the domestic preferences for fiscal austerity and societal disputes over the status of Quebec in the Canadian federation. Considering that Canada was nearly broke in the early to mid-1990s, there are few convincing arguments to be made that it enjoyed relative gains from sending a battalion-sized group to serve first under UN and then under NATO missions in the Balkans.[63] Rather, while enforcing the public good of regional stability in CEE and showing strong national preferences for enforcing human rights and security, Canada sought cooperation with other like-minded NATO states – not to increase its own benefits (relative gains) but to diminish its relative costs by sharing the burden in the Balkans with other allies.

There is no evidence from the case study that private benefits were paid to Canada or that they mattered in the formation of its preferences. NATO, conceived of as an international organization, played the role of facilitator of interstate cooperation. It provided an institutional advantage by offering a trans-Atlantic policy forum in which discussions and exchanges regarding European security matters were made possible. It also facilitated the exchange of information and decisions among the allies. Hence, the questions of values, cohesion, and absolute interests are valid. In the short term, Canada did not have much to gain from sending troops, resources, and equipment to the Balkans aside from keeping its membership in the alliance in good order and maintaining a seat at the table.[64] To the contrary, it had to shoulder additional costs while its own coffers were strained. It thus risked domestic disapproval of those foreign commitments; it is "hard politics" to defend international commitments when national budgets are being slashed.

As suggested above, the short-term gain of Canadian commitments was altruistic and rooted in the notion of external responsibility to NATO. Canada made a value-rational rather than an instrumentally rational decision to shoulder these burdens. On an international level, this responsibility included a strong preference for defending human

---

63 This also demonstrates that the distinction between domestic and international politics is artificially constructed. At the same time, the recognition of domestic politics or domestic preconditions as independent variables in liberal theory raises an important question: how much should foreign policy be accountable to its citizens? Aside from adhering to the liberal democratic theorem, this problem touches on the quest for efficiencies in the external relations of nation states versus improving the democratic participation of citizens in the policymaking process.

64 On this notion, see Sokolsky 1989, 2004b.

and humanitarian rights and halting the acts of manslaughter taking place in the Balkans. And the absence of a domestic upheaval in Canada – no demonstrations, protests, or petitions – speaks to the prominence of this external responsibility among Canadians and the existence of socially different states within a community of liberal states. It is in its ability to overcome the debate between divisive absolute versus relative gains that the strength of liberal IR theory is most clearly demonstrated.

Practical Implications

Given the nature of the empirical analysis and the theoretical debates, this study has practical implications for policymakers and Canadian government officials.

First of all, the case study, in conjunction with the framework of liberal IR theory, suggests a number of foreign policy goals to which government officials in democratic states can aspire. States can actively seek to democratize non-democratic states and bring them into the liberal community by increasing economic relations, spreading liberal values and beliefs, and building governance institutions. They can pursue ideational, commercial, and republican liberal preferences simultaneously to ensure a lasting democratic peace. In this way, the liberal state functions as a role model for non-liberal states, offering a certain attractiveness and respect. States can expand the liberal community of states but should remain cautious about the challenges and threats of complacency inherent in the liberal peace.

The EU's record in containing the ethnic conflicts in the Balkans is a good example here. Europe reacted in a complacent manner[65] to those civil wars, even though they took place on its doorstep and threatened its stability, especially the territorial sovereignty of some of its southern members (Italy, Austria, and Greece, for example). The EU was unable to act decisively, making only diplomatic efforts to manage the crisis, and the conflict spiralled out of control. NATO was asked to bring those civil wars to an end and contain the spread of further violence across Europe.

---

65 As realist scholars have pointed out, all it takes to offset the liberal peace is one democratic state acting offensively against another one.

The civilian and military burden-sharing analysis in chapters 5, 6, and 7 clearly demonstrates that second-tier powers shouldered an adequate burden of the Atlantic alliance, one that was consistent with their *relative* capabilities. The process of sharing burdens in an alliance requires a multidimensional and cross-level analysis that makes use of sophisticated analytical tools beyond the GDP/level of defence spending index. This point is of particular relevance to the current burden-sharing debates on NATO's mission in Afghanistan.

The new security environment of the post–Cold War era called for analytical tools beyond the conventional hard power indexes, and second-tier powers were right to point out the array of soft power tools and other contributions they made to international security governance. This has elevated their status since the end of the Cold War, especially since the United States gained superpower status. Once they are better organized among themselves and more aware of their relative importance, their views and policy ideas may gain more prominence in international politics. And international opinion leaders may revisit their predispositions towards second-tier NATO powers.

Canada's Balkan operations suggest that its battle group concept, which the EU has since adopted for its own military deployments, was a palpable, sustainable, and manageable way for second-ranked states to make military contributions to peace operations.[66] It is highly likely that in an increasingly complex, multidimensional, and multi-causal security environment, the demand for highly flexible and mobile armed forces will continue to grow. Because of the success of the battle group concept in the 1990s, NATO's second-tier powers are likely to use it in future military deployments for two reasons: it enables them to show activism and commitment to international security governance without overextending their relative national resources; and it allows them to keep the scope and extent of that commitment sustainable and manageable by restricting the number of troops and resources allocated to those operations.

---

66 A battle group consists of 1,000–1,500 highly trained soldiers. I am not suggesting that the EU has copied this model from Canada, but there seems to be a move to favour the battle group approach as a way to posture national forces effectively. Canada had experience with this concept since it first forwardly deployed its 4 Mechanized brigade to Germany in 1957.

This book has attempted to broaden the research into Atlantic burden sharing by examining the value-rational and instrumentally rational preferences of states to share the collective burden, but the empirical findings and especially Canada's felt external responsibility as a second-tier power need to be tested for the post-2001 period. NATO's crisis-management operations in Afghanistan (ISAF) and Libya (Operation UNIFIED PROTECTOR) are ideal test cases at a time when acts of terrorism are increasingly frequent. They, and their implications for the role of second-tier powers in the Atlantic alliance, would be a fruitful area of future investigation.

Bibliography

Air Force Association. "The Kosovo Campaign: Aerospace Power Made It Work." September 1999.

Alfano, Geraldine, and Gerald Marwell. "Experiments on the Provision of Public Goods by Groups III: Nondivisibility and Free Riding in 'Real' Groups." *Social Psychology Quarterly* 43 (1981): 300–9.

Allison, Graham T. *Essence of Decision: Explaining the Cuban Missile Crisis.* Boston: Little Brown, 1971.

Alt, James E., Randell L. Calvert, and Brian D. Humes. "Reputation and Hegemonic Stability: A Game-Theoretic Analysis." *American Political Science Review* 82 (1988): 445–66.

Anderson, Mary. *Do No Harm: How Aid Can Support Peace – or War.* Boulder, CO: Lynne Rienner Publishers, 1999.

Anthony, Ian. *The Future of the Defence Industries in Central and Eastern Europe.* Oxford: Oxford University Press, 1994.

Arora, Chaya. *Germany's Civilian Power Diplomacy: NATO Expansion and the Art of Communicative Action.* New York: Palgrave Macmillan, 2006.

Art, Robert J., and Kenneth Neal Waltz. *The Use of Force: Military Power and International Politics.* 6th ed. Lanham, MD: Rowman & Littlefield, 2004.

Ashley, Richard K. "The Poverty of Neorealism." In *Neorealism and Its Critics,* edited by Robert O. Keohane, 255–301. New York: Columbia University Press, 1986.

Asmus, Ronald D. Opening NATO's Door: How the Alliance Remade Itself for a New Era. New York: Columbia University Press, 2002.

– "Rebuilding the Atlantic Alliance." *Foreign Affairs* 82, no. 5 (2003): 20–31.

Asmus, Ronald D., Richard Kugler, and Stephen F. Larrabee. "Building a New NATO." *Foreign Affairs* 72, no. 4 (1993): 28–40.

Axelrod, Robert M. *The Evolution of Cooperation.* New York: Basic Books, 1984.

Axelrod, Robert M., and Robert O. Keohane. "Achieving Cooperation under Anarchy: Strategies and Institutions." In *Cooperation under Anarchy*, edited by Kenneth A. Oye, 226–54. Princeton, NJ: Princeton University Press, 1986.

Axworthy, Lloyd. "Canadian Foreign Policy: A Liberal Party Perspective." *Canadian Foreign Policy* 1, no. 1 (Winter 1992/93): 7–14.

– "Kosovo and the Human Security Agenda." In *Statements and Speeches 99/28*. Ottawa: Department of Foreign Affairs, 1999.

Babst, Dean V. "Elective Governments – A Force for Peace." *Wisconsin Sociologist* 3, no. 1 (1964): 9–14.

– "A Force for Peace." *Industrial Research* 14 (1972): 55–8.

Bailey, Kenneth. *Typologies and Taxonomies: An Introduction to Classification Techniques*. Thousand Oaks, CA: Sage Publications, 1994.

Baker, James Addison, and Thomas M. DeFrank. *The Politics of Diplomacy: Revolution, War, and Peace, 1989–1992*. New York: Putnam, 1995.

Baldwin, David A. "The Concept of Security." *Review of International Studies* 32 (1997): 5–26.

– *Neorealism and Neoliberalism: The Contemporary Debate*. New York: Columbia University Press, 1993.

– "Power Analysis and World Politics: New Trends versus Old Tendencies." *World Politics* 31, no. 2 (1979): 161–94.

Barany, Zoltan D., and Robert G. Moser. *Ethnic Politics after Communism*. Ithaca, NY: Cornell University Press, 2005.

Barnett, Michael M., and Jack S. Levy. "Domestic Sources of Alliances and Alignments: The Case of Egypt, 1962–73." *International Organization* 45, no. 3 (1991): 369–95.

Barston, R.P. *Modern Diplomacy*. London: Longman, 1988.

Bashow, David L., Dwight Davies, Andre Viens, John Rotteau, Norman Balfe, Ray Sotouffer, James Pickett, and Steve Harris. "Mission Ready: Canada's Role in the Kosovo Air Campaign." *Canadian Military Journal* (Spring 2000): 55–61.

Beardsworth, A. "Analysing Press Content: Some Technical and Methodological Issues." In *The Sociology of Journalism and the Press*, edited by H. Christian, 371–95. Keele: Keele University Press, 1980.

Beattie, Clayton E., and Michael S. Baxendale. *The Bulletproof Flag: Canadian Peacekeeping Forces and the War in Cyprus*. Maxville, ON: Optimum Publishing International, 2007.

Beharrell, P. "AIDS and the British Press." In *Getting the Message: News, Truth and Power*, edited by J. Eldridge, 210–41. London: Routledge, 1993.

Bellamy, Alex J., Paul Williams, and Stuart Griffin. *Understanding Peacekeeping*. Cambridge: Polity Press, 2004.

Bennett, Andrew, Joseph Lepgold, and Danny Unger. "Burden-Sharing in the Persian Gulf War." *International Organization* 48, no. 1 (1994): 39–75.

– *Friends in Need: Burden Sharing in the Persian Gulf War*. New York: St. Martin's Press, 1997.

Bennett, Christopher, Stephen Bennett, and Marie Dallam. *Yugoslavia's Bloody Collapse: Causes, Course and Consequences*. New York: New York University Press, 1995.

Bennett, D. Scott. "Testing Alternative Models of Alliance Duration, 1816–1984." *American Journal of Political Science* 41, no. 3 (1997): 846–78.

– "Toward a Continuous Specification of the Democracy-Autocracy Connection." *International Studies Quarterly* 50, no. 2 (2006): 313–38.

Bentham, Jeremy. *Plan for an Universal and Perpetual Peace*. London: Sweet & Maxwell, 1927.

Berelson, B. *Content Analysis in Communication Research*. New York: Free Press, 1952.

Betts, Alexander. "Public Goods Theory and the Provision of Refugee Protection: The Role of the Joint-Product Model in Burden-Sharing Theory." *Journal of Refugee Studies* 16, no. 3 (2003): 273–96.

Bin, Matthew. *On Guard for Thee: Canadian Peacekeeping Missions*. Toronto: BookLand Press, 2007.

Bishai, Linda S. "From Recognition to Intervention: The Shift from Traditional to Liberal International Law." Paper presented at the International Studies Association Annual Convention, Los Angeles, 2000.

Blanchette, Arthur E. *Canadian Peacekeepers in Indochina, 1954–1973: Recollections*. Rideau Series. Ottawa: Golden Dog Press, 2002.

Bland, Douglas L., and Sean M. Maloney. *Campaigns for International Security: Canada's Defence Policy at the Turn of the Century*. Montreal and Kingston: McGill-Queen's University Press, 2004.

Blechman, Barry M. "International Peace and Security in the Twenty-First Century." In *Statecraft and Security: The Cold War and Beyond*, edited by Ken Booth, 289–307. Cambridge: Cambridge University Press, 1998.

Bliss, Harry, and Bruce Russett. "Democratic Trading Partners: The Liberal Connection." *Journal of Politics* 60, no. 4 (1998): 1126–47.

Bloomfield, Alan, and Kim Richard Nossal. "Towards an Explicative Understanding of Strategic Culture: The Cases of Australia and Canada." *Contemporary Security Policy* 28, no. 2 (2007): 286–307.

Bobrow, Davis B. "Playing for Safety: Japan's Security Practices." *Japan Quarterly* 31, no. 1 (1984): 33–43.

Bohm, Peter. "Estimating Demand for Public Goods: An Experiment." *European Economic Review* 3, no. 2 (1972): 111–30.

Booth, Ken. *Critical Security Studies and World Politics.* Boulder, CO: Lynne Rienner Publishers, 2005.
– "Security and Emancipation." *Review of International Studies* 17, no. 4 (1991): 313–26.
Born, Hans, and Alexey Arbatov. *Parliamentary Oversight of the Security Sector: Principles, Mechanisms and Practices.* Geneva: Geneva Centre for the Democratic Control of Armed Forces / Inter-Parliamentary Union, 2003.
Borrus, Michael, Ken Conca, Wayne Sandholtz, Jay Stowsky, Steven Weber, and John Zysman. *The Highest Stakes: The Economic Foundations of the Next Security System.* New York: Oxford University Press, 1992.
Boulden, Jane. *Dealing with Conflict in Africa: The United Nations and Regional Organizations.* Basingstoke, UK: Palgrave Macmillan, 2003.
– *Peace Enforcement: The United Nations Experience in Congo, Somalia, and Bosnia.* Westport, CT: Praeger, 2001.
– *The United Nations and Mandate Enforcement: Congo, Somalia, and Bosnia.* Martello Papers, no. 20. Kingston, ON: Centre for International Relations, Queen's University; Laval, QC: Institut québécois des hautes études internationales, Université Laval, 1999.
Boutros-Ghali, Boutros. *An Agenda for Peace: Preventive Diplomacy, Peacemaking, and Peace-Keeping – Report of the Secretary-General Pursuant to the Statement Adopted by the Summit Meeting of the Security Council on 31 January 1992.* New York: United Nations, 1992.
– *Supplement to Agenda for Peace.* 2nd ed. New York: United Nations, 1995.
Boyer, Mark A. *International Cooperation and Public Goods: Opportunities for the Western Alliance.* Baltimore: Johns Hopkins University Press, 1993.
Brömmelhörster, Jörn. *Demystifying the Peace Dividend.* Baden-Baden: Nomos, 2000.
Brooks, Stephen G., and William Curti Wohlforth. *World out of Balance: International Relations and the Challenge of American Primacy.* Princeton, NJ: Princeton University Press, 2008.
Brown, Archie. *The Rise and Fall of Communism.* New York: HarperCollins, 2009.
Brown, Chris. "History Ends, Worlds Collide." *Review of International Studies* 25, no. 5 (1999): 41–57.
Brown, Michael E., Sean M. Lynn-Jones, and Steven E. Miller. *The Perils of Anarchy: Contemporary Realism and International Security.* Cambridge, MA: MIT Press, 1995.
Bueno de Mesquita, Bruce J., Robert W. Jackman, and Randolph M. Siverson. "Democracy and Foreign Policy: Community and Constraint." *Journal of Conflict Resolution* 35, no. 2 (1991): 181–6.

Bueno de Mesquita, Bruce J., and David Lalman. "Domestic Opposition and Foreign War." *American Political Science Review* 84, no. 3 (1992a): 747–66.

– *War and Reason: Domestic and International Imperatives*. New Haven, CT: Yale»University Press, 1992b.

Bull, Hedley. *The Anarchical Society: A Study of Order in World Politics*. London: Macmillan, 1977.

Burg, Steven L., and Paul Shoup. *The War in Bosnia-Herzegovina: Ethnic Conflict and International Intervention*. Armonk, NY: M.E. Sharpe, 1999.

Buteux, Paul. "Sutherland Revisited: Canada's Long-Term Strategic Situation." *Canadian Defence Quarterly* 24 (September 1994): 5–9.

Buteux, Paul, Michel Fortmann, and Pierre Martin. "Canada and the Expansion of NATO: A Study in Elite Attitudes and Public Opinion." In *Will NATO Go East? The Debate over Enlarging the Atlantic Alliance*, edited by David G. Haglund, 147–79. Kingston, ON: Centre for International Relations, Queen's University, 1996.

Buzan, Barry, Charles A. Jones, and Richard Little. *The Logic of Anarchy: Neorealism to Structural Realism*. New York: Columbia University Press, 1993.

Buzan, Barry, and Ole Waever. *Identity, Migration and the New Security Agenda in Europe*. London: Printer, 1993.

Cahen, Alfred, and Atlantic Council of the United States. *The Western European Union (WEU) and NATO: Strengthening the Second Pillar of the Alliance*. Occasional Paper Series. Washington, DC: Atlantic Council of the United States, 1990.

Campbell, Kurt M., and Celeste Johnson Ward. "New Battle Stations?" *Foreign Affairs* 82, no. 5 (2003): 95–103.

Canada. "Canada in the World: Government Statement." Sessional Paper 8525-351-24. Ottawa: Government of Canada, 1995.

Canada, Department of External Affairs. *Cooperative Security: A New Security Policy for Canada*. Ottawa: Department of External Affairs, 5 April 1991.

Canada, Department of External Affairs and International Trade. "Canada and the New Europe: Speech at Humber College, Toronto." *Statements and Speeches* 90, no. 9 (1990).

Canada, Department of Finance. "Budget 1989." Ottawa: Supply and Services Canada, 1989.

Canada, Department of National Defence. *Canadian Defence Policy*. Ottawa: 1992.

Canada, Parliament, House of Commons. *Debates, 35th Parliament, 1st Session*, vol. 3. Ottawa: Queen's Printer, 21 April 1994.

– *Debates, 36th Parliament, 1st Session*, no. 129. Ottawa: Queen's Printer, 30 September 1998.

- *Debates, 36th Parliament, 1st Session*, no. 205. Ottawa: Queen's Printer, 12 April 1999.

Canadian International Development Agency. *Canadian Opinions on Canadian Foreign Policy, Defence Policy and International Development Assistance*. Hull, QC: Minister of Supply and Services, 1995.

Caplow, Theodore. *Two against One: Coalitions in Triads*. Englewood Cliffs, NJ: Prentice-Hall, 1968.

Cardin, Jean-François. *Comprendre octobre 1970: Le FLQ, la crise et le syndicalisme*. Montreal: Éditions du Méridien, 1990.

Carpenter, Ted Galen. *The Future of NATO*. London: Frank Cass, 1995.

Carpenter, Ted Galen, and Barbara Conry. *NATO Enlargement: Illusions and Reality*. Washington, DC: Cato Institute, 2001.

Carroll, Michael K. *Pearson's Peacekeepers: Canada and the United Nations Emergency Force, 1956–67*. Vancouver: University of British Columbia Press, 2009.

Carter, Ashton B., William James Perry, and John D. Steinbruner. *A New Concept of Cooperative Security*. Brookings Occasional Papers Series. Washington, DC: Brookings Institution, 1992.

Chalmers, Malcolm. "The Atlantic Burden-Sharing Debate – Widening or Fragmenting?" *International Affairs* 77, no. 3 (2001): 569–85.

Chan, Steve. "Grasping the Peace Dividend: Some Propositions on the Conversion of Swords into Plowshares." *Mershon International Studies Review* 39, no. 1 (1995): 53–95.

- "In Search of Democratic Peace: Problems and Promise." *Mershon International Studies Review* 41, no. 1 (1997): 59–91.

- "Mirror, Mirror on the Wall ... Are the Freer Countries More Pacific?" *Journal of Conflict Resolution* 28, no. 6 (1984): 617–48.

Chapman, J.W., R. Drifte, and I.T. Gow. *Japan's Quest for Comprehensive Security: Defence-Diplomacy-Security*. New York: St. Martin's Press, 1982.

Chapnick, Adam. "The Gray Lecture and Canadian Citizenship in History." *American Review of Canadian Studies* 37, no. 4 (2007): 443–57.

- *The Middle Power Project: Canada and the Founding of the United Nations*. Vancouver: University of British Columbia Press, 2005.

Checkel, Jeffrey T. *Theoretical Synthesis in IR: Possibilities and Limits*. Simons Papers in Security and Development, No. 6/ 2010. Vancouver: School for International Studies, Simon Fraser University, September 2010.

Checkel, Jeffrey T., and Andrew Moravcsik. "A Constructivist Research Program in EU Studies?" *European Union Politics* 2, no. 2 (2001): 219–49.

Chipman, John. "The Links between Economics and Strategy." In *IISS 36th Annual Conference*. Vancouver, 8–11 September 1994.

Christiansen, Thomas, Knud Erik Jørgensen, and Antje Wiener. *The Social Construction of Europe*. London: Sage, 2001.

Chubin, S. "The South and the New World Order." In *Order and Disorder after the Cold War*, edited by Brad Roberts, 429–49. Cambridge, MA: MIT Press, 1995.

Cini, Michelle. "Intergovernmentalism." In *European Union Politics*, edited by Michelle Cini. 2nd ed. Oxford: Oxford University Press, 2003.

Clark, Ian. *The Post–Cold War Order: The Spoils of Peace*. Oxford: Oxford University Press, 2001.

Clark, Joe. "Canada's Stake in European Security." *NATO Review* (Web edition) 38, no. 5 (October 1990): 2–7. Accessed 8 July 2014. http://www.nato.int/docu/review/1990/9005-01.htm.

Clark, Wesley K. *Waging Modern War: Bosnia, Kosovo, and the Future of Combat*. New York: PublicAffairs, 2001.

– *Winning Modern Wars: Iraq, Terrorism, and the American Empire*. New York: PublicAffairs, 2004.

Clarkson, Stephen, and Marjorie Griffin Cohen. *Governing under Stress: Middle Powers and the Challenge of Globalization*. London: Zed Books, 2004.

– *Uncle Sam and Us: Globalization, Neoconservatism, and the Canadian State*. Toronto: University of Toronto Press, 2002.

Claude, Inis L. "Collective Legitimization as a Political Function of the United Nations." *International Organization* 20, no. 3 (1966): 367–79.

– *Power and International Relations*. New York: Random House, 1962.

Cline, Ray S. *The Power of Nations in the 1990s: A Strategic Assessment*. Lanham, MD: University Press of America, 1994.

– *World Power Assessment: A Calculus of Strategic Drift*. Washington, DC: Center for Strategic and International Studies, Georgetown University, 1975.

– *World Power Trends and U.S. Foreign Policy for the 1980s*. Boulder, CO: Westview Press, 1980.

Cohen, Andrew. *While Canada Slept: How We Lost Our Place in the World*. Toronto: McClelland & Stewart, 2004.

Cohen, Lenard J. "Blue Helmets, Green Helmets, Red Tunics: Canada's Adaptation to the Security Crisis in Southeastern Europe." In *NATO and European Security: Alliance Politics from the End of the Cold War to the Age of Terrorism*, edited by Alexander Moens, Lenard J. Cohen, and Allen G. Sens, 125–34. Westport, CT: Praeger, 2003.

Coker, Christopher. *Shifting into Neutral? Burden Sharing in the Western Alliance in the 1990s*. London: Brassey's, 1990.

Collins, John M. *Desert Shield and Desert Storm: Implications for Future U.S. Force Requirements*. CRS Report for Congress, 91-361 RCO. Washington, DC: Library of Congress Congressional Research Service, 1991.

Conference of Defence Associations Institute. "A Nation at Risk: The Decline of the Canadian Forces." Ottawa: Conference of Defence Associations Institute, 2002.

Connolly, Michael. "Public Goods, Externalities, and International Relations." *Journal of Political Economy* 78, no. 2 (1970): 279–90.

– "Trade in Public Goods: A Diagrammatic Analysis." *Quarterly Journal of Economics* 86, no. 1 (1972): 61–78.

Conybeare, John A. "Public Goods, Prisoners' Dilemmas and the International Political Economy." *International Studies Quarterly* 28 (1984): 5–22.

Cooper, Andrew Fenton, Richard A. Higgott, and Kim Richard Nossal. *Relocating Middle Powers: Australia and Canada in a Changing World Order.* Vancouver: University of British Columbia Press, 1993.

Cooper, Richard N. "Trade Policy as Foreign Policy." In *U.S. Trade Policies in a Changing World Economy*, edited by Robert M. Stern, 291–336. Cambridge, MA: MIT Press, 1987.

Cooper, Scott A. "Air Power and the Coercive Use of Force." *Washington Quarterly* 24, no. 4 (2001): 81–93.

Cornes, Richard, and Todd Sandler. "Easy Riders, Joint Production, and Public Goods." *Economic Journal* 94, no. 375 (1984a): 580–98.

– "The Theory of Public Goods: Non-Nash Behavior." *Journal of Public Economics* 23 (1984b): 367–9.

Cornish, Paul. "NATO: The Practice and Politics of Transformation." *International Affairs* 80, no. 1 (2004): 63–74.

Courchene, Thomas J. "Half-Way Home: Canada's Remarkable Fiscal Turnaround and the Paul Martin Legacy." *IRPP Policy Matters* 3, no. 8 (2002).

Courchene, Thomas J., and Edwin H. Neave, eds. *Reforming the Canadian Financial Sector: Canada in Global Perspective.* Policy Forum Series. Kingston, ON: John Deutsch Institute for the Study of Economic Policy, Queen's University, 1997.

Cowen, Deborah E. "Fighting For 'Freedom': The End of Conscription in the United States and the Neoliberal Project of Citizenship." *Citizenship Studies* 10, no. 2 (May 2006): 167–83.

Cox, Michael. *US Foreign Policy after the Cold War: Superpower without a Mission?* London: Royal Institute of International Affairs, 1995.

– "Whatever Happened to the 'New World Order'?" *Critique* 25, no. 1 (1997): 85–95.

Cox, Michael, Ken Booth, and Timothy Dunne. *The Interregnum: Controversies in World Politics 1989–1999.* Cambridge: Cambridge University Press, 1999.

Cox, Michael, and Doug Stokes. *US Foreign Policy.* Oxford: Oxford University Press, 2008.

Cox, Robert W., and Timothy J. Sinclair. *Approaches to World Order*. Cambridge: Cambridge University Press, 1996.

Crawford, Beverly. *Economic Vulnerability in International Relations: The Case of East-West Trade, Investment, and Finance*. New York: Columbia University Press, 1993.

Cushman, John H., Jr. "Splitting the Check for Allied Defense." *New York Times*, 8 May 1988.

Czempiel, Ernst Otto. *Friedensstrategien, Systemwandel durch internationale Organisationen, Demokratisierung und Wirtschaft*. Paderborn: Schönigh, 1986.

Daalder, Ivo H., and Michael E. O'Hanlon. *Winning Ugly: NATO's War to Save Kosovo*. Washington, DC: Brookings Institution Press, 2000.

Dahl, Robert A. "The Concept of Power." In *Political Power: A Reader in Theory and Research*, edited by Roderick Bell, David V. Edwards, and R. Harrison, 79–93. New York: Free Press, 1969.

– "The Concept of Power." *Behavioural Science* 2 (July 1957): 201–15.

Dalgaard-Nielsen, Anja. *Germany, Pacifism and Peace Enforcement*. Manchester: Manchester University Press, 2006.

David, Steven R. "Explaining Third World Alignment." *World Politics* 43, no. 2 (1991): 233–56.

– "Why the Third World Still Matters." *International Security* 17, no. 3 (1992/93): 127–59.

de Chastelain, A.J.G.D. "Wing-Walking Revisited: Canada's Defence Policy after the Cold War." *Canadian Defence Quarterly* 12 (June 1992): 7–13.

de Coning, Cedric. "Coherence and Coordination in United Nations Peacebuilding and Integrated Missions: A Norwegian Perspective." Oslo: Norwegian Institute of International Affairs, 2007.

de Nooy, G.C. *Cooperative Security, the OSCE, and Its Code of Conduct*. The Hague: Kluwer Law International, 1996.

Deutsch, Karl Wolfgang. *Political Community and the North Atlantic Area: International Organization in the Light of Historical Experience*. Princeton, NJ: Princeton University Press, 1957.

Dewing, Michael, and Corinne McDonald. "International Deployment of Canadian Forces: Parliament's Role." Ottawa: Library of Parliament, Parliamentary Research Branch, 2004.

DiCicco, Jonathan M., and Jack S. Levy. "The Power Transition Research Program." In *Progress in International Relations Theory: Appraising the Field*, edited by Colin Elman and Miriam Fendius Elman, 109–57. Cambridge, MA: MIT Press, 2003.

Diehl, Paul F. *Peace Operations*. Cambridge, MA: Polity Press, 2008.

Dingwerth, Klaus, and Philipp Pattberg. "Global Governance as a Perspective on World Politics." *Global Governance* 12, no. 2 (2006): 185–203.

Dixon, William J. "Democracy and the Management of International Conflict." *Journal of Conflict Resolution* 37, no. 1 (1993): 42–68.

– "Democracy and the Peaceful Settlement of Conflict." *American Political Science Review* 88, no. 1 (March 1994): 14–32.

– "Dyads, Disputes and the Democratic Peace." In *The Political Economy of War and Peace*, edited by Murray Wolfson, 103–26. Boston: Kluwer Academic Publishers, 1998.

Domke, William Kinkade. *War and the Changing Global System*. New Haven, CT: Yale University Press, 1988.

Donnelly, Jack. "Twentieth-Century Realism." In *Traditions in International Ethics*, edited by Terry Nardin and David A. Mapel, 85–111. Cambridge: Cambridge University Press, 1992.

Doran, Charles F. "Confronting the Principles of the Power Cycle: Changing Systems Structure, Expectations, and War." In *Handbook of War Studies*, edited by Manus I. Midlarsky, 332–68. Boston: Unwin Hyman, 1989.

– "Economics, Philosophy of History, and the 'Single Dynamic' of Power Cycle Theory: Expectations, Competition, and Statecraft." *International Political Science Review* 24, no. 1 (2003): 13–49.

– "Explaining Ascendancy and Decline: The Power Cycle Perspective." *International Journal* 60, no. 3 (2005): 685–701.

– *The Politics of Assimilation: Hegemony and Its Aftermath*. Baltimore: Johns Hopkins University Press, 1971.

– *Systems in Crisis: New Imperatives of High Politics at Century's End*. Cambridge: Cambridge University Press, 1991.

Doran, Charles F., and Wes Parsons. "War and the Cycle of Relative Power." *American Political Science Review* 74, no. 4 (1980): 947–65.

Dorussen, Han, Emil J. Kirchner, and James Sperling. "Sharing the Burden of Collective Security in the European Union." *International Organization* 63, no. 4 (2009): 789–810.

dos Santos, Theotonio. "The Structure of Dependence." *American Economic Review* 60, no. 2 (1970): 231–6.

Downs, Anthony. *An Economic Theory of Democracy*. New York: Harper and Row, 1957.

Doyle, Michael W. "Kant, Liberal Legacies, and Foreign Affairs." *Philosophy and Public Affairs* 12, no. 3 (1983a): 205–35.

– "Kant, Liberal Legacies, and Foreign Affairs, Part 2." *Philosophy and Public Affairs* 12, no. 4 (1983b): 323–53.

– "Liberalism and Foreign Policy." In *Foreign Policy: Theories, Actors, Cases*, edited by Steve Smith, Amelia Hadfield, and Timothy Dunne, 50–70. Oxford: Oxford University Press, 2008.

- "Liberalism and World Politics." *American Political Science Review* 80, no. 4 (1986): 1151–61.
- "Liberalism and World Politics Revisited." In *Controversies in International Relations Theory: Realism and the Neoliberal Challenge*, edited by Charles W. Kegley, 83–105. New York: St. Martin's Press, 1995.
- *Ways of War and Peace: Realism, Liberalism, and Socialism.* 1st ed. New York: Norton, 1997.
Draimin, Tim, and Betty Plewes. "Civil Society and the Democratization of Foreign Policy." In *Canada among Nations 1995: Democracy and Foreign Policy*, edited by Maxwell A. Cameron and Maureen Appel Molot, 63–82. Ottawa: Carleton University Press, 1995.
Duffield, John S. "NATO's Functions after the Cold War." *Political Science Quarterly* 109, no. 5 (1994–95): 763–87.
- "The North Atlantic Treaty Organization: Alliance Theory." In *Explaining International Relations since 1945*, edited by Ngaire Woods, 337–54. Oxford: Oxford University Press, 1996.
- *World Power Forsaken: Political Culture, International Institutions, and German Security Policy after Unification.* Stanford, CA: Stanford University Press, 1998.
Edmunds, Timothy. "NATO and Its New Members." *Survival* 45, no. 3 (2003): 145–66.
Eide, Espen B., Anja T. Kaspersen, Randolph Kent, and Karen von Hippel. "Report on Integrated Missions: Practical Perspectives and Recommendations." Oslo: Norwegian Institute for International Affairs, 2005.
Ek, Carl W. *NATO Common Funds Burdensharing: Background and Current Issues.* Report for Congress RL30150. Washington, DC: Library of Congress Congressional Research Service, 2006.
Elias, Norbert. *The Civilizing Process.* Oxford: B. Blackwell, 1982.
Elman, Colin. "Explanatory Typologies in the Qualitative Study of International Politics." *International Organization* 59, no. 2 (2005): 293–326.
Elman, Colin, and Miriam Fendius Elman. *Progress in International Relations Theory: Appraising the Field.* Cambridge, MA: MIT Press, 2003.
Elsässer, Jürgen, and Joschka Fischer. *Nie wieder Krieg ohne uns: Das Kosovo und die neue deutsche Geopolitik.* Hamburg: Konkret, 1999.
Elster, Jon. *Nuts and Bolts for the Social Sciences.* Cambridge: Cambridge University Press, 1989.
Engle, Sally Merry. "Transnational Human Rights and Local Activism: Mapping the Middle." *American Anthropologist* 108, no. 1 (2006): 38–51.
Enterline, Andrew. "Driving While Democratizing: A Rejoinder to Mansfield and Snyder." *International Security* 20, no. 4 (Spring 1996): 183–207.

Eyal, Jonathan. "NATO's Enlargement: Anatomy of a Decision." *International Affairs* 73, no. 4 (1997): 695–719.

Ferguson, Niall. *The War of the World: Twentieth-Century Conflict and the Descent of the West*. New York: Penguin Press, 2006.

Finkelstein, Lawrence S. "What Is Global Governance." *Global Governance* 1, no. 3 (1995): 367–72.

Finnemore, Martha. *National Interests in International Society*. Cornell Studies in Political Economy. Ithaca, NY: Cornell University Press, 1996.

– *The Purpose of Intervention: Changing Beliefs about the Use of Force*. Ithaca, NY: Cornell University Press, 2003.

Fiscarelli, Rosemary. "Europe Is Grabbing the Spoils of Peace." *New York Times*, 9 March 1990, A35.

Fischer, Joschka. *Die rot-grünen Jahre: Vom Kosovokrieg bis zum 11. September*. Köln: Kiepenheuer & Witsch, 2007.

Flynn, Gregory. *The Internal Fabric of Western Security*. Lanham, MD: Rowman & Littlefield, 1981.

Foot, Rosemary, John Lewis Gaddis, and Andrew Hurrell. *Order and Justice in International Relations*. Oxford: Oxford University Press, 2003.

Forage, Paul C. "Bombs for Peace: A Comparative Study of the Use of Air Power in the Balkans." *Armed Forces and Society* 28, no. 2 (2002): 211–32.

Forster, Peter Kent, and Stephen J. Cimbala. *The US, NATO and Military Burden-Sharing*. London: Frank Cass, 2005.

Foucault, Martial. "Does the European Defense Burden-Sharing Matter?" In *Conflict Management, Peace Economics, and Development*, edited by M. Chatterji and J. Fontanel, 299–317. London: Emerald, 2008.

Foucault, Martial, and Frédéric Mérand. "The Challenge of Burden Sharing." *International Journal* 67, no. 2 (2012): 423–9.

Frey, Frederick W. "Comment: On Issues and Nonissues in the Study of Power." *American Political Science Review* 65, no. 4 (1971): 1081–101.

Frieden, Jeffrey A. "Actors and Preferences in International Relations." In *Strategic Choice and International Relations*, edited by David A. Lake and Robert Powell, 39–76. Princeton, NJ: Princeton University Press, 1999.

Friedman, Thomas L. *The World Is Flat: A Brief History of the Twenty-First Century*. Rev. pbk. ed. New York: Picador, 2007.

Friis, Karsten, and Pia Jarmyr, eds. *Comprehensive Approach: Challenges and Opportunities in Complex Crisis Management*. NUPI Report. Security in Practice no. 11. Oslo: Norwegian Institute of International Affairs, 2008.

Fukuyama, Francis. "The End of History?" *National Interest* 16 (1989): 3–18.

– *The End of History and the Last Man*. New York: Free Press, 1992.

Gaddis, John L. *The Cold War: A New History*. New York: Penguin Press, 2005.

– "Toward the Post–Cold War World." *Foreign Affairs* 70, no. 2 (1991): 102–22.

Galbreath, David J. *The Organization for Security and Co-operation in Europe.* Abingdon, UK: Routledge, 2007.

Gammer, Nicholas. *From Peacekeeping to Peacemaking: Canada's Response to the Yugoslav Crisis.* Montreal and Kingston: McGill-Queen's University Press, 2001.

Gardam, John. *Canadians in War and Peacekeeping.* Burnstown, ON: General Store Publishing House, 2000.

Garnett, Ian. "NATO Response Force." *RUSI Journal* 148, no. 6 (2003): 20–5.

Garnham, David. "War-Proneness, War-Weariness, and Regime Type, 1816–1980." *Journal of Peace Research* 23, no. 3 (1986): 279–89.

Garthoff, Raymond. "Why Did the Cold War Arise, and Why Did It End?" In *The End of the Cold War: Its Meaning and Implications*, edited by Michael J. Hogan, 127–36. Cambridge: Cambridge University Press, 1992.

Gaubatz, Kurt T. "Democratic States and Commitment in International Relations." *International Organization* 50, no. 1 (Winter 1996): 109–39.

Gauvin, Charles-Julien. *Référendum 1995, avenir du Québec et du Canada: Séparation oui ou non?* Saint-Fulgence, QC: Quebec-Presse, 1994.

Gelpi, Christopher F., and Joseph M. Grieco. "Democracy, Interdependence, and the Sources of the Liberal Peace." *Journal of Peace Research* 45, no. 1 (2008): 17–36.

George, Alexander L. "Case Studies and Theory Development: The Method of Structured Focused Comparison." In *Diplomacy: New Approaches in History, Theory, and Policy*, edited by Paul Gordon Lauren, 43–68. New York: Free Press, 1979.

– "The Need for Influence Theory and Actor-Specific Behavioural Models of Adversaries." In *Know Thy Enemy: Profiles of Adversary Leaders and Their Strategic Cultures*, edited by Barry R. Schneider and Jerrold M. Post, 271–310. Maxwell Air Force Base, AL: USAF Counterproliferation Center, 2003.

George, Alexander L., and Andrew Bennett. *Case Studies and Theory Development in the Social Sciences.* Cambridge, MA: MIT Press, 2005.

Gheciu, Alexandra. "International Institutions as Agents of Socialization?" *International Organization* 59, no. 4 (2005a): 973–1012.

– *NATO in the "New Europe": The Politics of International Socialization after the Cold War.* Stanford, CA: Stanford University Press, 2005b.

– *Securing Civilization? The EU, NATO and the OSCE in the Post-9/11 World.* Oxford: Oxford University Press, 2008.

Giarra, Paul S. "The NATO Response Force Initiative." In *Transforming Defense Capabilities: New Approaches for International Security*, edited by Scott Jasper, 167–86. Boulder, CO: Lynne Rienner Publishers, 2009.

Gilboa, Eytan. "The CNN Effect: The Search for a Communication Theory of International Relations." *Political Communication* 22, no. 1 (2005): 27–44.

Gill, Stephen. *Globalization, Democratization, and Multilateralism.* New York: St. Martin's Press, 1997.

Gilpin, Robert G. "The Richness of the Tradition of Political Realism." In *Neorealism and Its Critics,* edited by Robert O. Keohane, 301–21. New York: Columbia University Press, 1986.

– "The Theory of Hegemonic War." In *The Origin and Prevention of Major Wars,* edited by Robert I. Rotberg and Theodore K. Raab, 15–37. Cambridge: Cambridge University Press, 1988.

– *War and Change in International Politics.* Princeton, NJ: Princeton University Press, 1981.

Gnesotto, Nicole. *European Defence: A Proposal for a White Paper.* Paris: European Union Institute for Security Studies, 2004.

Goldstein, Avery. "Discounting the Free Ride: Alliances and Security in the Post-War World." *International Organization* 49, no. 1 (1995): 39–71.

Gompert, David C., Richard L. Kugler, and Martin C. Libicki. *Mind the Gap: Promoting a Transatlantic Revolution in Military Affairs.* Washington, DC: National Defense University Press, 1999.

Gongora, Thierry, and Harald Von Riekhoff. *Toward a Revolution in Military Affairs? Defense and Security at the Dawn of the Twenty-First Century.* Westport, CT: Greenwood Press, 2000.

Gordon, Philip H. *NATO's Transformation: The Changing Shape of the Atlantic Alliance.* Lanham, MD: Rowman & Littlefield, 1997.

Göttert, Willi. *Die Bundeswehr im Wandel zum übernationalen Friedensschutz.* Münster: Lit Verlag, 1993.

Gottfried, Kurt. *Towards a Cooperative Security Regime in Europe: A Report.* Ithaca, NY: Cornell University, Peace Studies Program, 1989.

Gourevitch, Peter A. "The Second Image Reversed: The International Sources of Domestic Politics." *International Organization* 32, no. 4 (1978): 881–911.

Gowa, Joanne S. *Ballots and Bullets: The Elusive Democratic Peace.* Princeton, NJ: Princeton University Press, 1999.

– "Rational Hegemons, Excludable Goods, and Small Groups: An Epitaph for Hegemonic Stability Theory?" *World Politics* 41 (1989): 307–24.

Gowland, David, Arthur Turner, and Alex Wright. *Britain and European Integration since 1945: On the Sidelines.* New York: Routledge, 2009.

Græger, Nina. *The European Security and Defence Dimension: Dilemmas and Challenges for the EU, the WEU and NATO.* NUPI report. Oslo: Norwegian Institute of International Affairs, 1999.

Graham, John. "Black Past, Grey Future?" *International Journal* 53, no. 2 (1998): 204–20.

Granatstein, Jack L. *Who Killed the Canadian Military?* 2nd ed. Toronto: HarperPerennialCanada, 2004.

Gray, Colin S. *Strategy for Chaos: Revolutions in Military Affairs and the Evidence of History*. London: Frank Cass, 2002.

Grieco, Joseph M. "Anarchy and the Limits of Cooperation: A Realist Critique of the Newest Liberal Institutionalism." *International Organization* 42, no. 3 (1988): 485–507.

Gross, Eva. "EU and the Comprehensive Approach." In *DIIS Report 13*. Copenhagen: Danish Institute for International Studies, 2008.

Grubel, Herbert G. *Limits to Government: Controlling Deficits and Debt in Canada*. Toronto: C.D. Howe Institute, 1992.

Gulick, Edward Vose. *Europe's Classical Balance of Power*. New York: W.W. Norton, 1955.

Haas, Ernst B. "The Balance of Power: Prescription, Concept, or Propaganda?" *World Politics* 5, no. 4 (1953): 442–77.

Hacke, Christian. *Die Außenpolitik der Bundesrepublik Deutschland: Weltmacht wider Willen?* Frankfurt am Mein: Ullstein, 1997.

Haglund, David G. "Allied Force or Forced Allies? The Allies' Perspective." In *Alliance Politics, Kosovo, and NATO's War: Allied Force or Forced Allies?*, edited by Pierre Martin and Mark R. Brawley, 91–112. New York: Palgrave, 2001.

– "'Let's Call the Whole Thing Off'? Security Culture as Strategic Culture." *Contemporary Security Policy* 32, no. 3 (2011): 494–516.

– *Will NATO Go East? The Debate over Enlarging the Atlantic Alliance*. Kingston, ON: Centre for International Relations, Queen's University, 1996.

Hall, John A., and T.V. Paul. "The State and Future of World Politics." In *International Order and the Future of World Politics*, edited by T.V. Paul and John A. Hall, 395–408. Cambridge: Cambridge University Press, 1999.

Hall, Peter. "Some Reflections on Preference Formation." Memorandum for the Workshop on Rational Choice and Historical Institutionalism. New York: Russell Sage Foundation, 2000.

Hall, Rodney Bruce. "Moral Authority as a Power Resource." *International Organization* 51, no. 4 (1997): 591–622.

Halliday, Fred. *The World at 2000: Perils and Promises*. New York: Palgrave, 2001.

Hamilton, Keith, and Richard Langhorne. *The Practice of Diplomacy: Its Evolution, Theory, and Administration*. London: Routledge, 1995.

Hammond, Andrew. *The Balkans and the West: Constructing the European Other, 1945–2003*. Aldershot, UK: Ashgate, 2004.

Hansen, L., James C. Murdoch, and Todd Sandler. "On Distinguishing the Behaviour of Nuclear and Non-nuclear Allies in NATO." *Defence Economics* 1, no. 1 (1990): 37–55.

Harnisch, Sebastian, and Hanns Maull. *Germany as a Civilian Power? The Foreign Policy of the Berlin Republic.* Issues in German Politics. Manchester: Manchester University Press, 2001.

Hartley, Keith, and Todd Sandler. "NATO Burden-Sharing: Past and Future." *Journal of Peace Research* 36, no. 6 (1999): 665–80.

Hasenclever, Andreas, Peter Mayer, and Volker Rittberger. *Theories of International Regimes.* Cambridge: Cambridge University Press, 1997.

Hauser, Gunther, and Franz Kernic. *European Security in Transition.* Aldershot, UK: Ashgate, 2006.

Hawthorn, Geoffrey. "Liberalism since the Cold War: An Enemy to Itself?" *Review of International Studies* 25, no. 5 (1999): 145–60.

Hegre, Havard, Tanja Elligsen, Scott Gates, and Nils Peter Gleditsch. "Toward a Democratic Civil Peace? Democracy, Political Change, and Civil War, 1816–1992." *American Political Science Review* 95 (2001): 33–48.

Heinbecker, Paul. "Case Study: The Kosovo Air Campaign." In *Human Security and the New Diplomacy: Protecting People, Promoting Peace,* edited by Don Hubert and Rob McRae, 122–33. Montreal and Kingston: McGill-Queen's University Press, 2001.

– "Human Security." *Behind the Headlines* 56, no. 2 (1999): 4–9.

– "Human Security: The Hard Edge." *Canadian Military Journal* 1, no. 1 (2000): 11–16.

– "Kosovo." In *The UN Security Council: From the Cold War to the 21st Century,* edited by David Malone. Boulder, CO: Lynne Rienner Publishers, 2004.

Heisbourg, François. "American Hegemony? Perceptions of the US Abroad." *Survival* 41, no. 4 (1999): 5–19.

Hendrickson, Ryan C. *Diplomacy and War at NATO: The Secretary General and Military Action after the Cold War.* Columbia: University of Missouri Press, 2006.

Henius, Jakob, and Jacopo Leone McDonald. "Smart Defense: A Critical Appraisal." NDC Forum Paper 21. Rome: NATO Defense College, 2012.

Hewitt, Dawn M. *From Ottawa to Sarajevo: Canadian Peacekeepers in the Balkans.* Martello Papers, no. 18. Kingston, ON: Centre for International Relations, Queen's University, 1998.

Hickey, Donald R. *The War of 1812: A Forgotten Conflict.* Urbana: University of Illinois Press, 1989.

Hillier, Rick. *A Soldier First: Bullets, Bureaucrats and the Politics of War.* Toronto: HarperCollins Canada, 2009.

Hobolt, Sara Binzer. *Europe in Question: Referendums on European Integration.* New York: Oxford University Press, 2009.

Hobsbawm, Eric J. *Nations and Nationalism since 1780: Programme, Myth, Reality.* 2nd ed. Cambridge: Cambridge University Press, 1992.

Hoffmann, Peter. *Friedensverantwortung und Sicherheitsarchitektur in Europa: KSZE, NATO, WEU, EG/EU.* Aktuell-Kontrovers. Hanover: Niedersächsische Landeszentrale für Politische Bildung, 1992.

Hoffmann, Stanley. *Contemporary Theory in International Relations.* Englewood Cliffs, NJ: Prentice-Hall, 1960.

– *The State of War.* London: Pall Mall, 1965.

– *World Disorders: Troubled Peace in the Post–Cold War Era.* Lanham, MD: Rowman & Littlefield, 1998.

Hogan, Michael J. *The End of the Cold War: Its Meaning and Implications.* Cambridge: Cambridge University Press, 1992.

– *The Marshall Plan: America, Britain, and the Reconstruction of Western Europe, 1947–1952.* Cambridge: Cambridge University Press, 1987.

Holbraad, Carsten. *Middle Powers in International Politics.* New York: St. Martin's Press, 1984.

Holbrooke, Richard C. *To End a War.* New York: Random House, 1998.

Holland, Kenneth M. *Canadian–United States Engagement in Afghanistan: An Analysis of the "Whole of Government" Approach.* Clementsport, NS: Canadian Peacekeeping Press, 2009.

Hollis, Martin, and Steve Smith. *Explaining and Understanding in International Relations.* Oxford: Oxford University Press, 1990.

Holsti, Kalevi J. "The Coming Chaos? Armed Conflict in the World's Periphery." In *International Order and the Future of World Politics,* edited by T.V. Paul and John A. Hall, 283–310. Cambridge: Cambridge University Press, 1999.

– *The Dividing Discipline: Hegemony and Diversity in International Theory.* Boston: Unwin Hyman, 1985.

Holsti, Ole R. *Content Analysis for the Social Sciences and Humanities.* Reading, MA: Addison-Wesley, 1969.

Holsti, Ole R., P. Terrence Hopmann, and John D. Sullivan. *Unity and Disintegration in International Alliances: Comparative Studies.* New York: John Wiley, 1973.

Homer-Dixon, Thomas F. "Environmental Scarcities and Violent Conflict: Evidence from Cases." *International Security* 23, no. 3 (1994): 43–78.

Honig, Jan Willem, and Norbert Both. *Srebrenica: Record of a War Crime.* New York: Penguin Books, 1997.

Houweling, Henk, and Jan G. Siccama. "Power Transitions as a Cause of War." *Journal of Conflict Resolution* 32, no. 1 (1988): 87–102.

Howard, Michael. *War and the Liberal Conscience.* New Brunswick, NJ: Rutgers University Press, 1978.

– "When Are Wars Decisive?" *Survival* 41, no. 1 (1999): 126–35.

Human Security Centre. "Human Security Report 2005: War and Peace in the 21st Century." New York: Oxford University Press, 2005.

Hume, David. *Essays: Moral, Political, and Literary*. London: Oxford University Press, 1963. First published 1741–2.

Humphrey, T., ed. *Immanuel Kant: Perpetual Peace and Other Essays on Politics, History, and Morals*. Indianapolis, IN: Hackett Publishing, 1983.

Huntington, Samuel P. "No Exit: The Errors of Endism." *National Interest* 17 (Fall 1989): 3–11.

– "The Political Development and Political Decay." *World Politics* 17 (1965): 386–430.

Hurd, Ian. "Legitimacy and Authority in International Politics." *International Organization* 53, no. 2 (1999): 379–408.

Hurrell, Andrew. *On Global Order: Power, Values, and the Constitution of International Society*. Oxford: Oxford University Press, 2007.

– "Power, Principles and Prudence: Protecting Human Rights in a Deeply Divided World." In *Human Rights in Global Politics*, edited by Timothy Dunne and Nicholas J. Wheeler, 277–302. Cambridge: Cambridge University Press, 1999.

– "The Theory and Practice of Global Governance: The Worst of All Possible Worlds?" *International Studies Review* 13, no. 1 (2011): 144–54.

Hurrell, Andrew, and Benedict Kingsbury. *The International Politics of the Environment: Actors, Interests, and Institutions*. Oxford: Oxford University Press, 1992.

Hurrell, Andrew, and Ngaire Woods. *Inequality,Globalization, and World Politics*. Oxford: Oxford University Press, 1999.

Hyde-Price, Adrian G.V. *European Security in the Twenty-First Century: The Challenge of Multipolarity*. London: Routledge, 2007.

Ignatieff, Michael. *The Warrior's Honor: Ethnic War and the Modern Conscience*. New York: Metropolitan Books, 1998.

Ikenberry, G. John. "The Myth of Post–Cold War Chaos." *Foreign Affairs* 75, no. 3 (1996): 79–91.

Institute for National Strategic Studies, National Defense University. *Allied Command Structures in the New NATO*. Washington, DC: National Defense University Press, 1997.

International Institute for Strategic Studies. *Military Balance 1991/92*. London: IISS / Oxford University Press, 1992.

– *Military Balance – 1992/93*. London: IISS / Oxford University Press, 1993.

– *Military Balance – 1994/95*. London: IISS / Oxford University Press, 1994.

– *Military Balance – 1995/96*. London: IISS / Oxford University Press, 1995.

– *Military Balance – 1996/97*. London: IISS / Oxford University Press, 1996.

– *Military Balance – 1999*. London: IISS / Oxford University Press, 1999.

– *Military Balance – 2000*. London: IISS / Oxford University Press, 2000.

Ishizuka, Katsumi. *Ireland and International Peacekeeping Operations 1960–2000: A Study of Irish Motivation.* London: Frank Cass, 2004.

Jakobsen, Peter Viggo. "Focus on the CNN Effect Misses the Point: The Real Media Impact on Conflict Management Is Invisible and Indirect." *Journal of Peace Research* 37, no. 2 (2000): 131–43.

— "National Interest, Humanitarianism or CNN: What Triggers UN Peace Enforcement after the Cold War?" *Journal of Peace Research* 33, no. 2 (1996): 205–15.

Jenish, D'Arcy. *Money to Burn: Trudeau, Mulroney, and the Bankruptcy of Canada.* Toronto: Stoddart, 1996.

Jervis, Robert. "Realism, Neoliberalism, and Cooperation: Understanding the Debate." In *Progress in International Relations Theory: Appraising the Field,* edited by Colin Elman and Miriam Fendius Elman, 277–309. Cambridge, MA: MIT Press, 2003.

— "A Usable Past for the Future." In *The End of the Cold War: Its Meaning and Implications,* edited by Michael J. Hogan, 257–68. Cambridge: Cambridge University Press, 1992.

Jervis, Robert, and Jack L. Snyder. *Dominoes and Bandwagons: Strategic Beliefs and Great Power Competition in the Eurasian Rimland.* New York: Oxford University Press, 1991.

Jockel, Joseph T. *Canada and International Peacekeeping.* Significant Issues Series vol. 16, no. 3. Toronto: Canadian Institute of Strategic Studies; Washington, DC: Center for Strategic and International Studies, 1994.

Jockel, Joseph T., and Joel J. Sokolsky. *Canada and Collective Security: Odd Man Out.* The Washington Papers, no. 121. New York: Praeger, 1986.

— "Canada and the War in Afghanistan: NATO's Odd Man Out Steps Forward." *Journal for Transatlantic Studies* 6, no. 1 (2008): 100–15.

Joffe, Josef. "Collective Security and the Future of Europe: Failed Dreams and Dead Ends." *Survival* 34, no. 1 (1992): 36–50.

— *The Limited Partnership: Europe, the United States, and the Burdens of Alliance.* Cambridge, MA: Ballinger, 1987.

Johnston, Alastair Iain. "Treating International Institutions as Social Environments." *International Studies Quarterly* 45, no. 3 (2001): 487–515.

Judah, Tim. "Kosovo's Moment of Truth." *Survival* 47, no. 4 (2005–06): 73–84.

— *Kosovo: War and Revenge.* 2nd ed. New Haven, CT: Yale University Press, 2002.

— *The Serbs: History, Myth, and the Destruction of Yugoslavia.* New Haven, CT: Yale University Press, 1997.

Judt, Tony. *Postwar: A History of Europe since 1945.* New York: Penguin Press, 2005.

Kaldor, Mary. *The Disintegrating West.* New York: Hill and Wang, 1978.

- *New and Old Wars: Organized Violence in a Global Era*. Stanford, CA: Stanford University Press, 1999.
Kammel, Arnold, and Benjamin Zyla. "Looking for a 'Berlin-Plus in Reverse'? NATO in Search of a New Strategic Concept." *Orbis* 55, no. 4 (2011): 648–62.
Kant, Immanuel. *Kant: Political Writings*, edited by Hans Reiss. New York: Cambridge University Press, 1991.
- *Toward Perpetual Peace and Other Writings on Politics, Peace, and History*, edited by Pauline Kleingeld. Translated by David L. Colclasure. Rethinking the Western Tradition Series. New Haven, CT: Yale University Press, 2006.
Kaplan, Lawrence S. *NATO Divided, NATO United: The Evolution of an Alliance*. Westport, CT: Praeger, 2004.
Kaplan, Robert D. *The Coming Anarchy: Shattering the Dreams of the Post Cold War*. New York: Random House, 2000.
Kapstein, Ethan B. *The Political Economy of National Security: A Global Perspective*. New York: McGraw-Hill, 1992.
Karkoszka, Andrej. "Canada, Poland, and NATO Enlargement." In *Canada, Poland and NATO Enlargement*, edited by Jim Hanson and Susan McNish, 1–7. Toronto: Canadian Institute of Strategic Studies, 1997.
Karns, Margaret P., and Karen A. Mingst. *International Organizations: The Politics and Processes of Global Governance*. Boulder, CO.: Lynne Rienner Publishers, 2004.
Katzenstein, Peter J. *The Culture of National Security: Norms and Identity in World Politics*. New York: Columbia University Press, 1996.
Katznelson, Ira, and Barry R. Weingast, eds. Introduction to *Preferences and Situations: Points of Intersection between Historical and Rational Choice Institutionalism*. New York: Russell Sage Foundation, 2005.
Kaufman, Robert Gordon. "To Balance or to Bandwagon? Alignment Decisions in 1930s Europe." *Security Studies* 1, no. 3 (1992): 417–47.
Kaufman, Stuart J., Richard Little, and William Curti Wohlforth. *The Balance of Power in World History*. Basingstoke, UK: Palgrave Macmillan, 2007.
Kay, Sean. *Global Security in the Twenty-First Century: The Quest for Power and the Search for Peace*. Lanham, MD: Rowman & Littlefield, 2006.
- *NATO and the Future of European Security*. Lanham, MD: Rowman & Littlefield, 1998.
Keating, Michael, James Hughes, and European Forum (European University Institute). *The Regional Challenge in Central and Eastern Europe: Territorial Restructuring and European Integration*. Brussels: P.I.E.-Peter Lang, 2003.
Keating, Thomas F. *Canada and World Order: The Multilateralist Tradition in Canadian Foreign Policy*. 2nd ed. Don Mills, ON: Oxford University Press, 2002.

Keck, Otto. "The New Institutionalism and the Relative-Gains-Debate."
In *International Relations and Pan-Europe: Theoretical Approaches and Empirical Findings*, edited by Frank R. Pfetsch, 35–62. Münster: Lit, 1993.

Kegley, Charles W. *The Long Postwar Peace: Contending Explanations and Projections*. New York: HarperCollins, 1991.

Kegley, Charles W., and Gregory A. Raymond. *How Nations Make Peace*. New York: St. Martin's / Worth Publishers, 1999.

Kennedy, Paul. *The Rise and Fall of Great Powers: Economic Change and Military Conflict from 1500 to 2000*. New York: Random House, 1987.

Keohane, Robert O. *After Hegemony: Cooperation and Discord in the World Political Economy*. Princeton, NJ: Princeton University Press, 1984.

– "Beyond Dichotomy: Conversations between International Relations and Feminist Theory." *International Studies Quarterly* 42 (1998): 193–9.

– "Governance in a Partially Globalized World: Presidential Address, Annual Meeting of the American Political Science Association, 2000." *American Political Science Review* 95, no. 1 (2001): 1–13.

– *International Institutions and State Power: Essays in International Relations Theory*. Boulder, CO: Westview Press, 1989a.

– "International Institutions: Two Approaches." *International Studies Quarterly* 32, no. 4 (1988): 379–96.

– *Internationalization and Domestic Politics*. Cambridge: Cambridge University Press, 1996.

– "Lilliputians' Dilemmas: Small States in International Politics." *International Organization* 23, no. 2 (1969): 291–310.

– "Multilateralism: The Anatomy of an Institution." *International Journal* 45, no. 4 (Autumn 1990): 731–64.

– "Neoliberal Institutionalism: A Perspective on World Politics." In *International Institutions and State Power: Essays in International Relations Theory*, edited by Robert O. Keohane, 1–20. Boulder, CO: Westview Press, 1989b.

– *Neorealism and Its Critics: The Political Economy of International Change*. New York: Columbia University Press, 1986.

– "The Theory of Hegemonic Stability and Changes in International Economic Regimes, 1967–1977." In *Change in the International System*, edited by Ole R. Holsti, 131–62. Boulder, CO: Westview Press, 1980.

– *Transnational Relations and World Politics*. Cambridge, MA: Harvard University Press, 1972.

Keohane, Robert O., and Lisa L. Martin. "The Promise of Institutional Theory." *International Security* 20, no. 1 (1995): 39–51.

Keohane, Robert O., and Joseph S. Nye. "International Interdependence and Integration." In *Handbook of Political Science*, edited by Fred I. Greenstein and Nelson W. Polsby, 363–414. Andover, MA: Addison-Wesley, 1975.

- *Power and Interdependence: World Politics in Transition*. Boston: Little, Brown, 1977.
- "Transgovernmental Relations and International Organizations." *World Politics* 27, no. 1 (1974): 39–62.

Kiesling, Herbert J. "Public Goods and the Possibilities for Trade." *Canadian Journal of Economics* 7, no. 3 (1974): 402–17.

Kim, Hyung Min, and David L. Rousseau. "The Classical Liberals Were Half Right (or Half Wrong): New Tests of the 'Liberal Peace,' 1960–88." *Journal of Peace Research* 42, no. 5 (2005): 523–43.

Kim, Woosang. "Alliance Transitions and Great Power War." *American Journal of Political Science* 35, no. 4 (1991a): 833–50.
- "Power, Alliance, and Major Wars, 1816–1975." *Journal of Conflict Resolution* 33, no. 2 (1989): 255–73.
- "Power Transitions and Great Power War from Westphalia to Waterloo." *World Politics* 45, no. 1 (1992): 153–72.
- "Sanctions Imposed on Yugoslavia: Canada Backs European Community Bid for UN-Sponsored Oil Embargo." *Globe and Mail*, 1991b, A1.

Kimball, Anessa L. "Political Survival, Policy Distribution, and Alliance Formation." *Journal of Peace Research* 47, no. 4 (2010): 407–19.

Kindelberger, Charles. *The World in Depression: 1929–1939*. Berkeley: University of California Press, 1973.

King, Gary, Robert O. Keohane, and Sidney Verba. *Designing Social Inquiry: Scientific Inference in Qualitative Research*. Princeton, NJ: Princeton University Press, 1994.

Kirchner, Emil J. "The Challenge of European Security Governance." *Journal of Common Market Studies* 44, no. 5 (2006): 947–68.

Kirkpatrick, Jeane J. "Beyond the Cold War." *Foreign Affairs* 69, no. 1 (1989/1990): 1–16.

Kiss, Judit. *The Defence Industry in East-Central Europe: Restructuring and Conversion*. SIPRI Monographs. Oxford: Oxford University Press, 1997.

Klotz, Audie, and Deepa Prakash, eds. *Qualitative Methods in International Relations: A Pluralist Guide*. Basingstoke, UK: Palgrave Macmillan, 2008.

Kluger, Richard L. "Conventional Operations and Warfare: A New Era Ahead?" In *Strategic Assessment 1999: Priorities for a Turbulent World*. Washington, DC: Institute for National Security Studies, National Defense University, 1999.

Knutsen, Torbjørn L. *The Rise and Fall of World Orders*. Manchester: Manchester University Press, 1999.

Kondracke, Morton. "Who Needs NATO?" *New Republic* 5 (March 1990): 14–15.

Kotkin, Stephen, and Jan Tomasz Gross. *Uncivil Society: 1989 and the Implosion of the Communist Establishment.* New York: Modern Library, 2009.

Krahmann, Elke. "National, Regional, and Global Governance: One Phenomenon or Many?" *Global Governance* 9, no. 3 (2003): 323–46.

Krasner, Stephen D. *International Regimes.* Cornell Studies in Political Economy. Ithaca, NY: Cornell University Press, 1983.

Krauthammer, Charles. "The Unipolar Moment." *Foreign Affairs* 70, no. 1 (1990/91): 23–33.

Krepinevich, Andrew F. "Cavalry to Computer: The Pattern of Military Revolutions." *National Interest* 37 (Fall 1994): 30–42.

Krieger-Boden, Christiane, Edgar L.W. Morgenroth, and George Petrakos. *The Impact of European Integration on Regional Structural Change and Cohesion.* Abingdon, UK: Routledge, 2007.

Kugler, Jacek, and Douglas Lemke. *Parity and War: Evaluations and Extensions of "the War Ledger."* Ann Arbor: University of Michigan Press, 1996.

Kupchan, Charles A. "NATO and the Persian Gulf: Examining Intra-Alliance Behavior." *International Organization* 42, no. 2 (1988): 317–46.

Kupchan, Charles A., and Clifford A Kupchan. "Concerts, Collective Security, and the Future of Europe." *International Security* 16, no. 1 (1991): 114–61.

– "The Promise of Collective Security." *International Security* 20, no. 1 (1995): 52–61.

Lagassé, Philippe. "Specialization and the Canadian Forces." *Defence and Peace Economics* 16, no. 3 (2005): 205–22.

Lake, David A. "Leadership, Hegemony, and the International Economy: Naked Emperor or Tattered Monarch with Potential?" *International Studies Quarterly* 37 (1993): 459–89.

– "Powerful Pacifists: Democratic States and War." *American Political Science Review* 20, no. 1 (1992): 24–37.

– "Rightful Rules: Authority, Order, and the Foundations of Global Governance." *International Studies Quarterly* 54, no. 3 (2010): 587–613.

Lampe, John R. *Yugoslavia as History.* Cambridge: Cambridge University Press, 1996.

Lange, G. "The PCC: A New Player in the Development of Relations between NATO and Partner Nations." *NATO Review* 3 (May 1995): 3–33.

Larson, Deborah W. "Bandwagoning Images in American Foreign Policy." In *Dominoes and Bandwagons: Strategic Beliefs and Great Power Competition in the Eurasian Rimland,* edited by Robert Jervis and Jack L. Snyder, 85–111. New York: Oxford University Press, 1991.

Layne, Christopher. "Kant or Cant: The Myth of the Democratic Peace." *International Security* 19, no. 2 (Fall 1994): 5–49.

- "The Unipolar Illusion: Why New Great Powers Will Arise." *International Security* 17, no. 4 (1993): 5–51.
Lazarsfeld, Paul. "Some Remarks on the Typological Procedures on Social Research." *Zeitschrift für Sozialforschung* 6 (1937): 119–39.
Legault, Albert, and Manon Tessier. *Canada and Peacekeeping: Three Major Debates*. Clementsport, NS: Canadian Peacekeeping Press, 1999.
Lemke, Douglas. "The Continuation of History: Power Transition Theory and the End of the Cold War." *Journal of Peace Research* 34, no. 1 (1997): 23–36.
- *Regions of War and Peace*. Cambridge: Cambridge University Press, 2002.
Lemke, Douglas, and Suzanne Werner. "Power Parity, Commitment to Change, and War." *International Studies Quarterly* 40, no. 2 (1996): 235–60.
Letourneau, Paul, and Philippe Hebert. "NATO Enlargement: Germany's Euro-Atlantic Design." In *The Future of NATO: Enlargement, Russia, and European Security*, edited by Charles-Philippe David and Jacques Lévesque, 108–18. Montreal: McGill-Queen's University Press, 1999.
Levy, Jack S. "Alliance Formation and War Behaviour: An Analysis of the Great Powers, 1495–1975." *Journal of Conflict Resolution* 25 (1981): 581–613.
- "Domestic Politics and War." In *The Origin and Prevention of Major Wars*, edited by Robert I. Rotberg and Theodore Rabb, 79–99. New York: Cambridge University Press, 1989.
- "Preferences, Constraints, and Choices in July 1914." *International Organization* 15, no. 3 (1990–91): 151–86.
- "The Theoretical Foundations of Paul W. Schroeder's International System." *International History Review* 16, no. 4 (1994): 725–6.
Levy, Jack S., and Michael M. Barnett. "Domestic Sources of Alliances and Alignments: The Case of Egypt, 1962–1973." *International Organization* 45, no. 3 (1991): 369–95.
Levy, Marc A. "Is the Environment a National Security Issue?" *International Security* 20, no. 2 (1995): 35–62.
Liberal Party of Canada. "Creating Opportunity: The Liberal Plan for Canada." Ottawa: Liberal Party of Canada, 1993.
Lijphart, Arend. "Comparative Politics and the Comparative Method." *American Political Science Review* 65, no. 3 (1971): 682–93.
Lindblom, Charles Edward. *Politics and Markets: The World's Political Economic Systems*. New York: Basic Books, 1977.
Lindley-French, Julian. *A Chronology of European Security & Defence, 1945–2007*. Oxford: Oxford University Press, 2007.
- *The North Atlantic Treaty Organization: The Enduring Alliance*. New York: Routledge, 2006.

Lis, John J., and Zachary A. Selden. *NATO Burdensharing after Enlargement*. New York: Novinka Books, 2003.

Liska, George. *Nations in Alliance: The Limits of Interdependence*. Baltimore: Johns Hopkins University Press, 1962.

Locke, John. "Second Treatise." In *Two Treatises of Government*, edited by Peter Laslett. Cambridge: Cambridge University Press, 1988.

– *Two Treatises of Government*. New York: Cambridge University Press, 1963.

Loehr, William. "Collective Goods and International Cooperation: Comments," *International Organization* 27, no. 3 (1973): 421–30.

Lundestad, Geir. *No End to Alliance: The United States and Western Europe – Past, Present, and Future*. New York: St. Martin's Press, 1998.

– *The United States and Western Europe since 1945: From "Empire" by Invitation to Transatlantic Drift*. Oxford: Oxford University Press, 2003.

Maccloskey, Monro. *Pacts for Peace: UN, NATO, SEATO, CENTO, and OAS*. Military Research Series. New York: R. Rosen Press, 1967.

MacFarlane, S. Neil, and Yuen Foong Khong. *Human Security and the UN: A Critical History*. United Nations Intellectual History Project. Bloomington: Indiana University Press, 2006.

Macgregor, Douglas A. "The Balkan Limits to Power and Principle." *Orbis* 45, no. 1 (2001): 93–110.

MacInnis, John A. "Contrasts in Peacekeeping: The Experience of UNPROFOR and IFOR in the Former Yugoslavia." *Mediterranean Quarterly* 8, no. 2 (1997): 146–62.

MacKenzie, Lewis. *Peacekeeper: The Road to Sarajevo*. Vancouver: Douglas & McIntyre, 1993.

MacKinnon, Michael G. *The Evolution of US Peacekeeping Policy under Clinton: A Fairweather Friend?* London: Frank Cass, 2000.

Maloney, Sean M. *Canada and UN Peacekeeping: Cold War by Other Means, 1945–1970*. St. Catharines, ON: Vanwell Publishing, 2002.

– *The Hindrance of Military Operations Ashore: Canadian Participation in Operation Sharp Guard, 1993–1996*. Maritime Security Occasional Paper Series, no. 7. Halifax, NS: Centre for Foreign Policy Studies, Dalhousie University, 2000.

– "Operation Bolster: Canada and the European Community Monitor Mission in the Balkans, 1991–1994." The McNaughton Papers, no. 10. Toronto: Canadian Institute of Strategic Studies, 1997.

Mann, Michael. *The Dark Side of Democracy: Explaining Ethnic Cleansing*. New York: Cambridge University Press, 2005.

Mansfield, Edward D., and Jon C. Pevehouse. "Trade Blocs, Trade Flows, and International Conflict." *International Organization* 54, no. 4 (2000): 775–808.

Mansfield, Edward D., and Jack L. Snyder. "Democratization and the Danger of War." *International Security* 20, no. 1 (1995a): 5–38.

– "Democratization and War." *Foreign Affairs* 74, no. 3 (1995b): 79–97.

Maoz, Zeev. "Realist and Cultural Critiques of the Democratic Peace: A Theoretical and Empirical Re-assessment." *International Interactions* 24, no. 1 (1998): 38–44.

Maoz, Zeev, and Nasrim Abdolali. "Regime Types and International Conflict." *Journal of Conflict Resolution* 33, no. 1 (1989): 3–35.

Maoz, Zeev, and Bruce Russett. "Normative and Structural Causes of Democratic Peace, 1946–1986." *American Political Science Review* 87, no. 3 (September 1993): 624–38.

March, James G., and Johan P. Olsen. *Democratic Governance*. New York: Free Press, 1995.

– *The Logic of Appropriateness*. ARENA Working Papers WP 04/09. Oslo: ARENA Centre for European Studies, 2004.

Mariano, Stephen. *Untangling NATO Transformation*. Kingston, ON: Centre for International Relations, Queen's University, 2007.

Markham, James M. "For Europe, a New Look: Bush Fixes U.S. Role as More Modest One." *New York Times*, 20 July 1989, A9.

Markusen, Ann R., Sean DiGiovanna, and Michael C. Leary. *From Defense to Development? International Perspectives on Realizing the Peace Dividend*. London: Routledge, 2003.

Markwell, Donald J. "Sir Alfred Zimmern Revisited: Fifty Years On." *Review of International Studies* 12, no. 4 (1986): 279–92.

Marsh, Steve. "The United States and the Common European Security and Defence Policy." In *The United States and Europe: Beyond the Neo-conservative Divide?*, edited by John Baylis and Jon Roper, 89–106. New York: Routledge, 2006.

Marshall, Monty G., Keith Jaggers, and Ted Gurr. "Polity IV Project: Political Regime Characteristics and Transitions, 1800–2002." http://www.cidcm.umd.edu/inscr/polity.

Martin, Lisa L. "Interests, Power, and Multilateralism." *International Organization* 46, no. 4 (1992): 765–92.

– "The Rational State Choice of Multilateralism." In *Multilateralism Matters: The Theory and Praxis of an Institutional Form*, edited by John Gerard Ruggie, 91–121. New York: Columbia University Press, 1993.

Martin, Pierre, and Mark R. Brawley. *Alliance Politics, Kosovo, and NATO's War: Allied Force or Forced Allies?* New York: Palgrave, 2001.

Martin, Pierre, and Michel Fortmann. "Support for International Involvement in Canadian Public Opinion after the Cold War." *Canadian Military Journal* 2, no. 3 (Autumn 2001): 43–52.

Marwell, Gerald, and Ruth E. Ames. "Economists Free Ride, Does Anyone Else? Experiments on the Provision of Public Goods, IV." *Journal of Public Economics* 15, no. 3 (1981): 295–310.

– "Experiments on the Provision of Public Goods: I – Resources, Interest, Group Size, and the Free-Rider Problem." *American Journal of Sociology* 84, no. 6 (1979): 1335–60.

– "Experiments on the Provision of Public Goods: II – Provision Points, Stakes, Experience, and the Free-Rider Problem." *American Journal of Sociology* 85, no. 4 (1980): 926–37.

Mastanduno, Michael. *The Nuclear Revolution: International Politics before and after Hiroshima*. New York: Cambridge University Press, 1981.

– "Preserving the Unipolar Moment: Realist Theories and U.S. Grand Strategy after the Cold War." *International Security* 21, no. 4 (1997): 49–88.

Matthews, Jessica T. "Redefining Security." *Foreign Affairs* 68, no. 2 (1989): 162–77.

Matthews, Ron, and J.M. Treddenick. *Managing the Revolution in Military Affairs*. Basingstoke, UK: Palgrave, 2001.

Maull, Hanns W. "German Foreign Policy, Post-Kosovo: Still a 'Civilian Power'?" *German Politics* 9, no. 2 (2000): 1–24.

– "Germany and Japan: The New Civilian Powers." *Foreign Affairs* 69, no. 5 (1990): 91–106.

May, Ernest. "U.S. Government, a Legacy of the Cold War." In *The End of the Cold War: Its Meaning and Implications*, edited by Michael J. Hogan, 217–28. Cambridge: Cambridge University Press, 1992.

Mayhew, David R. *The Electoral Connection*. New Haven, CT: Yale University Press, 1974.

McCalla, Robert B. "NATO's Persistence after the Cold War." *International Organization* 50, no. 3 (1996): 445–75.

McCormick, James M. *American Foreign Policy and Process*. 4th ed. Belmont, CA: Thomson / Wadsworth, 2005.

McDougall, Barbara. "Canada, NATO, and the North Atlantic Cooperation Council." In *Canada and NATO: The Forgotten Ally?*, edited by Barbara McDougall, Kim Richard Nossal, Alex Morrison, and Joseph T. Jockel. Washington, DC: Brassey's, 1992a.

– "Meeting the Challenge of the New World Order." *International Journal* 47, no. 3 (Summer 1992b): 463–78.

McDougall, Barbara, Kim Richard Nossal, Alex Morrison, and Joseph T. Jockel, eds. *Canada and NATO: The Forgotten Ally?* Washington, DC: Brassey's, 1992.

McGuire, M.C. "Mixed Public-Private Benefit and Public-Good Supply with Application to the NATO Alliance." *Defence Economics* 1, no. 1 (1990): 17–35.

McRae, Rob. "Human Security, Connectivity, and the New Global Civil Society." In *Human Security and the New Diplomacy: Protecting People, Promoting Peace*, edited by Don Hubert and Rob McRae, 236–49. Montreal and Kingston: McGill-Queen's University Press, 2001.

Mearsheimer, John J. "Back to the Future: Instability after the Cold War." *International Security* 15, no. 1 (1990): 5–56.

– "The False Promise of International Institutions." *International Security* 19, no. 3 (1994–95): 5–49.

– "A Realist Reply." *International Security* 20, no. 1 (1995): 82–93.

– *The Tragedy of Great Power Politics*. New York: Norton, 2001.

Merritt, Richard L., and Dina A. Zinnes. "Validity of Power Indices." *International Interactions* 14, no. 2 (1988): 141–51.

Michta, Andrew A. *America's New Allies: Poland, Hungary, and the Czech Republic in NATO*. Seattle: University of Washington Press, 1999.

Middlemiss, Danford William, and Joel J. Sokolsky. *Canadian Defence: Decisions and Determinants*. Toronto: Harcourt Brace Jovanovich Canada, 1989.

Miller, J.D.B., and R.J. Vincent. *Order and Violence: Hedley Bull and International Relations*. Oxford: Oxford University Press, 1990.

Milner, Helen V. *Interests, Institutions, and Information: Domestic Politics and International Relations*. Princeton, NJ: Princeton University Press, 1997.

Mingst, Karen A., and Margaret P. Karns. *The United Nations in the Post–Cold War Era*. 2nd ed. Dilemmas in World Politics Series. Boulder, CO: Westview Press, 2000.

Mittrany, David. "The Functional Approach to World Organization." *International Affairs* 24, no. 3 (1948): 19–56.

– *A Working Peace System*. Chicago: Quadrangle, 1966.

Modelski, George, and William R. Thompson. "Long Cycles and Global War." In *Handbook of War Studies*, edited by Manus I. Midlarsky, 23–54. Boston: Unwin Hyman, 1989.

Moens, Alexander, Lenard J. Cohen, and Allen G. Sens. *NATO and European Security: Alliance Politics from the End of the Cold War to the Age of Terrorism*. Humanistic Perspectives on International Relations Series. Westport, CT: Praeger, 2003.

Moravcsik, Andrew. *The Choice for Europe: Social Purpose and State Power from Messina to Maastricht*. Ithaca, NY: Cornell University Press, 1998.

– "Liberal International Relations Theory: A Scientific Assessment." In *Progress in International Relations Theory: Appraising the Field*, edited by Colin Elman and Miriam Fendius Elman, 159–204. Cambridge, MA: MIT Press, 2003.

- "Preferences and Power in the European Community: A Liberal Intergovernmentalist Approach." *Journal of Common Market Studies* 31, no. 4 (1993): 473–524.
- "Taking Preferences Seriously: A Liberal Theory of International Politics." *International Organization* 51, no. 4 (1997): 513–53.

Morgan, Patrick M. "Multilateralism and Security: Prospects in Europe." In *Multilateralism Matters: The Theory and Praxis of an Institutional Form*, edited by John Gerard Ruggie, 327–64. New York: Columbia University Press, 1993.

Morgan, T. Clifton, and S.H. Campbell. "Domestic Structure, Decisional Constraints, and War: So Why Kant Democracies Fight?" *Journal of Conflict Resolution* 35, no. 2 (1991): 187–211.

Morgan, T. Clifton, and Valerie Schwebach. "Take Two Democracies and Call Me in the Morning: A Prescription for Peace?" *International Interactions* 17, no. 4 (1992): 305–20.

Morgenthau, Hans J. *Politics among Nations: The Struggle for Power and Peace.* New York: A.A. Knopf, 1948.

Morgenthau, Hans J., and Kenneth W. Thompson. *Politics among Nations: The Struggle for Power and Peace.* Brief ed. New York: McGraw-Hill, 1993.

Morrow, James D. "Modelling International Regimes: Distribution versus Information." *International Organization* 48, no. 3 (1994): 387–423.

Moses, Jonathon W., and Torbjørn L. Knutsen. *Ways of Knowing: Competing Methodologies in Social and Political Research.* Basingstoke, UK: Palgrave Macmillan, 2007.

Moskos, Charles C., John Allen Williams, and David R. Segal. "Armed Forces after the Cold War." In *The Postmodern Military: Armed Forces after the Cold War*, edited by Charles C. Moskos, John Allen Williams, and David R. Segal, 1–12. New York: Oxford University Press, 2000a.

- eds. *The Postmodern Military: Armed Forces after the Cold War.* New York: Oxford University Press, 2000b.

Mousseau, Michael. "Democracy and Compromise in Militarized Interstate Conflicts, 1816–1992." *Journal of Conflict Resolution* 42, no. 2 (April 1998): 210–30.

Mueller, John. *Retreat from Doomsday: The Obsolescence of Major War.* New York: Basic Books, 1994.

Murdoch, James C., and Todd Sandler. "Complementarity, Free Riding, and Military Expenditures of the NATO Allies." *Journal of Public Economics* 25, no. 1–2 (1984): 83–101.

- "A Theoretical and Empirical Analysis of NATO." *Journal of Conflict Resolution* 26, no. 2 (1982): 237–63.

Naim, Moises. "Clinton's Foreign Policy: A Victim of Globalization." *Foreign Policy* 109 (Winter 1997–98): 34–69.

National Defense University, Institute for National Strategic Studies. *Allied Command Structures in the New NATO*. Washington, DC: National Defense University, 1997.

NATO Defence College. *Co-operative Security Arrangements in Europe*. Frankfurt am Mein: Peter Lang, 1997.

Neack, Laura. "UN Peace-Keeping: In the Interest of Community or Self?" *Journal of Peace Research* 32, no. 2 (1995): 181–96.

Nicholson, Michael. "What's the Use of International Relations?" *Review of International Studies* 26, no. 2 (2000): 183–98.

Nincic, Miroslav. *Democracy and Foreign Policy: The Fallacy of Political Realism*. New York: Columbia University Press, 1992.

North Atlantic Treaty Organization. "Study on NATO Enlargement." Brussels: NATO, 3 September 1995.

North Atlantic Treaty Organization, Defence Planning Committee. "Enhancing Alliance Collective Security: Shared Risks, Roles, and Responsibilities in the Alliance." Brussels: NATO, 1988.

Nossal, Kim Richard. "The Democratization of Canadian Foreign Policy: The Elusive Ideal." In *Canada among Nations 1995: Democracy and Foreign Policy*, edited by Maxwell A. Cameron and Maureen Appel Molot. Ottawa: Carleton University Press, 1995.

– "A European Nation? The Life and Times of Atlanticism in Canada." In *Making a Difference? Canada's Foreign Policy in a Changing World Order*, edited by John English and Norman Hillmer, 79–102. Toronto: Lester Publishing, 1992.

– "'Middlepowerhood' and 'Middlepowermanship' in Canadian Foreign Policy." In *Canada's New Foreign and Security Policy Strategies: Re-examining Soft and Hard Dimensions of Middlepowerhood*, edited by Nikola Hynek and David Bosold, 20–34. Oxford: Oxford University Press, 2010.

– "Pinchpenny Diplomacy: The Decline of 'Good International Citizenship' in Canadian Foreign Policy." *International Journal* 54, no. 1 (Winter 1998–99): 88–105.

Nossal, Kim Richard, and Stéphane Roussel. "Canada and the Kosovo War: The Happy Follower." In *Alliance Politics, Kosovo, and NATO's War: Allied Force or Forced Allies?*, edited by Pierre Martin and Mark R. Brawley, 181–99. New York: Palgrave, 2001.

Nye, Joseph S. *Bound to Lead: The Changing Nature of American Power*. New York: Basic Books, 1990a.

– "Neorealism and Neoliberalism." *World Politics* 40, no. 2 (1988): 235–51.

- *The Paradox of American Power: Why the World's Only Superpower Can't Go It Alone.* Oxford: Oxford University Press, 2002.
- *Power in the Global Information Age: From Realism to Globalization.* London: Routledge, 2005a.
- *The Powers to Lead.* Oxford: Oxford University Press, 2008.
- "Soft Power." *Foreign Policy* 80, no. 79 (1990b): 153–71.
- *Soft Power: The Means to Success in World Politics.* New York: PublicAffairs, 2004.
- *Understanding International Conflicts: An Introduction to Theory and History.* 5th ed. Longman Classics in Political Science. New York: Pearson / Longman, 2005b.

Off, Carol. *The Ghosts of Medak Pocket: The Story of Canada's Secret War.* Toronto: Random House Canada, 2004.

Ohmae, Kenichi. *The Borderless World: Power and Strategy in the Interlinked Economy.* New York: Harper Business, 1990.

Olson, Mancur. *The Logic of Collective Action.* Cambridge, MA: Harvard University Press, 1965.

Olson, Mancur, and Richard Zeckhauser. "An Economic Theory of Alliances." *Review of Economics and Statistics* 48, no. 3 (1966): 266–79.

Oneal, John R. "Testing the Theory of Collective Action: NATO Defense Burdens, 1950–1984." *Journal of Conflict Resolution* 34, no. 3 (1990a): 426–48.
- "The Theory of Collective Action and Burden Sharing in NATO." *International Organization* 44, no. 3 (1990b): 379–402.

Oneal, John R., and Paul F. Diehl. "The Theory of Collective Action and NATO Defence Burdens: New Empirical Tests." In *Working Papers in International Studies.* Stanford: Hoover Institution, 1990.

Oneal, John R., and Mark A. Elrod. "NATO Burden Sharing and the Forces of Change." *International Studies Quarterly* 33, no. 4 (1989): 435–56.

Oneal, John R., Frances H. Oneal, Zeev Maoz, and Bruce Russett. "The Liberal Peace: Interdependence, Democracy and International Conflict, 1950–1985." *Journal of Peace Research* 33, no. 1 (1996): 11–28.

Oneal, John R., and Bruce Russett. "The Classical Liberals Were Right: Democracy, Interdependence and Conflict, 1950–85." *International Studies Quarterly* 41, no. 2 (1997): 267–94.

Oneal, John R., Bruce Russett, and Michael Berbaum. "Causes of Peace: Democracy, Interdependence, and International Organizations, 1885–1992." *International Studies Quarterly* 47, no. 3 (2003): 371–93.

Organski, A.F.K. *World Politics.* New York: Knopf, 1958.

Organski, A.F.K., and Jacek Kugler. *The War Ledger.* Chicago: University of Chicago Press, 1980.

Ottawa Citizen. "Bush Offers 'Hand of Friendship' to Soviets." 6 July 1990, A6.

Owen, John M. "How Liberalism Produces Democratic Peace." *International Security* 19, no. 2 (1994): 87–125.

– "How Liberalism Produces Democratic Peace." In *Debating the Democratic Peace*, edited by Michael E. Brown, Sean M. Lynn-Jones, and Steven E. Miller, 116–54. Cambridge, MA: MIT Press, 1996.

Oye, Kenneth A. *Cooperation under Anarchy.* Princeton, NJ: Princeton University Press, 1986.

Palmer, Glenn. "Deterrence, Defense Spending, and Elasticity: Alliance Contributions to the Public Good." *International Interactions* 7, no. 2 (1991): 157–69.

Panke, Diana, and Thomas Risse. "Liberalism." In *International Relations Theories: Discipline and Diversity*, edited by Timothy Dunne, Milja Kurki, and Steve Smith, 90–107. Oxford: Oxford University Press, 2007.

Paris, Roland. *At War's End: Building Peace after Civil Conflict.* Cambridge: Cambridge University Press, 2004.

– "Bringing the Leviathan Back In: Classical versus Contemporary Studies of the Liberal Peace." *International Studies Review* 8 (2006): 425–40.

Parker, Noel. *The Geopolitics of Europe's Identity: Centers, Boundaries and Margins.* New York: Palgrave Macmillan, 2008.

Patrick, Stewart, and Kaysie Brown. *Greater Than the Sum of Its Parts? Assessing "Whole of Government" Approaches to Fragile States.* New York: International Peace Academy, 2007.

Pauly, Mark V. "Optimality, 'Public' Goods, and Local Governments: A General Theoretical Analysis." *Journal of Political Economy* 78, no. 3 (1970): 572–85.

Pease, Kelly-Kate S. *International Organizations: Perspectives on Governance in the Twenty-First Century.* 3rd ed. Upper Saddle River, NJ: Pearson Prentice Hall, 2008.

Pentland, Charles C. "Odd Man In: Canada and the Transatlantic Crisis." *International Journal* 59, no. 1 (2003–04): 145–66.

Peters, John E., Stuart Johnson, Nora Bensahel, Timothy Liston, and Traci Williams, eds. *European Contributions to Operation Allied Force: Implications for Transatlantic Cooperation.* Santa Monica, CA: Rand, 2001.

Pollachek, Solomon. "Why Do Democracies Cooperate More and Fight Less? The Relationship between International Trade and Cooperation." *Review of International Economics* 5, no. 3 (August 1997): 295–309.

Pollack, Mark A., and Gregory C. Shaffer, eds. *Transatlantic Governance in the Global Economy.* Lanham, MD: Rowman & Littlefield, 2001.

Posen, Barry R. "Commandos of the Commons: Military Foundation of U.S. Hegemony." *International Security* 28, no. 1 (2003): 5–46.

Powell, Robert. "Absolute and Relative Gains in International Relations Theory." *American Political Science Review* 85, no. 4 (1991): 1303–20.

President of the United States of America. *A National Security Strategy of Engagement and Enlargement*. Washington, DC: White House, 1995.

Pugh, Michael. "Elections and 'Protectorate Democracy' in South-East Europe.'" In *The United Nations and Human Security*, edited by Edward Newman and Oliver P. Richmond, 190–207. Basingstoke, UK: Palgrave, 2001.

– "Protectorates and Spoils of Peace: Intermestic Manipulations of Political Economy in South-East Europe." In *Shadow Globalization, Ethnic Conflicts and New Wars: A Political Economy of Intra-state War*, edited by Dietrich Jung, 47–69. London: Routledge, 2003.

Putnam, Robert D. "Diplomacy and Domestic Politics: The Logic of Two-Level Games." *International Organization* 42 (1988): 427–60.

Rasmussen, Anders Fogh. "Building Security in an Age of Austerity." Keynote speech delivered by NATO Secretary General Anders Fogh Rasmussen at the 2011 Munich Security Conference, 4 February 2011.

Ravenhill, John. "Cycles of Middle Power Activism: Constraint and Choice in Australian and Canadian Foreign Policies." *Australian Journal of International Affairs* 52, no. 3 (1998): 309–27.

Ray, James Lee. *Democracy and International Conflict: An Evaluation of the Democratic Peace Proposition*. Columbia: University of South Carolina Press, 1995.

– "The Democratic Path to Peace." *Journal of Democracy* 8, no. 2 (1997): 49–64.

– "A Lakatosian View of the Democratic Peace Research Program." In *Progress in International Relations Theory: Appraising the Field*, edited by Colin Elman and Miriam Fendius Elman, 205–43. Cambridge, MA: MIT Press, 2003.

– "Wars between Democracies: Rare or Nonexistent?" *International Interactions* 18, no. 3 (Spring 1988): 251–76.

Raymond, Gregory A. "Democracies, Disputes, and Third Party Intermediaries." *Journal of Conflict Resolution* 38, no. 1 (1994): 24–42.

– "Demosthenes and Democracies: Regime-Types and Arbitration Outcomes." *International Interactions* 22, no. 1 (1996): 1–20.

Reed, William. "Alliance Duration and Democracy: An Extension and Cross-Validation of Democratic States and Commitment in International Relations." *American Journal of Political Science* 41, no. 3 (July 1997): 1072–8.

Reinhardt, Klaus. "Commanding KFOR." *NATO Review* 48, no. 2 (Summer/ Autumn 2000): 16–19.

Rempel, Roy. "Canada's Troop Deployments in Germany: Twilight of a Forty-Year Presence?" In *Homeward Bound? Allied Forces in the New Germany*, edited by David G. Haglund and Olaf Mager, 213–47. Boulder, CO: Westview Press, 1992.

Reus-Smit, Christian. "Human Rights and the Social Construction of
    Sovereignty." *Review of International Studies* 27, no. 4 (2001): 519–38.
Ricardo, David. *On the Principles of Political Economy and Taxation*. London: J.
    Murray, 1817.
Ringsmose, Jens. "NATO Burden-Sharing Redux: Continuity and Change after
    the Cold War." *Contemporary Security Policy* 31, no. 2 (2010): 319–38.
Risse-Kappen, Thomas. "Collective Identity in a Democratic Community:
    The Case of NATO." In *The Culture of National Security: Norms and Identity in
    World Politics*, edited by Peter J. Katzenstein, 357–99. New York: Columbia
    University Press, 1996.
– *Cooperation among Democracies: The European Influence on U.S. Foreign Policy*.
    Princeton Studies in International History and Politics. Princeton, NJ:
    Princeton University Press, 1995a.
– "Democratic Peace – Warlike Democracies? A Social Constructivist
    Interpretation of the Liberal Argument." *European Journal of International
    Relations* 1, no. 4 (1995b): 489–515.
Rittberger, Volker, and C. Freund. "Utilitarian-Liberal Foreign Policy Theory."
    In *German Foreign Policy since Unification: Theories and Case Studies*, edited by
    Volker Rittberger, 68–104. Manchester: Manchester University Press, 2001.
Rodik, Dani. *The Globalization Paradox: Democracy and the Future of the World
    Economy*. New York: W.W. Norton, 2011.
Roper, John. "NATO's New Role in Crisis Management." *International
    Spectator* 34, no. 2 (1999): 51–61.
Rosecrance, Richard. *The Rise of the Trading State: Commerce and Conquest in the
    Modern World*. New York: Basic Books, 1986.
Rosenau, James N. "Governance in the Twenty-First Century." *Global
    Governance* 1, no. 1 (1995): 13–33.
– *The Study of Global Interdependence: Essays on the Transnationalization of World
    Affairs*. New York: Nichols, 1980.
– *The Study of World Politics*. 2 vols. London: Routledge, 2006.
Rosenau, James N., and Ernst Otto Czempiel. *Governance without Government:
    Order and Change in World Politics*. Cambridge: Cambridge University Press,
    1992.
Ross, Douglas Alan. "Canada and the Future of European Security: From a
    Cheap Ride to a Free Ride to No Ride at All?" *International Journal* 50, no. 4
    (December 1995): 721–30.
– "Canada's Functional Isolationism and the Future of Weapons of Mass
    Destruction." *International Journal* 54, no. 1 (Winter 1998–99): 120–42.
Roussel, Stéphane. *The North American Democratic Peace: Absence of War and
    Security Institution-Building in Canada-US Relations, 1867–1958*. Kingston,

ON: School of Policy Studies and Centre for International Relations, Queen's University; Montreal: McGill-Queen's University Press, 2004.

Rudderham, M.A. "Canada and United Nations Peace Operations: Challenges, Opportunities, and Canada's Response." *International Journal* 63, no. 2 (2008): 359–84.

Rudolph, Christopher. "Constructing an Atrocities Regime: The Politics of War Crimes Tribunals." *International Organization* 55, no. 3 (2001): 655–91.

Ruggie, John Gerard. *Constructing the World Polity: Essays on International Institutionalization.* London: Routledge, 1998.

– "Multilateralism: The Anatomy of an Institution." *International Organization* 46, no. 3 (1992): 561–98.

– "Multilateralism: The Anatomy of an Institution." In *Multilateralism Matters: The Theory and Praxis of an Institutional Form,* edited by John Gerard Ruggie, 3–36. New York: Columbia University Press, 1993a.

– ed. *Multilateralism Matters: The Theory and Praxis of an Institutional Form.* New York: Columbia University Press, 1993b.

– *Winning the Peace: America and World Order in the New Era.* New York: Columbia University Press, 1996.

Rummel, Reinhardt. "Libertarianism and International Violence." *Journal of Conflict Resolution* 27, no. 1 (March 1983): 27–71.

– *Power Kills: Democracy as a Method of Nonviolence.* New Brunswick, NJ: Transaction, 1997.

– *Understanding Conflict and War, vol. 4.* Beverly Hills, CA: Sage Publications, 1979.

Russett, Bruce M. *Controlling the Sword: The Democratic Governance of National Security.* Cambridge, MA: Harvard University Press, 1990.

– *Grasping the Democratic Peace: Principles for a Post–Cold War World.* Princeton, NJ: Princeton University Press, 1993.

– *What Price Vigilance? The Burdens of National Defense.* New Haven, CT: Yale University Press, 1970.

Russett, Bruce M., and John R. Oneal. *Triangulating Peace: Democracy, Interdependence, and International Organizations.* New York: Norton, 2001.

Russett, Bruce M., and Harvey Starr. "From Democratic Peace to Kantian Peace: Democracy and Conflict in the International System." In *Handbook of War Studies II,* edited by Manus I. Midlarsky, 93–128. Ann Arbor: University of Michigan Press, 2000.

Russett, Bruce M., and James Sutterlin. "The UN in a New World Order." *Foreign Affairs* 70, no. 2 (1991): 69–83.

Salmon, Trevor. "Testing Times for European Political Cooperation: The Gulf and Yugoslavia, 1990–92." *International Affairs* 68, no. 2 (1992): 233–53.

Samuelson, Paul A. "The Pure Theory of Public Expenditure." *Review of Economics and Statistics* 36, no. 4 (1954): 387–9.

Sandler, Todd. *Collective Action: Theory and Applications*. Ann Arbor: University of Michigan Press, 1992.

– "Impurity of Defense: An Application to the Economics of Alliances." *Kyklos* 30, no. 3 (1977): 443–60.

Sandler, Todd, and Jon Cauley. "On the Economic Theory of Alliances." *Journal of Conflict Resolution* 19, no. 2 (1975): 330–48.

Sandler, Todd, Jon Cauley, and John F. Forbes. "In Defense of a Collective Goods Theory of Alliances." *Journal of Conflict Resolution* 24, no. 3 (1980): 537–47.

Sandler, Todd, and John F. Forbes. "Burden-Sharing, Strategy, and the Design of NATO." *Economic Inquiry* 18, no. 3 (1980): 425–44.

Sandler, Todd, and Keith Hartley. *The Economics of Defense*. Cambridge: Cambridge University Press, 1995.

– *The Political Economy of NATO: Past, Present, and into the 21st Century*. Cambridge: Cambridge University Press, 1999.

Sandler, Todd, and James C. Murdoch. "Defense Burdens and Prospects for the Northern European Allies." In *Constraints on Strategy: The Economics of Western Security*, edited by David B.H. Denoon, 59–113. Washington, DC: Pergamon-Brassey's, 1986.

Sandler, Todd, and Hirofumi Shimizu. "NATO Burden Sharing 1999–2010: An Altered Alliance." *Foreign Policy Analysis* 10, no. 1 (2014): 43–60.

– "Peacekeeping and Burden-Sharing, 1994–2000." *Journal of Peace Research* 39, no. 6 (2002): 651–68.

Schelling, Thomas C. *The Strategy of Conflict*. Cambridge, MA: Harvard University Press, 1960.

Scherr, Bruce A., and Emerson M. Babb. "Pricing Public Goods: An Experiment with Two Proposed Pricing Systems." *Public Choice* 23 (Fall 1975): 35–48.

Schimmelpfennig, Frank. *The EU, NATO and the Integration of Europe: Rules and Rhetorik*. Cambridge, MA: Cambridge University Press, 2003.

– "NATO Enlargement: A Constructivist Explanation." *Security Studies* 8, no. 2 (1999): 198–234.

Schumpeter, Joseph Alois. *Imperialism and Social Classes*. New York: A.M. Kelly, 1951.

– *Kapitalismus, Sozialismus und Demokratie*. Translated by Susanne Preiswerk. Mensch und Gesellschaft, vol. 7. Bern: A. Francke, 1946.

Schürr, Ulrich. *Der Aufbau einer europäischen Sicherheits- und Verteidigungsidentität im Beziehungsgeflecht von EU, WEU, OSZE und NATO*. Frankfurt am Main: Peter Lang, 2003.

Scott, J. *A Matter of Record*. Cambridge: Polity Press, 1990.

Seidelmann, Reimund. *EU, NATO and the Relationship between Transformation and External Behavior in Post-socialist Eastern Europe: The Cases of the Slovak Republic, Bulgaria, Romania and Ukraine*. Demokratie, Sicherheit, Frieden, vol. 144. Baden-Baden: Nomos, 2002.

Sens, Allen G. *NATO's Small Powers and Alliance Change after the Cold War*. Ottawa: National Library of Canada, 1993.

– "Saying Yes to Expansion: The Future of NATO and Canadian Interests in a Changing Alliance." *International Journal* 50, no. 4 (Autumn 1995): 675–700.

Sens, Allen G., and Albert Legault. "Canada and NATO Enlargement: Interests and Options." *Canadian Foreign Policy* 4, no. 2 (1996): 88–93.

Shea, Jamie. "NATO: Upholding Ethics in International Security Policy." *Cambridge Review of International Affairs* 15, no. 1 (2002): 75–82.

Shoup, Paul. *The East European and Soviet Data Handbook: Political, Social, and Developmental Indicators, 1945–1975*. New York: Columbia University Press, 1981.

Simard, Francis. *Talking It Out: The October Crisis from Inside*. Translated by David Homel. Montreal: Guernica, 1987.

Simmons, Beth A. "Compliance with International Agreements." In *Annual Review of Political Science*, edited by Nelson W. Polsby, 75–93. Palo Alto, CA: Annual Reviews, 1998.

Simon, Jeffrey. "Europe's Past, Europe's Future: Does Eastern Europe Belong in NATO?" *Orbis* (Winter 1993): 21–35.

Simon, Michael W., and Eric Gartzke. "Political System Similarity and the Choice of Allies." *Journal of Conflict Resolution* 40, no. 4 (December 1996): 617–35.

Simonds, Frank H., and Brooks Emeny. *The Great Powers in World Politics: International Relations and Economic Nationalism*. New York: American Book Company, 1937.

Singer, J.D. "Reconstructing the Correlates of War Dataset on Material Capabilities of States, 1816–1985." *International Interactions* 14, no. 2 (1988): 115–32.

Singer, Max, and Aaron Wildacsky. *The Real World Order: Zones of Peace, Zones of Turmoil*. Chatham, NJ: Chatham House Press, 1993.

Sivard, Ruth Leger. "World Military and Social Expenditures." Leesburg, VA: WMSE Publications, 1996.

Siverson, Randolph M., and Juliann Emmons. "Birds of a Feather: Democratic Political Systems and Alliance Choices in the Twentieth Century." *Journal of Conflict Resolution* 35, no. 2 (June 1991): 285–306.

Skidelsky, Robert J. *The World after Communism: A Polemic for Our Times*. London: Macmillan, 1995.

Slaughter, Anne-Marie. "International Law in a World of Liberal States."
  European Journal of International Law 6, no. 2 (Spring 1995): 503–38.
– *A New World Order*. Princeton, NJ: Princeton University Press, 2004.
– "The Real New World Order." *Foreign Affairs* 76, no. 5 (September/October
  1997): 183–97.
Sloan, Elinor C. *Bosnia and the New Collective Security*. Westport, CT: Praeger,
  1998.
– *The Revolution in Military Affairs: Implications for Canada and NATO*. Montreal
  and Kingston: McGill-Queen's University Press, 2002.
Sloan, Stanley R. *Defence Burden-Sharing: U.S. Relations with the NATO Allies
  and Japan*. Report no. 85-101 F. Washington, DC: Library of Congress
  Congressional Research Service, 1985a.
– *NATO, the European Union, and the Atlantic Community: The Transatlantic
  Bargain Challenged*. 2nd ed. Lanham, MD: Rowman & Littlefield, 2005.
– "NATO's Future in a New Europe: An American Perspective." *International
  Affairs* 66, no. 3 (1990): 495–511.
– *NATO's Future: Toward a New Transatlantic Bargain*. Washington, DC:
  National Defence University Press, 1985b.
– *NATO in the 1990s*. Washington, DC: Pergamon-Brassey's, 1989.
– *NATO and Transatlantic Relations in the 21st Century: Crisis, Continuity or
  Change?* New York: Foreign Policy Association, 2002.
Small, Melvin, and David J. Singer. "The War-Proneness of Democratic
  Regimes." *Jerusalem Journal of International Relations* 1, no. 4 (Summer 1976):
  50–69.
Smith, Adam. *An Inquiry into the Nature and Causes of the Wealth of Nations*, ed-
  ited by R.H. Campbell and A.S. Skinner. Oxford: Oxford University Press,
  1976.
Smith, Dan. *Towards a Strategic Framework for Peacebuilding: Getting Their Act
  Together*. Overview Report of the Joint *Utstein* Study of Peacebuilding.
  Evaluation Report 1/2004. Oslo: International Peace Research Institute,
  2004.
Smith, Michael J. "Liberalism and International Reform." In *Traditions of
  International Ethics*, edited by Terry Nardin and David R. Mapel, 201–24.
  Cambridge: Cambridge University Press, 1992.
Smith, Steve, and Patricia Owens. "Alternative Approaches to International
  Theory." In *The Globalization of World Politics: An Introduction to International
  Relations*, edited by John Baylis and Steve Smith, 271–324. Oxford: Oxford
  University Press, 2005.
Snidal, Duncan. "The Game Theory of International Politics." In *Cooperation
  under Anarchy*, edited by Kenneth A. Oye, 25–57. Princeton, NJ: Princeton
  University Press, 1986.

- "The Limits of Hegemonic Stability Theory." *International Organization* 39, no. 4 (1985): 579–614.
- "Relative Gains and the Pattern of International Cooperation." *American Political Science Review* 85, no. 4 (1991): 701–26.
Snyder, Glen H. *Alliance Politics*. Ithaca, NY: Cornell University Press, 1997.
- "Alliance Theory: A Neorealist First Cut." *Journal of International Affairs* 44, no. 1 (2002): 103–23.
- "The Security Dilemma in Alliance Politics." *World Politics* 36 (1984): 461–96.
Snyder, Jack L. "Averting Anarchy in the New Europe." *International Security* 14, no. 4 (Spring 1990): 5–41.
- *From Voting to Violence: Democratization and Nationalist Conflict*. New York: Norton, 2000.
Snyder, Jack L., and Edward D. Mansfield. "Democratization and the Danger of War." *International Security* 20, no. 1 (Summer 1995): 5–38.
Sogge, David. *Give and Take: What's the Matter with Foreign Aid?* London: Zed Books, 2002.
Sokolsky, Joel J. *The "Away Game": Canada–United States Security Relations outside North America*. IRPP Working Paper Series, no. 2004-091. Montreal: Institute for Research on Public Policy, 2004a.
- *Realism Canadian Style: National Security Policy and the Chrétien Legacy*. Montreal: IRPP, 2004b.
- "The Revolution in Military Affairs and the Future of Arms Control and Verification." Ottawa: International Security Bureau, Department of Foreign Affairs and International Trade, February 2001.
- "A Seat at the Table: Canada and Its Alliances." *Armed Forces and Society* 16, no. 1 (1989): 11–35.
Sørensen, Georg. "IR Theory after the Cold War." *Review of International Studies* 24, no. 5 (1998): 83–100.
Souva, Mark, and Brandon Prins. "The Liberal Peace Revisited: The Role of Democracy, Dependence, and Development in Militarized Interstate Dispute Initiation, 1950–1999." *International Interactions* 32, no. 2 (2006): 183–200.
Sperling, James, and Mark Webber. "NATO: From Kosovo to Kabul." *International Affairs* 85, no. 3 (2009): 491–511.
Spero, Joshua. "The Budapest-Prague-Warsaw Triangle: Central European Security after the Visegrad Summit." *European Security* 1, no. 1 (Spring 1992): 58–83.
Spiro, David E. "The Insignificance of the Liberal Peace." *International Security* 19, no. 2 (Fall 1994): 50–86.
Sprout, Harold Hance, and Margaret Tuttle Sprout. *Foundations of National Power: Readings on World Politics and American Security*. Princeton, NJ: Princeton University Press, 1945.

Staab, Andreas. *The European Union Explained: Institutions, Actors, Global Impact*. Bloomington: Indiana University Press, 2008.

Stam, Allan C., III. *Win, Lose, or Draw: Domestic Politics and the Crucible of War*. Ann Arbor: University of Michigan Press, 1996.

Stares, Paul B., and John D. Steinbruner. "Cooperative Security in the New Europe." In *The New Germany and the New Europe*, edited by Paul B. Stares, 218–48. Washington, DC: Brookings Institution, 1992.

Stein, Arthur. *Why Nations Cooperate: Circumstance and Choice in International Relations*. Ithaca, NY: Cornell University Press, 1990.

Strange, Susan. "The Defective State." *Daedalus* 124, no. 2 (1995): 55–74.

– "The Name of the Game." In *Sea Changes: American Foreign Policy in a Transformed World*, edited by Nicholas X. Rizopoulos. New York: Council on Foreign Relations, 1987a.

– "The Persistent Myth of Lost Hegemony." *International Organization* 41, no. 4 (1987b): 551–74.

Streit, Clarence K. *Union Now: A Proposal for a Federal Union of the Democracies of the North Atlantic*. New York: Harper & Brothers, 1939.

Sturm, Roland. *Public Deficits: A Comparative Study of Their Economic and Political Consequences in Britain, Canada, Germany, and the United States*. London: Longman, 1999.

Sullivan, Leonard. "A New Approach to Burden Sharing." *Foreign Policy* 60 (Autumn 1985): 91–110.

Sweeney, John W. "An Experimental Investigation of the Free Rider Problem." *Social Science Research* 2, no. 3 (1973): 277–92.

Tansey, Oisin. "Process Tracing and Elite Interviewing: A Case for Non-Probability Sampling." *PS: Political Science and Politics* 40, no. 4 (2007): 765–72.

Taylor, George Rogers. *The War of 1812: Past Justifications and Present Interpretations*. Westport, CT: Greenwood Press, 1980.

Thakur, Ramesh Chandra. *The United Nations, Peace and Security: From Collective Security to the Responsibility to Protect*. Cambridge: Cambridge University Press, 2006.

Thielemann, Eiko. "Between Interests and Norms: Explaining Patterns of Burden-Sharing in Europe." *Journal of Refugee Studies* 16, no. 3 (2003): 253–73.

Thornberry, Cedric. "Saving the War Crimes Tribunal." *Foreign Policy* 104 (Fall 1996): 72–85.

Tickner, J. Ann. "Continuing the Conversation ..." *International Studies Quarterly* 42, no. 1 (1998): 205–10.

Tochilovsky, Vladimir. "Cold War Foes Welcomed with Lukewarm Embrace." *Ottawa Citizen*, 9 November 1991, A6.

- "Diplomatic Initiative Sets New Formula." *Calgary Herald*, 7 November 1991, C9.
- "Globalizing Criminal Justice: Challenges for the International Criminal Court." *Global Governance* 9, no. 3 (2003): 291–9.

Trachtenberg, Marc. *A Constructed Peace: The Making of the European Settlement, 1945–1963*. Princeton, NJ: Princeton University Press, 1999.

Trainor, Bernard E. "Sharing the Defence Burden: Allies Are Listening." *New York Times*, 6 September 1988, B8.

Underdal, Arild. "The Concept of Regime Effectiveness." *Cooperation and Conflict* 27 (1992): 227–40.

United Nations. *The Blue Helmets: A Review of United Nations Peace-Keeping*. 3rd ed. New York: United Nations Department of Public Information, 1996.

United Nations, Department of Public Information. "United Nations Protection Force." New York: United Nations Publications, 1996.

United Nations Chronicle. "Fighting Escalates, UN Role in Question." Vol. 32, no. 3 (1995): 29–34.

United Nations Development Programme. *Human Development Report 1994*. New York: Oxford University Press, 1994.

United Nations General Assembly. *Report of the Secretary-General Pursuant to General Assembly Resolution 53/35: Srebrenica Report (1998)*. New York: UN Secretariat, 1998.

United States, Committee on Armed Services. *Interim Report of the Defence Burden Sharing Panel*, US House of Representatives, 100th Congress, Second Session, Committee Report No. 23. Washington, DC: US Government Printing Office, 1988.

United States, Library of Congress Congressional Research Service. "Kosovo and Macedonia: U.S. and Allied Military Operations." In *CRS Brief for Congress*. Washington, DC: Congress, 2003.
- "Kosovo and US Policy." In *Report for Congress*. Washington, DC: Congress, 2001.
- "NATO Burdensharing and Kosovo: A Preliminary Report." In *CRS Report for Congress*. Washington, DC: Congress, 3 January 2000.

United States, Department of Defense. *Report to Congress: Kosovo/Operation Allied Force After-Action Report*. Washington, DC: Department of Defense, 2000.

United States Information Service. "The New World Order: An Analysis and Document Collection of the Principal Texts in Which the Concept of the New World Order Is Described." London: United States Information Service of the American Embassy, 1991.

van Creveld, Martin. *Technology and War: From 2000 B.C. to the Present*. New York: Free Press, 1989.

van Evera, Stephen. "Offense, Defense, and the Causes of War." *International Security* 22, no. 4 (1998): 5–43.

van Ham, Peter. "The Lack of a Big Bully: Hegemonic Stability Theory and Regimes in the Study of International Relations." *Acta Politica* 27 (1992): 29–48.

van Oudenaren, John. "Transatlantic Bipolarity and the End of Multilateralism." *Political Science Quarterly* 120, no. 1 (2005): 1–32.

van Ypersele de Strihou, Jacques M. "Sharing the Defence Burden among Western Allies." *Review of Economics and Statistics* 49, no. 4 (1967): 527–36.

Vernon, Raymond. *Sovereignty at Bay: The Multinational Spread of U.S. Enterprises.* New York: Basic Books, 1971.

Viggo, Peter. "NATO's Comprehensive Approach to Crisis Response Operations: A Work in Slow Progress." In *DIIS Report 15.* Copenhagen: Danish Institute for International Studies, 2008.

Waever, Ole. "The Rise and Fall of the Inter-paradigm Debate." In *International Theory: Positivism and Beyond,* edited by Steve Smith, Ken Booth, and Marysia Zalewski, 149–85. Cambridge: Cambridge University Press, 1996.

Walker, R.B.J. *Inside/Outside: International Relations as Political Theory.* Cambridge: Cambridge University Press, 1993.

– "International Relations and the Concept of the Political." In *International Relations Theory Today,* edited by Ken Booth and Steve Smith, 306–27. University Park: Pennsylvania State University Press, 1995.

Wallander, Celeste A. "Institutional Assets and Adaptability: NATO after the Cold War." *International Organization* 54, no. 4 (2000): 705–35.

Wallerstein, Immanuel. "The Rise and Future Demise of the World Capitalist System." *Comparative Studies in Society and History* 16, no. 2 (1974): 387–415.

Walt, Stephen M. *The Origins of Alliances.* Ithaca, NY: Cornell University Press, 1987.

Waltz, Kenneth N. *Theory of International Politics.* Boston: McGraw-Hill, 1979.

Watson, William. "The Lessons of Kosovo." Interview with Michael Bliss and Janice Gross Stein. *Policy Options* (October 1999): 7–17.

Weart, Spencer R. *Never at War: Why Democracies Will Not Fight One Another.* New Haven, CT: Yale University Press, 1998.

Weber, Max. *Economy and Society: An Outline for Interpretive Sociology.* New York: Bedminster Press, 1968.

– *The Theory of Social and Economic Organization.* New York: Oxford University Press, 1947.

Weber, Max, and Edward Shils. *Max Weber on the Methodology of the Social Sciences.* Glencoe, IL: Free Press, 1949.

Weber, Steven. "Institutions and Change." In *New Thinking in International Relations Theory*, edited by Michael W. Doyle and G. John Ikenberry, 229–65. Boulder, CO: Westview Press, 1997.

Wedel, Janine. *Collision and Collusion: The Strange Case of Western Aid to Eastern Europe 1989–1998*. New York: St. Martin's Press, 1998.

Weede, Erich. "Democracy and War Involvement." *Journal of Conflict Resolution* 28, no. 1 (1984): 7–17.

– "Some Simple Calculations on Democracy and War Involvement." *Journal of Peace Research* 29, no. 4 (1992): 377–83.

Wendt, Alexander. "Constructing International Politics." *International Security* 20, no. 1 (1995): 71–81.

Wentz, Larry K., ed. *Lessons from Bosnia: The IFOR Experience*. Command and Control Research Program Publication Series. Washington, DC: Department of Defense, 1997.

– *Lessons from Kosovo: The KFOR Experience*. Command and Control Research Program Publication Series. Washington, DC: Department of Defense, 2002.

Whelan, Patrick. *Cross-Departmental Challenges: A Whole-of-Government Approach for the Twenty-First Century*. Dublin: Institute of Public Affairs, 2003.

Wight, Colin. *Agents, Structures and International Relations: Politics as Ontology*. Cambridge: Cambridge University Press, 2006.

Wight, Martin. "The Balance of Power and International Order." In *The Bases of International Order: Essays in Honour of C.A.W. Manning*, edited by Alan James, 85–115. Oxford: Oxford University Press, 1973.

– *Power Politics*. London: Royal Institute of International Affairs, 1946.

– *Systems of States*. Leicester: Leicester University Press, 1977.

Wight, Martin, Hedley Bull, and Carsten Holbraad. *Power Politics*. Leicester: Leicester University Press, 1978.

Williams, Michael C. "The Discipline of the Democratic Peace: Kant, Liberalism, and the Social Construction of Security Communities." *European Journal of International Relations* 7, no. 4 (2001): 525–53.

Williams, Michael C., and Iver B. Neumann. "From Alliance to Security Community: NATO, Russia, and the Power of Identity." *Millennium – Journal of International Studies* 29, no. 2 (2000): 357–87.

Wilson, Woodrow. *The Messages and Papers of Woodrow Wilson*, edited by Albert Shaw. New York: Review of Reviews Co., 1924.

Winess, Michael. "Report on NATO Calls on U.S. to Cut Its Forces by Two-Thirds." *New York Times*, 2 March 1991, 3.

Wohlforth, William C. *The Elusive Balance: Power and Perceptions during the Cold War*. Ithaca, NY: Cornell University Press, 1993.

Wolfers, Arnold. *Discord and Collaboration*. Baltimore: Johns Hopkins University Press, 1962.

Wright, Gerald. "Unspent Currency: Peacekeeping and Canada's Political Role." In *Bridges to Peace: Ten Years of Conflict Management in Bosnia*, edited by Charles C. Pentland, 195–212. Kingston, ON: Queen's Quarterly / Centre for International Relations, 2003.

Yarbrough, Beth V., and Robert M. Yarbrough. "Cooperation and the Liberalization of International Trade: After Hegemony What?" *International Organization* 41 (1987): 1–26.

Yost, David. "The New NATO and Collective Security." *Survival* 40, no. 2 (1998): 135–60.

Young, Oran. *International Cooperation: Building Regimes for Natural Resources and the Environment*. Ithaca, NY: Cornell University Press, 1989.

– *International Governance: Protecting the Environment in a Stateless Society*. Ithaca, NY: Cornell University Press, 1994.

Young, Oran, and Gail Osherenko. "International Regime Formation: Findings, Research Priorities, and Applications." In *Polar Politics: Creating International Environmental Regimes*, edited by Oran Young and Gail Osherenko, 223–61. Ithaca, NY: Cornell University Press, 1993.

Young, Robert A. *The Struggle for Quebec: From Referendum to Referendum?* Kingston, Montreal: McGill-Queen's University Press, 1999.

Zacher, Mark W., and Richard A. Matthew. "Liberal International Theory: Common Threads, Divergent Strands." In *Controversies in International Relations Theory: Realism and the Neoliberal Challenge*, edited by Charles W. Kegley, 107–50. New York: St. Martin's Press, 1995.

Zakaria, Fareed. *From Wealth to Power: The Unusual Origins of America's World Role*. Princeton, NJ: Princeton University Press, 1998.

Zangl, Bernhard. "Politik auf zwei Ebenen: Hypothesen zur Bildung internationaler Regime." *Zeitschrift für Internationale Beziehungen* 1, no. 2 (1994): 279–312.

Zeev, M., and N. Abdolali. "Regime Types and International Conflict, 1816–1976." *Journal of Conflict Resolution* 33, no. 1 (1989): 3–35.

Zimmern, Alfred. *The League of Nations and the Rule of Law, 1918–1935*. London: Macmillan, 1936.

Zürn, Michael. "Globalization and Global Governance: From Societal to Political Denationalization." *European Review* 11, no. 3 (2003): 341–64.

– *Regieren jenseits des Nationalstaates: Denationalisierung und Globalisierung als Chance*. Frankfurt am Mein: Suhrkamp, 1998.

Zyla, Benjamin. "Canada and Collective Action in Afghanistan: Theory Meets Practice." In *Statebuilding in Afghanistan: Multinational Contributions to*

Reconstruction, edited by Nik Hynek and Peter Marton, 104–23. London: Routledge, 2011.

- "Multilateralism à la Carte? The Bush II Administration and US Foreign Policy." *WeltTrends* 54, no. 15 (2007): 113–25.
- "NATO Doctrine and Canadian Special Operations." In *Choice of Force: Special Operations for Canada*, edited by David Last and Bernd Horn, 253–65. Montreal and Kingston: McGill-Queen's University Press, 2005.
- "NATO and Post–Cold War Burden-Sharing: Canada the Laggard?" *International Journal* 64, no. 2 (2009): 337–59.
- "Years of Free-Riding? Canada, the New NATO, and Collective Crisis Management in Europe, 1989–2001." *American Review of Canadian Studies* 40, no. 1 (2010): 22–39.

Zyla, Benjamin, and Joel J. Sokolsky. "Canada and the Atlantic Alliance in the Post–Cold War Era: More NATO Than NATO?" In *Canada's New Foreign and Security Policy Strategies: Re-examining Soft and Hard Dimensions of Middlepowerhood*, edited by Nikola Hynek and David Bosold. Oxford and Toronto: Oxford University Press, 2010.

Index